EU Competition Enforcement and Human Rights

Arianna Andreangeli

Lecturer in Law, Liverpool Law School, University of Liverpool, UK

Edward Elgar

Cheltenham, UK • Northampton, MA, USA

Published by
Edward Elgar Publishing Limited
The Lypiatts
15 Lansdown Road
Cheltenham
Glos GL50 2JA
UK

Edward Elgar Publishing, Inc.
William Pratt House
9 Dewey Court
Northampton
Massachusetts 01060
USA

A catalogue record for this book
is available from the British Library

Library of Congress Control Number: 2008927978

ISBN 978 1 84720 632 9

Typeset by Cambrian Typesetters, Camberley, Surrey
Printed and bound in Great Britain by MPG Books Ltd, Bodmin, Cornwall

Ai miei genitori e alla mia famiglia
– To my parents and family

Contents

Acknowledgements

This book is the outcome of research conducted between October 2003 and July 2007 and is based on a PhD thesis submitted to the School of Law, University of Birmingham, in July 2006. The degree was awarded without corrections in November 2006.

I am very grateful to my supervisor, Dr Julian Lonbay, for his help and support; to Dr Eleanor Spaventa and Prof. Panos Koutrakos, my teaching mentors during the time that I spent in the School of Law at the University of Birmingham, for their encouragement; to all colleagues at the School of Law in Birmingham for their encouragement throughout my PhD; to my examiners, Prof. Anthony Arnull, Head of the School of Law, University of Birmingham, and Mr Angus MacCulloch, of the School of Law, University of Lancaster, for the excellent feedback I received in the course of an exhaustive, and exhausting, examination; to Mr Luke Adams and Ms Nep Elverd, of Edward Elgar Publishing, for their editorial assistance.

The financial assistance of the School of Law of the University of Birmingham is gratefully acknowledged.

I would also like to thank a number of colleagues at Liverpool Law School, University of Liverpool, for their continuous assistance during the preparation of the manuscript, and also for their friendly encouragement: Prof. Michael Dougan, for his invaluable feedback; Miss Eleanor Drywood and Mr Bleddyn Davies, for proofreading significant parts of this work; Dr Samantha Currie, Prof. Anu Arora and Prof. Fiona Beveridge, for their ongoing support.

Finally, special thanks are owed to Dr Alistair Clark, of the School of Politics, International Relations and Philosophy of the Queen's University, Belfast, for having provided feedback on the manuscript at various stages and for his continuous care and kindness.

Table of cases

NUMERICAL LIST OF THE JUDGMENTS AND OPINIONS OF THE EUROPEAN COURTS

European Court of Justice

1/58, *Stork v High Authority*, [1959] ECR 19 **1**
25/62, *Plaumann v Commission*, [1963] ECR 95 **154**
32/62, *Alvis v Council*, [1963] ECR 49 **32**
56 and 58/64, *Consten & Grundig v Commission*, [1966] ECR 299 **37**
14/68, *Walt Wilhelm v Commission*, [1969] ECR 1 **193**
29/69, *Stauder v City of Ulm*, [1969] ECR 419 **2**
41/69, *ACF Chemiefarma v Commission*, [1970] ECR 661 **36**
45/69, *Boehringer Mannheim v Commission*, [1970] ECR 153 **36**
49/69, *BASF v Commission*, [1972] ECR 619 **37**
51/69, *Bayer v Commission of the European Communities*, [1972] ECR 745 **36**
11/70, *Internationale Handelsgesellschaft v Einfuhr und Vorratstelle fur Getreide und Futtermittel*, [1970] ECR 1125 **7**
41-42-43-44/70, *NV International Fruit Company and Others v Commission*, [1971] ECR 411 **154**
6/72, *Continental Can v Commission*, [1973] ECR 215 **37**
4/73, *Nold v Commission*, [1974] ECR 491 **7**
17/74, *Transocean Marine Paint Association v Commission,* [1974] ECR 1063 **33**
74/74, *CNTA SA v Commission*, [1975] ECR 533 **164**
43/75, *Defrenne v SABENA*, [1976] ECR 455 **4**
26/76, *Metro SB-Grossmarkte GmbH & Co KG v Commission*, [1977] ECR 1875 **154**
85/76, *Hoffmann La-Roche v Commission*, [1979] ECR 461 **63**
209-15 and 218/78, *Heinz van Landewyck Sarl v Commission*, [1980] ECR 3125 **23**
44/79, *Hauer v Land Rheinland-Pfalz*, [1979] ECR 3727 **17**
155/79, *AM & S Europe Limited v Commission of the European Communities*, [1982] ECR 1575 **93**
100–03/80, *Musique de Diffusion Française v Commission*, [1983] ECR 1825 **165**
60/81, *International Business*

Court of First Instance

European Court of Human Rights

National Courts

United Kingdom

House of Lords

Privy Council

Court of Appeal

High Court

Germany

United States of America

Table of legislation

EUROPEAN UNION

Council of Ministers

Regulations

Regulation No 17 of 6 February 1962, First Regulation implementing Articles 85 and 86 of the Treaty, [1959–62] OJ Spec. Ed. 57 **1**

Regulation (EEC) 4064/89 on the control of concentrations between undertakings, [1997] OJ C23/3 **1**

Regulation (EEC) No 990/93 of 26 April 1993 concerning trade between the EEC and the Federal Republic of Yugoslavia (Serbia and Montenegro), [1993] OJ L102/14 **12**

Regulation (EC) No 1310/97 of 30 June 1997 amending Regulation (EEC) No 4064/89 on the control of concentrations between undertakings, [1997] OJ L180/1 **1**

Regulation No 1 of 16 December 2002 on the implementation of the rules on competition laid down in Articles 81 and 82 of the Treaty, [2003] OJ L1/1 **1**

Regulation (EC) No 139/2004 of 20 January 2004 on the control of concentrations between undertakings, [2004] OJ L24/1 **1**

Directives

Directive No 91/308/EEC of 10 June 1991 on prevention of the use of the financial system for the purpose of money laundering, [1991] OJ L166/77 **107**

Directive 2001/97/EC of the European Parliament and of the Council of 4 December 2001 amending Council Directive 91/308/EEC on prevention of the use of the financial system for the purpose of money laundering, [2001] OJ L344/76 **107**

Commission of the European Communities

Commission Regulation No 99/63 EEC of 25 July 1963 on the hearings provided for in Article 19(1) and (2) of Council Regulation No 17, [1963] OJ P127/2268 **39**

Commission Regulation (EC) No 2842/98 of 22 December 1998 on the hearing of parties in certain proceedings under Articles 85 and 86 of the EC Treaty, [1998] OJ L354/18 **39**

Commission Regulation (EC) No 773/2004 of 7 April 2004 relating to the conduct of proceedings by the Commission pursuant to Articles 81 and 82 of the EC Treaty, [2004] OJ L123/18 **64**

LEGISLATIVE PROPOSALS AND RESOLUTIONS ADOPTED IN THE CONTEXT OF THE LEGISLATIVE PROCESS

Commission of the European Communities

European Parliament

NATIONAL LEGISLATION

United Kingdom

Other official documents

access to the file in cases pursuant to Article 85 and 86 of the EC Treaty, Articles 65 and 66 of the ECSC Treaty and Council Regulation (EEC) 4064/89, [1997] OJ C23/3 **66**

Guidelines on the method of setting fines imposed pursuant to Article 15(2) of Regulation No 17 and Article 65(5) of the ECSC Treaty, [1998] OJ C9/3 **163**

Notice on immunity from fines and reduction of fines in cartel cases, [2002] OJ C45/3 **28**

Guidelines of best practices on the conduct of EC merger control proceedings, available at: http://europa.eu.int/comm/competition/mergers/legislation/regulation/best_practices.pdf **42**

Notice on cooperation within the Network of competition authorities, [2004] OJ C101/43 **190**

Notice on cooperation between the Commission and the courts of the EU member states in the application of Articles 81 and 82 EC, [2004] OJ C101/54 **195**

Notice on the rules for access to the Commission file in cases pursuant to Articles 81 and 82 of the EC Treaty, Articles 53, 54 and 57 of the EEA Agreement and Council Regulation (EC) No 139/2004, [2005] OJ C325/7 **64**

Guidelines on the method of setting fines imposed pursuant to Article 23(2)(a) of Regulation No 1/2003, [2006] OJ C210/2 **28**

Notice on immunity from fines and reduction of fines in cartel cases, [2006] OJ C298/17 **196**

Reports

XI Report on Competition Policy, 1982: Brussels **35**

XII Report on Competition Policy, 1983: Brussels **37**

XIII Report on Competition Policy, 1984: Brussels **48**

XXIII Report on Competition Policy,1994: Brussels **48**

Other Documents

Dealing with the Commission: Competition Enforcement, 1997: Brussels: Official Publication Centre **36**

White Paper on Modernisation of the rules implementing Articles 85 and 86 [now 81 and 82] of the EC Treaty, [1999] OJ C132/1 **38**

Green Paper on the review of Council Regulation (EEC) No 4064/89, [2001] OJ C745/6 **44**

Submissions received on the Green Paper on the review of Council Regulation (EEC) no 4064/89, available at: http://ec.europa.eu/comm/competition/mergers/review/comments.html **44**

Green Paper on conflicts of jurisdiction and the principle of *ne bis in idem* in criminal proceedings, 23 December 2005, SEC(2005) 1767, COM(2005) final 696 **211**

UNITED KINGDOM

House of Lords Select Committee on the European Union

Office of Fair Trading

IRELAND

Irish Competition Authority

ITALY

1. Introduction

1. INTRODUCTION: AIMS AND OBJECTIVES

Since the inception of the European Economic Community Articles 81 and 82 of the EC Treaty have provided powerful tools for the establishment of genuine and undistorted competition and, overall, for the realisation of the Common Market.[1] In addition, the enactment in 1989 of the Merger Control Regulation[2] seeks to protect effective competition against changes in the structure of the relevant markets by establishing a compulsory system for ex ante screening of mergers and acquisitions liable to affect trade among the Member States.[3] However, the concentration of extensive investigative powers and of the decision-making function, including the power to impose substantial financial penalties in the hands of only one institution, the European Commission, has raised questions concerning the fairness of the procedures for the enforcement of the EC antitrust and merger rules.

The objective of this work is to examine the procedural rights enjoyed by the undertakings concerned by proceedings for the application of, respectively, Articles 81 and 82 of the EC Treaty and the Merger Control Regulation and to discuss their compliance with the notion of 'fair procedure' enshrined in the European Convention on Human Rights (hereinafter referred to also as ECHR). This assessment will be conducted in accordance with the 'composite approach' adopted by the European Court of Human Rights in its case law concerning the conformity of domestic administrative proceedings aimed at the 'determination of civil rights or obligations or of a criminal charge' with

---

[1] Council Regulation No 17 of 6 February 1962, First Regulation implementing Articles 85 and 86 of the Treaty, [1959–62] OJ Spec. Ed. 57, hereinafter referred to as Council Regulation No 17/62. Regulation 17/62 has been repealed by Council Regulation No 1 of 16 December 2002 on the implementation of the rules on competition laid down in Articles 81 and 82 of the Treaty ([2003] OJ L1/1), which entered into force on 1 May 2004. See, *inter alia*, SLOT, 'A view from the mountain: 40 years of developments in EC competition law', (2004) 41 *CMLRev* 443.

[2] Council Regulation No 4064 of 21 December 1989 on the control of concentrations between undertakings, [1989] OJ L395/1.

[3] For an examination of the Merger Control Regulation, see generally KERSE and COOK, *EC Merger Control*, 4th edn (2005) London: Sweet and Maxwell.

Article 6(1) ECHR. Consequently, it will require an examination of the scope of the rights enjoyed by the investigated parties during the administrative procedure as well as of their right to challenge the Commission decision before the Court of First Instance (CFI) and the European Court of Justice (ECJ).

2. THE ROLE OF THE COMMISSION IN COMPETITION ENFORCEMENT: A PROBLEM OF FAIRNESS

The application of the Community competition rules falls within the competence of the European Commission. With respect to the application of Articles 81 and 82 EC Treaty, the current Implementing Regulation, i.e. Council Regulation No 1/2003,[4] confers on the Commission extensive fact-finding, decision-making and sanctioning powers that are exercised in close cooperation with the competition authorities of Member States (hereinafter referred to also as NCAs) within the European Competition Network (hereinafter referred to also as ECN).[5]

Proceedings can be started either *proprio motu* or following a complaint. The first phase of the procedure aims at gathering of evidence through the exercise of investigative powers, allowing the Commission to request information from the investigated parties, to inspect their premises, to seize records and to ask for 'on-the-spot' explanations. The second phase of the procedure begins with the formal statement of the allegations of anti-competitive conduct on the part of the Commission and is articulated in a written and an oral hearing before a final decision is adopted.[6]

The procedure for controlling concentrations[7] starts with the notification to the Commission of the proposed transactions having a 'Community dimension'; the framework provides for a 'one-stop-shop' for assessing concentra-

---

4 Council Regulation No 1 of 16 December 2002 on the implementation of the rules on competition laid down in Articles 81 and 82 of the Treaty ([2003] OJ L1/1). The Regulation repealed Council Regulation No 17 of 6 February 1962, First Regulation implementing Articles 85 and 86 of the Treaty, [1959–62] OJ Spec. Ed. 57, hereinafter referred to as Council Regulation No 17/62.

5 Recitals II-III-IV, Preamble to Council Regulation (EC) No 1/2003. *Inter alia*, VENIT, 'Brave new world: the Modernisation and Decentralisation of enforcement under Articles 81 and 82 of the EC Treaty', (2003) 40 *CMLRev* 545 at 555–56.

6 For commentary on EC Antitrust Procedure, see generally KERSE and KHAN, *EC Antitrust Procedure*, 5th edn (2004) London: Sweet and Maxwell.

7 Council Regulation (EC) No 139/2004 of 20 January 2004 on the control of concentrations between undertakings (hereinafter referred to as the EC Merger Control Regulation), [2004] OJ L24/1.

tions that meet the prescribed turnover thresholds. It is articulated in two stages and according to tight time limits, namely 25 working days for phase I and 90 working days for phase II proceedings. The second phase of the procedure allows a full consideration of the merger in the event of 'serious doubts' as to its compatibility with the Common Market arising from the first, summary examination stage. For the purpose of outlining these concerns, a statement of objections is served so as to allow the concerned parties to submit written observations and to appear at an oral hearing before the adoption of a final decision. Extensive contact between Commission officials and the notifying undertakings is maintained throughout the procedure.[8]

That cursory examination of the structural characteristics of competition proceedings before the Commission highlights a common feature, namely, that in either context the Commission acts as investigator, prosecutor and decision-maker. The concentration of these functions in the hands of the same authority was criticised by commentators as potentially threatening the undertakings' right to a 'fair procedure' before the Commission.[9] Montag noted in 1996:

> A close look at the Commission's practice in infringement proceedings to date makes clear the necessity for reform in this area, especially when looked at from the perspective of the subjects of the proceedings, that is, from the undertakings' point of view. Undertakings often feel that they are treated unfairly and that their procedural rights are violated in the course of infringement proceedings.[10]

Several factors emerged as being the cause of these concerns,[11] namely the breadth of the Commission's investigative powers, the absence, in the context of the enforcement of Articles 81 and 82 EC Treaty, of precise deadlines for the adoption of a final decision on single cases and the absence of separation between the investigative and decision-making functions.[12] The purpose of the present work is therefore to explore whether these concerns are warranted by examining the procedural rights and safeguards available to the investigated parties in the course of antitrust and merger procedures in the light of standards of 'administrative due process' enshrined in the ECHR.

---

[8] For an examination of the Merger Control Regulation, see generally KERSE and COOK, *EC Merger Control*.

[9] *Inter alia*, MONTAG, 'The case for a radical reform of the infringement procedure under Regulation 17', (1996) 17 *ECLR* 428; WINCKLER, 'Some comments on procedures and remedies under EC merger control rules: something rotten in the kingdom of EC merger control?', (2003) 26 *W. Comp.* 219.

[10] MONTAG, 'The case for a radical reform of the infringement procedure under Regulation 17', at 428–29.

[11] *Id.*, p. 429.

[12] *Inter alia*, WESSELING, 'The Draft-Regulation modernising the competition rules: the Commission is married to one idea', (2001) 26 *ECLR* 357, at 361.

The remainder of Chapter 1 will thus address some general issues related to the protection of fundamental rights in the Community framework and the relevance of the ECHR in that context, including the extent to which the Convention can be applied to legal persons and especially to business entities and the nature of competition proceedings before the Commission for the purpose of the application of Article 6(1) ECHR.

Thereafter, Chapters 2, 3 and 4 will address the degree of protection afforded by EC law to, respectively, the right to be heard and to have access to the Commission file, the right to legal professional privilege and to the privilege against self-incrimination, and will assess them in the light of the standards enshrined in Article 6(1) of the Convention. This examination will illustrate, on the one hand, that the position adopted by EC law[13] is consistent with the 'composite approach' advocated by the European Court of Human Rights in articulating the concept of 'fair administrative procedure'.[14] On the other hand, it will raise significant issues with respect to the scope of the right to obtain access to the evidence held by the Commission and especially to the safeguards attending its exercise, the function of the hearing officer in this context and the extent to which Community law protects the confidentiality of lawyer-client correspondence[15] and the right against self-incrimination.[16]

Chapter 5 will examine the right to challenge Commission antitrust and merger decisions before the CFI and the ECJ and assess its scope in the light of the relevant principles provided by the ECHR as regards the right to obtain the judicial scrutiny of public authorities' decisions having a 'civil' or 'criminal' character. It will argue that whereas the more 'vigilant' attitude to judicial control in merger matters is to be welcomed,[17] the restrained approach adopted by the ECJ in the scrutiny of 'complex economic appraisals' made by the Commission in the antitrust context[18] could give rise to concerns in the light of the Convention. It will therefore suggest that the 'criminal' nature of proceedings for the application of Articles 81 and 82 EC Treaty may require the introduction of stricter standards of review, perhaps extending to the 'merits' of the Commission decisions.

---

13 *Inter alia,* case T-156/94, *Siderurgica Aristrain Madrid SL v Commission*, [1999] ECR II-645.

14 Appl. Nos 7299/75 and 7496/76, *Albert & LeCompte v Belgium*, [1983] 5 EHRR 533, para. 29.

15 Case 155/79, *AM & S Europe Limited v Commission of the European Communities*, [1982] ECR 1575.

16 Case 27/88, *Orkem v Commission*, [1989] ECR 3355.

17 *Inter alia,* case T-342/99, *Airtours plc v Commission*, [2002] ECR II-2585; joined cases 5 and 80/02, *Tetra Laval v Commission*, [2002] ECR II-4519.

18 *Inter alia,* joined cases T-68, 77-78/89, *Società Italiana Vetro SpA and Others v Commission*, [1992] ECR II-1403.

Chapter 6 will address some of the issues arising from the impact of the Modernisation Regulation on the extent of procedural rights enjoyed by the investigated parties and will highlight the risk that the right to a fair procedure enjoyed by the investigated undertakings could be eroded as a result of the absence of harmonisation of the rules concerning the admissibility of evidence, the procedure and the sanctions applicable to competition cases across the ECN.[19] It will be argued that, although the more proactive attitude of the European Court of Human Rights in assessing the 'equivalent protection' of human rights in the Community framework vis-à-vis the ECHR shown in *Matthews*[20] appears to have given way to a more hands-off approach in the later *Bosphorus* case,[21] there may still be doubts as regards the compliance of the measures of cooperation adopted by the NCAs to fulfil their obligations under Council Regulation No 1/2003.

Finally, Chapter 7 will discuss the current standards of 'administrative due process' provided by EC law in the area of competition enforcement and will suggest solutions to the perceived divergences from the principles enshrined in Article 6(1) ECHR. It will argue that, in consideration of the ongoing developments of fundamental rights protection in the EC legal system and especially of the increasing willingness of the Community courts to engage in an in-depth analysis of the ECHR,[22] a new 'Community due process' clause could be emerging, which may be increasingly consistent with the Convention. However, it will also demonstrate that these developments are likely to have a considerable impact not only on the legal standards governing the Commission's investigative powers and practices, but also on the current standards of judicial scrutiny applicable to competition decisions.

The chapter will argue that the need to ensure the 'Article-6-proofing' of EC antitrust proceedings in the light of emerging higher standards of 'due process' could also pose an ultimate challenge to the Council, who could perhaps reflect on whether to introduce wider-ranging reforms of the framework for the enforcement of Articles 81 and 82 EC Treaty. Consequently, it will examine some of the alternatives to the existing system, including the creation of a specialised judicial panel responsible for the review 'on the merits' of antitrust decisions, the conferral of fact-finding powers to a body

---

19 Commission Notice on cooperation within the Network of competition authorities, [2004] OJ C101/43; see also Recital XVI, Preamble to Council Regulation No 1/2003.

20 Appl. No 24833/94, *Matthews v United Kingdom*, [1999] 28 EHRR 361.

21 Appl. No 45036/98, *Bosphorus Hava Yollari Turizm ve Ticaret Anonim Sirketi v Ireland*, judgment of 30 June 2005, [2006] 42 EHRR 1.

22 E.g. case C-60/00, *Carpenter v Secretary of State for the Home Department*, [2002] ECR I-6279.

separate from the Commission and the internal reorganisation of DG Competition to ensure the separation of the investigation from the decision-making phase of the proceedings between two different units within the Directorate General.

Chapter 7 will conclude that, although in principle the creation of a 'jurisdiction on the merits' in the area of the enforcement of Articles 81 and 82 of the EC Treaty would constitute the most appropriate solution for ensuring conformity of the proceedings with Article 6(1) ECHR, due to its overarching institutional implications it may instead be more viable to opt for internal restructuring of DG Competition so as to establish a clear demarcation between the units responsible for the investigation and the adoption of decisions in antitrust cases, perhaps in conformity with the blueprint offered by the European Anti-Fraud Office.[23]

3. OUTLINE: THE PROTECTION OF HUMAN RIGHTS IN EC LAW AND COMPETITION PROCEEDINGS: GENERAL ISSUES

Illustrated above are the aims and objectives of the present work and the issues which it seeks to address. The remainder of this Chapter will address the general issues concerning the protection of fundamental rights in the EC legal system and the extent to which the ECHR can be considered relevant in the determination of applicable human rights standards. Thereafter, it will examine whether the Convention principles governing the concept of 'fair trial' and 'fair administrative procedure' are applicable to business entities affected by competition enforcement proceedings before the European Commission.

4. THE DEVELOPMENT OF FUNDAMENTAL RIGHTS STANDARDS IN THE COMMUNITY CONTEXT: PERSPECTIVES FROM THE ECJ

It is accepted that the protection of human rights was not a pressing concern in the early stages of the Community legal system. The silence of the

---

[23] Commission Decision 1999/352/EC, ECSC, Euratom of 28 April 1999, [1999] OJ L136/20; Regulation 1073/1999 of 25 May 1999 of the Council and the European Parliament, concerning investigations conducted by the European Anti-Fraud Office (OLAF), [1999] L136/1. Case C-11/00, *Commission v European Central Bank*, [2003] ECR I-7147.

Founding Treaty can be explained in relation to the perception of the Community as an organisation of limited remit that pursued objectives of an economic nature[24] and was therefore regarded as neutral vis-à-vis safeguarding the individual's fundamental rights.[25] However, the affirmation of the principles of supremacy and direct effect of EC law questioned that assumption of neutrality and raised concerns, especially at national level, that human rights guarantees could be affected by Community measures in a manner which was not compatible with the principles enshrined in domestic constitutions.[26]

In response to that challenge the ECJ developed 'Community-own' standards for the protection of human rights that would be binding on the EC institutions[27] and on the Member States in the implementation of Community law.[28] The Court acknowledged that the general principles of EC law provided autonomous human rights standards inspired by the 'constitutional traditions common to the Member States' [29] and by international treaties in which the Member States have collaborated or to which they have acceded,[30] and whose protection would be secured within the framework and objectives of the EC Treaty.[31]

Backed by expressions of commitment on the part of the political institutions,[32] the ECJ succeeded in maintaining the autonomy and supremacy of

---

24 DOUGLAS-SCOTT, *The Constitutional Law of the European Union* (2002) Longman, p. 432.

25 WEILER, 'Eurocracy and distrust: some questions concerning the role of the European Court of Justice in the protection of fundamental human rights within the legal order of the European Communities', (1986) 61 *Wash. Law Rev.* 1103 at 1111; see also DAUSES, 'The protection of fundamental rights in the Community legal order', (1985) 10 *ELRev* 398 at 400.

26 DAUSES, footnote 25, pp. 399–400. See e.g. case 11/70, *Internationale Handelsgesellschaft v Einfuhr und Vorratstelle fur Getreide und Futtermittel*, [1970] ECR 1125; cf. the adverse position of the German Constitutional Court, described, *inter alia,* in CROSSLAND, 'Three major decisions given by the Bundesverfassungsgericht (Federal Constitutional Court)', (1994) 19 *ELRev* 202, and reversed only in case 69/85, *Wunsche Handelsgesellschaft*, [1986] ECR 947. Also, see DOUGLAS-SCOTT, *The Constitutional Law of the European Union* (2002) Longman, p. 440.

27 Case 11/70, *Internationale Handelsgesellschaft*, [1970] ECR 1125, para. 4.

28 Case C-5/88, *Wachauf v Bundesamt fur Ernahrung und Fortwirtschaft*, [1989] ECR 2609, para. 19; see also case C-260/89, *ERT AE v DEP and Sotirios Kouvelas*, [1991] ECR I-2925, paras. 42–43.

29 Case 11/70, *Internationale Handelsgesellschaft*, [1970] ECR 1125, para. 4.

30 Case 4/73, *Nold v Commission*, [1974] ECR 491, para. 13.

31 *Inter alia,* HARTLEY, *The Foundations of European Community Law*, 5th edn (2003) Oxford University Press, p. 137.

32 E.g. Joint Declaration of the European Parliament, the Council and the Commission, [1977] OJ C301/1; Article F(2) [now 6(2)], Treaty of the European

Community law and, at the same time, in providing a degree of human rights protection inspired by principles already accepted at national level.[33] In this respect, the European Convention on Human Rights has a key role as a special source of inspiration.[34] Also, the increasing willingness of the Luxembourg Courts to engage in an in-depth analysis of its provision as well as of the European Court of Human Rights' case law can be read as demonstrating that, despite the absence of formal accession to the Convention, the European human rights discourse is developing toward progressively more common standards of protection.[35]

In the light of the above considerations the solemn proclamation of the EU Charter of Fundamental Rights[36] appears to be the culmination of this process of fundamental rights consolidation.[37] The drafting of an extensive and wide-ranging human rights catalogue applicable to the action of both the EU institutions and bodies and the Member States 'only when they are implementing Union law'[38] provides perhaps the highest expression of the *acquis communautaire* as regards fundamental rights protection.[39]

The importance of the Charter is also reflected in the case law of the Community Courts. In its recent *Re: Right to Family Reunification* judgment,[40] the ECJ clearly stated that the 'principal aim of the Charter' was 'to reaffirm rights as they result in particular from the common constitutional traditions and international obligations common to the Member States',[41]

Union. *Inter alia,* LENAERTS and VAN NUFFEL, *Constitutional Law of the European Union*, 2nd edn (2004) London: Sweet and Maxwell, pp. 720–721.

33 CRAIG and DeBÙRCA, *EU Law: text, cases and materials*, 3rd edn (2002) Oxford University Press, p. 324.

34 Case 4/73, *Nold v Commission*, [1974] ECR 491, para. 13.

35 See e.g. case C-60/00, *Carpenter v Secretary of State for the Home Department*, [2002] ECR I-6279, para. 42; for commentary, JACOBS, 'European Community Law and the European Convention of Human Rights', in CURTIN & HEUKELS (eds.), *Institutional Dynamics of European Integration*, Vol. II (1997) Dordrecht, London, Nijhoff, 516–72 at 563.

36 Part II, Treaty establishing a Constitution for Europe, [2003] OJ C169.

37 DeBÙRCA and ASCHENBRENNER, 'The development of European constitutionalism and the role of the EU Charter of Fundamental Rights', (2003) 9 *Colum. J. Eur. L.* 355 at 379.

38 Article 51(1), EU Charter of Fundamental Rights; see e.g. Case C-112/00, *E. Schmidtberger, Internationale Transporte und Planzuge v Austria*, [2003] ECR I-5659, paras. 56–57, 60 and 64. For commentary, see, *inter alia*, BIONDI, 'Free trade, a mountain road and the right to protest: European economic freedoms and fundamental individual rights', (2004) *EHRLR* 51 at 58–59.

39 LENAERTS & DeSMIJTER, 'A Bill of Rights for the European Union', (2001) 38 *CMLRev* 273 at 292.

40 Case C-540/03, *European Parliament v Council*, judgment of 27 June 2006, [2006] ECR I-5769.

41 *Id.*, para. 38.

including the 'case law of the Court and of the European Court of Human Rights.'[42] Accordingly it may be argued that the position occupied in its context by the Convention as the 'minimum standard' of protection of those rights that are common to both instruments[43] illustrates its continuity with the system of shared values and principles from which the *acquis* developed.[44]

In this respect, the circumstance that, in accordance with Article 6 of the Draft Constitutional Treaty approved at the Lisbon Inter-Governmental Conference in July 2007, the EU Charter for Fundamental Rights will become binding on the EU institutions and on the Member States when they implement Union law[45] can be interpreted as confirming the authority of the Charter as the point of arrival of the process of consolidation started by the ECJ with its *Internationale Handelsgesellschaft* and *Nold* judgments.[46] In addition, paragraph 2 of the same provision establishes the legal basis for the EU accession to the ECHR, as a result of which the EU measures will become challengeable before the European Court of Human Rights and, accordingly, demonstrates the centrality of the Convention in the European human rights discourse.[47]

---

42 *Ibid.* For commentary, see DRYWOOD, 'Giving with one hand, taking with the other: fundamental rights, children and the family reunification decision', (2007) 32(3) *ELRev* 396.

43 Article 52(3), EU Charter: 'Insofar as this Charter contains rights which correspond to rights guaranteed by the Convention for the Protection of Human Rights and Fundamental Freedoms, the meaning and scope of those rights shall be the same as those laid down by the said Convention. This provision shall not prevent Union law from providing more extensive protection.' For commentary, *inter alia*, LEMMENS, 'The relation between the Charter of Fundamental Rights of the European Union and the European Convention of Human Rights—Substantive aspects', (2001) 8 *Maastricht J. of Euro. and Comp. L.* 49 at 54. Also ARNULL, 'From Charter to Constitution and beyond: fundamental rights in the new European Union', (2003) *PL* Winter 774 at 786.

44 *Inter alia*, DOUGLAS SCOTT, 'The Charter of Fundamental Rights as a constitutional document', (2004) *EHRLR* 37 at 48–49; ARNULL, 'From Charter to Constitution and beyond', at 780.

45 *Inter alia*, EECKHOUT, 'The EU Charter of Fundamental Rights and the federal question', (2002) 39 *CMLRev* 945 at 968–69; also, DEFEIS, 'A Constitution for the European Union? A transatlantic perspective', (2005) 19 *Temp. Int'l & Comp. L J* 351 at 379–80.

46 WETZEL, 'Improving fundamental rights protection in the European Union: resolving the conflict and confusion between the Luxembourg and Strasbourg Courts', (2003) 71 *Fordham L. Rev.* 2823 at 2853.

47 For commentary, see, *inter alia*, CARRUTHERS, 'Beware of lawyers bearing gifts: a critical evaluation of the proposals on fundamental rights in the EU constitutional treaty', (2004) *EHRLR* 424 at 433–34; also, ARNULL, 'From Charter to Constitution and beyond', at 786.

It can be concluded that over the 50 years since the inception of the EEC, autonomous human rights standards have developed through the case law of the ECJ and are now a core element of the *acquis communautaire* of which the EU Charter of Fundamental Rights constitutes perhaps the most authoritative statement.[48] In this context the ECHR emerges as a key source of inspiration for the Community courts and for the Charter's drafters. However, the EC/EU is not a party to the Convention.[49] It is thus necessary to assess the position of the European Court of Human Rights with respect to the compliance of Community fundamental rights with the ECHR. This issue will be dealt with in the following section.

5. EC FUNDAMENTAL RIGHTS PRINCIPLES AND THE EUROPEAN CONVENTION ON HUMAN RIGHTS: THE VIEW FROM STRASBOURG

An in-depth analysis of the case law of the European Court of Human Rights concerning the compatibility of the Community fundamental rights with the ECHR is clearly beyond the scope of this work. Suffice to say, the approach adopted by the Strasbourg Court appears to have evolved from an overall attitude of trust towards the degree of protection provided at Community level to an increasing willingness to hold the Contracting States to account for allegations that Convention rights were not effectively protected in the EC context.[50]

Although the EC cannot be held responsible before the Court with respect to allegations that the Community institutions infringed the ECHR due to lack of jurisdiction *ratione personae*,[51] the Convention organs have not excluded in principle the responsibility of the Member States for an infringement of the Convention resulting from a Community measure. Rather, it was held that the Contracting States remain responsible for the observance of the ECHR even in

---

[48] DEFEIS, 'A Constitution for the European Union?', at 379–80; see also the Opinion of AG Mischo, joined cases C-20 and 64/00, *Booker Aquaculture v Scottish Ministers*, [2003] ECR I-7411, para. 126.

[49] Opinion 2/94, on *Accession of the Community to the ECHR*, [1996] ECR I-1759, para. 27. See, *inter alia*, YOUNG, 'The Charter, Constitution and human rights: is this the beginning or the end for human rights protection by Community law?', (2005) 11 *EPL* 219 at 226–27.

[50] *Inter alia*, CANOR, '*Primus inter pares*. Who is the ultimate guardian of fundamental rights in Europe?', (2000) 25 *ELRev* 3 at 4.

[51] Appl. No 8030/77, *CFDT v European Communities*, [1979] 13 D & R 231 at 240. But cf. Article 6, Draft Constitutional Treaty, IGC 1/2007, Brussels, 23 July 2007. *Infra*, Chapter 7, section 1.1.

respect of acts adopted in areas for which powers have been transferred to international organisations.[52]

Article 1 of the Convention was therefore interpreted as requiring that, in the event of such a transfer, human rights receive protection at least equivalent to that of the Convention within the framework of the international organisation.[53] In light of this approach, it was concluded in the *CFDT* decision that, in consideration of the human rights standards recognised by the general principles of EC law and of the judicial mechanisms to ensure their safeguard, the EC met that requirement of 'equivalent protection' and that as a result the European Court of Human Rights would not exercise its scrutiny powers with respect to the Community measures complained of.[54]

However, in later judgments the Strasbourg Court seemed to depart from its 'trusting approach' to the assessment of the adherence of EC action to the principles enshrined in the Convention.[55] In *Matthews v United Kingdom*[56] the Court held that, despite being unable to review the compliance of Community measures as such with the Convention, it remained competent to verify that Contracting States had 'secured the Convention rights in respect to European legislation'.[57] In that case it found a violation of the applicant's Convention rights in the circumstance that she had been left without a judicial remedy to vindicate her right to vote in parliamentary elections for the European Parliament, enshrined in Article 3 of Protocol I to the Convention.[58]

Matthews was hailed by some commentators as the first step towards the construction of a de facto 'vertical relationship between the ECJ and the European Court of Human Rights in respect of the protection of human rights vis-à-vis the EC institutions'.[59] Other authors, however, argued, perhaps less radically, that the conclusions adopted in that decision were motivated by the absence of any judicial remedy enabling the applicant to challenge the

---

52 Appl. 13258/87, *M & Co v Germany*, [1990] 64 D & R 138 at 145.

53 Appl. No 8030/77, *CFDT v European Communities*, [1979] 13 D & R 231 at 240.

54 *Ibid. Inter alia*, DUVIGNEAU, 'From Advisory Opinion 2/94 to the Amsterdam Treaty: Human Rights protection in the European Union', (1998) 25 *LIEI* 61 at 83.

55 E.g. Appl. No 17862/91, *Cantoni v France*, unreported, HUDOC case number 45/1995/551/637, para. 30.

56 Appl. No 24833/94, *Matthews v United Kingdom*, [1999] 28 EHRR 361.

57 *Id.*, para. 34.

58 *Id.*, para. 33. Also, *mutatis mutandis*, Appl. No 26083, *Waite and Kennedy v Germany*, [1999] 30 EHRR 261 at para. 68. For commentary, *inter alia*, SCHERMERS, *Matthews v United Kingdom*, judgment of 18 February 1999, case comment, (1999) 36 *CMLRev* 673 at 679.

59 CANOR, '*Primus inter pares*. Who is the ultimate guardian of Fundamental Rights in Europe?', (2000) 25 *ELRev* 3 at 4.

measure in question either before the national courts or before the ECJ.[60] Since the measure at issue was an annex to the Treaty of Amsterdam and as a result could not be challenged either in Luxembourg or in national courts, it was indispensable to redress that shortcoming in the protection of Mrs Matthews's human rights by allowing her access to the Strasbourg machinery.[61]

It is submitted that this interpretation appears to have been confirmed by the later *Bosphorus* judgment.[62] In *Bosphorus* the applicant had alleged that the impoundment by the Irish authorities of an aircraft belonging to the national airline company of the Former Republic of Yugoslavia, imposed to fulfil the obligations incumbent on Ireland as a result of the Council Regulation[63] enacted to give effect to the UN Resolution imposing economic sanctions on former Yugoslavia, violated its rights to enjoy property peacefully.[64]

The Strasbourg court reiterated that, although the Contracting States were allowed to transfer sovereign powers to international organisations, that transfer did not exonerate them from liability under the Convention.[65] Action taken to fulfil obligations arising from membership of such organisations would therefore conform to the ECHR so long as the relevant organisation provided protection at least equivalent to fundamental rights, having regard to both their substantive content and the mechanisms aimed at securing their observance.[66] In that context, the Court made it clear that 'equivalent' should be interpreted not as meaning 'identical' but rather 'comparable' with the degree of human rights protection provided by the ECHR in the circumstances of each case.[67]

On the merits the Court found no violation of the Convention. First, it stated that 'the finding of equivalence could not be final and would be susceptible to review in the light of any relevant change in fundamental rights protection'.[68] The Court then held that the substantive content of the EC general principles of law and the role played by the ECHR in that context, together

---

60 SCHERMERS, *Matthews v United Kingdom*, judgment of 18 February 1999, case comment, (1999) 36 *CMLRev* 673 at 679–80.

61 CANOR, '*Primus inter pares*. Who is the ultimate guardian of fundamental rights in Europe?', (2000) 25 *ELRev* 3 at 5.

62 Appl. No 45036/98, *Bosphorus Hava Yollari Turizm ve Ticaret Anonim Sirketi v Ireland*, judgment of 30 June 2005, [2006] 42 EHRR 1.

63 Council Regulation (EEC) No 990/93 of 26 April 1993 concerning trade between the EEC and the Federal Republic of Yugoslavia (Serbia and Montenegro), [1993] OJ L102/14.

64 Appl. No 45036/98, *Bosphorus Hava Yollari Turizm ve Ticaret Anonim Sirketi v Ireland*, judgment of 30 June 2005, [2006] 42 EHRR 1, part B and C of the judgment.

65 *Id.*, para. 154.

66 *Id.*, para. 155.

67 *Ibid.*

68 *Id.*, para. 155.

with the effectiveness of 'the mechanisms of control in place to ensure the observance of such rights',[69] secured a degree of protection provided by EC law 'comparable' to that of the ECHR.[70]

The European Court of Human Rights took the view that this 'presumption of equivalence' could be rebutted, and therefore the Court's jurisdiction would be exercised only if the applicant could prove that in the circumstances of the case the safeguarding of human rights in the Community context had been 'manifestly deficient'. However, the Court gave no indication of the circumstances in which this threshold would be met. Judge Ress suggested in his concurring opinion that a similar finding could be reached, for instance, in cases when the ECJ had no jurisdiction to review the measure in question, when the Court had adopted an 'excessively restrictive' view of the right claimed by the applicant or when it had departed from established case law of the Strasbourg Court without good reason.[71]

Just like *Matthews*, *Bosphorus* was widely discussed. Commentators criticised the European Court of Human Rights as being too lenient vis-à-vis the EC institutions and as setting the standards of proof necessary to rebut the presumption of equivalent protection too high and therefore not entirely consistent with the practical and effective protection of Convention rights.[72] Furthermore, concern was expressed at the possibility that this judgment could open the way to more frequent 'indirect human rights challenges' to EC measures,[73] with significant implications for the relationship between the European Court of Human Rights, the respondent states and the Community institutions.[74]

However, it is argued that the *Bosphorus* judgment could also be interpreted as demonstrating that, rather than adopting an activist stance in the scrutiny of EC measures through the medium of the Member States, the European Court of Human Rights may in fact have preferred a more restrained attitude to the review of claims stemming from EC action.[75] It was suggested that the general and abstract examination of the system of judicial protection

---

69 *Id.*, para. 160.

70 *Id.*, para. 164.

71 *Id.*, concurring separate opinion of Judge Ress, para. 3.

72 COSTELLO, 'The Bosphorus ruling of the European Court of Human Rights: fundamental rights and blurred boundaries in Europe', (2006) 6 *Hum. Rts. L. Rev.* 87 at 102.

73 HARMSEN, 'National responsibility for European Community acts under the European Convention on Human Rights: recasting the accession debate', (2001) 7 *EPL* 625 at 646.

74 *Id.*, p. 645.

75 See e.g. PHELPS, 'Reflections on Bosphorus and human rights in Europe', (2006) 81 *Tul. L. Rev.* 251 at 271–72.

provided by the EC Treaty before both the ECJ and the national courts, together with the standard of 'manifest deficiency' which should be satisfied before the Strasbourg Court can step in to review the act complained of, could be interpreted as indicating a hands-off, middle-ground approach to the scrutiny of similar cases.[76]

By assessing the 'guarantees offered and the mechanisms controlling their observance in the EC', the Court emphasised the 'systemic' equivalent protection of human rights in the Community framework and accordingly sent a strong signal to potential applicants that *Bosphorus*-type claims would stand a very limited chance of success.[77] However, it also demonstrated that it would continue to be vigilant on the degree of fundamental rights protection in the Community legal system and would exercise its jurisdiction if 'the specific circumstances of a case might reveal unexpected "shortcomings" in the EC's systems of human rights' protections [*sic*]'.[78]

Although admittedly it does not resolve all the issues arising from the possibility of human rights challenges to the EC action via the medium of the Member States, the *Bosphorus* decision can be interpreted as suggesting that the European Court of Human Rights is likely to be reluctant to engage in the detailed scrutiny of similar cases. It was suggested that, in a way which resembles the approach adopted by the German Constitutional Court in its *Solange* judgments,[79] the Court would only exercise a residual jurisdiction. It would therefore go beyond the presumption of 'equivalent protection of human rights' in the Community context only in the event of a breakdown in the safeguards provided by the ECJ and the domestic courts in respect of allegations of human rights breaches caused by EC measures.[80]

Accordingly, it can be concluded that, although significant questions concerning the interaction between the Community legal system and the Convention machinery remain open, the *Bosphorus* judgment appears to have marked an at least partial return by the European Court of Human Rights to the 'trusting approach' to the human rights supervision of EC action. This

---

[76] HOFFMEISTER, '*Bosphorus Hava Yollari Turizm Ve Ticaret Anonim Sirket v Ireland*', case comment, (2006) 100 *Am J Int'l L* 442 at 447.

[77] *Ibid.*

[78] *Ibid.*

[79] German Constitutional Court, judgment of 7 June 2000: 'Constitutional review of the EC Regulation on bananas', 102 BVerfGE 147 (2000). For commentary, HOFFMEISTER, Case comment to German Bundesverfassugsgericht: *Alcan*, Decision of 17 February 2000; *Constitutional review of EC Regulation on bananas*, Decision of 7 June 2000, (2001) 38 *CMLRev* 791 at 797–98.

[80] BANNER and THOMPSON, 'Human rights' review of state acts performed in compliance with EC Law: Bosphorus Airways v Ireland', (2005) 6 *EHRLR* 649 at 657.

outcome could, in turn, be explained as a consequence of the 'consolidation' of the EC/EU human rights discourse achieved over the years and of the vital role played by the ECHR itself in shaping the principles applied in this context by the ECJ.[81]

6. HUMAN RIGHTS AND BUSINESS ENTITIES: THE REACH OF THE EUROPEAN CONVENTION ON HUMAN RIGHTS IN THE CORPORATE CONTEXT

The previous sections briefly illustrated the degree of protection afforded to fundamental rights by EC law and in that context illustrated that, despite not being binding on the European institutions, the European Convention on Human Rights enshrines relevant standards for the assessment of their action in consideration of the Convention's role as a special source of guidance in shaping the EC general principles. However, it cannot be denied that the ECHR as a human rights catalogue was designed primarily as a means to protect natural persons from the arbitrary or excessive exercise of State power. Consequently, a preliminary question should be examined, namely to what extent the safeguards laid down in the Convention can be applied to non-individual actors and especially to business entities.[82]

It will be recalled that Article 1 ECHR obliges all the Contracting States to secure the human rights provided by the Convention to 'everyone' in their jurisdiction. Accordingly, it could be argued that the term 'everyone' can be read as encompassing both natural and legal persons, including commercial entities, provided that they find themselves within the reach of the respondent State.[83] However, it is submitted that, despite being apparently convincing, this literal argument is not wholly satisfactory. First, it could be argued that a literal reading of the Convention is not consistent with the approach adopted by the Strasbourg court itself, which often defies the literal wording of the ECHR and prefers a reading of its provisions 'in the light of its object and purpose' and of 'the present day conditions' in which they are to be applied.[84]

---

[81] See, e.g., BESSON, 'The European Union and human rights: towards a post-national human rights institution?', (2006) 6 *Hum. Rts. L. Rev.* 323 at 344–45; cf. PHELPS, 'Reflections on Bosphorus and human rights in Europe', (2006) 81 *Tul. L. Rev.* 251 at 275–76.

[82] For a general study of these issues, see most recently EMBERLAND, *The Human Rights of Companies*, (2005) Oxford University Press.

[83] EMBERLAND, pp. 33–34.

[84] *Inter alia*, OVEY and WHITE, *European Convention on Human Rights*, 3rd edn, (2002) Oxford University Press, pp. 34–35.

And second, this interpretation does not appear to take into adequate consideration the substratum of principles and values at the basis of the Convention and the extent to which they may be used to justify its application to protect corporate entities.[85]

Although the limited remit of this work does not allow for an exhaustive examination of these issues, it may be noted that the ECHR constitutes the expression of a specific system of values, among which the principles of individual dignity, democracy and the rule of law feature prominently. Commentators pointed out that democracy constitutes the 'spiritual bedrock of the Convention'[86] and the only political model contemplated as compatible with it, a model which is governed by principles such as free political debate, free elections and freedom of association.[87] The 'objective value' of the rule of law, applicable to all forms of exercise of public power,[88] also ensures that the action of government be restrained by law to avoid 'the arbitrary exercise of power and to secure equality and foreseeability (. . .)'.[89]

The values of the free market play a vital role within the model of liberal democracy at the foundation of the Convention by ensuring not only the personal but also the economic liberty of the individual.[90] In addition, it is acknowledged that there is no express reference to freedom of enterprise. However, the recognition in the Convention, albeit not unlimited, of the right to peaceful enjoyment of property, of freedom of association and of the right to receive and to impart information, including that of a 'commercial' nature,[91] seems to demonstrate the importance of business freedom as an aspect of the democratic society on which the ECHR is grounded.[92]

In this context, the emergence of the limited liability company as a vehicle through which freedom of enterprise can be exercised has played a key role in the economic development of the Contracting States.[93] However, it has also raised significant issues concerning the control of corporations in an economic and political system in which economic rights and freedoms are not unlimited

---

85 EMBERLAND (footnote 82), p. 25.

86 *Id.*, p. 40.

87 *Id.*, p. 41.

88 *Id.*, p. 47.

89 *Id.*, p. 45.

90 See, *inter alia*, OVEY and WHITE, *European Convention on Human Rights*, p. 302.

91 Appl. No. 10572/83, *Markt Intern Verlag GmbH and Klaus Bermann v Germany*, judgment of 20 November 1989, ser. A No 165, [1990] 12 EHRR 161; see *infra*, this section.

92 EMBERLAND (footnote 82), pp. 48–49.

93 *Ibid.*

and has consequently prompted the creation of often complex and pervasive systems for the regulation of the activities of private enterprises.[94]

Accordingly, it is submitted that it is in this context that the function of the Convention as a means through which corporate actors can seek protection of fundamental entitlements such as the right to fair and impartial legal process, freedom of association for the purpose of creating a juristic person and, albeit more controversially, the right to the protection of a sphere of privacy, should be understood.[95] Commentators forcefully argued that the recognition of the rule of law as an 'objective concept', as a result of which the ECHR becomes an instrument for the protection of 'everyone' from the arbitrary and excessive exercise of public power, provides a strong justification for the application of its provisions to the benefit of private enterprises, especially in the context of regulatory regimes.[96]

However, it is clear from its very text that not all of the Convention's safeguards are equally applicable to business entities: rules enshrining, for instance, the right to protection against torture or arbitrary detention or the right to respect for one's family life are clearly designed only for human beings. By contrast, 'classical' civil rights, such as the right to a fair trial, can be easily extended to corporate applicants.[97]

The practice of the European Court of Human Rights supports the view that the reach of the Convention should cover the business context and therefore 'secure' at least some of the rights listed therein not only in respect of individuals but also to legal persons. In the *Niemitz* case[98] the Court took the view that the notion of 'private life' could not be restricted 'to an "inner circle" in which the individual may live his own personal life as he chooses'[99] and should also encompass his or her 'right to establish and develop relationships with other human beings'. Consequently it was held that its meaning should be construed as also encompassing 'activities of a professional or business nature',[100] since it is in the course of such activities that individuals enjoy

---

[94] *Inter alia*, TRAINOR, 'A comparative analysis of a corporation's right against self-incrimination', (1994–1995) 18 *Fordham Int'l L J* 2139 at 2165–66.

[95] EMBERLAND (footnote 82), p. 51.

[96] *Ibid.*

[97] E.g. Appl. No 14369/88, *Noviflora Sweden AB v Sweden*, Commission Decision, [1993] 15 EHRR CD6; paras. 2(b) and 4. For commentary, *inter alia*, MacCULLOCH, 'The privilege against self-incrimination in competition investigations: theoretical foundations and practical implications', (2006) 26(2) *Legal Studies* 211 at 235.

[98] Appl. No 13710/88, *Niemitz v Germany*, ser. A No 251-B, [1993] 16 EHRR 17.

[99] *Id.*, para. 29.

[100] *Ibid.*

significant opportunities to build relations with the outside world.[101] As a result, the concept of 'home' laid down in Article 8 ECHR was read as comprising the applicant's business premises: a more restrictive interpretation would have impaired the function of that provision, which is to protect individuals against the arbitrary interference of the public authorities.[102]

This reading of the concept of 'home' for the purpose of the Convention was confirmed in the later *Ste Colas Est* judgment, which concerned the legality of competition inspection powers provided by French law.[103] The European Court of Human Rights held that in view of the broad connotation assigned to the word 'domicile' in the context of the French version of the Convention vis-à-vis the notion of 'home', the safeguards provided by Article 8 ECHR should extend to business premises or professional offices.[104] Accordingly, it was concluded that given the nature of the Convention as a 'living instrument',[105] Article 8 ECHR should be read as enshrining a 'right to respect for a company's registered office, branches or other business premises'.[106]

The application of the Convention's safeguards was also sought for the protection of freedom of commercial speech and expression, including advertising. In *Markt Intern*[107] the Court held that information of a commercial nature could not be excluded from the scope of Article 10 ECHR.[108] On the contrary, an active specialised press constituted an essential factor in a market economy, in as much as, by ensuring a degree of 'scrutiny of the [undertaking's] practices by its competitors',[109] it fostered 'the openness of business activities'.[110]

The later *Casado Coca* judgment[111] reiterated that Article 10 ECHR protected the freedom to impart information of whatever nature, including that

---

101 *Ibid.*

102 *Id.*, para. 31. See also, *mutatis mutandis*, Appl. No 10461/83, *Chappell v United Kingdom*, Report of the European Commission on Human Rights, 14 October 1987, [1989] 11 EHRR CD543, paras. 96–99; judgment of the European Court of Human Rights, 30 March 1989, [1990] 12 EHRR 1, para. 51.

103 Appl. No 37971/97, *Ste Colas Est and Others v France*, judgment of 16 April 2002, [2004] 39 EHRR 17.

104 *Id.*, para. 40.

105 *Id.*, para. 41.

106 *Ibid.*

107 Appl. No 10572/83, *Markt Intern Verlag GmbH and Klaus Bermann v Germany*, judgment of 20 November 1989, ser. A No 165, [1990] 12 EHRR 161.

108 *Id.*, para. 26.

109 *Id.*, para. 35.

110 *Ibid.*

111 Appl. No 15450/89, *Casado Coca v Spain*, ser. A No 285, [1994] 18 EHRR 1.

'of a commercial nature . . . and even light music and commercials transmitted by cable'.[112] The Court clearly extended the safeguards provided by Article 10 of the Convention to natural and legal persons engaged in economic activities,[113] namely to 'undertakings', to adopt terminology developed in the context of EC competition law.[114] It therefore embraced a purposive approach in the interpretation of the Convention and ensured that the function of its provisions would not be jeopardised.[115]

Nonetheless, it cannot be denied that the application of human rights guarantees to corporate entities gives rise to specific issues caused by the circumstance that these safeguards were originally developed to protect the life, physical integrity and human dignity of natural persons. Although it is acknowledged that certain rights are entirely applicable to corporate entities just as to individuals, the extension to legal persons of other guarantees is far more controversial.

It will be illustrated in later chapters that whether business enterprises can claim a 'right to silence' and not to incriminate themselves in the course of regulatory investigations and judicial proceedings constitutes a telling example of the difficulties stemming from the application of 'traditional' human rights standards to corporate entities.[116] This prompts the question of how to reconcile the competing interests of the effective functioning of regulatory frameworks and the protection of fundamental entitlements claimed by business entities.

---

112 *Ibid.*

113 But cf. Appl. No 10572/83, *Markt Intern Verlag GmbH and Klaus Bermann v Germany*, judgment of 20 November 1989, ser. A No 165, [1990] 12 EHRR 161 at paras. 33, 35 and 37 with Appl. No 9815/82, *Lingens v Austria*, judgment of 8 July 1986, ser. A No 103, [1986] 8 EHRR 103 at paras. 41–42.

114 *Inter alia*, case C-41/90, *Hofner and Elsner v Macroton*, [1991] ECR I-1979, para. 21.

115 See Appl. No 37971/97, *Ste Colas Est and Others v France*, judgment of 16 April 2002, [2004] 39 EHRR 17, para. 41. See also, *mutatis mutandis*, case C-185/95, *Baustahlgewebe v Commission*, [1998] ECR I-8417, per AG Leger, para. 33. For commentary, *inter alia*, VENIT and LOUKO, 'The Commission's new power to question and its implications on human rights', in HAWK (ed.), *International Antitrust Law and Policy, Annual Proceedings of the Fordham Corporate Law Institute* (2005) New York: Juris Publishing, p. 675 at 696–97. But cf. DEKEYSER and GAUER, 'The new enforcement system for Articles 81 and 82 and the rights of defence', in HAWK (ed.), *International Antitrust Law and Policy*, p. 549 at 562.

116 For an examination of the issue with respect to the protection of the right against self-incrimination, see, *inter alia*, TRAINOR, 'A comparative analysis of a corporation's right against self-incrimination', (1994–1995) 18 *Fordham Int'l L J* 2139; RILEY, '*Saunders* and the power to obtain information in Community and United Kingdom competition law', (2000) 25 *ELRev* 264; MacCULLOCH, 'The privilege against self-incrimination in competition investigations: theoretical foundations and practical implications', (2006) 26(2) *Legal Studies* 211.

It was suggested that the European Court of Human Rights may have responded to these concerns by adopting a 'more lenient' approach in the assessment of allegations of Convention breaches raised by business entities.[117] Judgments such as *Groppera Radio*[118] and perhaps more significantly *Markt Intern Verlag*[119] appear to indicate that in principle the Strasbourg Court looks favourably on the possibility for corporate applicants to rely on Article 10 ECHR against restrictions of their right to disseminate commercial information, such as advertising. However, the examination of the appraisal made by the Court of the legality of the interference with the applicants' right to freedom of expression suggests the adoption of a more deferential approach to the discretion exercised by the Contracting States' authorities in the regulation of the economic activities.[120]

Although the judgment will be examined in more detail in later chapters, it is noteworthy that in *Markt Intern Verlag*[121] the Court expressly stated that 'in commercial matters and in particular in an area as complex and fluctuating as that of unfair competition' its scrutiny would be confined 'to the question whether the measures taken on the national level are justifiable in principle and proportionate'.[122]

The position adopted in this judgment can be contrasted with other decisions taken in the context of the protection of 'political' speech, such as, for instance, *Silver*[123] or *Handyside*.[124] In these cases the Court was far less reluctant to engage in an analysis as to whether the restrictions on the applicants' right to free expression were necessary in a democratic society for the achievement of a legitimate aim, as prescribed by Article 10(2) ECHR.

Accordingly, it was held that, although the State authorities are best placed to assess the necessity in a democratic society of imposing restrictions on the exercise of certain fundamental rights and freedoms and for that purpose enjoy a measure of discretion, their 'margin of appreciation' is not unlimited but is

---

117 EMBERLAND (footnote 82), pp. 128–130.

118 Appl. No 10890/84, *Groppera Radio AG and others v Switzerland*, judgment of 28 March 1990, ser. A, No 173, [1990] 12 EHRR 321.

119 *Markt Intern Verlag GmbH and Klaus Bermann v Germany*, judgment of 20 November 1989, ser. A No 165, [1990] 12 EHRR 161.

120 EMBERLAND (footnote 82), pp. 129–30.

121 Appl. No 10572/83, *Markt Intern Verlag GmbH and Klaus Bermann v Germany*, judgment of 20 November 1989, ser. A No 165, [1990] 12 EHRR 161.

122 *Id.*, para. 33.

123 Appl. Nos. 5947/72 6205/73, 7052/75, 7061/75 7107/75, 7113/75, 7136/75, judgment of 25 March 1983, ser. A No 61, [1983] 5 EHRR 347.

124 *Handyside v United Kingdom*, judgment of 7 December 1976, ser. A No 24, [1979–80] 1 EHRR 737.

at all times subjected to the supervision of the Convention organs.[125] It would therefore fall within the Strasbourg Court's jurisdiction to consider whether the interferences with the Convention rights alleged by the applicant responded 'to a "pressing social need" and [were] "proportionate to the legitimate aim pursued" '.[126]

However, it is not entirely clear how the 'varying standards' for the scrutiny of State measures impinging on the freedom of speech adopted in the 'commercial' as opposed to the 'political' arena may be explained. Commentators argued that in 'commercial speech' cases the European Court of Human Rights did not adopt the 'substantive standard of control over the domestic authorities' assessment of "necessity" '[127] applicable to 'political' speech cases. Instead, and by reason of the different context in which the Contracting States exercised their margin of appreciation, it opted for a formal type of scrutiny, limited to verifying 'whether the proportionality assessment under the "necessity" criterion has (. . .) been undertaken at national level'.[128,129]

It cannot be denied that the adoption of such a generous standard of review leaves considerable discretion to the national authorities and raises the question whether it can be justified in the light of the function of the ECHR as a means to protect 'everyone' from the arbitrary and excessive exercise of powers by the public authorities.[130] Even though these issues will be directly addressed in later chapters, it is necessary to point out already at this stage that there may be compelling reasons for the recognition of a broader margin of appreciation on the part of the domestic authorities in the sphere of the regulation of economic activities.

As Emberland put it, 'the Convention's profound reverence for democratic processes'[131] and the recognition of a wide ambit of discretion enjoyed by the legislators of the Contracting States in making choices concerning the 'public regulation of private economic activity for the benefit of the common good'[132]

---

125 *Handyside v United Kingdom*, judgment of 7 December 1976, ser. A No 24, [1979–80] 1 EHRR 737, para. 48. For commentary, OVEY and WHITE, *European Convention on Human Rights*, pp. 210–11.

126 Appl. Nos. 5947/72 6205/73, 7052/75, 7061/75 7107/75, 7113/75, 7136/75, *Silver v United Kingdom* judgment of 25 March 1983, ser. A No 61, [1983] 5 EHRR 347, para. 97. For commentary, OVEY and WHITE, *European Convention on Human Rights*, pp. 276–77.

127 *Id.*, p. 166.

128 *Id.*, p. 167.

129 EMBERLAND (footnote 82), p. 165.

130 *Id.*, p. 177.

131 *Id.*, p. 184.

132 *Id.*, p. 192.

could constitute legitimate grounds for a more 'lenient' attitude on the part of the Strasbourg Court as regards claims brought by corporate applicants.[133] As a result, the concern for maintaining the 'social function' of private property and free enterprise,[134] together with the recognition that 'commercial speech' does not engage the value of democracy to the same extent as speech in the 'political arena',[135] could provide a convincing explanation for the adoption of less stringent standards for the review of allegations of infringement of the Convention raised by corporate entities acting in the commercial sphere.[136]

In the light of the analysis conducted so far it is concluded that the ECHR, being a human rights instrument rooted in principles such as democracy and the rule of law and embedded in the values of European liberalism, can in principle provide for the protection of certain fundamental rights to corporate entities engaged in commercial activities. However, a closer examination of the case law reveals that even though 'classical' human rights standards can be claimed by economic actors, such as the right to free speech, the standards of review applied by the European Court of Human Rights in examining the allegations raised by these applicants may not be as stringent as those adhered to outside the 'commercial arena'.

It could be argued that the 'lenient approach' to human rights adjudication emerging in the business context may be justified in the light of the 'social function of private property' and of the need to respect the integrity of the democratic decision-making processes in each Contracting State with respect to the determination of economic and regulatory choices. Nevertheless, the adoption of differing standards of review also raises questions concerning how the balance should be struck between the rights claimed by business entities and the common interests sought by the Contracting States in individual cases.

As a result, it is not entirely clear how the scope of rights such as the entitlement to a fair trial, the confidentiality of lawyer-client communications and the right to remain silent in the face of questioning, especially during regulatory investigations, should be fashioned. Nonetheless, before examining these issues in more detail, it is necessary to examine the extent to which the ECHR is applicable to the action of public authorities in the context of the regulation of economic activities and especially to the action of the European Commission in the area of competition enforcement. This other general question will be examined in the following section.

---

133 *Id.*, p. 193.
134 *Id.*, pp. 190–91.
135 *Id.*, p. 187.
136 *Id.*, p. 193.

7. COMPETITION ENFORCEMENT AND THE REACH OF ARTICLE 6(1) OF THE ECHR: THE NATURE OF THE ANTITRUST AND MERGER PROCEEDINGS IN EC LAW

The nature of the proceedings for the application of Articles 81 and 82 EC Treaty and of the Merger Regulation is widely disputed. The Community legislature constantly reiterated that the procedure before the Commission is 'administrative' in essence, as is demonstrated by Article 23(5) of Council Regulation No 1/2003, according to which decisions imposing financial penalties for antitrust violation 'shall not be of a criminal nature'.

Several commentators, however, challenged the legislative statement and alleged that since these proceedings can 'culminate in the imposition of fines having a criminal law character',[137] they actually 'relate to the determination of a criminal charge'.[138] Consequently, they argued that they did not comply with the requirements laid down by Article 6(1) ECHR, on account of the concentration of the investigative and decision-making functions on the Commission. However, the appeals brought against Commission competition decisions on grounds of a violation of Article 6(1) ECHR have been constantly dismissed by the Strasbourg organs.[139]

The possibility that the Convention could be successfully invoked in order to challenge a competition decision was also constantly denied by the ECJ[140] 'precisely because it [the Commission] is not independent of the executive'[141] and is entrusted with carrying out merely an administrative function.[142] The observance of the procedural guarantees laid down by the regulations governing the enforcement of competition law, together with the availability of the action for annulment before the CFI under Article 230 EC Treaty[143] was considered sufficient to meet the requirements of a fair hearing for the undertakings concerned.[144]

---

137 DRABEK, 'A fair hearing before EC institutions', (2001) 4 *Euro. Rev. of Private Law* 529 at 532.

138 *Id.*, p. 533.

139 E.g. Appl. 13258/87, *M & Co v Germany*, [1990] 64 D & R 138.

140 *Inter alia*, case 45/69, *Boehringer Mannheim v Commission*, [1970] ECR 153, para. 23; case T-11/89, *Shell v Commission*, [1992] ECR II-757, para. 39.

141 DRABEK, 'A fair hearing before EC institutions', (2003) 4 *ERPL* 529 at 533.

142 *Inter alia*, cases 100–103/80, *Musique de Diffusion Française v Commission*, [1983] ECR 1825, per AG Slynn, p. 1920.

143 Case T-156/94, *Siderurgica Aristrain Madrid SL v Commission*, [1999] ECR II-645, para. 102 and 109.

144 *Inter alia*, joined Cases 209-15 and 218/78, *Heinz van Landewyck Sarl v Commission*, [1980] ECR 3125, para. 81.

Nonetheless, the view that Article 6(1) ECHR would not in principle be relevant for competition proceedings before the Commission could be open to question in the light of the case law of the European Court of Human Rights. Although none of the Convention norms lay down specific 'administrative fairness' standards applicable to proceedings before non-judicial authorities, the Court was mindful of the fact that according to 'the administrative law of all contracting states . . . in numerous different fields public authorities are empowered by law to take various forms of action impinging on the private rights of citizens'.[145] It therefore adopted a substantive test to determine whether the exercise of administrative powers by public authorities could be considered to fall within the scope of Article 6(1) ECHR, so as to prevent the safeguards contained in the Convention and especially the right to a fair trial, being withheld merely due to national law classifications.[146]

With respect to the notion of 'criminal charge', the Strasbourg Court was often faced with controversial issues involving 'lesser offences (. . .) where a policy of decriminalisation is in operation'.[147] In these cases it took the view that the existence of a 'criminal charge' should be dependent on substantive factors, namely 'the nature and severity of the offence and the penalty' and 'the purpose of the fine', i.e. whether the latter 'was both deterrent and punitive (. . .)'.[148]

As a result, it was held in *Schmautzer*[149] that motoring offences, despite being classified by national law as belonging to 'the administrative sphere . . . are nevertheless criminal in nature'.[150] The Court pointed to several circumstances, namely, that national law 'refer[red] to administrative *offences* and administrative *criminal* procedure'[151] and that 'the fine imposed on the applicant was accompanied by an order for his committal to prison in the event of his defaulting on payment'.[152]

A similar approach was also adopted in the interpretation of the concept of

---

[145] Appl. No 7598/76, *Kaplan v United Kingdom*, Commission Decision, [1982] 4 EHRR 64, para. 150.

[146] BOYLE, 'Administrative justice, judicial review and the right to a fair hearing under the European Convention on Human Rights', (1984) *PL* 89 at 90.

[147] OVEY and WHITE, *Jacobs and White: The European Convention on Human Rights*, p. 141.

[148] *Ibid.*

[149] Appl. No 15523/89, *Schmautzer v Austria*, [1996] 21 EHRR 511.

[150] *Id.*, para. 28, emphasis in the original text.

[151] *Ibid.* Also Appl. No 8544/79, *Ozturk v Germany*, [1984] 6 EHRR 409, paras. 55–56.

[152] *Ibid.* Also, Appl. No 11598/85, *Stenuit v France*, [1992] ECC 401, paras. 56–57, 61; for an examination of the nature of domestic antitrust proceedings, *infra*, Chapter 2, footnote 205 and accompanying text.

a 'determination of civil rights and obligations'. In the *LeCompte, Van Leuven and de Meyere* judgment the European Court of Human Rights took the view that the French term ' "contestation" (dispute) . . . should not be construed too technically and (. . .) should be given a substantive rather than formal meaning'[153] and concluded that Article 6(1) ECHR should be applicable to all proceedings, be they judicial or administrative, whose 'result (. . .) [is] directly decisive'[154] for the existence or the exercise of a substantive right. Furthermore, provided that it was 'genuine and of a serious nature',[155] the dispute could 'relate not only to the actual existence of the right but also to its scope or the manner in which it may be exercised'.[156]

Therefore, in *Sramek*, the Court held that the outcome of proceedings before the Austrian Regional Property Transactions Authority 'was "decisive for private rights and obligations" '[157] of the applicant. In fact, the task of the authority was to rule as to whether the contract for the sale of land satisfied the statutory conditions in order to produce its legal effects and consequently its 'unfavourable decision (. . .) would – and did – mean that the transaction was null and void'. [158]

Having regard to the nature of competition proceedings, it is noteworthy that this issue was addressed by the now-defunct European Commission on Human Rights in the *Stenuit* case.[159] Although the Commission was aware of the circumstance that the French Conseil d'Etat had ruled that antitrust sanctions were not of a criminal nature,[160] it took the different view that, in consideration of the 'nature of the offence', the enforcement of French competition law nevertheless possessed a 'criminal aspect . . . for the purpose of the Convention'.[161]

The Human Rights Commission relied heavily on a 'combination of concordant factors'[162] including the goal of the provisions, which was 'to maintain free competition within the French market',[163] their general scope of application[164] and the deterrent nature of the penalty provided for those

---

153 Ser. A No 43, *LeCompte, Van Leuven and de Meyere v Belgium*, [1982] 4 EHRR 1, para. 45.

154 *Id.*, para. 47.

155 Appl. No 10426/83, *Pudas v Sweden*, [1988] 10 EHRR 380, para. 31.

156 *Ibid.*

157 Appl. No 8790/79, *Sramek v Austria*, [1985] 7 EHRR 351, para. 34.

158 *Ibid.*

159 Appl. No 11598/85, *Stenuit v France*, [1992] ECC 401.

160 *Id.*, para. 56.

161 *Id.*, para. 61.

162 *Id.*, para. 66.

163 *Id.*, para. 62.

164 *Id.*, para. 63.

responsible for competition infringements, i.e. 5 per cent of their total annual revenue.[165]

The position adopted in *Stenuit* supports the argument that the procedure for the enforcement of Articles 81 and 82 EC Treaty can also be considered to be 'criminal' in nature according to the ECHR. In fact, they concern the detection and sanction of violations of norms of general application[166] adopted in the general interest, namely the protection of free competition in the common market.[167] As to the nature and severity of the sanction which the concerned undertakings risk incurring, investigated firms may be fined up to 10 per cent of their worldwide turnover. It is therefore clear that such penalties are intended to be both deterrent and punitive.[168]

It may be argued that increasing awareness of the 'quasi-criminal' nature of antitrust proceedings has also emerged from the more recent case law of the ECJ and CFI. It is noteworthy that in his Opinion to the *Hercules Chemicals* case,[169] AG Vesterdorf argued that proceedings enforcing Articles 81 and 82 EC Treaty 'do in fact . . . have a criminal law character'[170] and should therefore comply with the requirements laid down by Article 6(1) ECHR. According to the Advocate General, it was 'vitally important' in the Community context 'that the ECJ should seek to bring about a state of legal affairs not susceptible of any justified criticism with reference to the European Convention for the Protection of Human Rights'.[171]

This view was shared by Advocate General Leger, who took the view in his Opinion in *Baustahlgewebe v Commission*[172] that 'in the light of the case law of the European Court of Human Rights . . . the present case involves a "crim-

---

165 *Id.*, para. 64. See also, *mutatis mutandis*, Appl. No 37971/97, *Ste Colas Est and Others v France*, judgment of 16 April 2002, para. 46, 48–49.

166 *Inter alia*, RILEY, 'Saunders and the power to obtain information in Community and United Kingdom competition law', (2000) 25 *ELRev* 264 at 271.

167 *Inter alia* WILS, 'The combination of the Investigative and prosecutorial function and the adjudicative function in EC Antitrust enforcement: a legal and economic analysis', (2004) 27 *W. Comp.* 201 at 208.

168 Case T-7/89, *SA Hercules Chemicals NV v Commission (Re: the Polypropylene Cartel)*, [1991] ECR II-1711; per AG Vesterdorf, reported in [1991] ECR II-867, para. I.3. See also, *mutatis mutandis*, Appl. No 69042/01, *OO Neste St Petersburg and Others v Russia*, decision of 3 June 2004 (third section), not yet reported, part 2(b).

169 Case T-7/89, *SA Hercules Chemicals v Commission*, [1991] ECR II-1711.

170 Per AG Vesterdorf, [1991] ECR II-867, para. I.3.

171 *Ibid.* See also, *mutatis mutandis*, case C-198/01, *Consorzio Italiano Fiammiferi v Autorità Garante della Concorrenza e del Mercato*, [2003] ECR I-8055, Opinion of AG Francis Jacobs, para. 52.

172 Case 185/95, [1998] ECR I-8417.

inal charge" ',[173] the appeal being directed at a Commission decision imposing fines for an antitrust breach. Consequently, the Advocate General concluded that the applicant was entitled to the protections enshrined in Article 6 of the European Convention.[174]

Similarly, in her recent Opinion to the *Dutch Electricians Federation* case[175] Advocate General Kokott suggested that, although Article 6(1) ECHR is not per se directly applicable to the proceedings before the Commission,[176] in assessing whether action had been taken 'within a reasonable time', as is required by the general principles of EC law, the ECJ will conform 'closely to the settled case law of the European Court of Human Rights' concerning that issue.[177]

It could be suggested that the CFI has shown an increasing awareness of the criminal nature of competition proceedings within the meaning given to the concept of a 'criminal charge' by the Strasbourg Court. In its recent *JFE v Commission* decision[178] the Court held with respect to the reach of the presumption of innocence in EC competition proceedings:

> given the nature of the infringements . . . and the nature and degree of severity of the ensuing penalties, the principle of the presumption of innocence applies in particular to the procedures relating to infringements of the competition rules relating to undertakings that may result in the imposition of fines or periodic penalty payments (. . .).[179]

In reaching this conclusion the CFI referred to judgments of the European Court of Human Rights such as *Lutz*[180] and *Ozturk*[181] which, like the *Schmautzer* case,[182] cited above, concerned the legality of proceedings for the

---

173 Per AG Leger, para. 31.

174 *Id.*, para. 30, 32. See HOGAN, 'The use of compelled evidence in European competition law cases', in HAWK (ed.), *International Antitrust Law and Policy*, p. 659 at 671–72.

175 Case C-105/04 P, *Netherlandse Feteratieve Vereigning voor de Goothandel op Elektrotechnisch Gebied v Commission*, Opinion of AG Kokott, delivered on 8 December 2005, [2006] ECR I-8725.

176 Per AG Kokott, para. 107, footnote 57.

177 *Id.*, para. 108. Cf. T-23/99, *LR AF 1998 A/S v Commission,* [2002] ECR II-1705, paras. 220–21; also, *mutatis mutandis*, T-9/99, *HFB v Commission*, [2002] ECR II-1487, paras. 390–91.

178 Case T-67/00, [2004] ECR II-2501.

179 *Id.*, para. 178.

180 Appl. No 9912/82, *Lutz v Germany*, judgment of 25 August 1987, [1988] 10 EHRR 182, para. 57.

181 Appl. No 8744/79, *Ozturk v Germany*, judgment of 21 February 1985, ser. A No 73, [1984] 6 EHRR 409, paras. 55–56.

182 Appl. No 15523/89, *Schmautzer v Austria*, [1996] 21 EHRR 511.

detection and repression of certain 'decriminalised' motoring offences that had been recognised as having a criminal character. Consequently, it is submitted that although the Court did not expressly define EC antitrust proceedings as criminal, the clear reference to the case law of the Strasbourg Court concerning administrative proceedings that are 'criminal in nature' would appear to support the view that the undertakings affected by competition proceedings before the Commission are entitled to the safeguards enshrined in the right to a fair hearing in accordance with Article 6(1) ECHR.[183]

It is submitted that the trend toward the criminalisation of cartels currently ongoing in the jurisdiction of some Member States, where violations of the prohibition of some forms of hardcore anti-competitive conduct are considered criminal offences, should also be taken into account. For instance, in the United Kingdom, according to s. 188 of the 2002 Enterprise Act, 'an individual is guilty of an offence if he dishonestly agrees with one or more persons to make or implement, or to cause to be made or implemented, arrangements' which would constitute so called 'hardcore' forms of anti-competitive conduct, namely price fixing, restrictions of output and supply, market partitioning or bid-rigging.

Commentators forcefully argued that the offence 'bears no resemblance to the [Chapter I] prohibition',[184] namely the prohibition of cartel behaviour or indeed to Article 81 EC Treaty.[185] However, the criminalisation of cartels in the laws of some of the Member States could be interpreted as a sign of the 'strong determination to robustly tackle hard-core cartel conduct'.[186] It also demonstrates that these forms of behaviour are perceived as extremely harmful to the public interest and the common economic welfare.[187] A similar trend appears also to be emerging in the context of the Commission's enforcement of Article 81 EC Treaty. The new Fining Guidelines[188] and the revised Leniency programme[189] demonstrate the Commission's commitment to the

[183] VENIT and LOUKO, 'The Commission's new power to question and its implications on human rights', in HAWK (ed.), *International Antitrust Law and Policy*, pp. 698–99.

[184] MacCULLOCH, 'The cartel offence and the criminalisation of United Kingdom competition law', (2003) *Journal of Business Law* Nov 616 at 619.

[185] *Id.*, pp. 620–21.

[186] NASH and FURSE, 'Partners in crime – the cartel offence in UK law', (2004) 15 *International Company and Commercial Law Review* 138 at 153.

[187] JOSHUA, 'A Sherman Act bridgehead in Europe, or a ghost ship in mid-Atlantic? A close look at the United Kingdom proposals to criminalise hardcore cartel conduct', (2002) 23 *ECLR* 231 at 245.

[188] Commission guidelines on the method of setting fines imposed pursuant to Article 23(2)(a) of Regulation No 1/2003, [2006] OJ C210/2.

[189] Commission Notice on the non-imposition or reduction of fines in cartel cases, [1996] OJ C207/04.

effective enforcement of Article 81 EC Treaty through, on the one hand, the imposition of financial penalties having a truly deterrent and punitive character and, on the other hand, the promise of immunity from fines as a means to encourage cooperation and as a result to boost cartel detection.[190]

By contrast with antitrust cases, no decision has been handed down to date on the question of the nature of merger proceedings. However, commentators suggested that merger proceedings may be classified as leading to the 'determination of civil rights and obligations'.[191] The purpose of merger control is to assess whether the notified concentration is capable of adversely affecting competition in the common market in particular by creating or strengthening a dominant position. Also the transaction is suspended, save in the exceptional cases listed in the Regulation,[192] until such time as the Commission adopts a decision.

A parallel can be drawn with those proceedings provided by the laws of some of the contracting states to the European Convention on Human Rights and aimed at the authorisation of land transactions, such as those at issue in the *Sramek* case,[193] examined above. In addition, in its other *Ringeisen* judgment the European Court of Human Rights held that a procedure aimed at approving the contract for the purchase of land fell within the scope of Article 6(1) ECHR, being concerned with the determination of civil rights and obligations and 'decisive for the relations in civil law' between the applicant and his counterpart in the land transaction.[194]

Merger proceedings, being aimed at verifying that the notified transaction is compatible with rules of free competition within the common market, are 'decisive for the relations in civil law' between the merging parties, by the same token to that in the procedure at issue in *Ringeisen*: in fact, it will depend on their outcome whether the parties will be allowed to carry out the concentration itself. They can thus be considered to be concerned with the determination of

---

[190] See, *inter alia*, GALE, 'The Leniency regime and the fight against cartels by the Directorate General for Competition', (2004) 25 *Company Lawyer* 324 at 327; also WILS, 'Leniency in antitrust enforcement: theory and practice', (2007) 30 *W. Comp.* 25; WILS, 'The European Commission 2006 Guidelines on antitrust fines: a legal and economic analysis', (2007) 30 *W. Comp.* 197.

[191] WAELBROECK and FOSSELARD, 'Should the decision-making power in EC Antitrust procedures be left to an independent judge? – The impact of the European Convention on Human Rights on EC Antitrust procedures', (1994) 14 *YEL* 111 at 124–25; and, more recently, WILS, 'The combination of the investigative and prosecutorial function and the adjudicative function in EC Antitrust enforcement: a legal and economic analysis', (2004) 27 *W. Comp.* 201 at 209.

[192] Article 7, EC Merger Control Regulation.

[193] Appl. No 8790/79, *Sramek v Austria*, [1985] 7 EHRR 351.

[194] Ser. A No 13, *Ringeisen v Austria*, [1979–80] 1 EHRR 455, para. 94.

the parties' civil rights and obligations and must be subject to the requirements laid down by Article 6(1) ECHR.

It can therefore be concluded that the adoption of the 'substantive' test elaborated with respect to administrative proceedings in the areas of, *inter alia*, town and environmental planning and repression of minor motoring offences, has allowed the European Court of Human Rights to extend the reach of Article 6(1) of the Convention to a variety of administrative proceedings. As a result, it may be convincingly argued that the standards of administrative fairness enshrined in the ECHR should provide a benchmark to assess the fairness of the competition procedures before the Commission. This assessment will be conducted in the following chapters.

2. The right to be heard in EC competition proceedings between 'administrative due process' and a right to a 'fair trial'

INTRODUCTION

This chapter seeks to examine the discipline of the right to be heard in antitrust and merger proceedings before the European Commission and to discuss its compliance with the standards provided by the European Convention on Human Rights with respect to administrative procedures having a civil or criminal character. After having investigated the genesis of the right to be heard as a general principle of EC law embodied in the 'constitutional traditions' common to the Member States, we will consider the corresponding requirements laid down in the ECHR. Thereafter, the examination will concentrate on highlighting areas of similarity and difference as well as issues of concern for the compliance of the right to a hearing in competition proceedings before the Commission with the European Convention standards.

The chapter will conclude that, although the right to be heard appears to be sufficiently established in the context of the EC competition enforcement, there are still significant problems concerning its effectiveness especially in the framework for merger control, given its tight deadlines, as well as more generally with respect to the completeness of the statement of objections and the involvement of the Hearing Officer in the context of Articles 81–82 EC Treaty cases.

1. THE RIGHT TO BE HEARD IN EC COMPETITION PROCEEDINGS: FROM THE 'GENERAL PRINCIPLES OF LAW' TO THE IMPLEMENTING REGULATIONS

1.1. '*Audi Alteram Partem*': the Foundations of the Right to a Hearing in EC Law

The standards of 'administrative fairness' in force in EC law are in significant part the product of judicial creation.[1] The ECJ was faced with a situation in which ad hoc procedural rules, including those determining the extent of the right to a 'fair hearing' before the Community institutions, had been enacted only in specific areas.[2] Consequently in the absence of rules set out in the Treaty or secondary legislation the Court had to strike a balance between the need to ensure the effective exercise of the rights of defence of those concerned by the proceedings with the goal of efficiency in administrative action.[3]

The Court was mindful of the need to reconcile differing trends and concepts developed in the legal systems of the Member States and especially of two rather different legal traditions:[4] on the one hand, the English tradition, grounded in the two principles of natural justice of *nemo judex in causa sua* and *audi alteram partem*,[5] and, on the other hand, the continental French tradition, which instead aims at achieving goals of efficiency in the interest of the common good.[6] However, these differences did not prevent the Court of Justice from acknowledging the existence vis-à-vis the Community employees of a 'generally accepted principle of administrative law in force in the Member States' according to which 'the administration . . . must allow their servants the opportunity of replying to the allegations before any disciplinary decision is taken concerning them'[7] in the interest of 'sound justice and good administration'.[8]

The ECJ was clearly influenced by the Anglo-Saxon tradition, which is rooted in the rule of law and in the principles of natural justice underpinning the power of the courts to assert their supervisory control of the procedures followed initially by courts of inferior jurisdiction and later by statutory bodies in the adoption of decisions liable to adversely affect the rights of indi-

---

1 *Inter alia*, LENAERTS & VANHAMME, 'Procedural rights of the private parties in the Community administrative process', (1997) 34 *CMLRev* 531 at 533.

2 *Ibid.*

3 SCHWARZE, 'Tendencies towards a common administrative law in Europe', (1991) 16 *ELRev* 3 at 5.

4 *Ibid.*

5 JOSHUA, 'The right to be heard in EEC Competition procedures', (1991–1992) 15 *Fordham Int'l L. J.* 16 at 21.

6 SCHWARZE, 'Tendencies towards a common administrative law in Europe', (1991) 16 *ELRev* 3 at 6. For commentary on the concept of 'procedural due process' in the Common law and especially in the North American legal tradition see generally MACDONALD, 'Judicial review and procedural fairness in administrative law', (1979–80) 25 *McGill L J* 520, (1980) 26 *McGill L J* 1.

7 Case 32/62, *Alvis v Council*, [1963] ECR 49, p. 55.

8 *Ibid.*

viduals.[9] The 'presumption of natural justice' developed in seventeenth-century England in the case law of the Court of King's Bench was held to encompass the rules of *audi alteram partem* and *nemo iudex in causa sua debet esse*,[10] namely the right to adequate notice precedent to an opportunity to be heard, and the right to an impartial and disinterested decision-maker[11] not only in judicial proceedings, but also in the context of administrative action.[12] Although the scope of the individuals' right to be heard is flexible and must be determined in relation to the context in which it must be exercised,[13] at a minimum it must confer a right to know the case against them, to be acquainted with the relevant evidence and to be given an opportunity to refute it.[14]

In the seminal *Transocean Marine Paint* judgment,[15] the ECJ was prepared to give these principles a firmer footing and to recognise their general application extending to areas in which the Community legislature had provided for ad hoc procedural laws, such as competition enforcement.[16] The Court expressly followed the advice of Advocate General Warner, according to whom:

> There is a rule embedded in the law of some of our countries that an administrative authority, before wielding a statutory power to the detriment of a particular person, must in general hear what that person has to say about the matter, even if the statute does not expressly require it.[17]

The ECJ concluded that in accordance with the 'general rule that a person whose interests are perceptibly affected by a decision taken by a public authority must

---

[9] *Inter alia*, MACDONALD, 'Judicial review and procedural fairness in administrative law: I', (1979–80) 25 *McGill L J* 520 at 529; REDISH and MARSHALL, 'Adjudicatory independence and the values of procedural due process', (1986) 95 *Yale L J* 455 at 459.

[10] MACDONALD, 'Procedural due process in Canadian constitutional law: natural justice and fundamental justice', (1987) 39(2) *U. Fla. L. Rev.* 217 at 235.

[11] *Ibid.*

[12] *Inter alia*, *Franklin v Minister of Town and Country Planning*, House of Lords, [1948] AC 87.

[13] *Alfred Thangarajah Durayappah of Chundikuly, Mayor of Jaffna v W.J. Fernando and Others*, Privy Council, [1967] 2 AC 337, per Lord Upjohn at p. 349.

[14] *Kanda v Government of Malaya*, House of Lords, [1962] AC 322, per Lord Denning at 337.

[15] Case 17/74, *Transocean Marine Paint Association v Commission*, [1974] ECR 1063.

[16] *Id.*, para. 15.

[17] Per AG Warner, Opinion available in [1974] 2 CMLR 469.

be given the opportunity to make his point of view known',[18] the applicants should have been granted the opportunity to be heard by the Commission before the adoption of an exemption decision, pursuant to Article 81(3) EC Treaty, although Regulation 17/62 did not expressly provide for their hearing in similar cases.

It follows that in proceedings leading to the adoption of a decision significantly affecting the position of individuals or undertakings, the latter must be afforded the possibility of making their views known as to the truth and relevance of the objections made by the competent EC institutions, even in the absence of rules governing the procedure in question.[19] The case law of the Community courts therefore indicates that the rule of *audi alteram partem* has now acquired the status of '*absolute* or *objective standard of good administration*',[20] which serves a twofold purpose: 'it contributes to the accuracy of the substantial outcome of the decision-making'[21] and at the same time 'it constitutes a process right designed to protect individual substantive rights and interests'.[22] Especially when the imposition of a sanction is concerned, the observance of the right to be heard constitutes a fundamental principle of Community law applicable in the course of administrative action.

The importance of the right to be heard is also reflected in more recent developments concerning the protection of fundamental rights in the EU. Article 41 of the EU Charter of Fundamental Rights, which establishes a 'right to good administration', namely the right of every person 'to have his or her affairs handled impartially, fairly and within a reasonable time by the institutions and bodies of the Union' includes, *inter alia*, the right 'to be heard before any individual measure which would affect him or her adversely is taken' and to have access to his or her individual file. The express recognition of this principle in an authoritative, albeit not legally binding, catalogue of human rights raises significant issues as regards its standing and the applicable standards of protection.

Commentators argued that an analogy could be drawn between the right to 'good administration' belonging to the Charter and the right to a fair trial guaranteed by Article 6 ECHR 'in providing an umbrella for a non-exhaustive list

---

18 *Id.*, para. 15 of the judgment.

19 Case C-135/92, *Fiskano v Commission of the European Communities*, [1994] ECR I-2885, para 39.

20 NEHL, *Principles of Administrative Procedure in EC Law* (1999) Oxford: Hart Publishing, p. 96 (emphasis in the original text).

21 *Id.*, p. 97.

22 *Ibid.* For the consequences of a violation of the 'due process' rules see, *inter alia*, joined cases 209-15 and 218/78, *Heintz van Landewyck v Commission*, [1980] ECR 3125.

of procedural guarantees'[23] applicable to administrative action and therefore suggested that Article 41 of the EU Charter of Fundamental Rights could lead to an interpretation of the principle of *audi alteram partem* progressively in line with the Convention standards.[24] However, the following sections will illustrate the extent to which this development could have far-reaching consequences on the current standards of 'fairness' applicable to competition proceedings before the Commission.

1.2. The Right to a Hearing in Antitrust Proceedings: the Statement of Objections and the Reply

The commitment of the Community legislature to safeguard appropriately the right to a hearing of undertakings concerned by antitrust proceedings before the European Commission is demonstrated by the preamble to Regulation No 1/03:

> The undertakings concerned should be accorded the right to be heard by the Commission, third parties whose interests may be affected by a decision should be given the opportunity of submitting their observations beforehand, and the decisions taken should be widely publicised (. . .).[25]

Accordingly, Article 27 states that the undertakings concerned must be afforded the opportunity to be heard on the allegations of anti-competitive conduct raised by the Commission against them. The implementing Commission Regulation states that the right to a hearing shall be exercised first and foremost in writing for reasons of administrative 'procedural economy',[26] whereas the oral hearing plays a supplementary role in completing the evidence and argument before the Commission.[27] It is submitted that the different role of the oral hearing vis-à-vis the written submissions can be interpreted as reflecting the administrative and not judicial nature of the

---

23 Lord MILLETT, 'The right to good administration in European Law', (2002) *PL* Summer 309 at 318.

24 *Inter alia*, KANSKA, 'Towards Administrative Human Rights in the EU. Impact of the Charter of Fundamental Rights', (2004) *ELJ* 296 at 306.

25 Recital XXXII, Preamble to Council Regulation No 1/2003.

26 See Article 10(3), Commission Regulation (EC) No 773/2004 of 7 April 2004 relating to the conduct of proceedings by the Commission pursuant to Articles 81 and 82 of the EC Treaty, [2004] OJ L123/18; Article 13(3), Commission Regulation (EC) No 802/2004 of 7 April 2004 implementing Council Regulation (EC) No 139/2004 on the control of concentrations between undertakings, [2004] OJ L133/1.

27 COMMISSION of the EUROPEAN COMMUNITIES, *XI Report on Competition Policy*, Brussels, 1982, p. 31.

competition procedure,[28] notwithstanding the emphasis placed by the Commission's administrative practice on the importance of oral submissions in the context of the 'administrative process'.[29]

Paramount to the exercise of the right to be heard is the 'meaningful participation' of the investigated undertakings in the procedure and the effective exercise on their part of the right to defend themselves against the allegations of anti-competitive conduct raised by the Commission.[30] Therefore it entails, on the one hand, the obligation for the Commission to notify in a clear and exhaustive manner its allegations of anti-competitive conduct against the concerned parties and, on the other hand, the right of the investigated undertakings to submit written observations and to be afforded the opportunity of an oral hearing.[31] The European Court of Justice has consistently indicated that the 'statement of objections' (hereinafter referred to also as SO) must satisfy minimum requirements as regards its contents.[32]

In *Boehringer Mannheim v Commission*[33] the ECJ held that the SO must at least set out 'clearly albeit succinctly the essential facts on which the Commission relies'[34] provided that, however, in the course of the administrative proceedings it 'supplies the details necessary to the defence'.[35] Another statement of objection will also be required when, following fresh investigations, new facts or evidence emerge which corroborate the Commission's case.[36]

---

28 KERSE, 'Procedures in EC Competition Cases: the oral hearing', (1994) 15 *ECLR* 40.

29 COMMISSION of the EUROPEAN COMMUNITIES, *Dealing with the Commission: Competition Enforcement*, 1997, Brussels: Official Publication Centre, p. 46.

30 Per AG Gand, Opinion in case 41/69, *ACF Chemiefarma v Commission*, [1970] ECR 661, p. 707.

31 *Inter alia,* GIANNAKOPOULOS, 'The right to be orally heard by the Commission in antitrust, merger, anti-dumping/anti-subsidies and State Aid Community Procedures', (2001) 24 *W Comp* 541 at 569.

32 *Inter alia*, case 41/69, *ACF Chemiefarma v Commission*, [1970] ECR 661; case 45/69, *Boehringer Mannheim v Commission* [1970] ECR 769; case C-62/86, *AKZO v Commission*, [1991] ECR I-3359; cases T- 10, 11, 12 and 15/92, *SA Cimenteries CBR & others v Commission*, [1992] ECR II-1571; cases 142 & 156/84, *BAT & Reynolds v Commission*, [1987] ECR 4487.

33 Case 45/69, [1970] ECR 769.

34 *Id.*, para. 9.

35 *Ibid.*

36 Case 51/69, *Bayer v Commission of the European Communities*, [1972] ECR 745, para. 11. Also case T-40/92, *Groupement CB & Europay International SA v Commission*, [1994] ECR II-49, paras. 57–58.

In later case law[37] the Community courts emphasised that the Commission would not only be obliged to spell out all the facts and legal arguments supporting its allegations[38] but would also have to explain the inferences that it has drawn from the evidence collected during the proceedings and on which it relies against the investigated undertakings.[39] To hold otherwise would amount to denying them the possibility to put forward their views as regards the probative value of that evidence.[40] It was primarily to comply with the revised position of the ECJ that the Commission modified its administrative practice in 1992 and began to attach the documentary evidence constituting the basis for the allegations made against the concerned firms to the SO.[41]

The very recent *Corus UK* judgment[42] added that, when the Commission proposes to inflict a pecuniary sanction on an undertaking, it will be obliged to give a brief assessment of the nature, the severity and the duration of the breach to allow the investigated party to foresee the dimension of the penalty that is likely to be inflicted on them and to challenge it in its submissions.[43] Confirming substantially this view, the ECJ held in the *SGL Carbon* appeal:

> (. . .) provided that the Commission sets out in the statement of objections the main elements of fact and of law capable of leading to the imposition of a fine, such as the gravity and the duration of the alleged infringement and also the circumstance that the infringement was committed deliberately or negligently, the Commission satisfies its obligation to observe the undertakings' right to be heard (. . .).[44]

However, it should be emphasised that not every divergence between the findings contained in the final decision and the allegations made in the statement of objections will give rise to the annulment of the decision. The ECJ

---

37 Case T-191/98, *Atlantic Container Line AB and others v Commission*, [2003] ECR II 3275.

38 *Id.*, para. 113.

39 *Id.*, para. 162.

40 *Id.*, paras. 172–73.

41 COMMISSION of the EUROPEAN COMMUNITIES, *XII Report on Competition Policy,* Brussels: 1993, pp. 40–41 (also cited in T-65/89, *BPB Industries plc and British Gypsum Ltd v Commission*, [1993] ECR II 389 at para. 29). See, *inter alia*, case 53/85, *Chemie BV and AKZO Chemie UK Ltd v Commission of the European Communities*, [1986] ECR 1965, para. 5.

42 Case T-48/00, *Corus UK v Commission*, judgment of the Court of First Instance (Second Chamber) of 8 July 2004, [2004] ECR II-2325.

43 *Id.*, paras. 144 and 146. See also, more recently, case T-340/03, *France Telecom v Commission*, judgment of 30 January 2007, not yet reported, para. 18.

44 Case C-328/05 P, *SGL Carbon AG v Commission*, judgment of 10 May 2007, not yet reported, para. 56. See also case T-109/02, *Bollore SA and others v Commission*, judgment of 26 April 2007, not yet reported, paras. 66–67.

recognises that the statement is merely provisional[45] and that the Commission is entitled, if not altogether obliged, to modify its contents as a result of new fact-finding measures or of the explanations given by the investigated parties in relation to the allegations or to the evidence.[46] The decision will thus be liable to annulment only if its divergences with the statement of objections concern new evidence or fresh allegations on which the investigated parties were not allowed to reply following the re-examination of the original statement.[47]

The case law of the ECJ and the administrative practice of the Commission demonstrate that the right to be heard constitutes an essential component of the rights of defence of the investigated undertakings[48] and encompasses a specific duty imposed on the Commission to 'observe the procedural safeguards provided for by the Community law'.[49] Complying with specific requirements as regards the contents of the statement of objections, the possibility to submit written observations and the opportunity to access an oral hearing are clearly among these guarantees. The stronger commitment to the disclosure of all the basic evidence constitutes an additional safeguard for the right to be heard of the investigated parties and accordingly contributes to the effective protection of the investigated parties' legitimate interests in the course of the procedure.

1.3. The Position of Third Parties in Antitrust Proceedings

EC antitrust enforcement relies greatly on the active role of complainants as a source of information on the basis of which the Commission can initiate proceedings.[50] The importance of their involvement is reflected in the need to ensure their close and constant involvement in the course of the procedure. According to Article 6 of the 2004 Commission's Implementing Regulation,

---

45 Case 60/81, *International Business Machines Corporation v Commission*, [1981] ECR 2639, para. 10: 'an act is open to review only if it is a measure definitively laying down the position of the Commission or of the Council on the conclusion of that procedure and not a provisional measure intended to pave the way for the final decision'.

46 Cases 142 & 156/84, *BAT & Reynolds v Commission*, [1986] ECR 1899, para. 27.

47 T-67/01, *JCB Service v Commission*, [2004] ECR II-49, paras. 50–51. Also case T-109/02, *Bollore SA and Others v Commission*, judgment of 26 April 2007, not yet reported, paras. 80–81.

48 *Inter alia,* GIANNAKOPOULOS, 'The right to be orally heard by the Commission', at 569.

49 *Ibid.*

50 See, *inter alia*, EUROPEAN COMMISSION, *White Paper on Modernisation of the rules implementing Articles 85 and 86 [now 81 and 82] of the EC Treaty, 28* April 1999, [1999] OJ L123/1.

complainants have the right to receive a non-confidential copy of the statement of objections, to submit observations in time and, where appropriate, to participate in the oral hearing.[51]

However, it should be emphasised that complainants are not entitled to obtain a final decision as to whether the facts that form the subject matter of that complaint disclose a violation of competition law.[52] The Commission, being an administrative authority, is allowed to assess the degree of priority of each case in accordance with the Community interest and therefore is only obliged 'to examine carefully the factual and legal aspects of which it is notified by the complainant in order to decide whether they indicate behaviour likely to distort competition in the Common Market'.[53] Consequently the Commission is entitled to reject a complaint on grounds of insufficient Community interest[54] having regard to a number of factors, namely the seriousness of the alleged infringement, the availability of the evidence and the scope of the investigation.[55]

It is recognised that, alongside complainants, other third parties (such as other competitors and customers) may be affected by the outcome of the procedure. However, their right to participate in the proceedings is limited to being informed in writing of the subject matter of the investigations and to making written submissions within a given deadline upon application to the Commission,[56] provided that they demonstrate a 'sufficient interest' in the proceedings.[57] On this point, it was held in the *Belgian Newsagents*[58] judgment that 'the Commission has a reasonable margin of discretion to decide how expedient it may be to hear persons whose evidence may be relevant to the inquiry'.[59]

---

51 Article 7, Commission Regulation No 2842/98 of 22 December 1998 on the hearing of parties in certain proceedings under Articles 85 and 86 of the EC Treaty, [1998] OJ L354/18; Article 6, Commission Regulation No 773/2004 of 7 April 2004 relating to the conduct of proceedings by the Commission pursuant to Articles 81 and 82 of the EC Treaty, [2004] OJ L123/18.

52 *Inter alia*, case T-24/90, *Automec v Commission*, [1992] ECR I-222, para. 79.

53 *Id.*, para. 85.

54 Case T-114/92, *BEMIM v Commission*, [1995] ECR II-147, para. 80.

55 *Id.* para. 86.

56 JELLEMA, 'The redheaded stepchild of Community competition law: the third party and its right to be heard in competition proceedings', (2002) 20 *Boston University International Law Journal* 211 at 262. Cf. Art. 13(1), Commission Regulation (EC) No 773/2004 of 7 April 2004 relating to the conduct of proceedings by the Commission pursuant to Articles 81 and 82 of the EC Treaty, [2004] OJ L123/18.

57 Case 43/85, *ANCIDES v Commission*, [1987] ECR 3131, para. 8.

58 Cases 43& 63/82, *VBBB & VBVB v Commission*, [1984] ECR 19.

59 *Id.*, para. 18. Cf. JELLEMA, 'The redheaded stepchild of Community competition law', *supra*, at 264.

Accordingly, before a third party can be allowed to participate in the inquiry, he or she must be able to demonstrate 'an economic or legal interest which is or may be detrimentally affected by the infringement of the Commission's decision'.[60] Before annulling a Commission decision on the grounds that the applicant had been denied the possibility to exercise the right to a hearing, he or she must therefore disclose 'evidence to show that in the circumstances the Commission, in not hearing' him or her 'unduly restricted the inquiry'.[61]

As regards the scope of their right to a hearing, in *Matra Hachette*[62] the CFI suggested that the procedural rights of third parties in competition proceedings were not as far reaching as those conferred on the investigated undertakings[63] and that in any event could not be exercised in a manner which resulted in weakening the right to a fair hearing enjoyed by the defendant undertakings.[64]

On this point, it is submitted that by entitling complainants to receive a non-confidential copy of the statement of objections, the Commission struck a fair balance between the need to ensure their meaningful participation in the procedure and the legitimate interests of the investigated parties,[65] since without going as far as to be acquainted with 'sensitive' aspects of the case, complainants are in any event capable of making their point of view known on the basis of sufficient information concerning the allegations made against the firms directly affected by the procedure.

Nevertheless, it is noteworthy that the Commission has never considered itself 'obliged to afford' third parties who have so applied 'a subsequent oral hearing, except when they are again able to show a legitimate interest in such a hearing'.[66] Although considerations of procedural economy and concerns for sound administration in the context of competition enforcement should not be overlooked, it could be argued that the rather limited possibility to access the

---

60 KERSE and KHAN, *EC Antitrust Procedure*, p. 194. See, e.g., case T-528, 542-43, 546/98, *Metropole Television SA & others v Commission*, [1996] ECR II-649, para. 61.

61 KERSE and KHAN, *EC Antitrust Procedure*, p. 58.

62 Case T-17/93, *Matra Hachette SA v Commission,* [1994] ECR II-595.

63 *Id.*, para. 35. Also T-65/96, *Kish Glass & Co Ltd v Commission*, [2000] ECR II-1885, para. 34.

64 JELLEMA, 'The redheaded stepchild of Community competition law', *supra*, at 272.

65 *Ibid.* Also, case 53/85, *AKZO Chemie BV v Commission*, [1986] ECR 1965, para. 28. For commentary, see KERSE and KHAN, *EC Antitrust Procedure,* p. 202; also JELLEMA, 'The redheaded stepchild of Community competition law', *ibid.* at 288–89.

66 COMMISSION of the EUROPEAN COMMUNITIES, *XI Report on Competition Policy*, Brussels: 1982, p. 31.

'oral' hearing constitutes a factor of some concern. In fact, the involvement of third parties can positively contribute to the full assessment of individual cases especially in this phase, which aims to examine more carefully facts and issues that have not been fully clarified in the written submissions.[67]

Undoubtedly, the final decision can be challenged before the CFI if third parties claim that their right to participate in the proceedings has been violated by the Commission's denial of a hearing. Nevertheless, the need to show that 'the Commission, in not hearing' the applicant 'unduly restricted the inquiry',[68] so as to successfully seek the annulment of the decision, appears to be a rather high threshold[69] which could eventually discourage third parties from vindicating their hearing rights.

1.4. The Right to a Hearing in Merger Cases

Just as in procedures applying Articles 81 and 82 EC Treaty, in merger cases 'the Commission is obliged to respect the parties' right to be heard since failure to do so constitutes an infringement of the parties' rights of defence'.[70] At the end of a Phase 1 investigation, they are therefore entitled to receive a statement of objections, to submit written representations and to have the opportunity to present their case at an oral hearing.[71]

With respect to the manner of exercise of the right to be heard, the Commission is committed to a policy of greater openness, transparency and close communication with the undertakings concerned.[72] The new Guidelines for Best Practice[73] state that 'DG Competition endeavours to give all parties involved in the proceeding ample opportunity for open and frank discussions and to make their points of view known throughout the procedure'.[74]

---

67 *Mutatis mutandis*, Appl. No 18064/91, *Ortenberg v Austria*, [1995] 19 EHRR 524, para. 26.

68 COMMISSION of the EUROPEAN COMMUNITIES, *XI Report on Competition Policy*, Brussels: 1982, p. 58.

69 Joined Cases 209-215 and 218/78, *Heintz van Landewyck v Commission*, [1980] ECR 3125, para. 47.

70 KEKELEKIS, 'The rights of notifying parties and third parties during the preliminary investigation procedures under the ECMR', (2003) *EBLRev* 429 at 435. See, *inter alia*, Case T-96/92, *Comité Central d'Enterprise de la Société Generale des Grandes Sources and Others v Commission of the European Communities*, [1995] ECR II-1213, para. 56.

71 Article 18, Council Regulation No 139/2004; see also Article 13(2) and (3), Implementing Commission Regulation No 804/2004, [2004] OJ L133/1.

72 *Id.*, para. 29.

73 COMMISSION of the EUROPEAN COMMUNITIES, DG Competition, *Best Practices on the Conduct of EC Merger Control Proceedings*.

74 *Id.*, para. 1.

It was emphasised that 'it is in the interests of DG Competition and the business and legal community to ensure that notification forms are complete from the outset'.[75] Consequently, 'preliminary contacts' between the case-handling officials and the undertakings concerned[76] play a pivotal role in ensuring that the proposed transaction is assessed thoroughly and that concerns vis-à-vis the rules of effective competition are avoided as early as possible.[77]

'State of Play' meetings[78] instead 'contribute to the quality and efficiency of the decision-making process and ensure transparency and communication between DG Competition and the notifying parties'.[79] They offer 'a forum for the mutual exchange of information between DG Competition and the notifying parties'[80] before and within two weeks of a decision opening a Phase 2 investigation, before the issuing of, as well as after the reply to, the Statement of Objections and the oral hearing and finally before the meeting of the Advisory Committee.[81] They also constitute a 'channel of contact' to discuss merger remedies to address the competition concerns raised by the Commission.[82]

It is noteworthy that the ECJ has interpreted the scope of the right to be heard in merger proceedings consistently with its case law concerning antitrust cases: on this point it was held that 'when the principle that the rights of the defence are to be protected is applied to' merger proceedings, 'it cannot result in any lesser right of access to documents in the Commission file'.[83]

However, one of the most significant differences between the two sets of proceedings concerns the involvement of third parties and their corresponding hearing entitlements. Since the clearance mechanism is triggered by the notification of a concentration, the role of complainants is far more limited than in antitrust proceedings. Third parties may still claim to have been adversely affected by the notified concentration.[84] For this reason the 2004 Merger

---

75 *Id.*, para. 7.

76 *Id.*, para. 5.

77 *Id.*, para. 1.

78 For commentary, *inter alia,* ANDREANGELI, 'Fairness and timing in merger control proceedings: will the 'stop-the-clock' clause work?', (2005) 26(7) *ECLR* 403.

79 COMMISSION of the EUROPEAN COMMUNITIES, DG Competition, *Best Practices on the Conduct of EC Merger Control Proceedings*, para. 30.

80 *Ibid.*

81 *Id.*, para. 33.

82 *Id.*, para. 41.

83 Case T-221/98, *Endemol Entertainment Holding BV v Commission of the European Communities*, [1999] ECR II-1299, para. 50.

84 COMMISSION of the EUROPEAN COMMUNITIES, DG Competition, *Best Practices on the Conduct of EC Merger Control Proceedings*, para. 105.

Regulation enshrines a limited right to be heard subject to evidence of 'sufficient interest' and provided that the Commission considers it necessary for the examination of the concentration.[85] As a result, they are entitled to receive 'sufficient information' concerning the notified concentration to assess the extent to which their interests are adversely affected by it and to submit their observations in writing to the Commission.[86]

Also, in accordance with the policy of greater openness and transparency adopted with the 2004 Merger Regulation, the revised Best Practice Guidelines provide for 'triangular' meetings[87] to which the case-handling officials can invite third parties to hear their views in the interest of the fact-finding investigation.[88] Their principal function is 'to enable DG Competition to reach a more informed conclusion'[89] on the compatibility of the proposed transaction with the Common Market in Phase 1 proceedings (before the Statement of Objections is issued), when the evidence at hand is somewhat conflicting or does not allow the Commission to reach a definitive decision on the notified merger.

The fact that the Merger Regulation confers on the recognised representatives of the employees of the undertakings concerned by the notified transaction the right to be heard constitutes one of its most interesting features.[90] As was recently emphasised by the House of Lords Select Committee on the European Union, its purpose is to provide for the consultation and the protection of employees in the event of a merger leading to restructuring so that its social impact can be assessed.[91]

Overall, it could be argued that, although significant aspects retain a degree of similarity with the discipline of the right to a hearing in antitrust proceedings, more recent developments indicate a trend towards more tailor-made standards reflecting the characteristics of merger proceedings and ensuring the

---

[85] Article 16, Commission Regulation No 802/2004. GIANNAKOPOULOS, 'The right to be orally heard by the Commission', at 557. See e.g. case T-290/94, *Kaysersberg SA v EC Commission*, [1997] ECR II-2137, para. 109.

[86] COMMISSION of the EUROPEAN COMMUNITIES, DG Competition, *Best Practices on the Conduct of EC Merger Control Proceedings*, para. 35. See also KEKELEKIS, 'The statement of objections as an inherent part of the right to be heard in EC merger proceedings: issues of concern', (2004) 25 *ECLR* 518 at 523.

[87] *Supra,* this section, footnote 73 and accompanying text.

[88] COMMISSION of the EUROPEAN COMMUNITIES, DG Competition, *Best Practices*, para. 38.

[89] *Id.*, para. 39.

[90] Article 18, Council Regulation No 139/2004.

[91] HOUSE of LORDS SELECT COMMITTEE on the EUROPEAN UNION, *XXXII Report: the Review of the EC Merger Regulation*, Session 2001/2002, 30/7/2002, para. 226.

exhaustive assessment of the notified concentration. Nonetheless, it is submitted that the extent to which the changes in the merger administrative practices are capable on their own of ensuring their fairness and the quality of the decision-making is not entirely clear. Recent decisions of the Court of First Instance[92] highlighted significant deficiencies in the assessment of evidence by the Commission[93] and prompted demands for improvements in the internal and the external checks and balances in an administrative process characterised by the dual role of the Commission as both investigator and decision-maker.[94]

The lack of appropriate scientific output in the appraisal of the notified transactions[95] and, perhaps more importantly, the negotiation and evaluation of proposed modifications to the merger[96] emerged as crunch points in the process of consultation, which led eventually to the enactment of the 2004 Merger Regulation. Having regard to the negotiations of commitments, representatives of the industry and several commentators argued that, in the context of merger control, recourse to judicial scrutiny of the Commission's decisions was less likely than in that of antitrust enforcement due to the commercial pressure involved and, as a result, the administrative decision was in fact final and beyond any control on the part of the European courts.[97]

Other authors suggested that the tight time limits governing the procedure often placed the notifying parties in a weak bargaining position vis-à-vis the Commission officials when it came to negotiating commitments to ensure clearance of the notified concentration. It was felt that, given the time involved in the judicial scrutiny of the decision, the undertakings concerned by the noti-

---

92 Case T-342/99, *Airtours plc v Commission*, [2002] ECR II-2585; joined cases 5 and 80/02, *Tetra Laval v Commission*, [2002] ECR II-4519.

93 See, *inter alia*, case T-342/99, *Airtours v Commission*, [2002] ECR II-2585, para. 65: '[i]t follows from the foregoing that the Commission made errors of assessment in its analysis of competition obtaining in the relevant market prior to the notification. First, it did not provide adequate evidence in support of its finding that there was already a tendency in the industry to collective dominance and, hence, to restriction of competition, particularly as regards capacity setting. Second, it did not take into account, as it should have done, the fact that the main tour operators' market shares have been volatile in the past and that such volatility is evidence that the market was competitive'.

94 RAGOLLE, '*Schneider Electric v Commission*: the CFI's response to the Green Paper on Merger Review', (2003) 24 *ECLR* 176 at 179.

95 HOFMANN, 'Good governance in EC merger control: due process and checks and balances under review', (2003) 24 *ECLR* 114 at 123.

96 BERG and OSTENDORF, 'The reform of EC merger control: substance and impact of the proposed new procedural rules', (2003) 24 *ECLR* 594 at 599–600.

97 HOUSE of LORDS SELECT COMMITTEE on the EUROPEAN UNION, *XIX Report: Strengthening the role of the Hearing Officer*, sess. 2000/2001, para. 32.

fied transaction had little choice but to accept any remedy suggested by the Commission just to secure the approval of the transaction.[98] Consequently, it was suggested that for justice to be seen to be done, the two phases of the merger procedure should be handled by separate case-handling teams.[99]

Further issues have arisen as regards the function of the statement of objections in merger proceedings: as is stated in Article 8 of the 2004 Regulation a statement of objection will be sent to the notifying undertakings when the Commission finds that the proposed concentration raises serious doubts as regards its compatibility with the Common Market. However, some authors have alleged that the Commission's view as to the compatibility of the notified concentration with the Common Market is already set when a statement of objections is sent out and that consequently, in practice, the case-handling officials 'focus on negotiating and market testing remedies'.[100] They argued that its effectiveness as a means to achieve the meaningful participation and the effective defence of the undertakings during the procedure would be seriously threatened.[101]

The case law of the Community courts concerning concentrations giving rise to a collective dominant position raises additional issues with respect to the right to a hearing of undertakings which, despite not being among the notifying parties, are found by the Commission to be members of an oligopoly together with the merged entity. Advocate General Tesauro pointed out in his Opinion in the *Re: Kali & Salz* case[102] that the firms 'which are presumed to be members of the oligopoly but are not parties to the concentration are not given any specific information'[103] and enjoyed only a very limited right to a hearing akin to that of all the other third parties.[104]

He argued, however, that these rights were insufficient to protect the interests of the jointly dominant undertakings[105] and suggested that, in consideration of the consequences that the declaration that they hold such a dominant position could have on the position of the undertakings, they should be entitled to a wider right of access to the file and to be heard by the Commission.[106]

---

98 *Ibid.*

99 *Id.*, para. 252. *Inter alia*, RAGOLLE, '*Schneider Electric v Commission*: The CFI's response to the Green Paper on Merger Review', (2003) 24 *ECLR*, 176 at p. 179.

100 KEKELEKIS, 'The statement of objections as an inherent part of the right to be heard in EC merger proceedings: issues of concern', (2004) 25 *ECLR* 518 at 524.

101 *Ibid.*

102 Joined Cases C-68/94 and 30/95, *France & Others v Commission*, [1998] ECR I-1375.

103 *Id.*, para. 91.

104 *Ibid.*

105 *Ibid.*

106 *Id.*, para. 92.

Nevertheless, the ECJ declined to follow the Advocate General's advice and decided that the undertakings found to be holding a joint dominant position as a result of the notified concentration should be heard as third parties in accordance with Article 18(4) of the Merger Regulation.[107]

It is submitted that the solution adopted by the ECJ appears unsatisfactory in the light of the approach adopted in decisions such as, *inter alia*, *Irish Sugar plc v Commission*[108] where it was held that even the conduct of one of the jointly dominant undertakings as a result of the merger could give rise to a violation of Article 82 EC Treaty, so long as it can be established that the conduct is 'capable of being identified as one of the manifestations of such a joint dominant position (. . .)'.[109] It could therefore be argued that the conclusions reached in *Re: Kali und Salz*[110] could lead to the rather objectionable result of giving the undertaking found to hold a joint dominant position together with the merged entity only a limited chance to be heard during the merger procedure, regardless of the resulting obligation not to engage, even unilaterally, in *prima facie* abusive conduct.[111]

The 2004 Merger Regulation attempted to address some of these concerns. Its Article 10 provides for the 'stop-the-clock' clause, i.e. for the possibility to extend the existing deadlines so as to allow a fuller consideration of the proposed commitments.[112] In addition, the Commission introduced new administrative practice directions to address the perceived lack of appropriate scientific input in the procedure[113] and the lack of quality in the decision-making by appointing a Chief Competition Economist and creating a peer review panel system for the scrutiny of merger decisions with a 'fresh pair of eyes at key points of the inquiry'.[114]

However, the new Merger Regulation failed to address the controversial questions arising from the *Kali & Salz* judgment. It is submitted that the ECJ

---

[107] *Ibid.* Also case T-125/97, *Coca Cola v Commission*, [2000] ECR II-1733, paras. 80–81.

[108] Case T-228/97, [1999] ECR II-2969.

[109] *Id.*, para. 66.

[110] Joined Cases 68/94 and 30/95, *France & Others v Commission*, [1998] ECR I-1375.

[111] *Id.*, per AG Tesauro, at para. 91.

[112] See HOUSE of LORDS SELECT COMMITTEE on the EUROPEAN UNION, *XXXII Report: the review of the EC Merger Regulation*, sess. 2001/2002, para. 197. Cf. case T-114/02, *BaByliss SA v Commission*, [2003] ECR II-1279 at paras. 136 to 140.

[113] BERG and OSTENDORF, 'The reform of EC merger control: substance and impact of the proposed new procedural rules', (2003) 24 *ECLR* 594 at 600.

[114] RYAN, 'Reform of the EU merger control system – a comprehensive package of proposals', (2003) *EC Competition Policy Newsletter*, Issue 1, 9, at 12.

position on the issue casts doubt on the effectiveness of this right[115] in the area of merger control and might require more extensive standards of protection being applied to cases in which third parties are found to be holding a joint dominant position as a result of the notified transaction.[116]

In the light of the above analysis, it can be concluded that the 2004 Merger Regulation together with the revised administrative practice rules constitute welcome developments for the purpose of ensuring procedural fairness and good-quality decision-making in the control of concentrations. Nonetheless, the extent to which these objectives can actually be achieved depends largely on their practical application as well as by the timeliness and effectiveness of the judicial scrutiny of the final decisions. In this specific respect, the recent debate on the establishment of an 'EU Competition Court'[117] responsible for merger review indicates that judicial scrutiny of the Commission's findings still constitutes the most fundamental check over the overall administrative procedure. This issue will be examined in greater detail in later chapters.

1.5. The Oral Hearing and the Hearing Officer

It was noted in section 1.2 that the oral hearing has gained increasing importance as a means to clarify and test the arguments and the evidence for and against the case made by the Commission in its Statement of Objections. In the context of merger control, this phase of the procedure acquires additional importance especially in the light of the new administrative practice guidelines, in as much as it constitutes a forum for the negotiation and market-testing of merger remedies.

However, especially in earlier years, the investigated undertakings raised concerns as to the extent to which the oral hearing could actually discharge its function. In particular, it was felt that if the hearing were to play an effective role towards the goal of a more transparent and fairer procedure, then it would have to be conducted by an official who displayed some guarantee of independence.

---

115 Joined Cases 68/94 and 30/95, *France & Others v Commission*, [1998] ECR I-1375.

116 *Inter alia,* case T-228/97, *Irish Sugar plc v Commission*, [1999] ECR II-2969, para. 66.

117 CBI Brief, 'The need for an EU Competition Court', 15 June 2006. HOUSE of LORDS SELECT COMMITTEE, *XV Report: an EU Competition Court*, session 2006–07, 23 April 2007 (hereinafter referred to as *XV Report*); the Report, the Minutes of Oral Evidence and the Written Evidence are available at: http://www.publications.parliament.uk/pa/ld200607/ldselect/ldeucom/75/75.pdf.

The Commission was not insensitive to this criticism and in its *XI Report on Competition Policy*[118] envisaged the appointment of 'Hearing Officers, duly authorised to chair hearings, vested with genuine autonomy and the right to direct access to the responsible member of the Commission'[119] to strengthen the 'objectivity of the procedure and any decision taken subsequently'.[120] According to the first Terms of Reference, the Hearing Officer was responsible only for the conduct of the hearing,[121] the gathering of 'fresh documents'[122] and for the production of a report on it.[123]

In its *XXIII Report on Competition Policy* the Commission proposed further reforms of the Hearing Officer's mandate[124] in order to strengthen her objectivity, independence and effectiveness in chairing the hearing and ensuring that the investigated parties be fully informed of the contents of the Commission's case.[125] However, it did not go as far as to allow her to be appointed outside the number of the Commission officials.[126] As a result, commentators argued that the degree of independence that the Officer enjoyed was not sufficient to comply with the concerns for the effectiveness of her 'guarantee role' during the proceedings.[127]

The manner in which the Hearing Officer may conduct the hearing was also criticised by the House of Lords Select Committee on the EU: the Committee considered that her inability to take an active part in the hearing and especially to ask questions to the Commission's officials on behalf of the investigated undertakings could prevent actual 'equality of arms' between the parties and thus hinder the overall fairness of competition cases.[128]

---

118 COMMISSION of the EUROPEAN COMMUNITIES, *XII Report on Competition Policy*, 1983: Brussels, p. 31.

119 *Id.*, p. 31.

120 *Ibid. Inter alia*, EHLERMANN, 'Developments in Community competition law procedures', (1994) 1 *EC Comp. Policy Newsl.* 2 at 3.

121 Article 2, Terms of Reference of the Hearing Officer, annexed to the *XI Report on Competition Policy*, Brussels: 1982.

122 Article 5.

123 Article 6.

124 COMMISSION of the EUROPEAN COMMUNITIES, Brussels: 1994, pp. 116–17.

125 Commission Decision 94/810/ECSC, EC, on the terms of reference of hearing officers in certain competition proceedings, [1994] OJ L330/67; see especially Articles 3–5.

126 HOUSE of LORDS SELECT COMMITTEE on the EUROPEAN UNION, *XIX Report: Strengthening the Role of the Hearing Officer*, sess. 1999/2000, para. 31.

127 LEVITT: 'Commission Hearings and the role of the Hearing Officer: suggestions for reform', (1998) 19 *ECLR* 397, pp. 404–05.

128 HOUSE of LORDS SELECT COMMITTEE on the EUROPEAN UNION, *XIX Report: Strengthening the Role of the Hearing Officer*, sess. 1999/2000 at para. 29.

In addition, the lack of disclosure of the Hearing Officer's report to the undertakings concerned constituted a considerable shortcoming[129] since it prevented significant procedural defects from being unveiled.[130] Overall, it was felt that, despite the significant number of new tasks conferred upon her by the 1994 Terms of Reference, the Hearing Officer had gained only relative strength and effectiveness vis-à-vis the case-handling officials and thus could not fully perform her functions.

It was primarily for these reasons that the Commission enacted new Terms of Reference in 2001.[131] By allowing the Officer to be chosen from 'outside' the Commission,[132] making her report available to the investigated parties[133] and empowering her to submit observations concerning a specific case at any stage of the proceedings[134] the Commission sought greater independence, procedural propriety and overall improved standards of fairness throughout the antitrust proceedings.[135] Commentators welcomed the current Mandate as striving to make the Hearing Officer the centrepiece of the competition procedure so as to protect adequately the undertakings' rights of the defence.[136]

The provision for a right to 'be kept informed by the director responsible for investigating the case . . . about the development of the procedure up to the stage of the draft decision to be submitted to the competent member of the Commission' and to 'present observations on any matter arising out of any Commission competition proceeding to the competent member of the Commission'[137] ensures that the proceedings are conducted in so far as possible fairly and under an independent supervisor.[138]

---

129 *Id.*, para. 37.

130 *Ibid.*

131 Commission Decision 2001/462/EC, ECSC, on the terms of reference of hearing officers in certain competition proceedings, [2001] OJ L162/21.

132 Articles 1–2. See, *inter alia*, VAN der WOUDE, 'Hearing Officers and EC antitrust procedures: the art of making subjective procedures more objective', (1996) 33 *CMLRev* 531 at 546.

133 Article 16. For commentary, see GIANNAKOPOULOS, 'The right to be orally heard by the Commission', at 552, 569.

134 Article 3.

135 HOUSE of LORDS SELECT COMMITTEE on the EUROPEAN UNION, *XIX Report: Strengthening the Role of the Hearing Officer*, sess. 1999/2000 at para. 58. See, *inter alia*, M. MONTI, 'European Commission strengthens the role of the Hearing Officer in competition proceedings' (Press Release), IP/01/736.

136 *Id.*, p. 569.

137 Article 3(2) and (3), Commission Decision 2001/462/EC, ECSC, on the terms of reference of hearing officers in certain competition proceedings, [2001] OJ L162/21.

138 HOUSE of LORDS SELECT COMMITTEE on the EUROPEAN UNION, *XIX Report: Strengthening the Role of the Hearing Officer*, sess. 1999/2000 at para. 58.

The position of the Hearing Officer raised separate questions in the context of the enforcement of the Merger Regulation. In the wake of the allegations of unfairness and lack of transparency of the commitments stage of Phase II proceedings,[139] the House of Lords Select Committee on the European Union suggested that the Officer's report should be disclosed to the notifying parties and, in case of a judicial challenge of the final decision, made available to the CFI so as to allow adequate checks as to the reasonableness of the demands made by the case-handling officials and the absence of any constraint.[140]

The Committee also proposed that the Hearing Officer be given a more autonomous and proactive role in conducting these negotiations to protect the notifying parties from any manifest unfairness[141] and foster trust throughout the negotiations.[142] Although the Commission representative supported this proposal during the Committee inquiry,[143] no reform to this effect was introduced with the 2004 Merger Regulation or the new administrative Best Practices. The lack of agreement over the extent of the powers that the Officer could exercise in the commitments negotiations is also regrettable.[144]

However the 2001 Terms of Reference introduced two generally applicable innovations likely to improve the fairness of Merger proceedings. Article 10 confers on the Hearing Officer the power to grant an extension to the time limit imposed on third parties for the purpose of replying to the statement of objection or to the Commission's letter informing them of the rejection of their complaint. This provision should grant additional flexibility to the procedural framework, especially during the negotiation of commitments.[145] In addition, the disclosure of the Hearing Officer's report[146] is likely to facilitate the judi-

---

See, *inter alia*, M. MONTI, 'European Commission strengthens the role of the Hearing Office in competition proceedings' (Press Release), IP/01/736.

139 HOUSE of LORDS SELECT COMMITTEE on the EUROPEAN UNION, *XIX Report: Strengthening the Role of the Hearing Officer*, sess. 1999/2000, paras. 64–65.

140 *Id.*, para. 65.

141 *Ibid.*

142 HOUSE of LORDS SELECT COMMITTEE on the EUROPEAN UNION, *XXXII Report: the Review of the EC Merger Regulation*, sess. 2001/2002, para. 211.

143 *Id.*, para. 209.

144 See RYAN, 'Reform of the EU Merger Control System – a comprehensive package of proposals', (2003) *EC Competition Newsletter*, issue 1, 9, at 13. Also HOUSE of LORDS SELECT COMMITTEE on the EUROPEAN UNION, *XIX Report: Strengthening the Role of the Hearing Officer*, sess. 1999/2000, para. 47.

145 HOUSE of LORDS SELECT COMMITTEE on the EUROPEAN UNION, *XXXII Report: the Review of the EC Merger Regulation*, sess. 2001/2002, para. 190.

146 Article 16, Commission Decision 2001/462/EC, ECSC, on the terms of reference of hearing officers in certain competition proceedings, [2001] OJ L162/21.

cial scrutiny of merger decisions, especially with respect to any allegation of procedural impropriety.[147]

It can therefore be concluded that the role of the Hearing Officer as a 'neutral chair' to the hearing constitutes a considerable improvement in ensuring the fairness of the proceedings. Her powers as regards the admission to the hearing and especially the disclosure of her report to the concerned parties are likely to increase the transparency of the procedure and ultimately to contribute to effective judicial scrutiny.[148] Nonetheless, the Officer's powers in relation to the disclosure of the evidence gathered by the Commission to the investigated undertakings are still liable to cause some concern, especially in view of the lack of any judicial supervision over their exercise. These issues will be considered in later sections.

2. THE RIGHT TO BE HEARD IN ADMINISTRATIVE PROCEEDINGS HAVING A 'CIVIL' OR 'CRIMINAL' NATURE UNDER THE ECHR: THE APPLICATION OF ARTICLE 6(1)

Chapter 1 illustrated the strict interrelationship between the European Convention on Human Rights and the doctrine of 'Community Fundamental Rights' developed by the ECJ and argued that the standards dictated by the Convention have provided an increasingly important source of inspiration for the Luxembourg courts in shaping the principles governing human rights protection in the Community context. On this point it was suggested that, as a result of the application of the 'substantive approach' developed by the European Court of Human Rights, antitrust and merger proceedings, despite being classified as 'administrative' by the legislature, may nonetheless be, respectively, 'criminal' and 'civil' in nature for the purposes of the European Convention.

Accordingly, it is necessary to determine which standards of 'fair procedure' are required by Article 6(1) ECHR to ensure compliance with the Strasbourg Court's case law.[149] This provision demands that the determination in question be carried out by an authority constituting 'an independent and

---

[147] For commentary, *inter alia*, GIANNAKOPOULOS, 'The right to be orally heard by the Commission', at 552.

[148] HOUSE of LORDS SELECT COMMITTEE on the EUROPEAN UNION, *XIX Report: Strengthening the Role of the Hearing Officer*, sess. 1999/2000 at para. 58. *Inter alia*, GIANNAKOPOULOS, *ibid.*, at 569.

[149] *Inter alia*, BOYLE, 'Administrative justice, judicial review and the right to a fair hearing under the European Convention on Human Rights', (1984) *PL* 89 at 90.

impartial tribunal established by law'. The European Court of Human Rights recognised that administrative bodies may come 'within the concept of a "tribunal" in the substantive sense of this expression',[150] provided that their 'function is to determine matters within its competence on the basis of rules of law, following proceedings conducted in a prescribed manner'.[151]

Nevertheless, the functional characteristics listed above do not suffice for the administrative proceedings to comply with the requirements of Article 6(1) ECHR: the authority in question must also meet guarantees of independence of the executive and impartiality of its members, in consideration of its composition, manner of appointment, duration of office and guarantees against bias.[152] Admittedly, this is not the case of many administrative authorities and bodies.[153] Therefore, the question becomes 'how to accommodate the relative inflexibility of Article 6 with the realities of administrative decision-making'.[154]

Article 6(1) ECHR could be read either as imposing 'a guarantee of due process at all stages of the administrative process',[155] and therefore the 'judicialisation' of the procedures before the administrative authorities, or as considering 'the initial exercise of administrative power as falling outside Article 6(1) [ECHR]',[156] whilst 'requir[ing] a right of appeal on the merits to a tribunal constituted according to the Article's procedural requirements'.[157]

In its *LeCompte, Van Leuven and de Meyere v Belgium* judgment the Court recognised that 'demands of flexibility and efficiency . . . may justify the prior intervention of administrative or professional bodies . . . which do not satisfy the said requirements in every respect'.[158] Nonetheless:

> the Convention calls at least for one of the two following systems: either the (administrative) organs themselves comply with the requirements of Article 6(1) or they do not comply but are subject to subsequent control by a judicial body that has full jurisdiction and does provide the guarantees of Article 6(1).[159]

---

150 Appl. No 8790/79, *Sramek v Austria*, [1985] 7 EHRR 351, para. 36.

151 *Ibid.*

152 *Inter alia,* Appl. No 9273/81, *Ettl v Austria*, [1988] 10 EHRR 255, paras. 38 and 41; Appl. No 19178/91, *Bryan v United Kingdom*, Commission report, [1996] 21 EHRR 342, paras. 37–38.

153 *Inter alia*, Appl. No. 8544/79, *Ozturk v Germany*, [1984] 6 EHRR 409 at paras. 49–50.

154 BOYLE, 'Administrative justice, judicial review and the right to a fair hearing under the European Convention on Human Rights', (1984) *PL* 89 at 99.

155 *Id.*, p. 100.

156 *Ibid.*

157 *Ibid.*

158 Appl. Nos 6878/75 and 7238/75, *LeCompte, Van Leuven and de Meyere v Belgium,* [1982] 4 EHRR 1, para. 51.

159 Appl. Nos 7299/75 and 7496/76, *Albert & LeCompte v Belgium*, [1983] 5 EHRR 533, para. 29.

Albert & LeCompte indicates that in the area of administrative decision-making the Strasbourg Court has interpreted Article 6(1) ECHR as enshrining 'a right to due process at *some* stage of the processings [*sic*], but not necessarily at the outset'.[160] All the Convention requires is that 'an administrative decision affecting civil rights . . . be amenable to a properly constituted tribunal with power to give full consideration to issues of law, facts and merits'.[161] The Court thus adopted a 'composite approach'[162] in the assessment of such proceedings: 'where there is a two-(or three) stage process involving an administrative decision-maker whose decision is subject to review by a court, regard must be had to both stages of the process'.[163]

With respect to the administrative stage, it was held in *W v United Kingdom*[164] (a case concerning care proceedings) that when measures interfering with the right to respect for family life are adopted, the authorities must ensure that the parents are 'involved in the decision-making process, seen as a whole, to a degree sufficient to provide them with the requisite protection of their interests'.[165] Likewise, in the area of urban planning and development[166] the Strasbourg Court pointed to 'the uncontested safeguards attending the procedure before the inspector'[167] as a decisive factor for upholding the conformity of the urban planning procedures with Article 6(1) ECHR.

The Court referred to 'the quasi-judicial character of the decision-making process' to indicate the provision of a set of procedural guarantees, namely, the right of the interested parties 'to appear, with or without legal representation, adduce evidence, both written and oral, and make submissions of both law and fact'.[168] The participation of the interested parties in the administrative procedure thus appears as an essential canon of fairness of administrative proceedings

---

160 BOYLE, 'Administrative justice, judicial review and the right to a fair hearing under the European Convention on Human Rights', at 100.

161 *Id.*, p. 105.

162 POUSTIE, 'The rule of law or the rule of lawyers? *Alconbury*, Article 6(1) and the role of courts in administrative decision-making', (2001) 6 *EHRLR* 657 at 663.

163 *Ibid.*

164 Appl. No 9749/82, [1988] 10 EHRR 29.

165 *Id.*, para. 64. Cf. also, Appl. No 10465/83, *Olsson v Sweden*, [1989] 11 EHRR 259, para. 71. See also, *mutatis mutandis*, Appl. No 11761/85, *Obermeier v Austria*, [1991] 13 EHRR 290, para. 69.

166 *Inter alia*, Appl. No 19178/91, *Bryan v United Kingdom*, [1996] 21 EHRR 342.

167 *Id.*, para. 46.

168 Commission Opinion, separate concurring Opinion of Mr N. Bratza, p. 354. See also joined Cases, *R (on the application of Holding & Barnes Plc), R (on the application of Premier Leisure UK), R (on the application of Alconbury Developments) v Secretary of State for the Environment, Transport and the Regions*, House of Lords, [2003] 2 AC 295, para. 46.

and a cumulative condition, together with the presence of a means of judicial review before an independent and impartial tribunal, which must be met to satisfy Article 6(1) ECHR.

The scrutiny of domestic 'administrative' proceedings in areas such as town planning and development also prompted the question of the extent to which third parties should be entitled, thanks to Article 6(1) ECHR, to make submissions to the public authorities alongside the parties directly concerned by the procedures, such as the applicants. In *Ortenberg*[169] the European Court of Human Rights held that in principle 'Article 6(1) applies when the subject matter of an action is "pecuniary" in nature . . . or [*inter alia*] where its outcome is "decisive for private rights and obligations" '.[170]

Accordingly it was concluded that, since the applicant enjoyed a right to 'object to the granting of planning permission by complaining that their personal rights will be infringed',[171] she was entitled to claim that her right to a 'fair and public hearing' had been violated. In fact, as the owner of neighbouring land she could establish that 'the decision on the relevant application had an immediate, and significant impact upon the right claimed'[172] and was thus entitled to make submissions and challenge the final decision.[173]

It may be concluded that Article 6(1) ECHR applies to any administrative proceedings relevant for the determination of civil rights and obligations or of a criminal charge, without, however, requiring their 'judicialisation'.[174] The Court has adopted a 'composite approach' [175] to assess whether national law complies with the Convention, according to which both the administrative and the judicial phases must be taken into account for the purpose of compliance with Article 6(1) ECHR.[176]

169 Appl. No 18064/91, *Ortenberg v Austria*, [1995] 19 EHRR 524.

170 *Id.*, para. 26.

171 *Ibid.*

172 CORNER and BROWN, 'Applying *Alconbury*: Article 6, third parties and development plans', (2002) *Journal of Planning and Environment Law*, Jun 661 at 663.

173 Appl. No 18064/91, *Ortenberg v Austria*, [1995] 19 EHRR 524, para. 28. But cf., *mutatis mutandis*, *R (Malster) v Ipswich and Ipswich Town FC*, High Court, [2001] EWHC Admin 711, subparas. VII–VIII; *Friends Provident Life & Pensions Ltd v Secretary of State for Transport, Local Government and Regions, Norwich City Council and Lend Lease Norwich Ltd*, High Court, [2001] EWHC Admin 820, paras. 94–95. For commentary, see CORNER and BROWN, 'Applying *Alconbury*', at 668.

174 BOYLE, 'Administrative justice, judicial review and the right to a fair hearing under the European Convention on Human Rights', at 100. *Supra,* chapter 1, section 5, footnote 145 and accompanying text.

175 *Inter alia*, Appl. Nos 7299/75 and 7496/76, *Albert & LeCompte v Belgium*, [1983] 5 EHRR 533, para. 29.

176 POUSTIE, 'The rule of law or the rule of lawyers?', at 663.

As regards the administrative stage, the Convention requires the Contracting States' authorities to afford the interested natural or legal persons a meaningful and effective right to be heard[177] and recognises in principle the right of third parties to make representations and to challenge the final decisions.[178]

3. 'ADMINISTRATIVE FAIRNESS' AND COMPETITION PROCEEDINGS: THE COMMISSION'S ENFORCEMENT ACTION AND ARTICLE 6(1)

3.1. Introductory Remarks

Section 1 above examined the scope of the right to be heard enjoyed by the undertakings concerned by the enforcement of the antitrust and merger rules before the European Commission and by third parties who may have a legitimate interest in the proceedings. With respect to the investigated parties, the right to be informed in full of the allegations made by the Commission against them, to make written submissions and to have the opportunity to be orally heard constitute the key elements of that right, in accordance with the general principle of *audi alteram partem.*

In this context, the presence of the Hearing Officer as a neutral chair to the oral hearing and as an overall supervisor to the procedure constitutes an additional guarantee to its overall fairness and transparency. Having regard to third parties, instead, their right to make representations to the case-handling official, despite being recognised in principle, appears to be more limited than that enjoyed by the investigated parties, by reason of procedural economy and confidentiality.

Sub-section 1.3 illustrated the ad hoc issues raised by the application of the Merger Regulation and highlighted the tight time limits and the negotiation of merger remedies as possible areas of concern for the fairness of these proceedings. It also examined the extent to which the adoption of new administrative practice rules could remedy, at least in part, the perceived shortcomings of the system for the control of concentrations by securing the meaningful involvement of the notifying parties and the overall good quality of the Commission's decision-making.

---

177 *Inter alia,* Appl. No 19178/91, *Bryan v United Kingdom*, [1996] 21 EHRR 342, para. 46.

178 Appl. No 18064/91, *Ortenberg v Austria*, [1995] 19 EHRR 524, para. 26. But cf., *inter alia, Friends Provident Life & Pensions Ltd v Secretary of State for Transport, Local Government and Regions, Norwich City Council and Lend Lease Norwich Ltd*, High Court, [2001] EWHC Admin 820, paras. 94–95.

Section 2 addressed the issue of the application of the right to a 'fair trial' to individuals and legal persons affected by procedures which, despite being defined as 'administrative' by domestic law, have a 'civil' or 'criminal' nature. It was argued that the Convention does not require the 'judicialisation' of these proceedings but has been interpreted as enshrining a composite approach in the interpretation of Article 6(1) ECHR. Nonetheless, it demands that the procedures before the non-judicial public authorities are assisted by such guarantees as the right to make submissions to the case-handling officials before a final decision is taken and the presence of an independent inspector responsible for the conduct of the hearing. It was also illustrated that, despite being entitled in principle to a written hearing, third parties do not enjoy rights as extensive as those enjoyed by the parties directly affected by the proceedings.

In view of the importance of the European Convention on Human Rights for the development of fundamental rights standards in EC law, this section will therefore assess the scope of the right to be heard enjoyed by the undertakings concerned and third parties in competition proceedings before the Commission in the light of the principles enshrined in Article 6(1) of the Convention.

3.2. EC Competition Proceedings and 'Fair Procedure': Elements for a Comparative Analysis

Considering the general issue of fairness of competition proceedings, the House of Lords Select Committee on the European Union noted that '[t]he perceived difficulty with the Commission's procedures, both under Article 81 and 82 and the Merger Control Regulation, arises because the Commission is at the same time both the prosecutor and decision-maker'.[179] Nevertheless, the Committee recognised that during that administrative procedure 'the Commission . . . is not without check, nor the parties without safeguards'.[180]

Thanks to the creative role of the ECJ, standards of fairness in administrative proceedings have been developed to reach 'a fair balance between an effective and capable administration on the one side and the secure and reliable protection of individual rights on the other'.[181] The Court was clearly influenced by the common law principles of natural justice, according to which 'a person whose interests are perceptibly affected by a decision taken

---

179 HOUSE of LORDS SELECT COMMITTEE on the EUROPEAN UNION, *XIX Report: Strengthening the Role of the Hearing Officer*, sess. 1999/2000, para. 55.

180 *Id.*, para. 8.

181 SCHWARZE, 'Tendencies towards a common administrative law in Europe', (1991) 16 *ELRev* 3 at 5.

by a public authority must be given the opportunity to make his point of view known'.[182]

However, it must be emphasised that competition proceedings were found by the Community Courts to comply with the requirements of Article 6 ECHR. In its decision in *Aristrain*[183] the CFI held that the fact that 'during the administrative proceedings before the Commission the latter is obliged to observe the procedural guarantees laid down by Community law',[184] considered together with the Court's unlimited jurisdiction in the scrutiny of decisions imposing pecuniary sanctions and periodic penalty payments in accordance with Article 229 EC Treaty,[185] secured the compliance of these enforcement mechanisms with the standards of Article 6.[186]

The position expressed by the Court, which is in line with that adopted by the European Court of Human Rights in its decision in *Albert & LeCompte v Belgium*,[187] discussed above,[188] supports the conclusion that even though the presence of effective safeguards undoubtedly benefits the fairness of these proceedings, the existence of a framework for judicial review before a Court having unlimited jurisdiction constitutes the main guarantee of the rights of the undertakings concerned.[189]

Nonetheless, the 'composite approach' adopted by the European Court of Human Rights suggests that, along with the vigilance of the Luxembourg courts, an improvement of the procedural rights of both the undertakings concerned and the relevant third parties would help ensure overall compliance with Article 6(1) ECHR.[190] On this point, the circumstance that the right to be heard is now definitely established in antitrust and merger proceedings ensures consistency with the Convention standards. The express recognition of a right to be heard for third parties could also be interpreted as providing a more

---

182 Case 17/74, *Transocean Marine Paint v Commission*, [1974] ECR 1063, para. 15.

183 Case T-156/94, *Siderurgica Aristrain Madrid SL v Commission*, [1999] ECR II-645.

184 *Id.*, para. 102.

185 *Id.*, para. 109.

186 *Id.*, para. 55.

187 Appl. Nos 7299/75 and 7496/76, *Albert & LeCompte v Belgium*, [1983] 5 EHRR 533 at para. 29.

188 *Supra*, sect. 2.

189 HOUSE of LORDS SELECT COMMITTEE on the EUROPEAN UNION, *XIX Report: Strengthening the Role of the Hearing Officer*, sess. 1999/2000, para. 56.

190 *Inter alia*, Appl. No 19178/91, *Bryan v United Kingdom*, [1996] 21 EHRR 342, para. 46. Also HOUSE of LORDS SELECT COMMITTEE on the EUROPEAN UNION, *XIX Report: Strengthening the Role of the Hearing Officer*, sess. 1999/2000, para. 96.

extensive degree of protection than that afforded by the ECHR,[191] especially in the light of the restrictive interpretation adopted by the English Courts under the 1998 Human Rights Act in the area of town development.[192]

Furthermore, the introduction of the Hearing Officer as a neutral chair to the hearing, especially the circumstance that her report will be disclosed to the concerned parties, is likely to increase the transparency of the procedure and ultimately to contribute to effective judicial scrutiny on the part of the Community courts.[193] It is submitted that, in view of the similarity between her function in the context of competition enforcement and the role of the independent inspector in charge of the conduct of the inquiries relating to new applications in the context of town planning proceedings, the Hearing Officer is likely to contribute to the compliance of EC proceedings with the ECHR standards, since the Strasbourg Court has recognised that the presence of that inspector constitutes an additional guarantee of due process.[194]

The analysis of the right to be heard in merger proceedings has, however, highlighted several areas of concern for the purposes of administrative due process. Section 1.4 illustrated that such proceedings present peculiar characteristics and therefore raise ad hoc issues as regards their fairness: the circumstance that they are triggered by a notification to the Commission results in the scope for the participation of third parties being far more limited than in antitrust enforcement and confined mainly to the submission of written observations to the Commission and the opportunity to take part in the 'triangular meetings' envisaged by the Best Practices Guidelines.[195]

Merger proceedings are characterised by significant room for negotiations between the Commission officials and the notifying parties, for which state-of-play and triangular meetings at key stages of the procedure provide a formal forum, and are governed by tight time limits within which a final decision must be adopted. It was therefore suggested that, while undoubtedly ensuring effi-

---

191 Cf. *inter alia*, Appl. No 18064/91, *Ortenberg v Austria*, [1995] 19 EHRR 524, para. 26 with, e.g., case T-290/94, *Kaysersberg SA v EC Commission*, [1997] ECR II-2137, para. 109.

192 *Inter alia, Friends Provident Life & Pensions Ltd v Secretary of State for Transport, Local Government and Regions, Norwich City Council and Lend Lease Norwich Ltd*, High Court, [2001] EWHC Admin 820, paras. 94–95.

193 HOUSE of LORDS SELECT COMMITTEE on the EUROPEAN UNION, *XIX Report: Strengthening the Role of the Hearing Officer*, sess. 1999/2000 at para. 58. *Inter alia*, GIANNAKOPOULOS, 'The right to be orally heard by the Commission', at 569.

194 *Inter alia.*, Appl. No 19178/91, *Bryan v United Kingdom*, [1996] 21 EHRR 342, para. 46.

195 COMMISSION of the EUROPEAN COMMUNITIES, DG Competition, *Best Practices on the Conduct of EC Merger Control Proceedings*.

ciency and timeliness in the assessment of the notified transactions, these strict deadlines could have an adverse effect on the market-testing of the proposed concentrations and on the bargaining powers of the notifying parties, and therefore raise questions as to the actual fairness of the proceedings.[196]

On this point, it is also submitted that the conformity of the negotiation of merger commitments with the canons of fairness laid down by Article 6(1) ECHR could legitimately be doubted in consideration of the case law of the European Court of Human Rights. In the *Deweer* judgment[197] the Court decided that when an individual forfeited her right to access to a court in the determination of a 'criminal charge' by accepting to pay an administrative fine,[198] particular care was needed in ensuring that the negotiations leading to that settlement were not tainted by constraint[199] and especially by pressures of an economic nature.[200]

It is suggested that the above decision, despite being concerned with the settlement of proceedings having a 'criminal nature', could be read as laying down a more general rule according to which individuals who enter into negotiations with the public authorities in the context of administrative action are entitled to expect that no constraint will be exerted on them. Consequently, it could be argued that the negotiations with the Commission officials should be subjected to a higher degree of scrutiny to ensure that no such compulsion was exercised on the notifying parties as a result of the structure of the proceedings and by the commercial convenience attending the execution of the transaction.

However, this conclusion could have significant consequences for the notifying undertakings in merger proceedings. The submissions presented by the representatives of the industry and the case law of the ECJ[201] constitute evidence that the notifying parties are often faced with the choice between accepting the commitments proposed by the Commission just to obtain the approval of the concentration and running the risk that the transaction may not be cleared in time to be carried out fruitfully and conveniently. On this point, it is submitted that the new 'Merger Control package'[202] strives to provide

---

196 *Inter alia*, HOUSE of LORDS SELECT COMMITTEE on the EUROPEAN UNION, *XXXII Report: the review of the EC Merger Regulation*, sess. 2001/2002, para. 211.

197 Ser. A No 35, *Deweer v Belgium*, [1979–1980] 2 EHRR 439.

198 *Id.*, para. 49.

199 *Ibid.*

200 *Id.*, paras. 51–52.

201 *Inter alia*, case T-5/02, *Tetra Laval BV v Commission*, [2003] ECR II-4519, para. 336.

202 Council Regulation (EC) No 139/2004 of 20 January 2004 on the control of concentrations between undertakings (the EC Merger Control Regulation), [2004] OJ L24/1. COMMISSION of the EUROPEAN COMMUNITIES, DG Competition, *Best Practices on the Conduct of EC Merger Control Proceedings*.

measures aimed at improving these standards by minimising the 'hot-house' effect, such as the 'stop-the-clock' provision,[203] the 'state-of-play' meetings and the 'peer-review panel' system.[204]

Nevertheless, it is not clear whether rules of mere administrative good practice are sufficient to minimise the possibility of constraints and ensure better compliance with the standards of fairness enshrined in Article 6(1) ECHR. As will be argued in later sections, it is suggested that the more vigilant approach to judicial review adopted by the CFI following the *Tetra Laval* appeal judgment could contribute to improving the system of checks and balances and thus safeguard more effectively the rights of the defence of the notifying parties[205] when the final decision is adopted as a result of the negotiation of merger remedies.

3.3. Summary Conclusions: the Right to be Heard before the Commission Between Effective EC Competition Enforcement and ECHR 'Administrative Fairness'

In the light of the above analysis it can be concluded that, given the importance of the principles of natural justice and in particular the rule of *audi alteram partem* and its scope resulting from Community legislation and case law, the right to be heard can nowadays be considered a well-established legal standard binding the Community institutions in the exercise of their powers. Its assessment in the light of the principles enshrined in Article 6(1) ECHR demonstrated that its scope and the safeguards attending its exercise are consistent with the standards developed by the case law of the Strasbourg Court, if not even more extensive, especially with respect to the position of third parties.

However, an analysis of the specific issues arising from the hearing of the notifying parties in the context of the control of concentrations highlighted significant concerns as regards the overall fairness of the negotiation of merger remedies and cast doubt on the effectiveness of the new administrative practice rules as a means of ensuring a level playing field in this phase of the proceedings, as well as on the overall good quality of the 'market testing' of the notified transaction or of any proposed modification.

---

203 Article 10, Council Regulation (EC) No 139/2004 of 20 January 2004 on the control of concentrations between undertakings (the EC Merger Control Regulation), [2004] OJ L24/1.

204 Paras. 32 and 41, COMMISSION of the EUROPEAN COMMUNITIES, DG Competition, *Best Practices on the conduct of EC merger control proceedings*.

205 *Inter alia*, case T-158/00, *ARD v Commission*, [2003] ECR II-3825, paras. 193–94.

Consequently, it was suggested that, ultimately, the only effective guarantee of the rights of notifying parties would lie in judicial scrutiny of the Commission decision. This specific issue, however, will have to be separately addressed in later chapters as the other essential element of the right to a 'fair procedure' enshrined in the composite approach to Article 6(1) ECHR adopted by the European Court of Human Rights in respect of administrative action aimed at the determination of civil rights and obligations or of criminal charges.

3. Access to the evidence in competition proceedings as a 'right of the defence' between professional secrecy and 'equality of arms'

INTRODUCTION

The previous chapter discussed the Community rules governing the right to be heard before the Commission in antitrust and merger proceedings and assessed them in the light of the principles enshrined in Article 6(1) of the European Convention on Human Rights applicable to proceedings before public non-judicial authorities having a 'civil' or 'criminal' character. The analysis illustrated the function of the right to be heard for the investigated undertakings, namely to participate meaningfully in the procedure to effectively present facts, evidence and arguments in their defence. In this context, being fully acquainted with the Commission's case via the Statement of Objections emerged as a key aspect of the investigated parties' rights.

This chapter will address another element of the rights of the defence of the undertakings affected by competition proceedings, namely the right to have access to the Commission's file containing the evidence gathered in the course of the investigation with a view to refuting the contents of the allegations made against them in their written and oral submissions.

Thereafter, the scope and the manner of exercise of this right will be examined in the light of the rules governing access to the evidence gathered by public authorities in the course of administrative proceedings relevant for the purposes of the ECHR.[1] It will emerge that although the right of access to the Commission's file is in principle solidly established, there are several areas of variance vis-à-vis the Convention standards which could give rise to concern as regards the overall fairness of the administrative procedure.

[1] *Inter alia*, Appl. No. 19178/91, *Bryan v United Kingdom*, [1996] 21 EHRR 342, para. 46.

1. THE FUNCTION AND THE LEGAL BASIS OF THE RIGHT OF ACCESS TO THE FILE

As noted in the previous chapter, the notification of the objections raised by the Commission to the undertakings concerned by competition proceedings constitutes an indispensable condition for the exercise of the right to be heard.[2] The right to access the documents gathered by the Commission during the investigations into its file serves the same purpose, since it allows the investigated parties to be acquainted with the information at the basis of the allegations made against them and to contest them accordingly.[3]

This right was initially recognised as part of the Commission's administrative practice[4] and expressed in the *XII Report on Competition Policy*.[5] In *Hercules Chemicals*[6] the CFI stated that 'the Commission may not depart from the rules which it has imposed on itself'[7] and therefore should have allowed the applicant to have access to all the documents contained in the file, with the exception of those containing business secrets of other firms, the Commission's internal documents and of other confidential information.[8]

However, in the later *Re: Soda Ash* judgment the Court was prepared to recognise it as a general principle of law.[9] In that decision it was held:

> [T]he purpose of providing access to the file in competition cases is to enable the addressees of Statements of Objections to examine evidence in the Commission's file so that they are in a position effectively to express their views on the conclusions reached by the Commission in its Statement of Objections on the basis of that evidence. Access to the file is thus one of the procedural safeguards intended to

2 TRIDIMAS, *The General Principles of EC Law* (1998) Oxford University Press, p. 254. *Inter alia*, case 41/69, *ACF Chemiefarma v Commission*, [1970] ECR 661, para. 56; case T-175/95, *BASF Coating Ag v EC Commission*, [1999] ECR II-1581, para. 45.

3 NEHL, *Principles of Administrative Procedure in EC Law* (1999) Oxford: Hart Publishing, p. 46. *Inter alia*, case 85/76, *Hoffmann-La Roche v Commission*, [1979] ECR 461, para. 5.

4 KERSE and KHAN, *EC Antitrust Procedure*, 5th edn (2004) London: Sweet & Maxwell, p. 216.

5 COMMISSION of the EUROPEAN COMMUNITIES, *XII Report on Competition Policy* (1983) Brussels, pp. 39–40.

6 Case T-7/89, *Hercules Chemicals NV v Commission* [1991] ECR II-1711.

7 TRIDIMAS, *The General Principles of EC Law* (1998) Oxford University Press, p. 264.

8 Case T-7/89, *Hercules Chemicals NV v Commission* [1991] ECR II-1711 at para. 54.

9 Case T-30/91, *Solvay SA v Commission*, [1995] ECR II-1175, para. 59; joined Cases T-10-12/92 and T-15/92, *SA Cimenteries CBR and Others v Commission*, [1992] ECR II- 2667 at para. 38.

> protect the rights of the defence (. . .). Respect for the rights of the defence in all proceedings in which sanctions may be imposed is a fundamental principle of Community law which must be respected in all circumstances, even if the proceedings in question are administrative proceedings.[10]

The Court therefore established a link between the right of access to the file to the complex of the rights of the defence enjoyed by the undertakings concerned by competition enforcement proceedings[11] and regarded it as 'one of the procedural guarantees intended . . . to ensure . . . that the right to be heard (. . .) can be exercised effectively'[12] by enabling the undertakings concerned 'to properly defend themselves against the objections made against them in the SO'.[13]

The same principles govern access to the file in merger proceedings. According to *Tetra Laval BV v Commission*,[14]

> access to the file in competition cases is intended in particular to enable the addressees of statements of objections to acquaint themselves with the evidence in the Commission's file, so that on the basis of that evidence they can express their views effectively on the conclusions reached by the Commission in its statement of objections.[15]

In addition, Article 7(1) of the 2004 Implementing Regulation confers a more limited right of access to Commission-held evidence by the complainant and other third parties involved in antitrust and merger procedures for the purpose of granting protection of their legitimate interests through their submissions.[16]

---

10 Case T-30/91, *Solvay SA v Commission*, [1995] ECR II-1175, para. 59.

11 *Id.*, para. 59.

12 Joined Cases T-10-12/92 and T-15/92, *SA Cimenteries CBR and Others v Commission*, [1992] ECR II- 2667 at para. 38.

13 *Ibid.* Also Case T-5/02, *Tetra Laval BV v Commission*, [2002] ECR II-4381, para. 89; also Case T-221/95, *Endemol Entertainment Holding BV v Commission*, [1999] ECR II-1299, para. 65. See ERLANDSSON, 'The defendant's right of access to the Commission's file in Competition cases', (1998) *LIEI* 139 at 141.

14 Case T-5/02, [2002] ECR II-4381.

15 *Id.*, para. 89. See also Commission Notice on the rules for access to the Commission file in cases pursuant to Articles 81 and 82 of the EC Treaty, Articles 53, 54 and 57 of the EEA Agreement and Council Regulation (EC) No 139/2004 (hereinafter referred to as Commission Notice on Access to the File), [2005] OJ C325/7, para. 1.

16 Article 7(1), Commission Regulation No 773/2004 of 7 April 2004 relating to the conduct of proceedings by the Commission pursuant to Articles 81 and 82 of the EC Treaty, [2004] OJ L123/18. Also Commission Notice on Access to the File, paras. 29–32.

It is thus apparent that this right is enshrined in the Community courts' case law and codified in secondary legislation, as well as in administrative practice, as part of the procedural rights enjoyed by the interested parties and retains a central role in proceedings before the Commission.[17] Furthermore, its recognition as a component of the 'right to good administration' granted by Article 41 of the EU Charter of Fundamental Rights reflects its higher status as part of the general principles of EC law and arguably calls for an increased degree of vigilance as regards its respect on the part of the Commission itself.[18]

2. THE SCOPE OF THE RIGHT OF ACCESS TO THE FILE IN ANTITRUST AND MERGER PROCEEDINGS

2.1. General Observations

According to Articles 26 and 27 of Regulation 1/2003, both the undertakings directly concerned by competition enforcement proceedings, i.e. the addressees of a Statement of Objections, and third parties showing a 'sufficient interest' and upon application to the Commission, enjoy a right to a hearing. Similar provisions are also contained in Article 18 of the Merger Control Regulation.

It should however be noted that the right of access to the Commission's file acquires a different significance in the field of antitrust as opposed to merger control. It was observed in previous sections that the proceedings enforcing Articles 81 and 82 EC Treaty, despite having been defined as 'administrative', possess strong 'criminal' connotations[19] and accordingly call for the provision of adequate procedural guarantees,[20] such as the right to be heard and to have access to the evidence on which the Commission's case rests so that the investigated parties can be given 'the opportunity to have knowledge of and comment on the observations filed and of the evidence adduced'[21] by the case-handling officials.

---

[17] Article 27(2), Council Regulation No 1/2003; Article 18(3), EC Merger Control Regulation.

[18] *Inter alia,* Lord MILLETT, 'The right to good administration in European Law', (2002) *PL* Summer 309 at 318.

[19] *Inter alia*, Appl. No 11598/85, *Stenuit v France*, Commission Report, [1992] ECC 401 at para. 57; Opinion of AG Vesterdorf, case T-7/89, *Hercules Chemicals v Commission*, [1991] ECR II-867, Part I, para. A., subpara. 3.

[20] *Inter alia*, HOUSE of LORDS SELECT COMMITTEE on the EUROPEAN UNION, *XIX Report: Strengthening the Role of the Hearing Officer in EC Competition cases*, sess. 1999/00, paras. 7–8.

[21] *Ibid.* Also, Appl. No 21497/93, *Mantovanelli v France*, judgment of 17 March 1997 (HUDOC Ref. No 8/1996/627/810), [1997] 24 EHRR 370 at para. 33.

Merger proceedings are instead initiated through a notification and conducted in close liaison with the undertakings concerned and the procedure is structured in two phases, of which only the second is initiated by a statement of objections. Consequently, it would appear that the right of access to the file acquires the significance of a 'right of the defence' for the notifying parties only in Phase 2 proceedings. Nonetheless, the CFI held in *Endemol*[22] that the application of 'the rights of the defence . . . to proceedings under Regulation No 4064/89 (. . .) cannot result in any lesser right of access to documents in the Commission's file'.[23]

Therefore, it is submitted that although the peculiar characteristics of merger proceedings must be taken into account, the discipline laid down for antitrust proceedings can be considered generally applicable also to merger cases. The following sections will address the notion of 'file' and, thereafter, the scope of the right of access to the evidence held by the Commission conferred respectively on the investigated undertakings and on third parties.

2.2. What is the 'File'?

The Commission Notice on Access to the File (hereinafter referred to also as 2005 Notice) defines 'file' as comprising 'all documents which have been obtained, produced and/or assembled by the Commission Directorate General for Competition during the investigation that has led the Commission to raise its objections'.[24] Access will thus extend to all the evidence gathered in it with the exception of internal documents, business secrets of other undertakings or other confidential information.[25]

It is submitted that the comprehensive concept of file proposed by the 2005 Notice appears to reflect to some degree the view expressed by the CFI in the *Re: Soda Ash* case,[26] according to which the investigated undertakings must be granted 'the opportunity to examine documents which may be relevant so that their probative value for the defence can be assessed'[27] and consequently should be allowed access to 'all documents which may be relevant to the

22 Case T-221/95, *Endemol Entertainment Holding BV v Commission*, [1999] ECR II-1299.

23 *Id.*, para. 50.

24 Commission Notice on Access to the File, para. 9.

25 *Ibid.* Cf. Commission Notice on the internal rules of procedure for processing requests for access to the file in cases pursuant to Article 85 and 86 of the EC Treaty, Articles 65 and 66 of the ECSC Treaty and Council Regulation (EEC) 4064/89, [1997] OJ C23/3 at C23/4.

26 Case T-30/91, *Solvay SA v Commission*, [1995] ECR II-1175, para. 81.

27 *Ibid.*

case'.[28] The concept of 'file' should therefore be intended as 'the sum of documents and other information of which there should be a written record and which, in accordance with the rights of defence, should be made available to the defence . . . wherever they may be located'.[29]

The right of access to that evidence, however, does not extend to 'sensitive' documents, namely the Commission's internal documents, business secrets of other undertakings and other confidential information. Although this issue will be addressed directly in later sections, it must be emphasised that this exception poses a considerable limit to their right to obtain the disclosure of evidence in accordance with the principle of 'equality of arms'[30] and consequently raises significant issues concerning how the protection of the legitimate interests of third parties as well as the secrecy of the deliberations of the Commission could be balanced against the undertakings' rights of the defence.[31]

Nonetheless, it is clear from the case law that once the Commission has withheld access to specific documents on grounds of protection of confidentiality, it cannot rely on them to find a breach of competition law since the investigated parties could not make known their views as to the significance and the probative value of those documents.[32] Having clarified what is intended as 'file', the next sections will address the scope and manner of exercise of the right of the investigated undertakings and third parties to obtain access to it.

2.3. The Right of Access to the File of Undertakings Concerned

The position of the Community courts and of the Commission appears clearly to have evolved from a rather restrictive to a more lenient approach vis-à-vis the undertakings concerned.[33] In the *Soda Ash* decision[34] the CFI rejected the Commission's allegation that 'although its officials themselves examined and re-examined all the documents…they found no evidence which might exculpate

---

28 LEVITT, 'Access to the file: the Commission's administrative procedures in cases under Articles 85 and 86', (1997) 34 *CMLRev* 1413, at 1421.

29 Case T-30/91, *Solvay SA v Commission*, [1995] ECR II-1175, para. 83.

30 LEVITT, 'Commission Notice on internal rules of procedure for access to the file', (1997) 18 *ECLR* 187 at 190.

31 *Inter alia*, case 85/76, *Hoffmann LaRoche v Commission*, [1979] ECR 461.

32 Joined cases 100-103/80, *SA Musique Diffusion Francaise and Others v Commission*, [1983] ECR 1825, at para. 29.

33 COMMISSION of the EUROPEAN COMMUNITIES, Brussels: 1982, p. 30. See, *inter alia*, Cases 56 and 58/64, *Consten & Grundig v Commission*, [1966] ECR 299.

34 Case T-30/91, *Solvay SA v Commission*, [1995] ECR II-1775.

the applicant',[35] and therefore 'there was no point in disclosing them'[36] and held, instead, that 'it cannot be for the Commission alone to decide which documents are of use for the defence'.[37]

Since competition cases very often require, 'as in the present case, difficult and complex appraisals . . . the Commission must give the advisers of the undertaking concerned the opportunity to examine documents which may be relevant so that their probative value for the defence can be assessed'.[38] Annulling the decision, the Court concluded:

> Having regard to the general principle of equality of arms, which presupposes that in a competition case the knowledge which the undertaking concerned has of the file used in the proceeding is the same as that of the Commission . . . it is not acceptable for the Commission alone to have had available to it, when taking a decision on the infringement, the documents . . . and for it therefore to be able to decide on its own whether or not to use them against the applicant, when the applicant had no access to them and was therefore unable likewise to decide whether or not it would use them in its defence.[39]

Although the impact of this judgment cannot be underplayed it should be emphasised that the principles it laid down do not allow the investigated parties to engage in any 'fishing expeditions': in principle the scope of the right of access to the file should be commensurate to the right to be heard[40] and cannot be interpreted as entailing any obligation on the Commission 'indiscriminately to hand over a firm's internal business records to its rivals'.[41] Regard should be had to the entire context in which the right is to be exercised, namely, on the one hand, the demands of a fair hearing and, on the other hand, the legitimate interests of third parties and the confidentiality of the deliberations of the Commission.

In *BASF Coating*[42] the CFI emphasised the need to strike a fair balance between these competing interests[43] and held that the Commission would be obliged at a minimum to send to the undertakings a list of all the relevant documents and to grant them the opportunity to inspect them at the

[35] *Id.*, para. 81.

[36] *Ibid.*

[37] *Ibid.*

[38] *Ibid.*

[39] *Id.*, para. 83.

[40] JOSHUA, 'Balancing the public interest: confidentiality, trade secret and disclosure of evidence in EC Competition procedures', (1994) 15 *ECLR* 68 at 71.

[41] Case 30/91, *Solvay SA v Commission*, [1995] ECR II-1775, para. 89.

[42] Case T-175/95, *BASF Coating v Commission*, [1999] ECR II-1581.

[43] *Inter alia*, ERLANDSSON, 'The defendant's right of access to the Commission's file in competition cases', (1998) *LIEI* 139 at 151.

Commission's premises so as to allow them to 'take cognisance of the existence of the document in question'[44] and, if necessary, to object to their non-disclosure.[45]

Accordingly, it appears that in the case of the investigated undertakings the right of access to the Commission file must be exercised to the widest possible extent in accordance with the principle of 'equality of arms'.[46] The *Re: Soda Ash* judgment suggests that any other solution would imperil the effectiveness of the right to a hearing and potentially jeopardise the undertakings' rights of the defence.[47]

It is also clear that responsibility for the provision of that access rests entirely with the Commission which, as the sole authority 'responsible for the proper investigation of a competition case (. . .), may not delegate that task to the undertakings, whose economic and procedural interests often conflict'.[48] Any cooperation among the parties 'cannot lessen the Commission's duty to ensure that the rights of the defence are observed'.[49]

Access must be allowed during the administrative proceedings so that the concerned firms can be fully and effectively heard before the adoption of a final decision. Any shortcoming in the disclosure of the documents contained in the file cannot be rectified at a later stage and especially not during the judicial proceedings before the CFI, which enjoys limited jurisdiction and cannot substitute its own assessment for that of the administrative decision.[50]

Nonetheless, EC law acknowledges that there may be good reasons why documents contained in the Commission's file should not be disclosed to the investigated undertakings: according to Article 287 of the EC Treaty, Commission officials are under a duty of professional secrecy with respect to the information they gather during the course of their functions. The extent to which that obligation affects competition investigations was clarified by the ECJ in the *Hoffmann LaRoche* judgment.[51] In that decision the Court held that the duty not to disclose documents or other information 'of the kind covered by the obligation of professional secrecy',[52]

---

[44] Case T-175/95, *BASF Coating v Commission*, [1999] ECR II-1581, para. 46.

[45] *Id.*, para. 50.

[46] *Inter alia*, Case 107/82, *AEG-Telefunken v Commission* [1983] ECR 3151, para. 24.

[47] Case T-30/91, *Solvay SA v Commission*, [1995] ECR II-1775, para. 83.

[48] Case T-30/91, *Solvay SA v Commission*, [1995] ECR II-1775 at para. 85.

[49] KERSE and KHAN, *EC Antitrust Procedure*, p. 221.

[50] Case T-30/91, *Solvay SA v Commission*, [1995] ECR II-1775 at para. 98. Cf. case 85/76, *Hoffmann LaRoche v Commission*, [1979] ECR 461, para. 15.

[51] Case 85/76, *Hoffmann LaRoche v Commission*, [1979] ECR 461.

[52] *Id.*, para. 13.

> by providing undertakings from whom information has been obtained with a guarantee that their interests which are closely connected with observance of professional secrecy, are not jeopardized, enables the Commission to collect on the widest possible scale the requisite data for the fulfilment of the task conferred upon it by Articles 85 and 86 [now 81 and 82] of the Treaty (. . .).[53]

However, the ECJ also emphasised that this obligation is not absolute but must be reconciled with the rights of the defence of the investigated parties.[54] Accordingly, it is necessary at this juncture to identify the notion of 'business secrets, internal documents and other confidential information', and thereafter to examine the manner in which the Commission seeks to reconcile 'the need to protect the rights of the defence of the investigated parties through the widest possible access to the file' with the 'confidentiality of "sensitive information" '.[55]

2.4. Protecting 'Sensitive Information': the Commission Practice and the Position of the Community Courts

The analysis of the scope of the right of access to the file enjoyed by the investigated undertakings indicated that, despite its importance, its extent is not unlimited but must be reconciled with the need to protect the business secrets of third parties.[56] The Commission will be required to assess whether considerations linked to the need to protect the economic interests of the undertakings from which the information originated could justify withholding the documents wholly or in part.[57]

Nonetheless, the Court recognised that this obligation must be reconciled with the right to be heard and cannot be invoked so as to frustrate the undertakings' rights of the defence[58] by permitting the Commission to deploy

> facts, circumstances or documents which it cannot in its view disclose if such a refusal of disclosure adversely affects the undertakings' opportunity to make known effectively its views on the truth and implications of those circumstances, on those documents or again on the conclusions drawn by the Commission from them.[59]

---

[53] *Id.*, para. 14.

[54] *Ibid.*

[55] Commission Notice on Access to the File, para. 24.

[56] Case 85/76, *Hoffmann LaRoche v Commission*, [1979] ECR 461, para. 14; also case 53/85, *AKZO Chemie BV and AKZO Chemie UK Ltd v Commission* [1986] ECR 1965, at para. 28.

[57] Case C310/93 P, *BPB Industries plc and British Gypsum Ltd v Commission*, [1995] ECR I-865, paras. 25–26.

[58] *Id.*, para. 13.

[59] *Ibid.*

Consequently, once access to evidence had been precluded on grounds of confidentiality the Commission could not subsequently use that evidence to find a breach of competition law against the investigated parties.[60]

However, no definition of evidence 'of the kind covered by professional secrecy' is given.[61] On this point, the case law suggests a 'substantive' approach to the definition of what constitutes a 'business secret'. In *Hercules Chemicals*[62] the CFI took the view that the Commission should reconcile the need to afford 'very special protection' to this kind of information with the effective safeguard of the investigated undertakings' rights of the defence[63] and that it could not 'use a general reference to confidentiality to justify a total refusal to divulge documents on its file'.[64]

Overall, it would appear that whether or not a piece of information can be classified as a 'business secret' depends on the extent to which its 'disclosure adversely affects the commercial interests of the owner of the information'.[65] What is accepted, however, is that confidential treatment cannot be granted to specific documents 'simply because they concern matters which the participants would prefer to keep private',[66] but must be balanced against the need for effective competition enforcement.[67]

The flexible approach adopted by the ECJ in defining 'business secret' seems to be reflected in the Commission's administrative practice. Paragraph 17 of the 2005 Access Notice indicates that the Commission will classify information as a 'business secret' insofar as its disclosure 'could result in a serious harm to the

---

60 Joined cases 100-103/80, *Musique Diffusion Française and Others v Commission*, [1983] ECR 1825, para. 29.

61 JOSHUA, 'Balancing the public interest', at 69.

62 Case T-7/89, *Hercules Chemicals NV v Commission* [1991] ECR II-1711 at para. 26.

63 *Id.*, para. 54.

64 Joined Cases T-305–07, 313-316, 318, 325, 328–29 & 335/94, *Lymburgse Vinyl Maatschappij NV & Others v Commission (Re: the PVC Cartel II)* [1999] ECR II-931, para. 1018. Also case T-30/91, *Solvay SA v Commission*, [1995] ECR II-1175 at para. 90.

65 EHLERMANN and DRIJBER, 'Legal protection of enterprises: administrative procedure, in particular access to files and confidentiality', (1996) 17 *ECLR* 375 at 382.

66 ERLANDSSON, 'The defendant's right of access to the Commission's file in Competition cases', at 149.

67 Case 53/85, *AKZO Chemie BV and AKZO Chemie UK Ltd v Commission* [1986] ECR 1965, para. 29. For commentary, *inter alia*, LAVOIE, 'The investigative powers of the Commission with respect to business secrets under Community Competition rules', (1992) 17 *ELRev* 20 at 31. *Infra*, this chapter, para. 2.4, footnote 120 and accompanying text.

same undertaking'.[68] The 2005 Notice[69] states that the Commission will decide whether to withhold access to any 'sensitive' evidence, such as:

- the relevance of the information in determining whether or not an infringement has been committed, and its probative value,
- whether the information is indispensable,
- the degree of sensitivity involved (to what extent would disclosure of the information harm the interests of the person or undertaking in question),
- the preliminary view of the seriousness of the alleged infringement.[70]

The Commission is thus obliged to act with due diligence in making the necessary evidence available for the defence of the investigated parties in a manner compatible with its obligation of professional secrecy by selecting, if necessary, suitable means for disclosing that evidence[71] and is bound to 'either annex to the statement of objections all the document which it wished to use to demonstrate the objections raised . . . or send the undertaking a list of relevant documents and grant it access "to the file", that is to say, allow it to inspect the documents at the Commission's premises'.[72]

A 'comprehensive list' of the relevant documents and their non-confidential versions will also be provided to allow the investigated parties to adjudge the relevance of the omitted information for its defence.[73] The list should indicate 'the degree of accessibility of the document and the parties with authorised access'[74] and for 'completely non-accessible documents' include a 'summary enabling the content and subject of the documents to be identified'[75] to facilitate their assessment by the concerned firms.

Persons submitting information to the Commission are obliged to 'clearly identify any material which it considers to be confidential, giving reasons, and to provide a separate non-confidential version'[76] of that material. It thus

---

[68] Commission 2005 Notice on access to file, cit., para. 17. Cf. Commission Notice on the internal rules of procedure for processing requests for access to the file in cases pursuant to Article 85 and 86 of the EC Treaty, Articles 65 and 66 of the ECSC Treaty and Council Regulation (EEC) 4064/89, [1997] OJ C23/3. For commentary, *inter alia*, KERSE and KHAN, *EC Antitrust Procedure*, pp. 231–32.

[69] Commission Notice on Access to the File, para. 23.

[70] *Ibid.*

[71] KERSE and KHAN, *EC Antitrust Procedure*, p. 223.

[72] Case T-30/91, *Solvay SA v Commission*, [1995] ECR II-1175 at para. 89.

[73] Commission Notice on Access to the File, para. 37.

[74] Notice on access to the file, para. 32.

[75] *Ibid.*

[76] *Id.*, para. 34.

appears that, whilst retaining a sufficient degree of flexibility in assessing what constitutes 'serious harm', the current practice is likely to provide a clearer indication as to the grounds on which this assessment should be based.[77]

With respect to internal documents, the rationale for their exclusion from the category of 'communicable documents' lies in the circumstance that they mainly consist of 'drafts, opinion or memos from the Commission's departments or other public authorities'.[78] Their non-disclosure is therefore justified by the need to ensure the secrecy of the Commission's deliberations and a 'space of free thinking' for its officials.[79] In the *BAT & Reynolds*[80] case the applicants were seeking access to the Commission's internal documents to sustain their allegations that the Commission's 'change of assessment'[81] in the final decision was attributable to undue pressure exerted on the Commission by the investigated parties at separate meetings.[82]

However the Court took the opposite view that the 'examination by the Court of the Commission's internal file with a view to verifying whether the Commission's decision was influenced by factors other than those indicated in the statement of reasons' constituted 'an exceptional measure of inquiry'[83] which would be admissible only if

> the circumstances surrounding the Decision in question gave rise to serious doubts as to the real reasons and in particular to suspicions that those reasons were extraneous to the objectives of Community law and hence amounted to a misuse of powers.[84]

Commentators criticised the narrow interpretation adopted by the ECJ and argued that when the applicant raised serious claims concerning the lawfulness of the decision and especially a plea of misuse of powers, the internal documents that are necessary to determine the validity of the allegations raised in the appeal should be disclosed.[85] Also, it was alleged that since 'the final decision is . . . an

---

77 JOSHUA, 'Balancing the public interest', at 72.

78 Commission Notice on Access to the File, para. 12, footnote 14.

79 *Inter alia*, LEVITT, 'Commission Notice on internal rules of procedure for access to the file', (1997) 18 *ECLR* 187 at 190.

80 Joined Cases 142 and 156/84, *British American Tobacco Company Ltd & RJ Reynolds Industries Inc v Commission of the European Communities*, (interim order) [1986] ECR 1899.

81 *Id.*, para. 10.

82 *Ibid.*

83 *Id.*, para. 11.

84 *Ibid.* Confirmed in, *inter alia*, case T-236/01, *Tokai Carbon and Others v Commission*, [2004] ECR II-1181, para. 40.

85 LEVITT, 'Access to the file: the Commission's administrative procedures in cases under Articles 85 and 86', (1997) 34 *CMLRev* 1413 at 1428.

act of the Commission as a whole',[86] the limit placed on the access of internal documents originating from Commission's Directorate Generals other than DG Competition could potentially affect the effective exercise of the rights of the defence, it being 'entirely possible that the information or views received by any of the Commissioners or their Directorates General may have an influence on the contents of the decision finally adopted'.[87]

The position of the Court in *BAT & Reynolds* can be contrasted with the later *NMH Stahlwerke*[88] decision, relating to the refusal on the part of the Commission to disclose certain internal documents during judicial proceedings. The CFI took the view that although the sound functioning of the EC institutions could be put at risk by the disclosure of the internal documents originating from that institution,[89] this possibility should be assessed with regard to two competing interests, namely on the one hand, the 'effectiveness of administrative action' and on the other hand the need for the 'judicial supervision of administrative acts'[90] and the respect for the rule of *audi alteram partem*.[91] Consequently, the Court concluded:

> the defendant should be asked to identify . . . the documents classified by it as internal in the file forwarded to the Court which, by reason of their specific nature or content, it considers may not be communicated to the applicants, while explaining in detail and specifically as regards each document the reasons which it considers to warrant such exceptional treatment and lodging, where appropriate, a non-confidential version of those documents . . . it must justify . . . the specific reasons for which it opposes the communication of that correspondence to the applicants . . . .[92]

The *Steel Beams* order therefore suggests that protection of the rights of the defence requires that internal documents which are relevant to issues upon which the Court must rule should be disclosed in their entirety to the undertakings concerned.[93] Even when 'the Commission can advance detailed and specific arguments as to why the disclosure of any specific internal documents would undermine the effectiveness of administrative action, non-confidential versions of the documents . . . should nonetheless be produced'.[94]

---

86 LEVITT, 'Commission Notice on internal rules of procedure for access to the file', (1997) 18 *ECLR* 187 at 190.

87 *Id.*, p. 189.

88 Joined Cases T-134, 136-138, 141, 145, 147-148, 151, 156-157, *NMH Stahlwerke and Others v Commission*, [1996] ECR II-537 (the *Steel Beams* order).

89 *Id.*, para. 73.

90 *Id.*, para. 74.

91 *Ibid.*

92 *Id.*, para. 76. *Inter alia*, LEVITT, 'Access to the file', at 1429.

93 LEVITT, *ibid.*, at 1429.

94 *Ibid.*

The importance of this decision cannot be understated: although it concerned the separate issue of the disclosure of Commission documents in proceedings before the Community courts, it is submitted that the rules laid down in the order could be equally applicable to the access to internal documents in the context of competition administrative proceedings.[95] The CFI relied on general principles such as *audi alteram partem*, 'equality of arms' and the protection of the rights of defence to reach remarkably similar conclusions to those of the *Re: Soda Ash* judgment.[96]

Against this background, it could be argued that the position expressed by the Commission in its 2005 Notice, according to which the investigated undertakings are precluded access to internal documents on the basis of a presumption that they lack evidential value,[97] is not entirely consistent with the view adopted by the CFI, which instead seems to support the thesis that a similar approach to that adopted vis-à-vis business secrets should be extended also to internal documents.[98]

The 2005 Notice on Access to the File defines 'other confidential information' as 'information other than business secrets which may be considered as confidential, insofar as its disclosure would significantly harm a person or undertaking'.[99] The Notice thus recognises that access may be withheld to information 'that would enable the parties to identify complainants or other third parties'[100] which may reasonably claim anonymity to avoid retaliatory measures being take against them especially in cases of an alleged abuse of a dominant position.[101]

This position was confirmed in *Tetra Laval v Commission*,[102] decided under the Merger Control Regulation. The CFI took the view that, faced with risks of being the target of retaliatory measures by a dominant undertaking, 'third parties who submit documents to the Commission in the course of its investigations, and who consider that reprisals might be taken against them as

---

95 *Inter alia*, LEVITT, 'Access to the file', at 1432.

96 Joined Cases T-134, 136–38, 141, 145, 147–48, 151, 156–57, *NMH Stahlwerke and Others v Commission*, [1996] ECR II-537 (the *Steel Beams* order) at para. 70.

97 Commission Notice on Access to the File, para. 12.

98 For the treatment of documents exchanged between the Commission and the National Competition Authorities, see *infra*, this paragraph, footnote 114 and accompanying text.

99 Commission Notice on Access to the File, para. 19.

100 *Ibid.*

101 ERLANDSSON, 'The defendant's right of access to the Commission's file in Competition cases', at 157.

102 Case T-5/02, *Tetra Laval BV v Commission (I)*, [2002] ECR II-4381.

a result, are entitled to expect that their request for confidentiality will be complied with'.[103]

It would appear that the Commission and the Community courts have interpreted strictly the duty to protect the anonymity of informants when a risk of retaliation exists. However, it is emphasised that, just as in the case of business secrets, the legitimate interests of third parties to the secrecy of their identity must be reconciled with the need to ensure the effective protection of the rights of the defence of the investigated undertakings and with the principle of 'equality of arms'.[104]

Recent decisions of the CFI have raised the issue of how the investigated undertakings can gain access to evidence gathered by the Commission as a result of informal meetings during cartel investigations. In *Groupe Danone*[105] the applicant alleged that respect by the Commission of the right of access to the file implied an obligation to 'draw up minutes of such meetings and make them available to the parties'.[106] Despite rejecting this contention,[107] the CFI made clear that 'the practice of using information provided orally by third parties cannot be permitted to infringe the rights of the defence'.[108]

Consequently, if evidence provided verbally was used to support allegations of anti-competitive conduct, the Commission would have to disclose it to the investigated undertakings by, if necessary, 'creat[ing] a written document to be placed in the file'.[109] On the merits the CFI found no violation of the applicant's rights of defence. However, the *Groupe Danone* judgment appears to suggest that there may be circumstances in which an obligation to keep minutes of informal meetings may arise.[110] It is submitted that this conclusion should be welcomed since it is likely to contribute to the meaningful protection of the undertakings' right to be heard whilst ensuring the efficiency of antitrust investigations.[111]

The enactment of the 'Modernisation' Regulation No 1/2003, introducing measures of closer cooperation between the Commission and the National

---

[103] *Id.*, para. 98. See also, more recently, case C-407/04, *Dalmine SpA v Commission*, judgment of 25 January 2007, not yet reported, paras. 46–47.

[104] Commission Notice on Access to the File, cit. (footnote 414), paras. 22 and 24. *Inter alia*, ERLANDSSON, 'The defendant's right of access to the Commission's file in Competition cases', at 157.

[105] Case T-38/02, *Groupe Danone v Commission*, [2005] ECR II-4407.

[106] *Id.*, para. 64.

[107] *Id.*, para. 66.

[108] *Id.*, para. 67.

[109] *Ibid.*

[110] *Inter alia*, joined cases T-191/98 and T-212-214/98, *Atlantic Container Line and Others v Commission*, [2003] ECR II-3275, para. 352.

[111] *Inter alia*, KERSE and KHAN, *EC Antitrust Procedure*, pp. 230–31.

Competition Authorities (NCAs) and amongst the NCAs themselves,[112] raises ad hoc issues as regards access to the evidence obtained by the Commission from other NCAs. Article 11 establishes a duty for each member of the European Competition Network (hereinafter referred to as ECN) to inform the other members of new cases concerning the application of Articles 81 and 82 EC Treaty. Article 12 gives them the power to exchange and use as evidence information collected in the course of their respective investigations, including confidential documents.

Although the implications of Council Regulation No 1/2003 for the protection of the rights of the defence will be addressed in more detail in later chapters,[113] it is appropriate to address at this juncture the extent to which the obligations of cooperation enshrined in Articles 11 and 12 of the Regulation affect the exercise of the right of access to the file.

The 2005 Notice defines the 'correspondence' between the Commission and the NCAs as a 'particular case of internal documents' that cannot therefore be revealed.[114] Nonetheless, the Commission declared that it would authorise their disclosure in exceptional circumstances and after consulting the entity that submitted the document. The investigated parties will be allowed access to these documents when they contain allegations against them or 'form part of the evidence in the investigative process'[115] and so far as they are relevant to the defence of the investigated undertakings.[116]

It is submitted that the position of the Commission could be interpreted as indicating a certain willingness to allow more extensive disclosure of documents obtained from the NCAs than it affords currently with respect to other internal documents. Accordingly, it appears consistent with the need to ensure that the undertakings directly concerned by antitrust proceedings are allowed access to 'inculpatory' and 'exculpatory' documents in accordance with the principle of 'equality of arms', whatever the origin of that evidence may be,[117] and thus goes some way towards reconciling the 'close cooperation' required by the 'modernised' competition enforcement framework with the need to ensure the effective protection of the rights of the defence of the investigated parties.[118]

---

112 See generally, *inter alia*, EHLERMANN, 'The Modernization of EC antitrust policy: a legal and cultural revolution', (2000) 37 *CMLRev* 537.

113 *Infra*, Chapter 6.

114 Commission Notice on Access to the File, para. 15.

115 *Id.*, para. 16.

116 *Ibid.* See also, para. 14, footnote 23 of the Notice as regards referral letters in merger proceedings.

117 *Mutatis mutandis,* joined Cases T-305–07, 313–16, 318, 325, 328–29 & 335/94, *Lymburgse Vinyl Maatschappij NV & Others v Commission (Re: the PVC Cartel II)*, [1999] ECR II-931, para. 1017–18.

118 KERSE and KHAN, *EC Antitrust Procedure*, p. 230.

Overall, it can be concluded that the right of access to the file enjoyed by the investigated undertakings entitles them in principle to obtain disclosure of all the evidence held by the Commission.[119] Nevertheless, the scope of that right must be reconciled with the duty of professional secrecy imposed on Commission officials vis-à-vis third parties. The case law of the ECJ requires the Commission to allow access to 'doctored' versions of confidential documents or when necessary to summaries, to ensure the effectiveness of the undertakings' rights of the defence.[120]

The almost outright refusal on the part of the Commission to allow the disclosure of internal documents in the course of competition proceedings raises, instead, some concern in as much as it would appear to be inconsistent with the case law of the CFI[121] and with the general principle of 'equality of arms' which should inform the exercise of the right of access to the documents relevant for the Commission's allegations.[122] In this specific respect, it is suggested that the approach adopted for the disclosure of documents obtained by other competition enforcement agencies in accordance with the Modernisation Regulation should be welcomed as providing evidence of a more flexible attitude which may, over time, be extended to other types of 'internal documents'.

2.5. Access to the File by Third Parties: Between Confidentiality and 'the Needs of the Inquiry'

The possibility for third parties having a 'sufficient interest' in the proceedings to be heard by the Commission demands that they be allowed access to the file. However, this poses questions relating to the scope of their procedural rights. With respect to complainants, the European Court of Justice held in the *Re: FEDETAB* case[123] that they enjoyed only 'a right to be heard and not a right to receive confidential information'.[124]

---

119 Case T-30/91, *Solvay SA v Commission*, [1995] ECR II-1775, para. 83.

120 Joined Cases T-305–07, 313–16, 318, 325, 328–29 & 335/94, *Lymburgse Vinyl Maatschappij NV & Others v Commission (Re: the PVC Cartel II)*, [1999] ECR II-931, paras. 1017–18.

121 Joined Cases T-134, 136–38, 141, 145, 147–48, 151, 156–57, *NMH Stahlwerke and Others v Commission*, [1996] ECR II-537 (the *Steel Beams* order), para. 76.

122 ERLANDSSON, 'The defendant's right of access to the Commission's file in Competition cases', at 157.

123 Joined Cases 209 to 215 and 218/78, *Heinz Van Landewyck Sàrl and Others v Commission (re: FEDETAB)*, [1980] ECR 3125.

124 *Id.*, para. 46.

Consequently, the Commission could 'communicate to such a party certain information covered by the obligation of professional secrecy', but only 'in so far as it is necessary to do so for the proper conduct of the investigation'.[125] It follows that, although the right of access to the file by third parties is clearly linked to the need to ensure a meaningful exercise of their right to be heard, its scope is by no means equivalent to that enjoyed by the investigated undertakings. In fact, the ECJ was concerned to avoid the possibility that third parties might raise complaints to the Commission only for the purpose of obtaining access to the trade secrets of their competitors.[126]

The more limited interpretation of that right with respect to third parties is also consistent with the non-judicial nature of competition proceedings before the Commission. It was held in the *BAT & Reynolds* judgment[127] that competition investigations were not 'adversary proceedings' between complainants and the investigated undertakings, but administrative proceedings 'commenced by the Commission . . . in fulfilment of its duty to ensure that the rules of competition are observed'.[128] Consequently, even though it is recognised that a competition decision is likely to affect the position of third parties and thus justifies their right to be heard, the procedural rights will not extend to documents classified as 'confidential' by the Commission.[129]

As a result, the ECJ held in *AKZO Chemie* that access to confidential documents can be granted to competitors only upon a formal decision on the part of the Commission and after having given the investigated parties both the opportunity to be heard and to bring an action for the annulment of that decision.[130] In accordance with the position adopted by the Community courts, the Commission 2005 Notice indicates that complainants cannot claim a right of access to the file to the same extent as the investigated parties, nor are they entitled to the disclosure of any confidential information gathered by the Commission.[131] Nonetheless, when the Commission proposes to reject their

---

[125] Case 53/85, *AKZO Chemie BV and AKZO Chemie UK Ltd v Commission* [1986] ECR 1965, para. 26.

[126] *Id.*, para. 28. See also, more recently, case T-204/03, *Haladjian Freres SA v Commission*, judgment of 26 September 2006, not yet reported, para. 210.

[127] Joined Cases 142 and 156/84, *BAT & Reynolds v Commission* [1987] ECR 4487.

[128] *Id.*, para. 21.

[129] *Id.*, para. 28. *Mutatis mutandis*, case T-9/99, *HFB and Others v Commission*, [2002] ECR II-1487, paras. 391–92. For commentary, SCHWARZE, *European Administrative Law*, 1992, London, Sweet & Maxwell, pp. 1326–27.

[130] Case 53/85, *AKZO Chemie BV and AKZO Chemie UK Ltd v Commission* [1986] ECR 1965, para. 29. For commentary, *inter alia* JOSHUA, 'Balancing the public interest', at 77.

[131] Commission Notice on Access to the File, para. 30.

complaint, they are granted an opportunity to scrutinise 'the documents on which the Commission has based its provisional assessment' for the purpose of preparing their reply.[132]

Commentators suggested that although 'the complainants must . . . be given the opportunity to defend their legitimate interests in the course of the administrative proceedings',[133] their 'procedural rights . . . are not as far-reaching as the right to a fair hearing of the companies which are the object of the Commission's investigation'[134] and must be limited 'where they begin to interfere with those companies' right to a fair hearing'.[135] Although their participation in the procedure may be necessary for the 'proper conduct' of the case,[136] it cannot result in the undue disclosure of 'commercially sensitive' information to the detriment of the investigated parties.[137]

2.6. The Consequences of a Violation of the Right to Access to the File

Having regard to the impact of a violation of the right of access to the file, the case law of the Community courts indicates that allegations related to the withholding of the documents retained by the Commission can be raised by the applicants in the appeal proceedings against the final decision,[138] and that whether or not a violation of the right of access to the Commission's file can cause the final decision to be annulled will depend on the extent to which the possibility of the undertakings to defend themselves in the proceedings was significantly affected by the lack of access to the relevant evidence in the circumstances of each case.[139]

---

[132] *Id.*, para. 31. See also Commission Notice on the internal rules of procedure for processing requests for access to the file in cases pursuant to Article 85 and 86 of the EC Treaty, Articles 65 and 66 of the ECSC Treaty and Council Regulation (EEC) 4064/89, [1997] OJ C23/3, para. II.D.1.

[133] SCHWARZE, *European Administrative Law* (1992) London: Sweet & Maxwell, p. 1326.

[134] Joined Cases 142 and 156/84, *BAT & Reynolds v Commission* [1987] ECR 4487, para. 20.

[135] SCHWARZE, *European Administrative Law* (1992) London: Sweet & Maxwell, p. 1326.

[136] Case 53/85, *AKZO Chemie BV and AKZO Chemie UK Ltd v Commission* [1986] ECR 1965, para. 26.

[137] Joined Cases 142 and 156/84, *BAT & Reynolds v Commission*, [1987] ECR 4487.

[138] Cases T-10-12/92 & 15/92, *Cimenteries CBR SA and others v EC Commission*, [1993] ECR II-1571, para. 47.

[139] KERSE and KHAN, *EC Antitrust Procedure*, p. 225. Cf., *inter alia*, case 30/91, *Solvay SA v Commission*, [1995] ECR II-1775 at para. 104.

A distinction was drawn between the failure to disclose inculpatory – namely, documents used by the Commission to substantiate its allegations of anti-competitive conduct – and exculpatory documents – i.e. evidence that the investigated parties may wish to rely on to contradict the Commission's case.[140] In the *AEG-Telefunken* case[141] the ECJ held that the failure to disclose to the investigated undertakings an inculpatory document would lead to that evidence being 'inadmissible' in the proceedings[142] and thus would cause the annulment of the impugned decision only if the Commission relied on them as proof of anti-competitive conduct and therefore substantially jeopardised the decision-making process or the rights of the defence of the undertakings concerned.[143]

With respect to the unlawful lack of disclosure of exculpatory documents, in *Re: Soda Ash*[144] the CFI considered that any alleged breach of the rights of the defence had to 'be examined in relation to the specific circumstances of each particular case'[145] and especially to 'the objections raised by the Commission in order to prove the infringement'.[146]

Since the documents whose disclosure (or lack thereof) was at issue 'might have shown that the passive conduct alleged against the applicant was based on its own independent decisions'[147] and not on the alleged conscious parallel conduct with its competitors, the Court concluded that 'the applicant's defence was affected in a general way by the unlawful failure to disclose certain documents which . . . might have been useful in its defence'[148] and therefore annulled the decision.[149]

It is noteworthy that in the recent *Groupe Danone* decision,[150] the CFI

[140] *Inter alia,* ERLANDSSON, 'The defendant's right of access to the Commission's file in Competition cases', at 172.

[141] Case 107/82, *AEG-Telefunken v Commission* [1983] ECR 3151.

[142] *Id.*, para. 27.

[143] *Ibid.* ERLANDSSON, 'The defendant's right of access to the Commission's file in Competition cases', at 172. See more recently, Opinion of AG Mischo, delivered on 25 October 2001, in case C-247/99 P, *Elf Atochem SA v Commission*, [2002] ECR I-8375, paras. 81–82; also, T-38/02, *Groupe Danone v Commission*, judgment of 25 October 2005, not yet reported, available in [2004] 4 CMLR 25, para. 35.

[144] Case T-30/91, *Solvay SA v Commission*, [1995] ECR II-1775.

[145] *Id.*, para. 60.

[146] *Ibid.*

[147] *Id.*, para. 77.

[148] *Id.*, para. 97.

[149] KERSE and KHAN, *EC Antitrust Procedure*, p. 227. See also T-38/02, *Groupe Danone v Commission*, judgment of 25 October 2005, not yet reported, available in [2006] 4 CMLR 25, para. 36.

[150] Case T-38/02, *Groupe Danone v Commission,* judgment of 25 October 2005, not yet reported, available in [2006] 4 CMLR 25.

emphasised that if documents that the applicant alleges contain exculpatory evidence are not among those making up the Commission file, it would be incumbent on the applicant to apply for access to them before the Commission.[151] In the opinion of the Court, 'failure to do so during the administrative procedure will mean that its right in that respect is barred in any action for annulment which may be brought against the final decision'.[152]

3. ENSURING THE EFFECTIVE EXERCISE OF RIGHT OF ACCESS TO THE FILE: THE ROLE OF THE HEARING OFFICER

3.1. Introductory Remarks

Chapter 2 argued that the position of the Hearing Officer was introduced in competition proceedings to ensure the effective exercise of the right to be heard of the investigated undertakings and of third parties. The current Terms of Reference have strengthened the Officer's authority and independence and provided also for powers concerning the disclosure of evidence to the parties concerned by the proceedings[153] in order to make the exercise of this right more effective.[154] The present section will examine the role of the Hearing Officer with respect to access to the Commission's file and assess his or her ability to ensure a fair and transparent disclosure of that evidence to the interested parties.

---

151 *Id.*, para. 37.

152 *Ibid.* See KERSE and KHAN, *EC Antitrust Procedure*, p. 225. Cf., *inter alia*, Case 30/91, *Solvay SA v Commission*, [1995] ECR II-1775 at para. 104. In the area of merger control see also, *inter alia*, case T-464/04, *IMPALA v Commission*, [2006] ECR II-2289, para. 40.

153 Article 5, Terms of Reference of the Hearing Officer, annexed to the *XI Report on Competition Policy*, Brussels: 1982. Article 7(3), Commission Decision 94/810/ECSC, EC on the terms of reference of hearing officers in certain competition proceedings, [1994] OJ L330/67; Article 12(3), Commission Decision 2001/462/EC, ECSC on the terms of reference of hearing officers in certain competition proceedings, [2001] OJ L162/21.

154 Article 7(3), Commission Decision 94/810/ECSC, EC on the terms of reference of hearing officers in certain competition proceedings, [1994] OJ L330/67; Article 12(3), Commission Decision 2001/462/EC, ECSC on the terms of reference of hearing officers in certain competition proceedings, [2001] OJ L162/21.

3.2. The Hearing Officer's Powers Concerning the Admission of Evidence

In 1994, the Commission conferred on the Hearing Officer the power to rule on requests for access to the file and for confidential treatment of the evidence gathered by the Commission[155] and to gather fresh documents during the hearing.[156] However, the 1994 Terms of Reference were strongly criticised on the ground that allowing the Officer to admit fresh evidence to the hearing may in fact jeopardise the undertakings' right to be heard on the allegations originally contained in the Statement of Objections.[157]

Commentators thus suggested that this clause should be interpreted as allowing new material to be presented in sufficient detail at the hearing only to the extent that it related to allegations already notified.[158] The interested parties should also be granted a reasonable opportunity to comment on the new evidence.[159]

It was also argued that these decisions should be open to judicial scrutiny to increase the transparency of the Officer's decision-making function and to allow allegations of procedural unfairness to be dealt with at an early stage.[160] However, the CFI took the opposite view that any allegations concerning infringement of the right to be heard enjoyed by the undertakings to which the statement of objections had been addressed, including those relating to access to the evidence retained by the Commission, could only be raised with the appeal against the final decision.[161] It was held in the *Cimenteries* judgment:

> . . . any infringement of the right of the addressees of an SO [statement of objections] effectively put forward their views on the objections made by the Commission and on the evidence intended to support those objections is capable of producing binding legal effects of such a nature as to affect the interests of the undertakings and associations of undertakings concerned only if and when the

---

155 Article 5, Commission Decision 94/810/ECSC, EC on the terms of reference of hearing officers in certain competition proceedings, [1994] OJ L330/67.

156 Article 5, Terms of Reference of the Hearing Officer, annexed to the *XI Report on Competition Policy*, Brussels: 1982; also, in the same terms, Article 4, 1994 Terms of Reference, as above.

157 *Inter alia*, case 45/69, *Boehringer Mannheim v Commission*, [1970] ECR 769, para. 9.

158 LEVITT: 'Commission hearings and the role of the Hearing Officer: suggestions for reform', at 405.

159 *Ibid.*

160 HOUSE of LORDS SELECT COMMITTEE on the EUROPEAN UNION, *XIX Report: Strengthening the Role of the Hearing Officer,* sess. 1999/2000, para. 50.

161 Cases T-10-12/92 & 15/92, *Cimenteries CBR SA and Others v EC Commission*, [1992] ECR II -2667 at para. 47.

> Commission has adopted a decision or decisions finding the existence of the infringement of which it accuses them.[162]

The Court had distinguished the case at hand from the ECJ *AKZO Chemie*[163] decision, where it was stated that 'the decision in which the Commission considered that the documents in question did not qualify for the confidential treatment guaranteed by Community law . . . is definitive in nature'.[164] Unlike *AKZO*, which concerned a decision on confidential treatment adopted at the interlocutory stage of the proceedings and thus 'unconnected with any decision'[165] on the merits, the *Cimenteries* decision recognised that the Commission could 'rectify any procedural irregularities by subsequently granting access to the file after initially declining to do so'[166] up to the final decision.

However, commentators argued that 'there exists a real disparity of protection between the various elements of the Commission's process of discovery or communication of documents which affects necessarily the rights of the investigated party'.[167] Whereas in *AKZO Chemie* 'the investigated party is able to obtain an annulment at the interlocutory stage concerning the protection of business secrets',[168] it cannot, as a result of *Cimenteries* seek the immediate annulment of a decision concerning the 'general discovery of documents'.[169]

Perhaps regrettably, the Commission failed to deal with the issues of concern outlined above in the 2001 Terms of Reference.[170] Article 12(3) reproduces the provision laid down by Article 7(3) of the previous Terms of Reference, according to which 'the hearing officer shall decide [*inter alia*] whether fresh documents should be admitted during the hearing (. . .)'.[171] Furthermore, despite the significant changes introduced by the 2001 Mandate

---

162 *Ibid.*

163 Case 53/85, *AKZO Chemie v Commission*, [1985] ECR 1965.

164 *Id.*, para. 20.

165 *Id.*, para. 22.

166 Cases T-10-12/92 & 15/92, *Cimenteries CBR SA and Others v EC Commission*, [1992] ECR II-2667 at para. 47. Also, Case T-90/96, *Automobiles Peugeot SA v Commission*, [1997] ECR II-663, paras. 32, 34 and 37.

167 CUMMINGS, 'Automobiles Peugeot SA v Commission of the European Communities', case comment, (1998) 19 *ECLR* 106, at 107.

168 *Id.*, p. 108.

169 *Ibid.*

170 VAN der WOUDE, 'Hearing Officers and EC antitrust procedures: the art of making subjective procedures more objective', (1996) 33 *CMLRev* 531 at 546.

171 Case 45/69, *Boehringer Mannheim v Commission*, [1970] ECR 769, para. 9. See, *inter alia*, LEVITT, 'Commission hearings and the role of Hearing Officer: suggestions for reform', at 405.

with respect to the independence and effectiveness of the role of the Hearing Officers, the CFI declined to reconsider the position expressed in the *Cimenteries* judgment, mentioned above.[172]

In the *Reisebank*[173] case the applicant had alleged that, by preventing the applicant from bringing an action for annulment of the decision of the Hearing Officer it would not be 'possible to guarantee the independence of the hearing officer and the autonomy of the hearing procedure'[174] and that the procedural rights of defence would be persistently and irreversibly damaged.[175] Despite the apparent strength of the applicant's arguments, the President of the Court dismissed the application and held that 'although they may constitute an infringement of the rights of the defence',[176] the decisions refusing access to the file are merely preparatory and not liable to judicial challenge. Consequently, only the final decision would be open to review by the Court of First Instance on procedural grounds.[177]

The Court declined to consider the argument based on the increased independence of the Hearing Officer resulting from the 2001 Terms of Reference on the ground that the applicant had not 'put forward any weighty considerations that would enable the Court to hold that the case-law cited above on access to file in competition cases is no longer applicable'.[178] It is submitted that the position adopted by the CFI sounds rather formalistic and does not appear to reflect the stronger powers enjoyed by the Hearing Officer after the 2001 Mandate.

The above analysis thus suggests that, although the role of the Hearing Officer as 'neutral' chair to the hearing has brought clear benefits for the disclosure of the documents contained in the Commission's file, by improving the objectivity of the assessment of what constitutes 'accessible' evidence, there are still several issues that may impair her function in this particular context. Later sections will illustrate the extent to which the absence of judicial supervision over decisions adopted by the Officer on requests for access

---

[172] Cases T-10-12/92 & 15/92, *Cimenteries CBR SA and others v EC Commission*, [1992] ECR II-2667 at para. 47. See also, *mutatis mutandis*, case 310/93P, *BPB & British Gypsum v Commission*, [1997] ECR I-865, available at [1997] 4 CMLR 238, per AG Leger, footnote 101, p. 262.

[173] T-216/01, *Reisebank AG v Commission*, [2001] ECR II-3481.

[174] *Id.*, para. 34.

[175] *Id.*, para. 35.

[176] *Id.*, para. 46.

[177] *Id.*, paras. 46–47. Confirmed in T-219/01, *Commerzbank AG v Commission*, [2001] ECR II-3501, paras. 38–40. Also *mutatis mutandis*, T-198/03 P, *Bank Austria Creditanstalt AG v Commission*, [2003] ECR II-4879, paras. 31–32, 34.

[178] *Id.*, para. 50. See also, more recently, case T-213/01, *Österreicische Postsparkasse AG v Commission*, [2006] ECR II-1601, paras. 142, 151.

to the file may not be entirely consistent with the requirements of 'fair procedure' enshrined in Article 6(1) of the European Convention on Human Rights.

4. THE DISCLOSURE OF EVIDENCE GATHERED IN THE COURSE OF 'ADMINISTRATIVE' PROCEDURE UNDER THE ECHR: A PRINCIPLE OF 'EQUALITY OF ARMS' STRASBOURG STYLE?

4.1. General Remarks

The analysis of the case law of the European Court of Human Rights concerning the application of Article 6(1) ECHR to the administrative action of public, non-judicial authorities conducted in the previous chapter emphasised the function of the right to be heard as a means through which the parties concerned can participate meaningfully in the proceedings so as to influence their outcome.[179] However, to achieve that objective it is also essential that the interested natural or legal persons be afforded an opportunity to acquaint themselves with the evidence at the basis of the authorities' case.

This section will illustrate the extent to which Article 6(1) ECHR confers on the affected parties the right to obtain access to the documents and other evidence retained by the public authorities. Thereafter, it will compare the standards enshrined in the Convention with those guaranteed by EC law in the context of competition enforcement before the Commission. It will demonstrate that the meaning of the concept of 'equality of arms' developed by the ECJ may not be entirely consistent with that enshrined in the case law of the Strasbourg Court, especially in consideration of the different safeguards attending the imposition of restrictions on the right enjoyed by the interested parties to obtain the disclosure of evidence relevant for their defence.

4.2. The Right to Obtain Disclosure of Evidence and the Principle of 'Equality of Arms' in the European Convention on Human Rights

The European Court of Human Rights has constantly reiterated that, to ensure effective and meaningful participation in the administrative proceedings leading to the determination of a 'criminal charge' or of 'civil rights and obligations',[180] the concerned parties must be afforded the opportunity to have

[179] *Supra*, Chapter 2, section 3.2. *Inter alia*, Appl. No 9749/82, *W v United Kingdom*, [1988] 10 EHRR 29.

[180] Appl. No 9749/82, *W v United Kingdom*, [1988] 10 EHRR 29.

access to the evidence gathered by the authorities so as to be able to influence the outcome of the procedure.[181] It was held that, although the admissibility of evidence should be left primarily to national law, and as a general rule it is the task of the national authorities, and especially the courts, to assess the evidence before them, the Strasbourg Court will exercise a power of supervision on the overall fairness of the proceedings.[182]

When evidence is withheld from the interested parties the European Court of Human Rights will assess that the procedure presents adequate safeguards to ensure the meaningful participation of those affected by the proceedings.[183] It was held in *Jasper*, a case concerning the fairness of criminal proceedings, that, although in principle the right to obtain disclosure of evidence retained by the investigating authorities must be informed by the principle of 'equality of arms',[184] 'there may be competing interests . . . which must be weighed against the rights of the accused',[185] including the need to preserve other individuals' rights.

However, 'only such measures restricting the rights of the defence which are strictly necessary are permissible',[186] and must be adopted so as to counterbalance 'any difficulties caused to the defence by a limitation on its rights . . . [through] the procedures followed by the judicial authorities'.[187] It is noteworthy that this conclusion was extended to national competition proceedings in the *Fortum* decision, according to which the failure of the competent national court to deal in its judgment with the applicant's pleas that his right of access to the file had been violated infringed Article 6(1) ECHR.[188]

Similar views were adopted as regards the determination of 'civil' matters. The Court held in *Olsson* that the possibility for the applicants 'to submit such materials and arguments as they saw fit'[189] and to obtain disclosure of the

---

181 *Inter alia,* Appl. no 27052/95, *Jasper v United Kingdom*, [2000] 30 EHRR 441, para. 52; also Appl. No 16424/90, *McMichael v United Kingdom*, ser. A No 308, [1995] 20 EHRR 205, para. 80.

182 *Inter alia*, Appl. No 33900/96, *PS v Germany*, judgment of 20 December 2001, [2003] 36 EHRR 61, para. 19; Appl. No 18978/91, *Miailhe v France*, judgment of 26 September 1996, [1997] 23 EHRR 491, para. 43.

183 Appl. 16424/90, *McMichael v United Kingdom*, ser. A No 308, [1995] 20 EHRR 205, paras. 80, 83, 91; Appl. No 39482/98, *Dowsett v United Kingdom*, judgment of 24 June 2003, [2004] 38 EHRR 41, paras. 42–43.

184 Appl. No 39482/98, *Dowsett v United Kingdom*, [2004] 38 EHRR 41, paras. 50–51.

185 Appl. No 27052/95, *Jasper v United Kingdom*, [2000] 30 EHRR 441, para. 52.

186 *Ibid.*

187 *Ibid.*

188 Appl. No 32559/96, *Fortum Corp v Finland*, judgment of 15 July 2003, [2004] 38 EHRR 36, paras. 41 and 43.

189 Appl. No 10465/83, *Olsson v Sweden*, [1989] 11 EHRR 259, para. 90.

evidence, especially from experts, submitted in the course of care proceedings was an essential factor for the overall fairness of the procedure.[190] The lack of disclosure to applicants of documents lodged with the decision-making authorities could thus be liable to result in a violation of their rights in so far as it adversely affected their 'ability (. . .) to influence the outcome' of the procedure.[191]

Accordingly, it is clear that a 'fair procedure' demands that the interested parties be allowed access to the evidence retained by the competent authorities in accordance with the principle of 'equality of arms'.[192] However, that right is not absolute, for the public interest may warrant a limitation of the scope of disclosure; nonetheless, in those circumstances appropriate procedural features, such as the judicial supervision over any such restriction, must be ensured to avoid that the parties' rights are not unduly burdened.[193]

4.3. 'Equality of Arms' in Strasbourg and in Luxembourg: Elements for a Comparative Analysis

Section 3 above illustrated the scope and manner of exercise of the right of access to the file enjoyed by the investigated undertakings and, albeit to a more limited degree, by third parties, and demonstrated its position 'at the heart' of the concept of EC 'due process' governing the competition proceedings before the Commission. The role of the Hearing Officer in the adoption of decisions concerning requests for disclosure of the documents held in the file emerged as an additional safeguard for the objectivity of this particular phase of the proceedings, although it was also emphasised that her decisions were not subject to direct and 'immediate' judicial scrutiny by the CFI.[194]

Section 4.2 instead examined the extent to which the European Court of Human Rights recognises a right to obtain the disclosure of the relevant evidence retained by public authorities in proceedings having a 'civil' or 'criminal' character. The Court emphasised that appropriate procedural safeguards must attend the imposition of any restrictions on the reach of that right,

---

[190] *Inter alia*, Appl. No 17383/90, *Johnasen v Norway*, [1997] 23 EHRR 33, para. 66. For commentary, FELDMAN, 'The developing scope of Article 8 of the European Convention on Human Rights', (1997) 3 *EHRLR* 265 at 267–69.

[191] Appl. 16424/90, *McMichael v United Kingdom*, ser. A No 308, [1995] 20 EHRR 205, para. 80.

[192] *Inter alia*, Appl. No 39482/98, *Dowsett v United Kingdom*, judgment of 24 June 2003, [2004] 38 EHRR 41, paras. 50–51.

[193] *Inter alia*, Appl. No 32559/96, *Fortum Corp v Finland*, [2004] 38 EHRR 36, para. 43.

[194] *Inter alia*, Case T-216/01, *Reisebank AG v Commission*, [2001] ECR II-3481, paras. 35–36.

especially by ensuring continuous judicial supervision over the adoption of any measure impinging upon it, in accordance with the principle of 'equality of arms'.[195]

In this specific respect, it is perhaps telling that the CFI used the same expression in its *Re: Soda Ash* judgment[196] to define the scope of the right of access to the file enjoyed by the investigated parties in competition proceedings. However, a closer examination of the case law demonstrates that there are significant differences in the interpretation of that concept. On the one hand, the case law of the Luxembourg courts clearly acknowledges that the right of access to the file may only be restricted in the interest of the protection of the confidentiality of 'sensitive information' and that, before refusing access outright, the Commission should make available to the investigated parties a 'non-confidential' version of the documents from which the 'sensitive' passages have been deleted.[197]

Nonetheless, although the 2001 Terms of Reference confer the power to adopt decisions as regards access to the Commission's file to the Hearing Officer after hearing the affected parties' submissions[198] in a manner similar, in some respects, to the safeguard offered by an 'independent adjudicator',[199] this power raises concern since the Officer's determinations are not amenable to immediate judicial review before the Community courts.[200]

On the other hand, the European Court of Human Rights emphasised that the circumstance that the questions concerning the disclosure of evidence in criminal proceedings were subject to the constant review of the trial judgment was considered essential to protect the rights of the accused to have access to the prosecution's brief according to the rule of 'equality of arms'.[201]

Against this background, the fact that the Hearing Officer can adopt determinations affecting the exercise of the right of the investigated undertakings to obtain disclosure of the evidence contained in the case file without judicial

---

195 *Inter alia*, Appl. No 32559/96, *Fortum Corp v Finland*, [2004] 38 EHRR 36, para. 43.

196 Case T-30/91, *Solvay SA v Commission*, [1995] ECR II-1775, para. 83. (*Soda Ash* was the name originally given to the investigation by the Commission.)

197 Case T-175/95, *BASF Coating v Commission*, [1999] ECR II-1581, para. 92.

198 Article 5, Commission Decision 2001/462/EC, ECSC, on the terms of reference of hearing officers in certain competition proceedings, [2001] OJ L162/21.

199 Appl. No 27052/95, *Jasper v United Kingdom*, [2000] 30 EHRR 441, para. 52.

200 Cases T-10-12/92 & 15/92, *Cimenteries CBR SA and Others v EC Commission*, [1992] ECR II-1571. Also Case T-216/01, *Reisebank AG v Commission*, [2001] ECR II-3481, para. 34.

201 Appl. No 39482/98, *Dowsett v United Kingdom*, judgment of 24 June 2003, [2004] 38 EHRR 41, paras. 50–51.

supervision[202] seems inconsistent with the need to ensure the effective protection of their right of access to the file in accordance with the principle of 'equality of arms' and ultimately with the right to a 'fair procedure' in the context of administrative action aimed at the determination of a 'criminal charge' as intended by the European Court of Human Rights.

5. THE RIGHT OF ACCESS TO THE COMMISSION'S FILE IN THE LIGHT OF THE ECHR: TENTATIVE CONCLUSIONS

The examination conducted in this chapter has demonstrated that the right to obtain access to the evidence gathered by public authorities in the course of administrative proceedings that have a 'civil' or 'criminal' nature and, in the EU context, of merger and antitrust procedures constitutes an essential instrument through which the interested parties and, to a more limited degree, third parties can participate meaningfully in them, with a view to influencing their outcome.

However, the comparative analysis of the right of access to the Commission file provided by EC law and of the right to obtain the disclosure of evidence especially in the course of criminal proceedings enshrined in the ECHR demonstrated that the principle of 'equality of arms', which should inspire the manner of exercise of these rights in both legal systems, has been interpreted differently. Whereas the European Court of Human Rights has favoured a broad reading of that principle so as to include the right to seek judicial scrutiny of decisions impinging upon the right to obtain the disclosure of the relevant evidence, the ECJ denied that the relevant decisions of the Hearing Officer could be challenged immediately before the CFI.

Accordingly, it may be concluded that without judicial supervision of the decisions of the Hearing Officer concerning access to the file of the investigated parties, it could be doubted that their right to be acquainted with the evidence in conditions of parity with the Commission is effective to the extent required by the Convention. It may be argued that the recent developments in the area of the protection of fundamental rights in the EU and the importance of the ECHR in this context could demand that the CFI allow for the judicial scrutiny of the Hearing Officer's decisions related to the disclosure of evidence.[203] However, most recent case law[204] suggests that a similar devel-

---

202 T-216/01, *Reisebank AG v Commission*, [2001] ECR II-3481, paras. 35–36.

203 *Inter alia*, Lord MILLETT, 'The right to good administration in European Law', (2002) *PL* (Summer) 309 at 318; ANDREANGELI, 'Strasbourg versus Brussels:

opment is less than likely and this is liable to cast doubt on the overall fairness of the 'administrative stage' of the competition proceedings before the Commission.

Human Rights, the right of access to the file and the protection of legal professional privilege', (2004) 11(2) *IJEL* 362 at 370.

204 T-216/01, *Reisebank AG v Commission*, [2001] ECR II-3481.

4. Protection against forced disclosure of 'sensitive evidence': the legal professional privilege and the privilege against self-incrimination in EC competition investigations and procedure

INTRODUCTION

The previous chapter examined the extent to which EC law confers on the undertakings being investigated by the Commission for suspected breaches of competition law the right to have access to the evidence gathered in the course of the investigations, and assessed it in the light of the principles enshrined in Article 6(1) ECHR and applicable to administrative procedures having a 'civil' or 'criminal' nature. In the course of the examination, it emerged that although this right is inspired by the principle of 'equality of arms', it may be limited in order to safeguard the legitimate interests of third parties or of the investigated parties themselves to the protection of their 'commercially sensitive' information.

The demands of fairness of the Commission proceedings may also require that information be protected against forced disclosure to the competition officials in other circumstances: such is the case with communications between the investigated undertakings and their legal advisers and with information which may be incriminating. This chapter will examine the extent to which, respectively, EC law and the European Convention on Human Rights protect the confidentiality of lawyer–client correspondence and the privilege against self-incrimination. Thereafter, it will assess whether the Community legal standards comply with the Convention requirements as regards these two safeguards.

1. THE CONFIDENTIAL TREATMENT OF LAWYER–CLIENT CORRESPONDENCE IN EC LAW

1.1. Introductory Remarks

The concept of legal professional privilege (hereinafter referred to also as LPP) in EC law has long been debated. Although the 2004 interim order in the *AKZO Nobel and Ackros Chemicals* case[1] appeared to signal a trend toward the reformulation of the standards of protection enshrined in the *A.M. & S. v Commission*[2] decision, the recent final judgment in *AKZO* reaffirmed the existing position. At the same time, the Community legislature, despite repeated calls for reform, declined to modify the remit of the privilege in the context of reforms of the framework for the enforcement of Articles 81 and 82 of the EC Treaty and of the Merger Regulation.

This section will examine the concept of LPP in Community law and consider the reasons for and against an extension of its scope to protect communications emanating from employed legal advisers. In conclusion, an attempt will be made to place the present trends developed in the area of competition enforcement in the wider context of the Community legislative measures enacted to facilitate the fight against organised crime and to speculate on the possible developments of the scope of the privilege.

1.2. *A.M. & S. v Commission*: a 'Community View' of Legal Professional Privilege

The concept of legal professional privilege was established in Community law as a 'judicial creation' of the ECJ. In *A.M. & S. Europe v Commission* the Court held that although Regulation 17/62 had conferred 'on the Commission wide powers of investigation and of obtaining information' and of requiring 'production of business records, that is to say, documents concerning the market activities of the undertakings',[3] the undertakings concerned could rely on the exception of confidentiality to prevent the disclosure of 'written communications between lawyer and client'[4] to enable 'any person . . . without constraint,

[1] Case T-125/03, *AKZO Nobel Chemicals Ltd and Ackros Chemicals Ltd v Commission*, [2003] ECR II-4771.

[2] Case 155/79, *AM & S Europe Limited v Commission of the European Communities*, [1982] ECR 1575.

[3] JOSHUA, 'Balancing the public interest: confidentiality, trade secret and disclosure of evidence in EC Competition procedures', (1994) 15 *ECLR* 68 at 72.

[4] Case 155/79, *AM & S Europe Limited v Commission of the European Communities*, [1982] ECR 1575, para. 18.

to consult a lawyer whose profession entails the giving of independent legal advice to all those in need of it'.[5]

The ECJ acknowledged however that 'although the principle of such protection is generally recognized, its scope and the criteria for applying it vary'[6] across the Community:

> Whilst in some of the Member States the protection against disclosure afforded to written communications between lawyer and client is based principally on a recognition of the very nature of the legal profession, inasmuch as it contributes towards the maintenance of the rule of law, in other Member States the same protection is justified by the more specific requirement (which, moreover, is also recognized in the first-mentioned states) that the rights of the defence must be respected.[7]

The Court consequently adopted a solution 'at Community level'[8] on the basis of 'the principles and concepts common to the laws'[9] of the Member States according to which lawyer–client communications 'exchanged after the initiation of the administrative procedure under Regulation no 17',[10] including 'earlier written communications which have a relationship to the subject-matter of that procedure',[11] would be privileged provided that they 'are made for the purposes and in the interests of the client's rights of defence and . . . emanate from independent lawyers, that is to say, lawyers who are not bound to the client by a relationship of employment'[12] and are entitled to 'practise [their] profession in one of the Member States, regardless of the Member State in which the client lives'.

Despite recognising legal professional privilege in Community law, *A.M.& S.* leaves open several issues as regards its scope. First, the ECJ expressly refers only to communications between lawyer and client.[13] Therefore, litigation privilege, namely the protection against forced disclosure of communications with third parties, including expert reports made for the dominant purpose of litigation[14] would not be included. However, it could be argued that the general exception of confidentiality of business secrets could be deployed to prevent their disclosure when they contain 'sensitive' data about the undertakings concerned.

---

5 *Ibid.*
6 *Id.*, para. 19.
7 *Id.*, para. 20.
8 *Id.*, para. 30.
9 *Id*, para. 18.
10 *Id.*, para. 23.
11 *Ibid.*
12 *Id.*, para. 21.
13 *Ibid.*
14 PATTENDEN, 'Litigation privilege and expert opinion evidence', (2000) 4 *Int'l J. of Ev. and Proof* 213.

Second, the ECJ justified the requirement of independence of the legal adviser, namely the absence of 'a relationship of employment'[15] with the client, on the basis of the nature of the legal profession and of the role of the counsel as 'collaborating in the administration of justice by the courts and as being required to provide, in full autonomy, and in the overriding interests of that cause, such legal assistance as the client needs'.[16] To fulfil this function the lawyer must therefore be bound by 'rules of professional ethics and discipline (. . .) laid down and enforced in the general interest by institutions endowed with the requisite powers for that purpose'.[17]

The ECJ pointed out that 'financial reliance on a single employer' is viewed in some Member States, such as France or Italy,[18] as a 'surrender of ethical autonomy' by the lawyer[19] and a ground for exclusion from the legal profession[20] as a result of which they would no longer be 'subjected to the deontology applicable to self-employed practitioners'.[21]

The restriction of the privilege to documents emanating from a lawyer authorised to practise the legal profession in a Member State is instead justified in relation to 'the common rules on the exercise of the legal profession as laid down in Council Directive 77/429/EEC of 22 March 1977'[22] and to the general principle of 'mutual recognition by all the Member States of the national legal concepts of each of them on this subject'.[23] The lack of 'common basis' for the rules governing the legal profession could therefore have constituted a factor leading to the exclusion from the scope of the privilege of communications emanating from lawyers authorised to practise in a non-Member State.[24]

---

15 Case 155/79, *AM & S Europe Limited v Commission of the European Communities*, [1982] ECR 1575 at para. 21.

16 *Id.*, para. 24.

17 *Ibid.*

18 See CCBE, 'The professional secret, confidentiality and legal professional privilege in the nine Member States of the European Community', report published by the Consultative Committee of the Bars and Societies of the European Community, 1976 – David EDWARD, p. 6. The version updated by John FISH is available at: http://www.ccbe.org/en/comites/in_house_en.htm.

19 DALY, 'The cultural, ethical and legal challenges in lawyering for a global organization: the role of the general counsel', (1997) 46 *Emory L. J.* 1057 at 1102.

20 JOSHUA, 'Privilege in multi-jurisdictional cartel investigations: are European courts missing the point?', (2004) 7 *Global Comp. Rev.* 39.

21 FENNELLY, 'Lawyers and employed lawyers: the application of legal professional privilege', (1998) 1 *Irish Bus. L.* 2 at 7.

22 Case 155/79, *AM & S Europe Limited v Commission of the European Communities*, [1982] ECR 1575, para. 26.

23 *Ibid.*

24 CARR, 'Should in-house lawyers have lawyer-client privilege?', (1996) 24 *Int'l Business Lawyer* 522 at 525.

Commentators suggested that the approach of the ECJ appears to focus more on 'the form (i.e. uniform application of Community protection of confidentiality)',[25] than on 'the substance',[26] namely the need to safeguard the confidentiality of the communications of any counsel who have been duly authorised to practise and are subject to appropriate rules of professional ethics[27] and that, due to its general character, withholds privilege from communications with in-house lawyers who, under the national laws of some of the Member States, are allowed to be members of the legal profession.[28]

That is the case in England and Wales, where in contrast with the concept of 'professional secrecy' developed in continental jurisdictions,[29] the privilege is conceived as a 'right of clients in the course of the administration of justice'.[30] Consequently, both barristers and solicitors who are employed by their 'client' are subject to the same obligations and endowed with the same rights as their independent colleagues 'by virtue of their qualification'.[31]

Similarly, in Ireland there is no distinction between employed and independent legal professionals who belong to – and are therefore regulated by – the Law Society of Ireland.[32] Other countries, such as Portugal[33] and Spain,[34] allow salaried legal professionals to become members of the national Bar, sometimes subject to an undertaking of independence. Following their admission to the Bar, they are treated as 'regulated legal professionals' for the purpose of privilege. In-house lawyers are also allowed to become members of the national 'Bar' in the Netherlands.[35] Consequently, an 'advocaat' in the

---

25 HILL, 'A problem of privilege: in-house counsel and the attorney-client privilege in the United States and the European Community', (1995) 27 *Case W. Res. J. of Int'l L.* 145 at 191.

26 *Ibid.*

27 *Ibid.*

28 *Inter alia*, FAULL, 'In-house lawyers and legal professional privilege: a problem revisited', (1998) 4 *Colum. J. of Eur. L.* 139 at 142.

29 E.g. France; see CCBE, *Regulated legal professionals and professional privilege within the European Union, the European Economic Area and Switzerland and certain other European Jurisdictions* – John FISH (February 2004), available at: http://www.ccbe.org/en/comites/in_house_en.htm, pp. 25–27.

30 CCBE, *Regulated legal professionals and professional privilege within the European Union, the European Economic Area and Switzerland, and certain other European jurisdictions*, p. 48.

31 *Id.*, p. 48.

32 *Id.*, p. 33.

33 *Id.*, p. 42.

34 *Id.*, p. 44.

35 *Id.*, p. 39.

Netherlands enjoys the same rights and is bound by the same duties regardless of whether or not he or she is employed by the client.[36]

It should be added that the test laid down in *A.M. & S* contrasts with the Opinion of AG Slynn in *A.M. & S.*, according to whom 'provided he is subject to rules of professional ethics, the salaried lawyer should . . . be treated in the same way as the lawyer in private practice'[37] for privilege purposes. Commentators added that the current notion creates considerable difficulties for companies and is likely to impair their role as advisers 'best-placed to encourage compliance with the law from their vantage point within the company'.[38]

Furthermore, the abolition of the notification procedure resulting from Regulation 1/2003 has forced undertakings to rely increasingly on self-assessment of their practices and therefore has called for a more proactive role for their legal advisers.[39] Consequently, it could be argued that denying the protection of confidentiality to communications emanating from employed counsel is likely to hamper the achievement of better self-compliance with Community competition rules in a framework where the 'safe harbour' of exemptions is no longer available.[40]

A.M. & S. presents further problems with respect to the procedure to decide whether certain communications are covered by the privilege. The ECJ held that only the Commission could determine whether or not the disclosure of a specific document should be withheld on grounds of privilege[41] and that the investigated party should produce 'relevant material' to substantiate the claim of privilege.[42] Some authors suggested that, although this assessment could not be based on the 'simple assertion on the part of a company that all the prerequisites for the protection of confidentiality had been met', the investigated undertakings would not be obliged to reveal the contents of the documents to the investigating officials.[43]

---

36 Case T-125/03, *AKZO Nobel Chemicals Ltd and Ackros Chemicals Ltd v Commission*, [2003] ECR II-4771, paras. 126–27.

37 Case 155/79, *AM & S Europe Limited v Commission of the European Communities*, [1982] ECR 1575, per AG Slynn, p. 1611.

38 FAULL, 'In-house lawyers and legal professional privilege: a problem revisited', at 140.

39 POWER, 'Representing clients after the Modernisation of EC Competition law', (2003) 14 *ICCLR* 335 at 336.

40 *Ibid.*

41 Case 155/79, *AM & S Europe Limited v Commission of the European Communities*, [1982] ECR 1575, para. 17.

42 *Id.*, para. 29.

43 CHRISTOFOROU, 'Protection of legal privilege in EEC competition law: the imperfections of a case', (1985–86) 9 *Fordham Int L J* 1, 47. Also Case T-125/03, *AKZO Nobel Chemicals Ltd and Ackros Chemicals Ltd v Commission*, [2003] ECR II-4771, paras. 133–34.

Nevertheless, it was argued that, given the nature of the conditions dictated in the *A.M. & S.* test,[44] the only way to conduct that assessment would be for the Commission's officials themselves to examine the document.[45] The possibility for the Commission to cast a 'cursory glance' on the evidence was however viewed as a potential threat to both the privilege and the overall fairness of the proceedings. Commentators pointed out that by viewing even 'cursorily' potentially confidential documents, the case-handling officials 'may consciously or unconsciously give a different direction to the investigation'[46] and thus called for adequate procedural guarantees to ensure that the assessment of the nature of the evidence does not endanger the rights of defence of the investigated undertakings.[47]

Additional problems are also likely to arise from the application of measures of cooperation enshrined in the Modernisation Regulation in the context of the European Competition Network. Although this topic will be considered in more detail in later chapters, it is noteworthy that Council Regulation No 1/2003, despite conferring on the Commission and the National Competition Authorities (hereinafter referred to as NCAs) a wide-ranging power to exchange evidence collected during competition proceedings, for the purpose of it being used during investigations in a different jurisdiction, does not lay down any rule governing the use of the evidence so obtained.[48]

Vesterdorf observed extra-judicially that Regulation 1/2003 in substance allows information to be deployed against the investigated undertakings 'even if it has been collected under rules which are less protective than those of the Commission or the receiving NCA'[49] subject only to the limits established by Article 12(3) for the protection of individuals.[50] Consequently, if the

---

44 Case 155/79, *AM & S Europe Limited v Commission of the European Communities*, [1982] ECR 1575, para. 29.

45 GIPPINI FOURNIER, 'Legal professional privilege in competition proceedings before the European Commission: beyond the cursory glance', (2005) 28 *Fordham Int'l L J* 967, at 1020.

46 *Id.*, p. 1021.

47 *Ibid.* Cf. DEKEYSER and GAUER, 'The new enforcement system for Articles 81 and 82 and the rights of defence', in HAWK (ed.), *International Antitrust Law and Policy*, p. 573.

48 *Infra*, Chapter 7, para. 3.1, footnote 89 and accompanying text.

49 VESTERDORF, 'Legal professional privilege and the privilege against self-incrimination in EC Law: recent developments and current issues', in HAWK (ed.), *International Antitrust Law and Policy*, at 721.

50 'Information exchanged pursuant to paragraph 1 can only be used in evidence to impose sanctions on natural persons where: – the law of the transmitting authority foresees sanctions of a similar kind in relation to an infringement of article 81 or article 82 of the Treaty or, in absence thereof, – the information has been collected in a way which respects the same level of protection of the rights of the defence of natural

Commission were to transmit communications between an investigated undertaking and its in-house counsel to another jurisdiction, the competent NCA could deploy that evidence in the proceedings, regardless of the higher degree of protection afforded in its jurisdiction to lawyer–client confidentiality.

A similar conclusion could however have unsavoury consequences for undertakings because it would permit NCAs, or indeed the Commission itself, to use evidence 'collected . . . under a specific standard of LPP'[51] although the law applicable in the receiving jurisdiction grants higher protection to the privilege.[52] Recourse to Article 12(1), Regulation 1/2003, may prevent the concerned firms from claiming the protection against forced disclosure of these communications not only vis-à-vis the Commission, but also vis-à-vis the receiving national competition authority in proceedings enforcing Articles 81 and 82 EC Treaty, since it would result in their inability to benefit from more extensive standards of privilege potentially available in the jurisdiction where that evidence is received.[53]

The legal implications arising from the increasing bilateral cooperation between the European Commission and the US Department of Justice were interpreted as providing additional support to the case for a reformulation of legal professional privilege.[54] In the United States of America in-house lawyers are allowed to be members of the Bar in the state of residence, having long been valued as an effective means to ensure self-compliance with the law.[55] Consequently they are subject to the same rules of professional ethics

persons as provided for under the national rules of the receiving authority. However, in this case, the information exchanged cannot be used by the receiving authority to impose custodial sanctions' (Article 12(3), Council Regulation (EC) No 1/2003). See OFFICE of FAIR TRADING, *Powers of Investigation,* Draft competition law guidelines for consultation, April 2004, OFT 404a, para. 6.3.

[51] VESTERDORF, 'Legal professional privilege and the privilege against self-incrimination in EC Law', p. 722.

[52] Also OFFICE of FAIR TRADING, *Powers of Investigation,* Draft competition law guidelines for consultation, April 2004, OFT 404a, para. 6.3.

[53] VESTERDORF, 'Legal professional privilege and the privilege against self-incrimination in EC law', p. 722. Cf. joined Cases T-125/03 and 253/03, *AKZO Nobel and Ackros Chemicals Ltd v Commission*, judgment of 17 September 2007, *infra*, section 3.

[54] *Inter alia*, LAMBERT, 'Parallel antitrust investigations: the long arm of the DOJ from the perspective of an EU defence counsel', (2002) 14 *Loy. Consumer L. Rev.* 509 at 514–15.

[55] *Id.*, p. 186. Cf. also AIBEL, 'Corporate counsel and business ethics: a personal review', (1994) 59 *Mo. L. Rev.* 427 at 439–40. For an examination of the role of in-house counsel in the reality of US corporations, see DALY, 'The cultural, ethical and legal challenges in lawyering for a global organization: the role of the general counsel', (1997) 46 *Emory L. J.* 1057.

and 'permitted the same rights'[56] as counsel in private practice.[57] By contrast, *A.M. & S.* compels undertakings established in non-Member States to employ an independent local counsel through whom advice can be channelled only in order to protect it from disclosure,[58] to the detriment of the smooth running of international commercial transactions.[59]

The above analysis suggests that the *A.M. & S.* judgment constituted a breakthrough for the establishment in EC law of a form of protection of the confidentiality of lawyer–client correspondence. However, its limited scope may no longer provide an effective safeguard against the forced disclosure of these communications in all circumstances. It could be disputed whether the current concept of privilege constitutes an adequate response to the needs of the reformed structure for the application of EC competition law resulting from the 'Modernisation' Regulation No 1/2003 and to the changing role of in-house counsel in the present business environment.[60] The debate on its reform will be considered in the following sections.

1.3. The *AKZO Nobel* Interim Order: Towards a Redefinition of Legal Professional Privilege?

In light of the above, the interim order of the CFI in the case of *AKZO Nobel and Ackros Chemicals v Commission*[61] clearly boosted the expectation of a

---

56 HILL, 'A problem of privilege: in-house counsel and the attorney-client privilege in the United States and the European Community', (1995) 27 *Case W. Res. J. of Int'l L.* 145 at 168. Also, BRAND, 'Professional responsibility in a transnational transactions practice', (1998) 17 *J. L. & Com.* 301 at 314.

57 Cf., *inter alia*, *United States v Louisville & N.R.R.*, (1915) 236 US 318 at 336; also *United States v United Shoe Machinery Corp.*, 89 F. Supp. 357 (D. Mass. 1950) at 360. For commentary, GIESEL, 'The legal advice requirement of the attorney-client privilege: a special problem for in-house counsel and outside attorneys representing corporations', (1997) 48 *Mercer L. Rev.* 1169 at 1208.

58 DALY, 'The cultural, ethical and legal challenges in lawyering for a global organization: the role of the general counsel', (1997) 46 *Emory L. J.* 1057 at 1108.

59 *Inter alia,* DOLMANS, 'Attorney-client privilege for in-house counsel: a European proposal', (1998) 4 *Colum. J. of Eur. L.* 125 at 134. For an examination of the implications of US/EU cooperation for the protection of privileged information, see most recently CURTIN, SAVRIN and BIGELOW, 'Collateral consequences of expanded European antitrust investigative authority for defendants in US proceedings', in HAWK (ed.), *International Antitrust Law and Policy*, p. 533 at 537–38 and 544–45.

60 DALY, 'The cultural ethical and legal challenges in lawyering for a global organization', at 1058. Also, ANDREANGELI, 'Strasbourg versus Brussels: Human Rights, the right of access to the file and legal professional privilege', (2004) 11 *IJEL* 362 at 378–79.

61 Case T-125/03, *AKZO Nobel Chemicals Ltd and Ackros Chemicals Ltd v Commission*, [2003] ECR II-4771.

more generous reformulation of the notion of legal professional privilege so as to cover communications emanating from employed legal advisers on the basis of the same rationale as *A.M. & S.,* according to which the scope of legal professional privilege is linked to the lawyers' obedience to binding rules of professional ethics in the interests of the administration of justice.[62] The President of the CFI considered whether written communications between the second applicant's General Manager and a member of the legal department of the first applicant could be covered by legal professional privilege in consideration of the 'numerous changes in the professional rules of the Member States . . . tending . . . to extend the cover of professional privilege to the activities of certain in-house lawyers'.[63] In that case, the legal adviser was 'a member of the Netherlands Bar, subject to professional obligations as regards independence and respect for the rules of the Bar comparable to those of an external lawyer'.[64]

On the basis of the evidence before the Court, the President held:

> there is no presumption that the link of employment between a lawyer and an undertaking will always, and as a matter of principle, affect the independence necessary for the effective exercise of the role of collaborating in the administration of justice by the courts, if, in addition, the lawyer is bound by strict rules of professional conduct, which where necessary require that he observe the particular duties commensurate with his status.[65]

Accordingly, he concluded that the pleas presented by the applicants and the interveners could justify reconsidering the extent to which communications between an undertaking and its in-house counsel can 'be protected by professional privilege, provided that the lawyer is subject to rules of professional conduct equivalent to those imposed on an independent lawyer'.[66]

Although the order in *AKZO Nobel* may appear a 'modest procedural victory for the applicants'[67] its potential for a future redefinition of legal professional privilege could not be overlooked. The reasoning of President Vesterdorf seemed to support the view that the scope of professional privilege should be defined solely on the basis of the allegiance on the part of the lawyer to binding rules of ethics[68] with evident benefits for the effective compliance

---

62 FAULL, 'In-house lawyers and legal professional privilege', at 142.

63 *Id.*, para. 80.

64 *Ibid.*

65 *Id.*, para. 126.

66 *Id.*, para. 127.

67 MURPHY, 'CFI signals possible extension of professional privilege to in-house lawyers', (2004) 25 *ECLR* 447 at 453.

68 HILL, 'A problem of privilege: in-house counsel and the attorney-client priv-

with competition law. In fact, the suggested definition would prevent disclosure of communications provided by employed counsel in the course of the legal self-assessment of *prima facie* anti-competitive practices.[69]

The interim order also addressed the problems raised by the procedure to determine whether the documents concerned are covered by LPP and the legitimacy of the possibility for the Commission officials to 'cast a cursory glance' over the evidence.[70] The President acknowledged that there may be cases in which 'the confidentiality of the documents (. . .) is not clear from external indications such as a lawyer's letterhead or a clear reference by that lawyer to their confidentiality' and that the only way for the Commission to appraise their nature would be to read them.[71] Nonetheless, he took the view that, at least when disagreement exists between the investigating officials and the concerned party, the officials should 'refrain from casting even a cursory glance over the documents' whose privileged nature is disputed[72] and concluded that a *prima facie* case had been made as regards the seizure of the evidence.[73]

Perhaps regrettably, the ECJ annulled the CFI's interim order on the grounds of lack of serious and irreparable harm. The Court opined that the 'mere reading' of the communication in question 'without that information being used' as evidence,[74] despite being in principle 'capable of affecting professional privilege',[75] was not 'sufficient to establish the existence of serious and irreparable harm'[76] because the Commission officials had already 'cast their cursory glance' over the documents.[77]

Commentators suggested that the analysis of the 'possible harm' conducted by both the CFI and the ECJ was consistent with the concept of LPP 'as a

---

ilege in the United States and the European Community', (1995) 27 *Case W. Res. J. of Int'l L.* 145 at 191.

69 But cf. WILS, 'Powers of investigation and procedural rights and guarantees in EU antitrust enforcement – the interplay between European and national legislation and case law', (2006) 29(1) *W. Comp.* 3 at 20–21; also DEKEYSER and GAUER, 'The new enforcement system for articles 81 and 82 and the rights of the defence', in HAWK (ed.), *International Antitrust Law and Policy*, p. 549 at 568–69.

70 Case T-125/03, *AKZO Nobel Chemicals Ltd and Ackros Chemicals Ltd v Commission*, [2003] ECR II-4771, para. 137.

71 *Id.*, para. 138.

72 *Id.*, para. 139.

73 *Ibid.* But cf. DEKEYSER and GAUER, 'The new enforcement system for articles 81 and 82 and the rights of the defence', p. 572–73.

74 Case C-7/04 P (R), *Commission v AKZO Nobel and Ackros Chemicals*, [2004] ECR I-8739, para. 43.

75 *Ibid.*

76 *Ibid.*

77 *Ibid.*

corollary of the rights of defence'[78] and concurred that even a 'cursory glance' could hinder the privilege.[79] However, the ECJ order left open the question whether the possibility for the investigating officials to examine, even cursorily, documents whose privileged nature is alleged, is consistent with the effective protection of lawyer–client confidentiality.[80]

It was argued that perhaps the Hearing Officer could resolve the 'proof dilemma'[181] by being granted the power to access the disputed evidence to assess whether legal professional privilege should attach to it, subject to the review of the CFI[82] and therefore avoiding that the officials in charge of a particular case be acquainted with the contents of the disputed documents.[83] Although this suggestion did not lack merit in principle,[84] it should be emphasised that, to date, judicial scrutiny has not been extended to the decisions of the Hearing Officer relating to access to the evidence gathered by the Commission and adopted under Article 9 of the 2001 Terms of Reference.[85] Consequently, it is not clear whether the Officer's involvement in the area would be subject to sufficiently cogent supervision as regards the adoption of decisions in this area.[86]

The circumstance that the ECJ did not examine the grounds of appeal concerning the *prima facie* case raised expectations as to the possibility of a reformulation of LPP in Community law,[87] although it did not shed any light as to which conditions will govern the new notion of privilege. Suggestions as to which conditions should govern the new notion of legal professional privilege were drawn from the US legal experience. In *Renfield v Remy Martin*[88]

---

78 GIPPINI FOURNIER, 'Legal professional privilege in competition proceedings before the European Commission: beyond the cursory glance', (2005) 28 *Fordham Int'l L J* 967, p. 1023.

79 *Id.*, pp. 1024–25.

80 *Inter alia*, DEKEYSER and GAUER, 'The new enforcement system for articles 81 and 82 and the rights of the defence', p. 572.

81 GIPPINI FOURNIER, 'Legal professional privilege in competition proceedings before the European Commission', p. 1025.

82 *Id.*, p. 1026–27.

83 *Id.*, p. 1026.

84 *Id.* , p. 1027.

85 Cases T-10-12/92 & 15/92, *Cimenteries CBR SA and Others v EC Commission*, [1992] ECR II-2667, para. 47; case T-90/96, *Automobiles Peugeot SA v Commission*, [1997] ECR II-663, paras. 32, 34 and 37.

86 Cf., *mutatis mutandis*, Appl. No 27052/95, *Jasper v United Kingdom*, [2000] 30 EHRR 441, para. 52.

87 Case C-7/04 P (R), *Commission v AKZO Nobel and Ackros Chemicals*, [2004] ECR I-8739, para. 28–29.

88 *Renfield Corp and Renfield Importers, Ltd v E. Remy Martin & Co, SA, Remy Martin Amerique Inc, Glenmore Distilleries Co and Foreign Vintages Inc*, US District Court, D. Delaware, (1982) 98 FRD 442.

the Delaware District Court had to decide 'whether the privilege is available where the attorney is a French "in-house counsel"'.[89] The plaintiff had relied on the fact that in France, unlike the United States, no such communication would be protected because an employed lawyer could not be a member of the legal profession.[90]

However, the Delaware District Court took the different view that, since 'the organization of the French legal profession is unlike that in the United States'[91] the criterion of membership in a 'bar'[92] was not decisive. Consequently, it stated that 'the requirement is a functional one of whether the individual is competent to render legal advice and is permitted by the law to do so'[93] and concluded that the communications in question should be privileged: 'French "in-house counsel" certainly meet this test; like their American counterparts, they have legal training and are employed to give legal advice to corporate officials on matters of legal significance to the corporation.'[94]

The test laid down in *Renfield* therefore rested on the question 'whether the individual is competent to render legal advice and is permitted by law to do so'.[95] The requirement of 'independence' and the resulting admission to a 'bar', far from being the decisive element of the test, as in *A.M. & S.*, constituted 'just one of the elements to be weighed up in deciding whether the communication involves legal advice'[96] for privilege purposes. Commentators argued that this could provide a reasonable and balanced alternative to the *A.M. & S.* test. It would have the advantage of not requiring total convergence of the legal systems of the various Member States as regards the admission of in-house counsel to the legal profession and would take into account the circumstance that, in the reality of business, 'a link of employment may not always exclude independence'.[97] It could also be sufficiently flexible to allow for the extension of the privilege to lawyers admitted to the bars of non-Member States, with evident benefits for the smooth running of international business and effective cooperation with foreign enforcement agencies.[98]

It was added that this 'functional' approach could provide adequate protection to lawyer–client confidentiality in the context of the decentralised appli-

---

89 *Id.*, para. 2.
90 *Ibid.*
91 *Ibid.*
92 *Ibid.*
93 *Ibid.*
94 *Ibid.*
95 JOSHUA, 'Privilege in multi-jurisdictional cartel investigations: are European courts missing the point?', (2004) 7 *Global Comp. Review* 39 at 40.
96 *Ibid.*
97 *Id.*, p. 41.
98 *Ibid.*

cation of EC competition law. Although the issues arising from the exchange of evidence within the ECN will be addressed in Chapter 6,[99] it should be noted at this stage that adopting a 'functional test' for LPP might enable the legal adviser to resist successfully the disclosure of her communications with the client that have been acquired by an NCA on the basis of Article 12, Regulation 1/2003. Also, the investigated undertakings could foresee the consequences of the transmission of information in the context of the network and the benefit from the more extensive level of protection available under the national law of the collecting authority.[100]

Nevertheless, it cannot be denied that the application of a '*Renfield*-type' approach fosters legal uncertainty as regards the boundaries of privilege. It was suggested that, due to his or her role within the corporate structure of the undertaking, it could sometimes be difficult to distinguish between legal and business advice given by an employed lawyer,[101] although it could be argued that this assessment would not be substantially different from that ordinarily carried out under by the current *A.M. & S.* requirement that communications be 'made for the purposes and in the interests of the client's rights of defence'.[102]

It must be recognised that the major difficulty with the *Renfield* set of conditions lies in its failure to address the issue of how to protect the ethical integrity and the independence of counsel. By not regarding allegiance to the local Bar as a decisive condition for the protection of the privilege, the test overlooks the need to ensure that appropriate ethical standards are enforced on employed counsel to avoid lawyer–client confidentiality being used as a 'shield' to withhold disclosure of evidence of episodes of corporate malpractice.[103]

In the United States of America this problem was highlighted by the ENRON scandal, as a result of which Congress adopted the Sarbanes-Oxley

---

99 *Infra*, Chapter 6, sect. 3.2.

100 JOSHUA, 'Privilege in multi-jurisdictional cartel investigations', at 41. Also, VESTERDORF, 'Legal professional privilege and the privilege against self-incrimination in EC Law', p. 722. But cf. joined Cases T-125/03 and 253/03, *AKZO Nobel Ltd and Ackros Chemicals Ltd v Commission*, judgment of 17 September 2007; *infra*, section 3.

101 COHEN, 'In-house counsel and the attorney-client principle: how Sarbanes-Oxley misses the point', (2004) 9 *Stanford Journal of Law, Business and Finance* 297 at 317.

102 Case 155/79, *AM & S Europe Limited v Commission of the European Communities*, [1982] ECR 1575 at para. 21.

103 ANDREANGELI, 'The protection of legal professional privilege in EU law and the impact of the rules on the exchange of information within the European Competition Network on the secrecy of communications between lawyer and client: one step forward, two steps back?', (2005) 2(1) *CompLRev* 32 at 51.

Act.[104] Section 307 of the Act imposes on corporate lawyers the duty to report evidence of certain forms of corporate misconduct committed by directors to 'the chief legal counsellor' or the chief executive officer of the company, and, if no appropriate measures are taken on the basis of that evidence, to the audit committee of the board of directors of the company.[105]

Despite being prompted by the need to counter the negative effects of serious corporate malpractice, the solution adopted by the US Congress was widely criticised. Commentators argued that the peculiar characteristics of the role of employed counsel threaten the efficacy of the reporting duty as a means to secure his or her allegiance to rules of professional conduct,[106] especially because the inherent economic dependence of the counsel on his or her client-employer and the resulting perceived risk of the possible loss of employment may act as a deterrent against the reporting itself.[107]

Consequently, it was questioned whether, were it to be imposed on European in-house counsel, the obligation to report 'up on the ladder', namely to the corporate officers that are hierarchically superior to the employed counsel, could be effective at all.[108] On this point, it was suggested that the general crime-fraud exception, as a result of which legal advice given to aid or abet the commission of a crime is no longer immune from forced disclosure,[109] could ensure the more effective reporting of episodes of corporate misfeasance[110] and thus could be more suited to the need to secure appropriate standards of ethics in business practice.[111]

It is thus clear that the *AKZO Nobel* interim order raised hopes for the possibility to introduce a more generous notion of LPP in the EU legal frame-

---

104 For commentary, *inter alia*, 'Developments in the Law – Corporations and Society: IV. Lawyer conduct and corporate misconduct', (2004) 117 *Harvard Law Review* 2227.

105 COHEN, 'In-house counsel and the attorney-client principle', at 308–09.

106 *Id.*, p. 318.

107 *Ibid.* Also, CURTIN, et al., 'Collateral consequences of expanded European antitrust investigative authority for defendants in US proceedings', in HAWK (ed.), *International Antitrust Law and Policy*, p. 533 at 546–47.

108 *Inter alia*, BAUM, 'An economic analysis of corporate lawyer client privilege', paper presented at the EALE Conference, Ljubjana, Slovenia, on 14 September 2005, pp. 34–35.

109 *Inter alia*, MAHER, 'Professional privilege – without prejudice letters and statutory inroads on the common law', (1990) 35(3) *Journal of the Law Society of Scotland* 108 at 110.

110 HILL, 'A problem of privilege: in-house counsel and the attorney-client privilege in the United States and the European Community', (1995) 27 *Case W. Res. J. of Int'l L.* 145 at 191.

111 ANDREANGELI, 'The protection of legal professional privilege in EU law', at 51–52.

work. However, parallel legislative developments did not seem entirely consistent with these expectations. The EU legislation on money laundering provides a telling example of a trend towards carving significant inroads into the scope of lawyer–client confidentiality.

The first Directive 'on the prevention of the use of the financial system for the purpose of money laundering',[112] was introduced in 1991 as part of an international concerted effort to fight the financing of organised crime[113] and laid down an obligation applicable to banks and other financial institutions to identify customers who carried out cash transactions of value exceeding the threshold set out in the Directive, to keep a record of these transactions and to report any 'suspicious operations' to the competent authorities.[114]

It was, however, the second Directive, adopted in 2001, that imposed the first significant limitation on the scope of lawyer–client confidentiality.[115] Its Article 2 extended the duty to report suspicious transactions to 'independent legal professionals' when they assist clients in the planning or execution of transactions concerning the sale or acquisition of property, the management of money or assets, the organization of contributions necessary for setting up or managing companies or trusts and real property transactions in which the lawyer has acted for or on behalf of his or her client.[116]

Although this obligation clearly aims to encourage lawyers to perform a 'gate-keeping' role,[117] its scope was widely criticised as potentially impairing the trust and loyalty existing between legal advisers and their clients.[118] It was acknowledged that Member States are allowed to exclude from the reporting duties information received 'in the course of ascertaining the legal

---

112 Council Directive of 10 June 1991 on prevention of the use of the financial system for the purpose of money laundering, No 91/308/EEC, [1991] OJ L166/77.

113 G-7 Task Force to make Recommendations on Curbing Money Laundering – Paris Economic Summit: Economic Declaration, 16 July 1989, published in (1989) 28 *ILM* 1293. Financial Action Task Force (hereinafter referred to as FATF) 40 Recommendations, contained in the 1990–1991 FATF Report (31 May 1991), available at: http://www.fatf-gafi.org/dataoecd/20/18/33643115.pdf. See BARBOT, 'Money laundering: an international challenge', [1995] 3 *Tul. J. Int'l & Comp L* 161 at 163–64 and 173ff.

114 *Inter alia*, MORTMAN, 'Putting starch in European efforts to combat money laundering', (1992) 60 *Fordham L Rev* S429 at S432–33.

115 Directive 2001/97/EC of the European Parliament and of the Council of 4 December 2001 amending Council Directive 91/308/EEC on prevention of the use of the financial system for the purpose of money laundering, [2001] OJ L344/76.

116 Article 2(2).

117 KRAULAND and HUTMAN, 'Money laundering enforcement and policy', (2004) 38 *Int'l Law.* 509 at 516.

118 SHAUGHNESSY, 'The new EU money laundering directive: lawyers as gatekeepers and whistle-blowers', (2002) 34 *Law & Pol'y Int'l Bus.* 25 at 35–36.

position for the client or performing their task of defending the client in, or concerning legal proceedings, including advice on instituting or avoiding legal proceedings (. . .)'.[119]

However, several commentators argued that the boundaries of that discretion were not sufficiently defined[120] and therefore suggested that it should be mandatory for the Member States to restrict the scope of the reporting obligations only to communications relating to 'transactional' activities carried out by the lawyer in the interests of the client,[121] so as to safeguard the rationale of legal professional privilege.[122]

Despite the criticism directed against the 2001 Directive, the Commission introduced a proposal for a new Directive in 2004, which left unaltered the reporting obligations imposed on independent legal professionals. It did not, once again, indicate a minimum limit on the value of the transactions that should be reported.[123] The Council of the Bars and Law Societies of the European Union (hereinafter referred to as CCBE), despite not being opposed in principle to an obligation to report information concerning 'suspicious transactions' acquired in the context of 'transactional business', objected to the breadth of discretion conferred on the Member States and argued that the position adopted in the proposal was very likely to threaten the very essence of lawyer–client confidentiality.[124]

---

[119] Article 2(5), Directive 2001/97/EC of the European Parliament and of the Council of 4 December 2001 amending Council Directive 91/308/EEC on prevention of the use of the financial system for the purpose of money laundering, [2001] OJ L344/76.

[120] *Id.*, p. 44.

[121] CCBE, Action Points for EU Bars and Law Societies on the implementation of the Money Laundering Directive, January 2002, available at: www.ccbe.org/doc/En/action_points_220102_en.pdf, p. 4/23. See also SHAUGHNESSY, 'The new EU money laundering directive: lawyers as gate-keepers and whistle-blowers', (2002) 34 *Law & Pol'y Int'l Bus.* 25 at 38–39.

[122] CCBE, Position on the requirements of a lawyer to report suspicions of money laundering and on the European Commission Proposal for a third EU Directive on Money Laundering Regulations, November 2004, available at: www.ccbe.org/doc/En/ccbe_position_paper_money_laundering_%20051104_en.pdf, para. 7. Also, CCBE, Position on the Consultation Paper of the FATF Forty Recommendations, September 2002, available at www.ccbe.org/doc/En/ccbe_response_110902_en.pdf, para. 3.

[123] Respectively, Articles 2(1)(b) and 20(2). See also CCBE, Position of the Council of the Bars and Law Societies of the European Union on the requirements on a lawyer to report suspicions of money laundering and on the European Commission Proposal for a Third EU Directive on Money Laundering Regulations, November 2004, available at: www.ccbe.org/doc/En/ccbe_position_paper_money_laundering_%20051104_en.pdf, pp. 4–5.

[124] *Id.*, pp. 7–8.

This is not the appropriate place to discuss in detail all the issues arising from the EC legislation concerning money laundering. Nevertheless, the brief analysis conducted above illustrates that the 2001 Directive has made a significant inroad into legal professional privilege. It is suggested that the reporting obligation provided by the Anti-Money-Laundering Directive could have far-reaching consequences for the scope of lawyer–client confidentiality as well as, more generally, for the future of the relationship of trust which constitutes the backbone of an effective legal representation.[125]

1.4. The AKZO Nobel Judgment: is this the Last Word for the Community Concept of Legal Professional Privilege?

The previous sections illustrated that, if on the one hand, the *AKZO Nobel* interim order suggested the apparent willingness of the CFI to adopt a more generous test for LPP, current legislative trends in the field of the fight against money laundering, on the other hand, resulted in significant inroads being carved into the scope of the privilege. Consequently the annulment of the interim order by the ECJ left the Court of First Instance to resolve this matter. However, in its judgment[126] the CFI declined to reconsider the requirements governing the scope of the Community concept of privilege.

The CFI reiterated that in *A.M. & S.* the ECJ had restricted the protection of LPP only to those communications emanating from 'independent' counsel, namely from a lawyer who is not bound to his or her client by a relationship of employment.[127] In other words, that requirement of 'independence' was defined as a 'negative' concept, focused on the absence of links between counsel and client, and not, as the applicant had suggested, as a 'positive' one, i.e. 'on the basis of membership of a Bar or Law Society' or 'of being subject to professional discipline and ethics'.[128]

The CFI also pointed out that in a large number of Member States the protection of lawyer–client confidentiality was still withheld from in-house counsel and that the latter were not allowed membership of local Law Societies in several jurisdictions.[129] Perhaps most importantly, the Court emphasised that the privilege constitutes an exception to the extensive investigation powers enjoyed by the Commission, powers that are aimed at targeting the most serious infringements of the Treaty competition rules.[130]

---

125 *Id.*, p. 2.

126 Joined cases T-125/03 and 253/03, *AKZO Nobel Ltd and Ackros Chemicals Ltd v Commission*, judgment of 17 September 2007, not yet reported.

127 *Id.*, para. 167.

128 *Id.*, para. 168.

129 *Id.*, para. 171.

130 *Id.*, para. 172.

Consequently, the Court concluded that, if on the one hand the enactment of the Modernisation Regulation had increased the importance of self-assessment of potentially anti-competitive commercial practices and had made it necessary for undertakings to devise 'compliance programmes', it had not, on the other hand, resulted in a substantial change in the role of, respectively, in-house and independent counsel.[131] In the words of the CFI:

> (. . .) such exercises of self-assessment and strategy definition may be conducted by an outside lawyer in full cooperation with the relevant departments of the undertakings, including the internal legal department. In that context, *communications between in-house lawyers and outside lawyers* are in principle protected under LPP, provided that they are made for the purpose of the undertaking's exercise of the rights of defence.[132]

Nor was the CFI convinced by the arguments, advanced by the applicants and by some of the interveners, that 'the personal scope of the Community concept of confidentiality should be governed by national law'.[133] On the contrary, the Court took the view that protection of secrecy of lawyer–client correspondence 'directly affects the conditions under which the Commission may act in a field as vital to the functioning of the common market as that of compliance with the rules on competition'.[134] Consequently, it concluded that to make the scope of that protection subject to conditions laid down by domestic law would jeopardise 'the uniform application of the Commission's powers in the common market' and ultimately be at odds with the principle of supremacy of EC law.[135]

It is acknowledged that the conclusions of the CFI in its judgment may sound disappointing. Despite the apparent strength of the arguments raised by the parties and by its President in its interim order, the Court declined to reconsider the *A.M. & S.* test for privilege. More generally, it may be suggested that in striking a balance between the need to protect the rights of defence of the investigated parties and the interest of the effective enforcement of the competition rules, the CFI clearly appeared to tip the scales in favour of the full exercise of the Commission's investigative powers. The emphasis on the need to ensure the effective application of Council Regulation No 1/2003 across the Common Market in accordance with the principle of supremacy was decisive to this end.[136]

---

131 *Id.*, para. 173.
132 *Ibid.* Emphasis added.
133 *Id.*, para. 176.
134 *Ibid.*
135 *Ibid.*
136 See especially paras. 176–77 of the judgment.

However, it is submitted that this judgment remains highly significant for a number of reasons, concerning especially the manner in which the Commission should exercise its powers to compel disclosure of potentially privileged evidence. First of all, the CFI made it plain that the decision with which the Commission officials determine whether the documents seized from the investigated parties should be protected by LPP constitutes a 'reviewable act' for the purpose of bringing an action under Article 230 EC Treaty.[137]

According to the Court, that decision not only brings to an end an ad hoc procedure focused on the assessment of the nature of that evidence. It also produces irreversible and potentially adverse legal consequences for the undertakings' rights of defence that cannot be made good by a later challenge to (and annulment of) the final decision,[138] and this regardless of whether the decision had been adopted expressly or tacitly, i.e. by seizing the document and placing it on the investigation file without taking a formal decision on its nature.[139]

Secondly, the CFI in *AKZO Nobel* took the opportunity to clarify the procedure which the Commission should follow in assessing the nature of the communications for which the protection of LPP is sought. It held that, when an undertaking wished to claim that evidence is covered by privilege, while not being obliged to disclose its contents, it is nonetheless bound to produce sufficient and relevant material to support its claim.[140] If, however, the Commission considered that the information adduced is not sufficient to ground a claim for privilege, it would be entitled to order the production of the actual documents and to cast a 'cursory look' on them to establish whether they are privileged or not on the basis of external indicia such as the 'layout, heading, title or other superficial features'.[141]

The CFI also recognised that in cases in which the privileged nature of the evidence is not immediately apparent even a 'cursory look' could result in the undertakings' rights of defence being irremediably prejudiced. Accordingly, it held that in these cases the Commission should place the documents in a sealed envelope, with a view to this being reopened at a later stage for the purpose of resolving the matter.[142] The Court forcefully reiterated that, in any event, the Commission officials should not read the contested evidence until such time as the undertaking concerned has been given the opportunity to

137 *Id.*, paras. 45, 48.
138 *Id.*, para. 46.
139 *Id.*, para. 49.
140 *Id.*, para. 79.
141 *Id.*, para. 81.
142 *Id.*, para. 83.

challenge the decision in Court and, if an action is brought, until the Court has handed down a judgment.[143]

To hold otherwise would irremediably impair the undertakings' rights of defence and especially the right to consult a lawyer without constraint, since the harm resulting from the disclosure of privileged documents could not be made good by challenging the final decision.[144] As the Court pointed out:

> Even if that document is not used as evidence in a decision imposing a penalty under the competition rules (. . .) [it] might be used by the Commission, directly or indirectly, in order to obtain new information or new evidence without the undertaking in question always being able to identify or prevent such information or evidence from being used against it.[145]

The *AKZO Nobel* judgment can thus be interepreted as suggesting that the CFI has now set more stringent boundaries for the possibility enjoyed by the Commission to cast a 'cursory look' over potentially privileged material. Not only are the investigating officers required to avail themselves of the 'sealed envelope' practice in all cases in which there are doubts as to the nature of the evidence, but also the Commission must allow the investigated parties an opportunity to seek judicial control of the decision on the part of the CFI before that 'envelope' can be opened and the documents placed on the file. The emphasis placed on ensuring the judicial supervision over the Commission decisions rejecting the claim of LPP is to be welcomed since it seeks to subject the powers of investigation to adequate checks and balances in a manner consistent, *inter alia*, with the standards enshrined in the ECHR.[146]

The CFI also shed some light on the circumstances in which a communication can be deemed to have been made 'for the purpose of the exercise of the client's rights of defence'.[147] The Court took the view that in principle even documents prepared solely by the client for the purpose of seeking legal advice from an independent lawyer may be covered by privilege. However, the communications contained therein must be aimed exclusively at 'gathering information which will be useful or essential to that lawyer for an understand-

---

[143] *Id.*, para. 88.

[144] *Id.*, para. 87.

[145] *Ibid.*

[146] See, *inter alia*, Appl. No 27052/95, *Jasper v United Kingdom*, [2000] 30 EHRR 441, para. 52. Cf., *mutatis mutandis*, Cases T-10-12/92 & 15/92, *Cimenteries CBR SA and Others v EC Commission*, [1992] ECR II-2667, para. 47; case T-90/96, *Automobiles Peugeot SA v Commission*, [1997] ECR II-663, paras. 32–37.

[147] Joined Cases T-125/03 and 253/03, *AKZO Nobel Ltd and Ackros Chemicals Ltd v Commission*, judgment of 17 September 2007, not yet reported, para. 117.

ing of the context, nature and scope of the facts for which his assistance is sought'[148] and must have been drafted solely in order to obtain the necessary legal assistance.[149]

Consequently, it is not sufficient to demonstrate that the contents of the communications were discussed with outside counsel;[150] nor that they were prepared in the context of a 'compliance programme', albeit one coordinated by independent counsel. What is required, instead, is clear proof that the documents were drafted exclusively with a view to providing counsel with sufficient information on the facts for which his or her advice is required and for the purpose of obtaining that advice.[151]

It is argued that the CFI's remarks on this point should be welcome not only as providing more guidance for the assessment of the boundaries of privilege but also as suggesting that, in principle, even purely internal communications may benefit from privilege, provided that, however, the fact that they were prepared solely for the purpose of seeking legal advice is apparent from their content. Accordingly, it is submitted that the findings made in *AKZO Nobel* clearly represent an attempt to reconcile the need to uphold the very essence of the privilege as a means for every person to be 'able without constraint, to consult a lawyer' in the interest of the sound administration of justice[152] with the legitimate interest of the effective enforcement of the Treaty competition rules.[153]

It may be concluded that even though it did not redefine the notion of LPP so as to include communications emanating from in-house counsel, the *AKZO Nobel* judgment was not a completely missed opportunity for the rights of defence of the investigated firms. The great emphasis on the need for judicial supervision of the Commission decisions rejecting claims of lawyer–client confidentiality and the clearer guidance on both the 'cursory look' procedure and the requirement that communications be made for the purpose of seeking legal advice demonstrate the Court's continuing commitment to the protection of the right to a fair procedure, whilst at the same time taking into due account the needs of effective competition enforcement.

---

148 *Id.*, para. 122.
149 *Id.*, para. 123.
150 *Id.*, para. 124.
151 E.g., *id.*, paras. 130–32.
152 *Id.*, para. 121.
153 See also, *mutatis mutandis*, case T-30/89, *Hilti AG v Commission* (interim order), [1990] ECR II-163, paras. 17–18.

1.5. Legal Professional Privilege in EC Law between the Protection of the Rights of the Defence and the Fight against Corporate Misfeasance: Summary Conclusions

The examination of the Community concept of legal professional privilege illustrated the difficulties faced by the undertakings concerned in protecting their communications with their legal adviser from disclosure to the Commission. Whereas the interim order of the CFI demonstrated the willingness of the Community courts to reconsider the boundaries of legal professional privilege in the light of recent developments in domestic law, the enactment of the Second Anti-Money-Laundering Directive could be interpreted as a potential threat to the integrity of the loyalty of the lawyer to his or her client.[154]

Furthermore, it would appear that the differing standards laid down by Community law as opposed to those applicable in the national jurisdictions as regards in-house counsel are likely to play havoc with legal certainty in the context of the decentralised enforcement of Articles 81 and 82 of the EC Treaty[155] and could jeopardise its effective protection in the framework of operation of the European Competition Network.[156] Against this background, the interim order in *AKZO Nobel*[157] appeared to be a turning point in the redefinition of LPP as extending to communications emanating from employed counsel.

However, the final judgment was not consistent with these expectations. Although the CFI greatly emphasised the function of the judicial supervision over Commission decisions concerning LPP as a 'check' on the respect of the rights of defence and gave clearer guidance as regards the procedure for the assessment of potentially privileged evidence, it declined to reconsider the conditions governing the scope of the privilege.

In addition, the Court reaffirmed that the supremacy of EU law and need to ensure the *effet utile* of Council Regulation No 1/2003 required a narrow reading of the existing notion of privilege as an exception to the Commission's wide powers of investigation. The following sections will therefore address the extent to which the European Convention on Human Rights could provide additional support for the reformulation of lawyer–client confidentiality in

---

[154] CCBE, Position on the Consultation Paper of the FATF Forty Recommendations, September 2002, available at www.ccbe.org/doc/En/ccbe_response_110902_en.pdf, p. 1.

[155] *Inter alia*, ECLA, 'Legal privilege for in-house lawyers', position paper, December 2002, available at http://www.ecla.org/pages/position_paper.html.

[156] VESTERDORF, 'Legal professional privilege and the privilege against self-incrimination in EC law', p. 722.

[157] Case T-125/03, *AKZO Nobel Chemicals Ltd and Ackros Chemicals Ltd v Commission*, [2003] ECR II-4771.

Community law, after having examined the conditions governing privilege in accordance with Article 6(1) of the Convention.

2. THE PROTECTION OF LAWYER–CLIENT CONFIDENTIALITY IN THE EUROPEAN CONVENTION ON HUMAN RIGHTS

2.1. Legal Professional Privilege in the ECHR as an Expression of the Right to a Fair Trial

Traditionally legal professional privilege, namely the protection against disclosure to other parties and to the adjudicator in legal proceedings of communications exchanged between lawyer and client,[158] was viewed as inextricably linked to the confidentiality of the relationship between an individual and his or her legal adviser[159] and, in broad terms, has been given a utilitarian and a fundamental rights-based interpretation. According to the utilitarian approach, protection from compulsory disclosure of communications generated in the course of that relationship is essential to ensure candour of the client vis-à-vis his or her lawyer and thus allow the effective provision of advice on the law.[160] In turn, the provision of that legal advice is thought to be capable of fostering the efficient administration of justice by encouraging self-compliance with the law.[161]

In the light of this reading, privilege is considered as being created 'by lawyers and for lawyers' for the purpose of ensuring the autonomous observance of the law and efficiency in the administration of justice.[162] The fundamental rights-based approach, instead, considers privilege as 'an individual entitlement, a right to confidentiality bestowed upon the client'[163] whose rationale rests in the right of that individual to be heard 'fairly' in legal proceedings, including those before administrative authorities.[164]

According to the European Court of Human Rights the protection against

---

158 *Inter alia*, GIPPINI FOURNIER, 'Legal professional privilege in competition proceedings before the European Commission', at 970.

159 WILLIAMS, 'Four questions of privilege: the litigation aspect of legal professional privilege', (1990) 9 (APR) *CJQ* 139 at 141.

160 *Ibid.*

161 GIPPINI FOURNIER, 'Legal professional privilege in competition proceedings before the European Commission', at 980.

162 WILLIAMS, 'Four questions of privilege', at 141.

163 GIPPINI FOURNIER, 'Legal professional privilege in competition proceedings before the European Commission', at 982.

164 See, *inter alia*, GIPPINI FOURNIER, pp. 996ff.

the compulsory disclosure of the communications between lawyer and client constitutes an essential element of the right to legal representation and assistance, which is in turn an indispensable condition for a 'fair hearing' within the meaning of Article 6(1) of the Convention.[165] It was held in *Golder*[166] that the refusal on the part of the Home Secretary to grant the applicant leave to consult a solicitor represented a hindrance of the applicant's right to access to a Court,[167] which 'constitutes an element . . . inherent in the right stated by Article 6(1)'[168] and a 'part of the basic requirements of a fair trial in a democratic society'.[169]

By a similar token, the European Court of Human Rights held in *Kopp v Switzerland*,[170] a case concerning the application of Article 8 ECHR, that the interception of telephone conversations was held to constitute an interference with the applicant's right to respect for 'private and family life, home and correspondence' contrary to the Convention since it was not 'prescribed by law' and 'necessary in a democratic society' for the achievement of a legitimate aim.[171] The insufficient clarity and precision of the national law allowing for phone-tapping meant that the applicant 'as a lawyer did not enjoy the minimum degree of protection required by the rule of law in a democratic society'.[172] The measure in question thus violated Article 8 ECHR, since the Authorities had failed to safeguard 'the special status of lawyers'[173] and their central position in the administration of justice as intermediaries between the public and the courts.[174]

The above analysis therefore suggests that the Strasbourg Court favours the

---

165 *Inter alia*, Appl. 19380/92, *Bentham v United Kingdom*, [1996] 22 EHRR 293.

166 *Golder v United Kingdom*, ser. 1, No 18, [1979–80] 1 EHRR 524.

167 *Id.*, para. 26.

168 *Id.*, para. 36.

169 Appl. 12629/87, *S v Switzerland*, [1992] 14 EHRR 670, para. 48. Also Appl. 13590/88, *Campbell v United Kingdom*, [1993] EHRR 137, para. 46. See also, *inter alia*, *R (Daly) v Secretary of State for the Home Department*, House of Lords, [2001] 2 AC 532, per Lord Bingham of Cornhill, para. 10; also *R (on the application of Morgan Grenfell & Co Ltd) v Special Commissioner of Income Tax*, [2002] HRLR 42, para. 7; most recently, *Three Rivers DC v Bank of England (No 6)*, [2004] UKHL 48, per Lord Philips, para. 14; per Baroness Hale, para. 62; quoting Lord Justice Taylor, *Balabel v Air India* (CA), [1988] Ch. 317 at 330. For commentary, *inter alia*, ANDREWS, 'Legal advice privilege's broad protection – the House of Lords in *Three Rivers* (no. 6)', (2005) 24 (APR) *CJQ* 185.

170 Appl. No 23224/94, [1999] 27 EHRR 91.

171 *Id.*, para. 75.

172 *Ibid.*

173 Appl. No 31611/96, *Nikula v Finland*, [2004] 38 EHRR 45, para. 45.

174 *Ibid.*

establishment of an extensive degree of protection[175] of the confidentiality of lawyer–client correspondence. The case law indicates that paramount to the Court's interpretation is the need to make the Convention rights 'practical and effective'[176] and to foster 'the public interest that in the administration of justice truth should be established'[177] in accordance with rules of adversary litigation[178] and consistently with the principle of the autonomy of each litigant to choose and pursue the best defence strategy.[179]

2.2. Lawyer–client Confidentiality and Rules of Professional Ethics: Defining the Boundaries of Privilege

The previous section illustrated the basic rationale for the recognition of the confidentiality of lawyer–client correspondence and the generous interpretation prevailing in the case law of the European Court of Human Rights, which is in turn motivated by the need to safeguard the 'special status' of legal advisers. In *AB v Netherlands*[180] the search and seizure by the prison authorities of correspondence between the applicant and his representative – a former inmate – in proceedings before the Strasbourg organs was held to be incompatible with Article 8 ECHR. The Court emphasised that 'neither the Convention nor the Rules of Procedure of the European Commission of Human Rights at the material time required the representatives of applicants to be practising lawyers'[181] and concluded that the correspondence at issue remained confidential.

That conclusion was reiterated in the recent *Nikula* judgment – concerning the application of Article 10 ECHR – a case in which a lawyer, who was acting as defence counsel despite being not registered with the local Bar, had been the target of libel actions for comments and other statements made before a court. The European Court of Human Rights affirmed that the 'restriction of defence counsel's freedom of expression could not be accepted as necessary in

---

175 Cf., *inter alia*, Appl. No 12629/87, *S v Switzerland*, [1992] 14 EHRR 670, para. 48.

176 Appl. No 37328/97, *AB v Netherlands*, [2003] 37 EHRR 48, para. 86.

177 *R v Derby Magistrates Court ex parte B*, [1996] 1 AC 487, per Lord Taylor CJ, p. 507.

178 MAHER, 'Professional privilege – without prejudice letters and statutory inroads on the common law', (1990) 35 *Journal of the Law Society of Scotland* 108 at 110.

179 GIPPINI FOURNIER, 'Legal professional privilege in competition proceedings before the European Commission', at 1002.

180 Appl. No 37328/97, *AB v Netherlands*, [2003] 37 EHRR 48.

181 *Id.*, para. 86.

a democratic society',[182] according to Article 10(2) ECHR, except in exceptional circumstances and despite the applicant not belonging to the local Bar or Law Society.[183]

However, in this case the Court attached considerable importance to the circumstance that, even though the applicant was not at the time subject to the disciplinary powers of the Bar council, she was nevertheless under the supervision of the trial court.[184] It is therefore unclear whether the protection of the 'special status' in question can be extended in all circumstances to legal advisers who do not belong to professional organisations responsible for upholding appropriate ethical standards in the public interest.

It is noteworthy that in its earlier *Casado Coca* decision the Court had held that those safeguards required that lawyers be subject to adequate restrictions on their conduct, including 'the monitoring and supervisory powers vested in Bar councils'.[185] Consequently, the *dictum* of *Nikula* could be interpreted as suggesting that, although formal membership does not constitute an essential condition for the protection of the lawyer's 'special status', a certain degree of control should nonetheless be exercised to 'ensure professional integrity commensurate to [her] role and position'.[186]

Overall, it may be concluded that the European Court of Human Rights has developed a notion of legal professional privilege strongly rooted in the right of each individual to a fair trial by obtaining full and frank legal advice from their legal advisers. Lawyers are recognised as holding a 'special position' as 'intermediaries' between the court system and the public and accordingly enjoy ad hoc safeguards allowing them to pursue their clients' interests zealously. At the same time, the Convention recognises that appropriate legal standards should be enforced to ensure ultimately the proper administration of justice. Allegiance to supervisory bodies such as the local Bar or Law Society is thus considered to be one, but perhaps not the only condition according to which that function may be fulfilled.

Having thus determined the scope and the conditions governing lawyer–client confidentiality in the ECHR framework, the Convention princi-

---

182 *Id.*, para. 55.

183 *Id.*, para. 53.

184 *Ibid.* Also, *mutatis mutandis*, Appl. No 52562/99 and 52620/99, *Sorensen v Denmark* and *Rasmussen v Denmark*, judgment of 11 January 2006, [2006] 20 BHRC 258.

185 Appl. No 15450/89, *Casado Coca v Spain*, ser. A No 285, [1994] 18 EHRR 1, para. 54.

186 Appl. No 31611/96, *Nikula v Finland*, [2004] 38 EHRR 45, para. 45. For commentary, see *inter alia*, ANDREANGELI, 'The protection of legal professional privilege in EU law', at 41–42. For the position in EU law see *supra*, this chapter, para. 1.2, footnote 3 and accompanying text.

ples will be used as a benchmark to examine the requirements of legal professional privilege in force in EC law with a view to assessing the extent to which they may justify a more generous reformulation of the *A.M. & S. Europe* criteria.

3. LEGAL PROFESSIONAL PRIVILEGE IN EC LAW AND IN THE ECHR: TOWARDS A REDEFINITION OF *A.M. & S.*?

3.1. Lawyers and Clients in Luxembourg and Strasbourg: Elements for a Comparative Analysis

Section 1 of this chapter illustrated how, despite constituting a remarkable achievement for the protection of the rights of the undertakings investigated by the Commission, the *A.M. & S. Europe v Commission* decision[187] was criticised as giving rise to a gap in the protection of lawyer–client confidentiality by not preventing the disclosure of documents containing legal advice given by in-house counsel[188] even in those jurisdictions where in-house counsel are allowed to be members of the local Bar or Law Society and are consequently entitled to the same rights as independent lawyers.[189] It was also noted that the *AKZO Nobel* judgment disappointed expectations of a more generous reformulation of the conditions governing privilege. Although the CFI reaffirmed the importance of LPP as an indispensable element of the undertakings' rights of defence, its reasoning emphasised the link between the availability of privilege and a 'negative' concept of 'independence'. The latter was interpreted as absence of a relationship of employment with the client rather than as a commitment to observe binding rules of professional ethics.

The current notion of legal professional privilege resulting from Community law can be contrasted with the position of the European Court of Human Rights, examined in section 2. The European Court of Human Rights emphasised the importance of the privilege in the context of the notion of 'fair trial' and 'fair procedure' enshrined in Article 6(1) ECHR and took the view

---

187 Case 155/79, *AM & S Europe Limited v Commission of the European Communities*, [1982] ECR 1575.

188 *Id.*, paras. 18–21.

189 See CCBE, *Regulated legal professionals and professional privilege within the European Union, the European Economic Area and Switzerland and certain other European Jurisdictions* – John FISH (February 2004), available at: http://www.ccbe.org/en/comites/in_house_en.htm, p. 48. *Inter alia*, FAULL, 'In-house lawyers and legal professional privilege: a problem revisited', at 142.

that legal advisers enjoy a 'special status' as intermediaries between the public and the courts so that the efficient administration of justice can be ensured.[190]

As a result, it was suggested that the allegiance to the national Bar or Law Society is not regarded as a precondition for the legal adviser to enjoy that 'special status',[191] provided that he or she is subject to control aimed at ensuring his or her professional integrity and independence[192] and regardless, it would appear, of the existence of a link of employment with the client.

Accordingly, it could be argued that the current position adopted by the European Court of Human Rights appears to justify a more generous reformulation of the Community notion of legal professional privilege so as to cover communications emanating from all legal advisers, whether employed or not, who are subject to appropriate standards of ethical integrity and independence.[193]

On the other hand, it is submitted that in view of the lack of a uniform discipline across the Member States, the adoption of this solution could result in significant uncertainty as regards the boundaries of privilege and ultimately hinder any existing degree of protection and also be inconsistent with the principle of supremacy of EU law. It is undeniable, however, that there exists a degree of variance between the EU concept of privilege and the notion recognised by the ECHR. The following section will therefore consider the available options for reform and will assess them in the light of the need to ensure the effective and uniform safeguard of lawyer–client confidentiality and the current legislative and jurisprudential trends in EC law and in the framework of the European Convention on Human Rights.

3.2. Legal Professional Privilege before the Commission: Options for Reform

The previous sections illustrated that despite having been presented with a key opportunity to rethink the *A.M. & S.* test, the CFI declined to reconsider the matter and instead reaffirmed the existing position. Although the need for the effective enforcement of competition law cannot be overlooked, it is however suggested that, in view of the importance of LPP as a right of defence in EU antitrust proceedings, it may still be preferable to reformulate its current scope in a manner which is more consistent with the existing ECHR requirements.

---

190 *Inter alia*, Appl. No 31611/96, *Nikula v Finland*, [2004] 38 EHRR 45, para. 45.

191 *Id.* para. 54.

192 *Inter alia*, Appl. No 15450/89, *Casado Coca v Spain*, ser. A No 285, [1994] 18 EHRR 1, para. 54.

193 *Ibid.*

It could be argued that if the primary duty of counsel is 'to defend their clients' interests zealously',[194] it is necessary to protect their 'special status' even when they do not belong to the local Bar or Law society, providing that they are subject to some degree of control, such as the supervision of the trial court,[195] to ensure the integrity of his or her function for a proper administration of justice.[196]

Accordingly, it is suggested that the current conditions governing privilege should be replaced by more flexible requirements allowing for the assessment of whether the lawyer, in the light of the circumstances of the case and especially of the rules in force in the jurisdiction in which he or she is authorised to practise, is subject to binding rules preserving her professional integrity and independence of the client[197] and commensurate with her status.[198] It is submitted that, whilst not overlooking the lack of uniformity existing among the rules governing the legal profession in each Member State, the proposed solution could reduce the risks for legal certainty and uniformity in the protection of lawyer–client confidentiality during Commission proceedings as well as across the European Competition Network[199] and be more consistent with the general principles governing the secrecy of lawyer–client correspondence enshrined in Article 6(1) ECHR.[200]

However, it is acknowledged that, despite sounding promising, the proposed solution could increase the fragmentation of the notion of privilege, since it would be left to the Member States to decide whether or not to allow in-house counsel to be admitted to the national Bar or Law Society. In this specific respect, the fact that similar proposals made in the context of the debate started by the Commission's White Paper on Modernisation of the rules implementing Articles 81 and 82 EC Treaty and of the review of the 1989 Merger Regulation were met with staunch opposition on the part of the Member States is particularly telling.

---

194 Appl. No 31611/96, *Nikula v Finland*, [2004] 38 EHRR 45 at paras. 54–55.

195 *Id.*, para. 55.

196 *Id.*, para. 45. Appl. No 15450/89, *Casado Coca v Spain*, ser. A No 285, [1994] 18 EHRR 1 at para. 54. For commentary, ANDREANGELI, 'The protection of legal professional privilege in EU law', at 41–42.

197 ANDREANGELI, *id.*, at 48.

198 *Id.*, para. 126.

199 *Inter alia*, ECLA, 'Legal privilege for in-house lawyers', position paper, December 2002, available at http://www.ecla.org/pages/position_paper.html; also, VESTERDORF, 'Legal professional privilege and the privilege against self-incrimination in EC Law', at 722.

200 *Inter alia*, Appl. No 37328/97, *AB v Netherlands*, judgment of 29 January 2002, [2003] 37 EHRR 48 at paras. 85–86; also Appl. No 31611/96, *Nikula v Finland*, [2004] 38 EHRR, 45 at para. 53. *Inter alia,* ANDREANGELI, 'The protection of legal professional privilege in EU law', at 42.

Although the White Paper on Modernisation examined in some depth the scope of the Commission's powers of investigations, it did not make any reference to the problems arising from *A. M. & S. Europe*.[201] However, in the course of the consultation that followed, many interested parties proposed without success that the legislature take the opportunity offered by the replacement of Council Regulation No 17/62 to adopt a harmonised approach to the concept of legal professional privilege[202] and perhaps extend its cover to communications emanating from in-house counsel.[203]

A further attempt to amend the conditions governing privilege was made in the context of the debate for the reform of the 1989 Merger Regulation, starting with the publication of the Commission's Green Paper in 2001.[204] It should be emphasised that the proposal was met with the support of the European Parliament, which in its Opinion suggested the following amendment to the Draft Regulation:

> (. . .) Communications between undertakings and associations of undertakings and outside or in-house counsel containing or seeking legal advice shall be privileged provided that the legal counsel is properly qualified and is subject to adequate rules of professional ethics and discipline which are laid down and enforced in the general interest by the professional association to which the legal counsel belongs. (. . .)[205]

---

201 EUROPEAN COMMISSION, *White paper on Modernisation of the rules implementing Articles 85 and 86 [now Articles 81 and 82] of the EC Treaty*, [1999] OJ C132/1, paras. 109–16; see especially para. 113.

202 See, e.g., Competition Law Forum, British Institute for International and Comparative Law, 'Supplemental submission to the European Competition Network regarding the Modernisation Package', available at: http://ec.europa.eu/comm/competition/antitrust/legislation/procedural_rules/comments/competition_law_forum_en.pdf, pp. 4–5.

203 See, e.g., ECLA, 'Comments on the draft Commission Regulation, Notices and Guidelines regarding Regulation 1/2003, December 2003', available at: http://ec.europa.eu/comm/competition/antitrust/legislation/procedural_rules/comments/ecla_en.pdf; also Joint Working Party of the Bars and Law Societies of the UK on Competition Law, comments, available at: http://ec.europa.eu/comm/competition/antitrust/legislation/procedural_rules/comments/jclwp_coop_en.pdf, p. 7; AFEP, 'Observations on the Draft Council Regulation and the Draft Commission Regulation and Notices', available at: http://ec.europa.eu/comm/competition/antitrust/legislation/procedural_rules/comments/afep_en.pdf, pp. 14–15.

204 EUROPEAN COMMISSION, *Green Paper on the Review of Council Regulation (EEC) No 4064/89*, available at: http://ec.europa.eu/comm/competition/mergers/review/green_paper/en.pdf.

205 EUROPEAN PARLIAMENT, *Report on the proposal for a Council regulation on the control of concentrations between undertakings*, Committee on Economic and Monetary Affairs (the 'della Vedova Report'), A5-0257/2003 FINAL, 9 July 2003, p. 9.

In its Report, the Economic and Monetary Affairs Parliamentary Committee justified its proposal in the light of the need to ensure 'fairness and due process' and the protection of the rights of the defence of the notifying parties and pointed out that it was indispensable to avoid the undertakings' executives becoming discouraged from consulting their legal advisers, whether independent or employed, only 'because confidential deliberations risk being disclosed'.[206]

However, that proposal was rejected by the Council of Ministers. It could be argued that the opposition of the Member States was probably motivated by the need to ensure uniformity in the reformulation of *A.M. & S.* and thus to make it applicable not only to merger cases but also to antitrust investigations,[207] as well as by the more general, ongoing lack of cross-border support for the recognition of the increased independence of in-house counsel.[208]

It could therefore be argued that, although the *AKZO Nobel* judgment appears to adopt a solution consistent with the conservative stance adopted by several Member States, it may still create the potential for future litigation concerning the position of those employed lawyers that are allowed to benefit from the same guarantees as independent counsel. It is concluded that despite appearing as the last word on the concept of EU legal professional privilege, *AKZO Nobel*, with its emphasis on the need for continuous judicial checks over the Commission's decisions concerning privilege, does not rule out the possibility for a future reconsideration of these issues.

4. THE PRIVILEGE AGAINST SELF-INCRIMINATION IN EC COMPETITION PROCEEDINGS

4.1. General Remarks: the Development of the Privilege in the Corporate Context

The privilege against self-incrimination constitutes another safeguard available to the undertakings investigated by the Commission for alleged breaches of Articles 81 and 82 EC Treaty. Despite not being explicitly provided for by

---

206 *Id.*, p. 10.

207 *Inter alia*, BERG, 'The new EC merger regulation: a first assessment of its practical impact', (2004) 24 *Nw. J. of Int'l L. and Bus.* 683 at 707.

208 See CCBE, *Regulated legal professionals and professional privilege within the European Union, the European Economic Area and Switzerland and certain other European Jurisdictions* – John FISH (February 2004), available at: http://www.ccbe.org/en/comites/in_house_en.htm; see especially pp. 25–27, 48, 50.

the relevant implementing legislation, it was recognised by the ECJ as part of the general principles of EC law, as a means of protecting the undertakings' rights of defence not only in the context of the formal procedure, namely of that phase of the proceedings following the service of the statement of objections, but also during the preliminary investigations leading to the gathering of the necessary evidence.[209]

An examination of the historical development of the privilege as an essential component of the right to a fair trial according to adversarial principles[210] is clearly beyond the scope of this work. It is sufficient to say that the privilege responds to the need to protect individuals subjected to criminal proceedings from forms of compulsion exercised by the authorities seeking to force them to confess to the crime of which they had been accused.[211] Conceived primarily as a reaction to the use of the 'oath ex officio' in the English Ecclesiastical courts in the fifteenth and sixteenth centuries,[212] it is now viewed as an internationally recognised standard and an essential requirement of a fair trial and procedure.[213]

The privilege against self-incrimination was explained as either an instrument to ensure adherence to the principles underlying the accusatorial criminal process or as a means to protect human autonomy from improper coercion and, generally, from the 'cruel choices' of the State.[214] According to the first theoretical strand, the privilege constitutes a 'functional necessity' within the criminal justice system,[215] since it ensures that the prosecution seek to prove the case against the defendant and that the latter not be obliged to give evidence that may incriminate him or her and thereby reflect the importance in a democratic society of the values of human freedom and dignity.[216] The privilege against self-incrimination is thus directly linked to the presumption of innocence and is concerned with preventing the authorities from forcing the accused to produce inculpatory evidence which would be impossible to obtain

---

[209] Case 27/88, *Orkem v Commission*, [1989] ECR 3355, para. 28, 33–34.

[210] *Inter alia*, Case 43/1994/490/572, *Saunders v United Kingdom*, [1997] 23 EHRR 313, para. 68.

[211] For an examination of the genesis of the privilege in Common law, see, *inter alia*, DENNIS, 'Instrumental protection, human right or functional necessity? Reassessing the privilege against self-incrimination', (1995) 54 (2) *CLJ* 342 at 348ff.

[212] *Inter alia*, TRAINOR, 'A comparative analysis of a corporation's right against self-incrimination', (1994–1995) 18 *Fordham Int'l L J* 2139 at 2144–45.

[213] OVEY and WHITE, *Jacobs and White: The European Convention on Human Rights* (2002) Oxford University Press, p. 174.

[214] DENNIS, 'Instrumental protection, human right or functional necessity?', at 348.

[215] *Id.*, p. 376.

[216] *Id.*, p. 353.

if not for his or her cooperation.[217] It seeks to avoid the reversal of the burden of proof and thus to prevent unfairly obtained convictions.[218]

The other theoretical strand, instead, links the privilege against self-incrimination to the right of each individual to a sphere of privacy, which also entails a 'right to control the provision of information about ourselves'.[219] According to this view, the privilege seeks to protect the individual's self-knowledge, personal identity and autonomy and consequently prevents the exercise of coercive powers that can thwart that autonomy.[220]

Despite having received varying degrees of support, both explanations have been criticised. Commentators suggested that an excessive reliance on the presumption of innocence as a basis to claim privilege may lead the state to 'be denied access to a good deal of relevant and reliable evidence',[221] even though the methods used to obtain it may not be necessarily oppressive and result in the adjudication process being less accurate. In other words, it was argued that this approach can lead to an over-inclusive interpretation of the privilege, which cannot be reconciled with, for example, the admissibility of evidence other than oral testimony which is obtained through methods that are potentially just as coercive, such as home and personal searches and the taking of bodily samples.[222]

The supporters of this thesis pointed out that the privilege, seen in this light, prevents the authorities from compelling the accused to 'bring into existence incriminating communications' which would otherwise remain unavailable, with a view to securing his or her conviction.[223] By contrast, evidence which exists 'independently of the suspect's communications', such as samples, pre-existing documents or fingerprints, even though it may be incriminating, would not be covered by the privilege because it could be acquired by the authorities through the exercise of compulsory powers without the active contribution of the individual concerned.[224]

With respect to the 'privacy-based' rationale, instead, it was argued that limiting the scope of the privilege to the communications 'generated' by the accused is not entirely sustainable. Although it was suggested that this interpretation

---

217 *Id.*, p. 355.

218 MacCULLOCH, 'The privilege against self-incrimination in competition investigations: theoretical foundations and practical implications', (2006) 26 (1) *LS* 211 at 220–21.

219 *Id.*, p. 216.

220 DENNIS, 'Instrumental protection, human right or functional necessity?', at 356.

221 *Id.*, p. 354.

222 *Id.*, p. 355.

223 *Ibid.*

224 *Ibid.*

stems from a narrow reading of privacy as encompassing only 'mental privacy', other commentators pointed out that, again, the taking of fingerprints or of bodily samples, which would be deployable later in trial, could perhaps be even more invasive of the individual's 'right to be left alone'.[225] In addition, it was argued that if privilege was given a 'privacy-based' explanation, its scope would become uncertain since it would depend on how the balance is struck between the individual's claim to preserve his or her 'private space' and the need to protect the community at large.[226]

Although, given the limited remit of this work, it is not possible to investigate further its rationale, it is submitted that both approaches can provide useful insights into the issue of how privilege can be justified and in that respect, how it can be applied in the context of regulatory investigations and with respect to corporate actors. As will be examined in detail in later sections, the case law of the European Court of Human Rights links the availability of the privilege to the need to protect the will of the accused against improper forms of coercion or oppression exercised by the authorities for the purpose of ensuring a 'fair trial'.[227] It was held in *Saunders*:

> The right not to incriminate oneself (. . .) presupposes that the prosecution in a criminal case seek to prove their case against the accused without resort to evidence obtained through methods of coercion or oppression in defiance of the will of the accused. (. . .)
>
> [It] is primarily concerned, however, with respecting the will of an accused person to remain silent. (. . .) [I]t does not extend to the use in criminal proceedings of material which may be obtained from the accused through the use of compulsory powers but which has an existence independent of the will of the suspect, such as, inter alia, documents acquired pursuant to a warrant, breath, blood and urine samples and bodily tissues for the purpose of DNA testing.[228]

It is submitted that the European Court of Human Rights, by emphasising the need to protect the will and the personal autonomy of the accused, appears to favour a 'privacy-based' interpretation of the privilege while at the same time taking into account the requirements of the accusatorial criminal justice system, namely the presumption of innocence and maintaining the burden of proof of the alleged offence on the prosecution. Accordingly, the Court,

---

225 *Id.*, pp. 357–58.

226 MacCULLOCH, 'The privilege against self-incrimination in competition investigations', at 218–19.

227 *Id.*, p. 231.

228 Case 43/1994/490/572, *Saunders v United Kingdom*, [1997] 23 EHRR 313, paras. 68–69. See also Appl. Nos. 15809/02 and 25624/02, *O'Halloran and Francis v United Kingdom*, judgment of 29 June 2007, not yet reported, para. 47.

despite being concerned with protecting that personal autonomy, also seeks to maintain the coherence of the privilege with the principles inspiring the concept of 'fair trial' enshrined in Article 6 ECHR.[229]

It could be argued, however, that the emphasis on the privacy rationale does not appear suitable to the application of the privilege to corporate actors, especially in the context of regulatory proceedings, including competition investigations. Although, as was argued in earlier sections, antitrust proceedings possess characteristics that make them criminal in nature and therefore bring them under the umbrella of Article 6(1) ECHR, it is also clear that some aspects of the privilege itself do not seem entirely suitable for application to legal persons.[230]

The debate concerning the possibility of extending the reach of the privilege against self-incrimination to benefit legal persons in the business framework may be traced back to the emergence of the corporation as a vital tool and as a progressively independent actor in the economic life of society, which in turn called for the establishment of systems for the regulation of corporate behaviour[231] aimed at the efficient prosecution of corporate misfeasance through a variety of instruments, including investigative and sanctioning powers.[232]

Although the creation of these control structures was in principle justified, it raised the issue of how to ensure an adequate balance of powers between the authorities and the investigated undertakings especially through the provision of procedural rights.[233] As was discussed in earlier sections,[234] the applicability of the human rights standards contained in the European Convention on Human Rights to corporate entities may be justified in relation to the values underlying the Convention system.[235] In that context the rule of law principle ensures that governmental action be 'subjected to law in order to prevent arbitrary exercise of power and to secure equality and foreseeability'.[236]

Accordingly, it can be interpreted as supporting the application of standards enshrined in the ECHR to corporate entities by seeking to prevent the excessive wielding of public power against legal as well as natural persons. Against this background, it is submitted that the extension of the privilege

---

229 DENNIS, 'Instrumental protection, human right or functional necessity?', at 375–76.

230 MacCULLOCH, 'The privilege against self-incrimination in competition investigations', at 233.

231 *Inter alia*, TRAINOR, 'A comparative analysis of a corporation's right against self-incrimination', (1994–1995) 18 *Fordham Int'l L J* 2139 at 2165–66.

232 *Id.*, pp. 2183–84.

233 *Id.*, p. 2166.

234 *Supra*, Chapter 1, Part 2, section 3.

235 EMBERLAND, *The Human Rights of Companies*, pp. 42–43.

236 *Id*, p. 45.

against self-incrimination to corporate entities imposes 'a reasonable limit on the state's power to pursue its otherwise legitimate goals' and therefore preserves 'an equitable balance of power between the state and the corporation'[237] in the context of investigations and regulatory and judicial procedures.[238]

However, although the objective nature of some of the values underlying the Convention provides strong support for the application of the privilege to legal persons, it was argued that this conclusion may not be entirely consistent with the 'privacy-based' rationale of the privilege. Commentators pointed out that this justification, despite being convincing in principle, is clearly linked to the protection of the individual's self-knowledge and personal privacy, elements which, if extended to legal persons, are 'strained if not lost entirely'.[239]

The 'privacy-based' interpretation of the privilege may be contrasted with the 'process-based' approach. It was suggested that this rationale allows a more inclusive reading of the privilege and could therefore provide a more suitable basis for its application to the corporate context. However, it should also be noted that it may be more difficult to reconcile it with the position adopted by the courts and especially by the ECJ, who have clearly favoured a more restrictive interpretation of the scope of the privilege.[240]

In conclusion, the privilege against self-incrimination constitutes a uniformly recognised international human rights standard that aims to protect the will and the autonomy of persons from improper coercion or oppression on the part of the state authorities in the context of primarily judicial but also regulatory proceedings.[241] Its recognition can therefore be justified in the light of the concept of the rule of law at the basis of a democratic society which, by virtue of its objective nature, is liable to further extension to corporate entities.[242] However, the analysis has also highlighted several problems stemming from the perceived uncertainty concerning the rationale at the basis of the privilege.[243] The following sections will examine the approaches to the scope of the privilege adopted by, respectively, the ECJ and the European Court of

[237] TRAINOR, 'A comparative analysis of a corporation's right against self-incrimination', at 2185.

[238] *Id.*, pp. 46–47.

[239] MacCULLOCH, 'The privilege against self-incrimination in competition investigations', at 234.

[240] *Id.*, pp. 235–36.

[241] TRAINOR, 'A comparative analysis of a corporation's right against self-incrimination', at 2185.

[242] EMBERLAND, pp. 42–43.

[243] *Inter alia*, WARD and GARDNER, 'The privilege against self-incrimination: in search of legal certainty', (2003) 4 *EHRLR* 388 at 394.

Human Rights and discuss the current standards enshrined in EC law in the light of those established under the Convention.

4.2. Privilege Against Self-incrimination in Competition Proceedings: Between the Rights of the Defence and Effective Antitrust Enforcement?

As noted in the previous section, EC law, whilst conferring on the Commission extensive investigative powers to uncover evidence of antitrust infringements, did not expressly recognise the privilege against self-incrimination as one of the procedural guarantees available to the investigated undertakings. Nonetheless, in its *Orkem* judgment[244] the ECJ was prepared to acknowledge the existence of a degree of protection against self-incrimination among the general principles of EC law for the purpose of respecting the rights of the defence enjoyed by the parties concerned, not only after the statement of objections was served to them, but also in the preliminary stages of the proceedings.[245]

In *Orkem* the applicants had objected to a Commission decision adopted in accordance with Article 11 of Council Regulation 17/62 requesting information concerning an alleged breach of Article 81(1) EC Treaty on the grounds that the Commission was seeking to compel the undertakings to give evidence against themselves.[246] They claimed that the impugned decision infringed their right not to incriminate themselves, which was upheld by the laws of the Member States and recognised by international human rights' instruments such as the European Convention on Human Rights and the UN International Covenant of Civil and Political Rights (hereinafter referred to as ICCPR).[247]

The question before the Court concerned therefore whether EC law recognised that right in the context of the Commission's competition investigations. The ECJ started by examining the nature of the investigative powers conferred on the Commission under Regulation 17/62 and held that their aim was 'to enable it to carry out its duty under the EEC Treaty of ensuring that the rules on competition are applied in the Common Market'.[248]

To achieve that objective Regulation 17/62 laid down a two-stage procedure for the enforcement of the Treaty antitrust rules: the first stage was of a preparatory nature and allowed the Commission to gather the necessary evidence to establish 'the actual existence and scope of a specific factual and

---

244 Case 27/88, *Orkem v Commission*, [1989] ECR 3355.
245 *Id.*, para. 28.
246 *Id.*, para. 3.
247 *Id.*, para. 18.
248 *Id.*, para. 19.

legal situation'.[249] The second stage, instead, namely the formal phase of the proceedings, was initiated with the service of the statement of objections and provided the investigated parties with an opportunity to contest the Commission case by way of written submissions and an oral hearing.[250]

The ECJ recognised that during the first phase of the procedure the Commission enjoyed wide powers of investigation and that the investigated parties would be under a corresponding obligation to cooperate with the officials so as not to frustrate the effectiveness of the investigative measures.[251] Among the available measures, Article 11, Regulation No 17/62, expressly empowered the Commission to request all the necessary information from the concerned undertakings and, in the event of non-compliance, authorised it to issue a decision requesting that information, with penalties in the event of further refusal.[252]

Nonetheless, the Court acknowledged that the Commission's powers are not unlimited. The Implementing Regulation, while it does not allow the undertaking 'to evade the investigation on the ground that the results thereof might provide evidence of an infringement by it of the competition rules',[253] confers on the investigated parties a set of procedural safeguards not only during the formal stage of the procedure but also in the preliminary, investigative stage, such as, *inter alia*, the right to be heard before the adoption of a decision imposing on it financial penalties for non-compliance with an Article 11 decision.[254] In that context, the question was whether the general principles of EC law recognised a right for the investigated parties not to give evidence and thus contribute to incriminating themselves.[255]

The Advocate General, after a thorough review of the national laws on the existence and the scope of the privilege across the Member States and, on the basis of the evidence before him, concluded that although the right not to give evidence against oneself was enshrined in all the considered jurisdictions, that principle became 'less common as one moves away from the area of (. . .) classic criminal procedure'.[256] In the judgment, the ECJ took the similar view that, whereas the right not to incriminate oneself was well established in the context of domestic criminal proceedings against natural persons, it could not be found

---

249 *Id.*, para. 21.
250 Case 27/88, *Orkem v Commission*, [1989] ECR 3355, para. 20.
251 *Id.*, para. 22.
252 *Id.*, para. 23.
253 *Id.*, para. 27.
254 *Id.*, para. 26.
255 *Id.*, para. 28.
256 *Id.*, Opinion of AG Darmon, available in [1991] 4 CMLR 502 at 534.

that the laws of the Member States conferred a similar right on legal persons in a regulatory context, and especially in that of antitrust enforcement.[257]

In response to the arguments drawn on the basis of the international human rights treaties advanced by the applicants, the Court held with respect to the ECHR that Article 6 did not expressly provide for the privilege.[258] As regards the ICCPR, instead, the ECJ held that although the Covenant expressly recognised the right against self-incrimination, it also limited its reach to individuals charged with criminal offences in judicial proceedings, and was therefore not susceptible of extension to the framework for the investigation of competition infringements.[259]

Finally the ECJ addressed the question of whether any implied limitations to the Commission's investigative powers could be derived from the undertakings' rights of defence that are part of the general principles of EC law so as to justify recognition of the privilege. The Court noted that these rights, despite being effective primarily during the formal stage of the proceedings, may equally be compromised in the course of preliminary investigations. Due to the importance of the fact-finding procedures as a means to obtain often decisive evidence of anti-competitive conduct, it would be therefore indispensable to limit the scope of the Commission's powers even during the preliminary stage of the inquiry, while at the same time preserving the effectiveness of the investigative powers in question.[260]

The ECJ concluded that, although the Commission was entitled to force the investigated undertakings to disclose information and provide documents concerning facts that may be known to them, even though the evidence so gathered may be used to establish the existence of an antitrust infringement, it could not by means of an Article 11 decision undermine the undertakings' rights of defence:[261] '(. . .) the Commission may not compel an undertaking to provide it with answers which might involve an admission on its part of the existence of an infringement which it is incumbent upon the Commission to prove'.[262]

The Court concluded that the impugned decision was partly unlawful and should be annulled[263] since in it the Commission was seeking to obtain information as regards 'the purpose of the action taken and the objective pursued'[264] by the undertakings and therefore was in essence forcing the

---

257 Case 27/88, *Orkem v Commission*, [1989] ECR 3355, para. 29.
258 *Id.*, para. 30.
259 *Id.*, para. 31.
260 *Id.*, paras. 32–33.
261 *Id.*, para. 34.
262 *Id.*, para. 35.
263 *Id.*, para. 42.
264 *Id.*, para. 38.

applicant to admit to participation in an agreement prohibited by Article 81(1) of the EC Treaty.[265]

The importance of the *Orkem* judgment cannot be understated: by acknowledging that the reach of the rights of the defence extended also to the preliminary, fact-finding stage of the proceedings the ECJ was able to recognise a limited right not to incriminate oneself during competition proceedings and, at the same time, to preserve the *effet utile* of Article 11, Regulation 17/62, namely the effectiveness of the investigative powers enjoyed by the Commission.[266]

However, the circumstance that the privilege attaches only to replies to 'leading questions', namely questions concerning the objective and purpose of action taken by the investigated parties, and still allows for 'factual' questions, was criticised by commentators who argued that even purely factual evidence may be equally damning.[267] Furthermore, the circumstance that the ECJ indicated, among the reasons at the basis of its decision, the absence from Article 6 ECHR of any reference to the privilege raised the question of whether the Court could have reached a different conclusion had the European Court of Human Rights already acknowledged the existence of a right not to incriminate oneself.[268]

As will be examined in later sections, the case law of the Strasbourg Court now expressly acknowledges the existence of the privilege as an essential element of the right to a fair trial and of the presumption of innocence.[269] However, these developments have not led the ECJ to reconsider its position. In the later *Mannesmannrohren-Werke v Commission* judgment,[270] the CFI declined to depart from the ECJ's conclusions in *Orkem*. After reiterating that it had no jurisdiction *ratione personae* to apply the Convention,[271] the Court held that although the rights of the defence should not be irremediably impaired during the preliminary phase of the procedure,[272] the investigated

---

265 *Id.*, paras. 38–39.

266 Van OVERBEEK, 'The right to remain silent in competition investigations: the *Funke* decision of the Court of Human Rights makes revision of the ECJ's case law necessary', (1994) 15(3) *ECLR* 127 at 128.

267 *Inter alia*, RILEY, '*Saunders* and the power to obtain information in Community and United Kingdom competition law', (2000) 21 *ELRev* 264 at 269.

268 *Inter alia*, WILS, 'Self-incrimination in EC antitrust enforcement: a legal and economic analysis', (2003) 26 *W. Comp.* 567 at 575–76.

269 See Appl. No 10828/84, *Funke v France*, ser. A-256/A, [1993] 16 EHRR 297; Case 43/1994/490/572, *Saunders v United Kingdom*, [1997] 23 EHRR 313. *Infra*, section 4.3.

270 Case T-112/98, *Mannesmannrohren Werke v Commission*, [2001] ECR II-729.

271 *Id.*, para. 59.

272 *Id.*, para. 64.

parties have no right to evade the Commission's investigations.[273] To the contrary, it was stated:

> To acknowledge the existence of an absolute right to silence (. . .) would go beyond what is necessary in order to preserve the rights of defence of undertakings and would constitute an unjustified hindrance to the Commission's performance of its duty (. . .) to ensure that the rules on competition within the common market are observed.[274]

Consequently, the protection against self-incrimination could only prevent the Commission officials from asking questions and requesting evidence concerning the purpose of the undertakings' actions, since these types of requests could only result in the undertaking being compelled to admit to the alleged violation.[275] Purely factual questions and the compliance with a request to hand pre-existing documents to the Commission officials, instead, would still be compatible with the principle of respect for the rights of defence.

According to the Court, even if the undertakings were obliged to disclose that evidence it would always be open to them to show, either in the context of the formal stage of the administrative proceedings or before the Community courts, that 'the facts set out in his replies or the documents produced by him have a different meaning from that ascribed to them by the Commission'.[276] As a result, the CFI annulled the impugned decision in the parts in which the Commission had obliged the applicant to answer questions concerning the purpose of the meetings to which it had taken part and the decisions adopted in the course of them.[277]

The decision in *Mannesmannrohren Werke* was strongly criticised as being unable to provide effective protection to the rights of the defence of the investigated parties. Commentators argued that, by adopting what was termed as a 'conscious policy decision not to extend to Commission investigations the safeguards against self-incrimination',[278] the CFI confirmed a narrow interpretation of the privilege which does not place any limit on the Commission's investigative powers with the sole exception of leading questions.[279]

---

273 *Id.*, para. 62.
274 *Id.*, para. 66.
275 *Id.*, para. 71.
276 *Id.*, para. 78.
277 *Id.*, para. 71.
278 WILLIS, '"You have the right to remain silent . . ." or do you? The privilege against self-incrimination following *Mannesmannrohren-Werke* and other recent decisions', (2001) 22 *ECLR* 313.
279 RILEY, '*Saunders* and the power to obtain information in Community and United Kingdom competition law', at 269.

In later cases the Court elaborated on the manner in which the existence of an infringement of the privilege should be assessed. In the *PVC II* appeal[280] the ECJ took the view that, in accordance with its existing case law and that of the European Court of Human Rights, the applicant would have to prove 'first, the exercise of coercion against the suspect in order to obtain information from him and second establishment of the existence of an actual interference with the right which they define'.[281]

On that basis, the ECJ found no infringement of the privilege on the grounds that, first of all, the complaint made by the applicant concerned a simple request of information, to which the applicant was not obliged to answer, and not a decision,[282] and second, that the illegality of those questions that the CFI had found to be offensive to the privilege had not affected the legality of the final decision. In fact, the investigated parties had either refused to give an answer to them or had denied the facts on which they had been questioned.[283]

Broadly similar conclusions were also reached in the *SGL Carbon* judgment[284] where the ECJ not only stressed the duty of active cooperation incumbent on the investigated undertakings in the course of the preliminary stage of the proceedings[285] but also reiterated that the judgments handed down by the Strasbourg Court after *Orkem* could not put in question the position hitherto maintained by the Luxembourg courts as regards the scope of the privilege.[286]

Accordingly, the more recent decisions of the ECJ suggest that, for there to be a violation of the privilege against self-incrimination there must be first of all evidence of coercion on the part of the Commission. In other words, if a potentially self-incriminating question was contained in a simple request for information, this would not be sufficient to establish a violation since a simple request is not binding on the party to which it is addressed. And second, there must be an 'actual interference'[287] with the right of the undertaking concerned to 'fair legal process'.[288] This condition was interpreted as requiring the applicant to prove that the illegality of the decision requesting the incriminating information affected the lawfulness of the final decision, and to that end to

280 Case C-238/99, *LVM NV and Others v Commission*, [2002] ECR I-8375.
281 *Id.*, para. 275.
282 *Id.*, para. 279.
283 *Id.*, para. 282.
284 Case C-301/04 P, *Commission v SGL Carbon AG*, judgment of 29 June 2006, not yet reported, available at [2006] 5 CMLR 15.
285 *Id.*, para. 40.
286 *Id.*, para. 43.
287 Case C-238/99, *LVM NV and Others v Commission*, [2002] ECR I-8375 at para. 275.
288 Case T-112/98, *Mannesmannrohren Werke v Commission*, [2001] ECR II-729 at para. 77.

show that the evidence in question was relied upon by the Commission to prove the existence of a violation of Articles 81 and 82 EC Treaty.[289]

It could be argued that the first requirement enshrined in the *PVC II* appeal decision appears consistent with the rationale of the privilege as protecting primarily the investigated party from the exercise of coercion or oppression by the authority in charge of the investigation.[290] As regards the second, it will be shown in the next section that, in the *Saunders* judgment, the European Court of Human Rights emphasised the circumstance that the privilege may be infringed, *inter alia*, by deploying incriminating statements in proceedings other than those in which they were gathered to support the prosecution's case.[291] The manner in which the evidence was obtained under compulsion was therefore central to the finding that the applicant's right under Article 6(1) ECHR had unlawfully been interfered with.[292]

However, although it would appear from more recent judgments that the Luxembourg courts have preferred a view of the privilege against self-incrimination which is more consistent with that emerging from the case law of the European Court of Human Rights, the limitations as regards the nature of the evidence attracting that safeguard, established by the *Orkem* judgment, have been expressly confirmed.

The approach of the ECJ therefore raises several questions with respect to the actual effectiveness of the privilege as a right of defence and more generally to the compliance of the concept of 'due process' in competition cases as enshrined in EC law vis-à-vis the human rights standards established by the European Convention on Human Rights. The next sections will thus illustrate the conditions governing the privilege against self-incrimination provided by Article 6 ECHR and thereafter will examine the EC law concept of privilege in the light of the Strasbourg Court's approach as it emerges from the *Funke* and *Saunders* judgments.

4.3. Article 6 of the ECHR and the Privilege Against Self-incrimination

As was noted in earlier sections, the European Convention on Human Rights did not expressly provide for any protection against self-incrimination. It was only with the *Funke v France* judgment[293] that the European Court of Human

---

289 Case C-238/99, *LVM NV and Others v Commission*, [2002] ECR I-8375 at para. 282.

290 VESTERDORF, 'Legal professional privilege and the privilege against self-incrimination in EC law', pp. 715–16.

291 Case 43/1994/490/572, *Saunders v United Kingdom*, [1997] 23 EHRR 313, para. 71.

292 *Ibid.*

293 Appl. No 10828/84, ser. A-256/A [1993] 16 EHRR 297.

Rights acknowledged the existence of a right to silence and not to contribute to incriminate oneself as part of the concept of 'fair procedure' enshrined in Article 6 of the Convention.[294] In *Funke* the Court examined the extent to which the search and seizure powers enjoyed by the French customs officials for the purpose of acquiring evidence necessary to establish tax evasion complied with Article 6.[295]

The applicant had complained that the fact that he had been prosecuted and fined for the refusal to hand in to the officials specific documents which they had requested to reinforce their allegations of tax and currency evasion was incompatible with his right to remain silent and not to incriminate himself, which despite not being expressly recognised by the Convention, constituted 'a general principle enshrined both in the legal orders of the Contracting States and in the European Convention and the International Covenant of Civil and Political Rights'.[296]

The respondent State in its defence alleged that even if it was acknowledged that these guarantees were implied by the ECHR, the powers to search premises and seize evidence enjoyed by the customs officials during tax investigations would not be incompatible with the concept of a 'fair trial' contained in Article 6: first of all, the exercise of these powers was under the strict supervision of the judiciary and, second, it was not aimed at forcing the investigated individual to confess to an offence, but merely to give 'particulars of evidence found by their officers', including specific documents.[297]

However, the Strasbourg Court took the different view that the conviction of the applicant was incompatible with the notion of 'fair trial' contained in the Convention: according to the Court, the authorities had 'secured Mr Funke's conviction in order to obtain certain documents' which they could not acquire by other means and therefore had in essence attempted to compel the applicant to provide the evidence of the offences of which he was suspected.[298] It was concluded that Mr Funke's right to remain silent and not to incriminate himself had been infringed in consideration of the 'special features of customs law' and of the degree of compulsion to which he had been subjected by means of the conviction.[299]

Despite having been welcomed as the first recognition of the existence of the privilege against self-incrimination in the framework of the Convention,[300]

---

294 *Id.*, para. 44.
295 *Id.*, paras. 30–31.
296 *Id.*, para. 41.
297 *Id.*, para. 42.
298 *Id.*, para. 44.
299 *Ibid.* Cf. Report of the European Commission on Human Rights, para. 43.
300 *Inter alia*, DENNIS, 'Instrumental protection, human right or functional necessity?', at 371.

the *Funke* judgment was extensively criticised. Commentators argued that the complaint concerned only the conviction inflicted on Mr Funke for the failure to hand in that evidence, regardless of the use to which the documents in question would later be put. On this point, Ward and Gardner noted:

> (. . .) It is hard to see how the use of compulsory powers to obtain information could involve Article 6(1). (. . .) If no trial takes place or no use is made of the compulsorily obtained material, then on the fact of it Article 6(1) is simply not engaged: the use of compulsory powers is not relevant to the determination of any criminal charge.[301]

The *Funke* judgment was also questioned in consideration of the nature of the evidence for which the privilege was claimed: the applicant's complaint concerned pre-existing documents, not oral evidence. On this point, it could be argued that, in the light of the considerations in section 4.1, the compelled handing over of documentary evidence should not engage application of the privilege: if one identifies the rationale of the privilege as being concerned with protection of the privacy and human dignity of the accused, only evidence which is 'produced' by the accused would be shielded from forced disclosure.[302] By contrast, evidence which exists outside the 'mental privacy' of the individual concerned, such as that at issue in *Funke*, should be open to compulsory access by the authorities.[303]

In the later *Saunders* judgment[304] the European Court of Human Rights took the opportunity to elaborate on the scope of the privilege. As is well known, *Saunders* concerned the use of statements made under compulsion in the course of non-judicial proceedings to the inspectors of the Department of Trade and Industry by the accused in his subsequent criminal trial.[305] The applicant argued that by deploying that evidence, which had been given during a separate investigation under threat of criminal sanctions for refusal to cooperate with the inspectors against him during the trial, his right not to incriminate himself had been violated.[306]

The European Court of Human Rights reiterated that, despite not being expressly mentioned, the right to silence and not to contribute to incriminating

---

301 WARD and GARDNER, 'The privilege against self-incrimination: in search of legal certainty', (2003) 4 *EHRLR* 388 at 391.

302 *Ibid.*

303 See also STESSENS, 'The obligation to produce documents versus the privilege against self-incrimination: human rights protection extended too far', (1997) 22 SUPP (Human Rights survey), text to fn. 78–79.

304 Case 43/1994/490/572, *Saunders v United Kingdom*, [1997] 23 EHRR 313.

305 *Id.*, para. 67.

306 *Id.*, para. 60.

oneself was enshrined in the Convention as a core element of the notion of a fair trial. The Court found its rationale in the protection of the accused against forms of improper coercion exercised by the authorities with a view to avoiding miscarriages of justice and to respecting the adversarial nature of the criminal trial, as a result of which it is incumbent on the prosecution to 'seek to prove their case against the accused'.[307] It was thus indispensable to prevent the authorities from relying on 'evidence obtained through methods of coercion or oppression in defiance of the will' of the suspect.[308]

It was therefore held that the scope of the privilege, being concerned with respecting the will of an accused person to remain silent, extended to statements made under threat of compulsion but did not go as far as to prevent the authorities from deploying against the individual concerned evidence 'which has an existence independent of the will of the suspect', including, *inter alia*, 'documents acquired pursuant to a warrant' and bodily samples for testing.[309]

In the light of the above, whether the right of the accused not to contribute to incriminating oneself has been breached would depend on the circumstances of the case. It would have to be assessed, first, whether the accused was compelled to give the incriminating evidence and second, whether that evidence was used during the trial in a manner 'which offended the basic principles of a fair procedure inherent in Article 6(1)' ECHR.[310] In the case at hand the Court found a violation of the Convention: with respect to the element of coercion, it was clear that Mr Saunders had been forced to give evidence to the DTI inspectors under threat of criminal prosecution for contempt of court.[311]

With respect to the second condition, before the Court the Government had pleaded that the answers given by the applicant to the inspectors were not of an incriminatory nature and therefore, although they had been extracted under threat of criminal sanctions, their use in the course of the trial was not such as to engage the privilege.[312] However, the Court took a different view: what was essential for a finding that the applicant's right not to incriminate oneself had been infringed was not so much the content of the testimony and the extent to which the latter may be directly incriminating, but rather, its use in the course of the trial[313] and especially whether the applicant could prove that the prosecution deployed that evidence in a manner that was actually incriminating.[314]

---

307 *Id.*, para. 68.
308 *Ibid.*
309 *Id.*, para. 69.
310 *Ibid.*
311 *Id.*, para. 70.
312 *Id.*, paras. 62–63.
313 *Id.*, para. 71.
314 *Ibid.*

The Strasbourg Court concluded that even those statements which were not actually of an incriminating nature, once used against Mr Saunders, had resulted in his right to a fair trial being undermined in as much as they had been read directly to the jury despite the defence's objections and had thus contributed to the strength of the prosecution's case by adversely affecting the applicant's credibility and generally his defence.[315]

Commentators observed that, despite reiterating its existence as one of the guarantees of a fair trial in the context of the ECHR, the Strasbourg Court in *Saunders* adopted a view of the privilege against self-incrimination which was less extensive than that adopted in previous decisions.[316] Partly in contrast with the *Funke* decision,[317] the *Saunders* judgment made clear that the right to remain silent, being aimed at the protection of the human dignity and autonomy of the will of the accused, prevented the use in trial of evidence 'generated' by the individual, but not of pre-existing documents obtained as a result of the exercise of compulsory powers.[318]

However, later case law does not seem to clarify the actual impact of *Saunders* on the scope of the privilege under the ECHR.[319] In *JB v Switzerland*[320] the applicant had complained that his prosecution for failure to hand to the national tax authorities all the documents concerning the subject matter of proceedings initiated against him and to declare the source of his income, had violated his right not to incriminate himself. The Strasbourg Court found a breach of Article 6 ECHR with respect to the sanctions imposed for the refusal to abide by both requests without, however, drawing any distinction between the 'fresh information' and the case of existing documents.[321]

In addition, the Court dismissed almost out of hand the argument raised by the respondent Government that the privilege should not attach to the requested documentary evidence as a result of the application of *Saunders*, only on the ground of the 'persistence' with which the authorities had attempted to obtain the documents.[322] It is also unclear whether, for there to be an infringement of the privilege, the evidence should be actually deployed in the course of the proceedings against the applicant. The judgment in *Saunders* clearly suggests that this should be the case. By contrast, in *JB* it

---

315 *Id.*, para. 72.

316 *Inter alia*, STESSENS, 'The obligation to produce documents versus the privilege against self-incrimination', text to fn. 78–79.

317 Case A/256-A, *Funke v France*, [1993] 16 EHRR 297, paras. 30–31, 44.

318 Case 43/1994/490/572, *Saunders v United Kingdom*, [1997] 23 EHRR 313, para. 69.

319 WARD and GARDNER, 'The privilege against self-incrimination', at 394.

320 Appl. No 31827/97, judgment of 8 March 2001, reported in 3 ITL Report 663.

321 *Id.*, para. 66.

322 *Id.*, para. 69.

emerged that the applicant later reached a settlement with the authorities as a result of which the evidence was not deployed against him, and yet the Court reached the conclusion that Article 6 ECHR had been violated.[323]

In the very recent *O' Halloran and Francis* judgment,[324] the European Court of Human Rights re-examined the scope of the privilege against self-incrimination and adopted an approach to the assessment of the existence of an infringement which was largely modelled on the lines of *Saunders*. The applicants had complained that the obligation imposed on the owner of a car to reveal the name of the individual driving it in the event of him or her being caught speeding on pain of financial penalties was contrary to Article 6 ECHR. They pleaded that the monetary sanctions which could be threatened for failing to answer that question or for providing incorrect information 'extinguished' their right against self-incrimination.[325]

The Court reviewed its previous case law on the issue[326] and found that, although the privilege is mainly concerned with protecting the will of the accused against forms of improper coercion or oppression, not every form of compulsion will give rise to a violation of Article 6 ECHR.[327] Rather, it held: 'While the right to a fair trial under Article 6 is an unqualified right, what constitutes a fair trial cannot be the subject of a single unvarying rule but must depend on the circumstances of the particular case.'[328]

Consequently, the Court took the view that whether the obligation to disclose the identity of the driver, in the event of a speeding offence contained in the UK Road Traffic Act, constituted an infringement of the applicants' right not to incriminate themselves had to be assessed on the basis of the type and degree of compulsion exercised on the will of the accused, the presence of procedural safeguards and the use to which the resulting evidence was put.[329]

On the merits, however, no breach of Article 6 of the Convention was found: in the Court's opinion, the coercion exercised on the applicants by the threat of penalties envisaged by the Act, despite being direct, was a consequence of the circumstance that, by choosing to drive a car, the applicants had voluntarily subjected themselves to a regulatory regime and, as a result, to a set of obligations and responsibilities justified by the needs of public safety.[330]

---

323 *Ibid.* See Appl. No 31827/97, *JB v Switzerland*, judgment of 8 March 2001, para. 62.

324 Appl. Nos. 15809/02 and 25624/02, *O' Halloran and Francis v United Kingdom*, judgment of 29 June 2007, not yet reported.

325 *Id.*, paras. 40–42.

326 *Id.*, paras. 45–52.

327 *Id.*, para. 53.

328 *Ibid.*

329 *Id.*, para. 55.

330 *Id.*, para. 57.

In addition, the inquiry conducted by the police was of limited remit, being aimed only at eliciting the identity of the driver in the event of an offence and the penalty for failure to answer to the questioning was 'moderate and non-custodial'.[331]

Finally, with respect to the manner in which the evidence could be used, the Court emphasised that the identity of the driver constitutes only one element of the offence of speeding. It was thus incumbent on the prosecution to prove the infringement 'beyond any reasonable doubt in ordinary proceedings, including protection against the use of unreliable evidence and evidence obtained by oppression'.[332] The defendant maintained his right to call witnesses and be cross-examined during the trial and no conviction could be secured solely on the basis of the evidence obtained through section 172 of the Road Traffic Act.[333]

It is premature to attempt to gauge the full implications of the *O'Halloran and Francis* decision for the scope of the privilege against self-incrimination. However, it is suggested that this judgment may be interpreted as demonstrating that, just as the Court had held in *Saunders*,[334] any allegation that the privilege has been infringed will be assessed in the light of all the circumstances of the case and having regard to the existence and the degree of coercion exercised on the will of the accused, to the safeguards attending the acquisition of that evidence and to the use to which the latter would be put.

It could, however, be argued that the European Court of Human Rights seems to have departed from previous statements concerning the context in which the investigations had taken place. In *Saunders*, the Court had taken the view that the complexity of the crimes being investigated could not justify the use of evidence obtained under compulsion from an individual in a manner which can incriminate her and thus infringe Article 6 of the Convention.[335] By contrast, in *O' Halloran and Francis* the Court appeared to accept that the 'special nature of the regulatory regime' in question could call for a more limited interpretation of the privilege.[336]

Accordingly, it may be concluded that, although the privilege against self-incrimination is now an established principle inherent to the concept of fair trial enshrined in the Convention, there are still significant doubts as regards

---

[331] *Id.*, para. 58.
[332] *Id.*, para. 60.
[333] *Ibid.*
[334] Case 43/1994/490/572, *Saunders v United Kingdom*, [1997] 23 EHRR 313, paras. 71–72.
[335] *Id.*, para. 74.
[336] Appl. Nos. 15809/02 and 25624/02, *O' Halloran and Francis v United Kingdom*, judgment of 29 June 2002, not yet reported, para. 62.

its reach. However, it is submitted that, if the right to silence is construed as a bulwark of personal autonomy and as an instrument to protect the privacy of the individual,[337] adherence to the *Saunders* approach emerges as most likely to provide a reasoned rule of thumb to determine the scope of the privilege, in the light of the circumstances of each case.[338]

5. PRIVILEGE AGAINST SELF-INCRIMINATION IN EC LAW AND IN THE EUROPEAN CONVENTION: IN SEARCH OF CONSISTENCY?

The previous sections briefly illustrated the main terms of the debate concerning the rationale of the privilege against self-incrimination and examined the approach adopted by the European Convention on Human Rights and EC law to the determination of its scope. Section 4.3 demonstrated that the European Court of Human Rights favours an interpretation of the privilege as an essential component of the right to a fair trial and as a safeguard against improper coercion or oppression of the will of the accused in the course of criminal investigations.

The protection from forced disclosure should therefore extend to all the evidence originating from the accused and obtained through compulsive interrogation methods, but not to evidence that exists independently of the accused's will, such as, *inter alia*, pre-existing documents.[339] However, it was also noted that the *Saunders* view of the privilege has not always been borne out by later case law, especially in respect of the type of evidence that should be shielded from forced disclosure to the authorities and use in the following criminal trial.[340]

By contrast, the ECJ has constantly reiterated that the investigated undertakings are under a duty of active cooperation with the Commission officials in the course of the preliminary stage of the competition proceedings, as a result of which they are obliged to hand over incriminating documents and to give such answers as may be requested from them even if they may be used as

337 *Inter alia,* MacCULLOCH, 'The privilege against self-incrimination in competition investigations', at 234.

338 *Inter alia*, see *R v Hertfordshire CC ex parte Green Environmental Industries Ltd*, [2002] 2 AC 412, per Lord Hoffmann, p. 423.

339 Case 43/1994/490/572, *Saunders v United Kingdom*, [1997] 23 EHRR 313, paras. 62–63, 71.

340 WARD and GARDNER, 'The privilege against self-incrimination: in search of legal certainty', at 394. See Appl. No 31827/97, *JB v Switzerland*, judgment of 8 March 2001, para. 62.

evidence of facts constituting a breach of Articles 81 or 82 EC Treaty, with the only exception of answers to questions[341] which could potentially involve an admission of responsibility for an infringement which it is for the Commission to prove.[342]

The approach adopted by the ECJ has been widely criticised. Commentators argued that, although in principle it is capable of protecting the investigated parties from coercive forms of interrogation or other 'oppressive behaviour' adopted by the Commission's officials, the current notion of privilege against self-incrimination does not create any 'inhibition on the Commission provided that leading questions are avoided'.[343] In addition, even if the view was taken that *Funke* had been in substance overruled by the later *Saunders* decision and that, as a result, privilege was limited only to oral evidence originated from the accused,[344] significant inconsistencies would remain with respect to the requests for oral explanations on the spot which may be made during a dawn raid and to which the undertakings' representatives are obliged to answer.

In the light of the conclusions reached in *Saunders*,[345] it is submitted that the distinction between factual and leading questions does not appear to provide a sufficient degree of protection of the right to a fair procedure and of the rights of defence enjoyed by the undertakings investigated for alleged breaches of Articles 81 and 82 EC Treaty. In fact, it allows the Commission not only to obtain incriminating documents – which in itself would not be incompatible with the Convention, at least in the light of *Saunders* – but also to extract incriminating information of a factual nature by way of asking on-the-spot explanations from the undertakings' representatives, an outcome which, were it to occur in the course of investigations before domestic authorities, would be precluded.[346]

Supporters of the *Orkem* notion of privilege against self-incrimination have argued, not without some merit, that the right to a fair trial and to a fair procedure is not absolute and can be limited to pursue legitimate aims such as the prevention of disorder and crime and the protection of the well-being

---

341 Case 27/88, *Orkem v Commission*, [1989] ECR 3355, paras. 22, 34.

342 *Id.*, paras. 34–35, 66.

343 RILEY, '*Saunders* and the power to obtain information in Community and United Kingdom competition law', at 269.

344 *Inter alia*, WILS, 'Self-incrimination in EC antitrust enforcement: a legal and economic analysis', at 575.

345 Case 43/1994/490/572, *Saunders v United Kingdom*, [1997] 23 EHRR 313, para. 71.

346 WILLIS, '"You have the right to remain silent . . ." or do you?', at 321.

of the country,[347] provided that any such restriction does not impair the very essence of the right and bears a reasonable relation of proportionality with its objectives.[348]

Accordingly, the question would be whether the restrictive view adopted by the ECJ can constitute a justifiable restriction on the scope of privilege in the light of the Convention principles. It is noteworthy that in *Mannesmannrohren-Werke v Commission* the CFI held that recognising an absolute right to silence in competition investigations would go 'beyond what is necessary (. . .) to preserve the rights of defence of undertakings and (. . .) constitute an unjustified hindrance to the Commission's performance of its duty' in the application of the Treaty antitrust rules.[349] The Court thus dismissed the applicant's argument that the degree of protection provided by EC law would not be 'equivalent' to that provided by the Convention and affirmed that the application of the general principles of 'the rights of defence and the right to fair legal process' ensured compliance with the principles enshrined in Article 6 ECHR.[350]

There seems to be little doubt that the effective enforcement of the Treaty competition rules throughout the Common Market constitutes a legitimate aim also within the meaning of the Convention.[351] However, it is less clear whether the limitations placed on its scope by the ECJ case law could constitute a 'proportionate interference' with the right against self-incrimination in a manner which is compatible with the Convention.

Vesterdorf, speaking extrajudicially, suggested that the CFI statement in *Mannesmannrohren Werke* could be read as 'a signal to the effect that the [ECJ]'s interpretation of certain rights in competition proceedings did not have to coincide exactly' with the standards elaborated by the European Court of Human Rights in respect to criminal proceedings against individuals.[352]

In a similar vein, Wils argued that at least in cases where the investigated undertaking is a legal person, the *Orkem* case law would not be incompatible

---

347 Appl. No 8225/78, *Ashingdane v United Kingdom*, [1985] 7 EHRR 528, para. 57.

348 *Ibid.* See McBRIDE, 'Access to justice and Human Rights treaties', (1998) 17 *CJQ* (Jul) 235 at 239. See also, *mutatis mutandis*, Appl. Nos 15809/02 and 25624/02, *O' Halloran and Francis v United Kingdom*, judgment of 29 June 2002, not yet reported, para. 62.

349 Case T-112/98, *Mannesmannrohren Werke v Commission*, [2001] ECR II-729, para. 66.

350 *Id.*, para. 77.

351 See, *mutatis mutandis*, *inter alia*, Appl. No 11598/85, *Stenuit v France*, Commission Report, [1992] ECC 401, para. 53.

352 VESTERDORF, 'Legal professional privilege and the privilege against self incrimination in EC law', p. 713.

with the Convention.[353] Although neither the complexity of the antitrust investigations nor the non-judicial nature of the investigation constitute acceptable grounds for a restrictive reading of the privilege,[354] the exacting standards of protection for the right to remain silent established in *Saunders* concern the use in criminal proceedings of incriminating evidence against a natural person.[355] He thus proposed that the 'stricter case law of the European Court of Human Rights' would have to be applied only to cases involving 'an undertaking consisting of an unincorporated business', whereas the EC concept of privilege would continue to be relevant in cases concerning legal persons.[356]

It could be argued that the proposed solution is not totally inconsistent with the case law of the European Court of Human Rights which appears to evidence a 'more lenient' standard of review with respect to 'commercial matters' involving legal persons.[357] It will be recalled[358] that in its *Markt Intern Verlag GmbH* judgment,[359] concerning the right to freedom of expression in the commercial context, the European Court of Human Rights emphasised the need to leave to the national authorities a certain margin of appreciation in assessing a restriction of any of the freedoms enjoyed by the applicant under the Convention 'in particular, in an area as complex and fluctuating as that of unfair competition'.[360]

Accordingly, to remain consistent with its mandate the Strasbourg Court's review should be limited 'to the question whether the measures taken on the national level are justified in principle and proportionate'.[361] It was illustrated in Chapter 1 that the *Markt Intern* 'necessity test' differs from the criteria laid down in the *Handyside* decision,[362] according to which, for an interference to be 'necessary in a democratic society' for the purposes of the ECHR, the measure should correspond to a 'pressing social need' and 'be proportionate to the legitimate aim pursued' and should be narrowly interpreted.[363]

Consequently, it was suggested that the adoption of a more lenient standard

---

353 WILS, 'Self-incrimination in EC antitrust enforcement', at 577.

354 Case 43/1994/490/572, *Saunders v United Kingdom*, [1997] 23 EHRR 313, para. 75.

355 WILS, 'Self-incrimination in EC antitrust enforcement', at 577.

356 *Ibid.*

357 EMBERLAND, p. 164.

358 *Supra*, Chapter 1, section 6, footnote 118 and accompanying text.

359 Appl. No 10573/82, *Markt Intern Verlag GmbH and Klaus Beermann v Germany*, ser. A, No 165, [1990] 12 EHRR 161.

360 *Id.*, para. 34.

361 *Ibid.* See EMBERLAND, p. 164.

362 *Handyside v United Kingdom*, ser. A No 24, [1979–80] 1 EHRR 737.

363 *Id.*, para. 97.

of scrutiny[364] for assessing national measures interfering with rights protected by the ECHR in the business arena as opposed to other contexts could be justified in relation to the nature of commercial speech, which does not engage the values of democracy to the same degree as, for instance, 'political expression'[365] and, more generally, to the limited nature of 'economic rights'. It was argued that this less intensive degree of control could have been developed as a result of a 'spill-over'[366] from the approach adopted by the Strasbourg Court in the interpretation of the right of peaceful enjoyment of property, provided by Article 1, Protocol I to the ECHR[367] and by the Court's general view of choices of economic policies as closely linked to the needs of individual states and, accordingly, as better regulated through domestic democratic processes.[368]

On the basis of the above analysis it could be argued that the more restrictive view of the privilege against self-incrimination in the context of competition enforcement and as against legal persons could be regarded as a legitimate interference with the right not to incriminate oneself for the purpose of promoting, through the action of competition agencies such as the Commission, the economic well-being of the Community,[369] and therefore may be reconciled with the Convention.

However, it could be doubted that the application of a more lenient standard of privilege to legal as opposed to natural persons may be consistent with the current case law.[320] Commentators argued that the ECJ, by requiring, firstly, proof of coercion being exercised on the investigated undertaking on the part of the Commission and, secondly, the existence of an 'actual interference' of the undertaking's right to 'fair legal process' in competition proceedings, namely the use of the evidence so acquired to sustain the allegations of anti-competitive conduct in the final decision, seems to prefer an interpretation of the privilege which is increasingly consistent with the Strasbourg Court's judgment in *Saunders*.[371]

---

364 EMBERLAND, p. 166.

365 *Id.*, pp. 186–87.

366 EMBERLAND, pp. 192–93.

367 See e.g. Appl. No 7151/75 and 7152/75, *Sporrong & Lonnroth v Sweden*, Ser. A No 52, [1983] 5 EHRR 35, para. 61.

368 EMBERLAND, pp. 192–93.

369 *Ibid.* See also WILS, 'Self-incrimination in EC antitrust enforcement', at 577.

370 Case C-238/99, *LVM NV and others v Commission*, [2002] ECR I-8375, para. 275; Case C-301/04 P, *Commission v SGL Carbon AG*, judgment of 29 June 2006, not yet reported, available at [2006] 5 CMLR 15, para. 40, 43.

371 VESTERDORF, 'Legal professional privilege and the privilege against self-incrimination in EC law', at 715–16. See case 43/1994/490/572, *Saunders v United Kingdom*, [1997] 23 EHRR 313, paras. 61–62, 71.

Accordingly, it could be argued that, rather than upholding differing standards applicable, respectively, to individuals and to corporate entitites, the ECJ may be developing a unitary test to determine the reach of the privilege, in a manner which seeks to reconcile the need to protect the concerned parties from improper coercion on the part of the investigating officers with the effectiveness of the Commission's functions.[372] Although this argument may sound convincing, it cannot be denied that the substantive limitations to the scope of the privilege as protecting the investigated undertaking from the compulsion to answer 'leading questions' and not 'purely factual' ones constitutes the principal difference between the position of the Luxembourg courts and the concept of privilege against self-incrimination recognised by the European Court of Human Rights.[373]

Finally, it is not excluded that the differences between the approaches to the privilege adopted by EC law and the ECHR may give rise to considerable questions with respect to the decentralised enforcement of Articles 81 and 82 EC Treaty. The impact of the application of the obligations of cooperation imposed on the NCAs and on the Commission by Articles 11 and 12 of Council Regulation 1/2003 on the protection of the rights of defence, and in that context of the right against self-incrimination will be discussed in detail in later chapters. At this stage, however, it is necessary to note that in the *Otto v Postbank* preliminary ruling,[374] the ECJ held that the *Orkem* concept of privilege against self-incrimination is not applicable to judicial proceedings before the national courts involving the application of Articles 81 and 82 EC Treaty.[375]

The Court drew a clear distinction between the procedural guarantees enjoyed by litigants during domestic civil proceedings and the rights of defence conferred on them in the administrative procedures before the European Commission.[376] Whereas the former concern the determination of 'private relations between individuals and cannot lead to the imposition of a penalty by a public authority', the latter allow the Commission to gather the necessary evidence with a view to a finding of an infringement of EC competition law and the imposition of serious financial sanctions.[377]

The ECJ also pointed out that, unlike in civil proceedings, where the procedural rights are a matter for national law, the parties investigated by the Commission are under a duty to cooperate actively with the Commission in

---

372 VESTERDORF, *supra*, footnote 371, at pp. 717–18.
373 See also KERSE and KHAN, *EC Antitrust Procedure*, pp. 141–43.
374 Case C-60/92, *Otto v Postbank*, [1993] ECR I-5683.
375 *Id.*, para. 16, 19.
376 *Id.*, para. 15.
377 *Id.*, para. 17.

the fact-finding stage of the case. It followed that in this context the right to avoid answering questions that may involve an admission of responsibility for a competition violation constitutes an essential component of the rights of defence aimed at protecting the individual from 'coercive' investigation measures.[378]

On account of the significant differences between the two sets of proceedings and of the resulting different procedural guarantees assisting them, the ECJ concluded that the right not to incriminate oneself crafted by the *Orkem* judgment could not be transposed to civil proceedings before domestic courts.[379] Nonetheless, the Court acknowledged that information obtained in the course of national court proceedings may become known to the Commission. In that case, it excluded, however, that evidence so obtained could be deployed by the Commission against the concerned parties, for that would be in contravention with the rules enshrined in *Orkem* which remain fully applicable to the Commission's enforcement action.[380]

The *Otto v Postbank* judgment could be interpreted as demonstrating that since the *Orkem* concept of privilege against self-incrimination cannot apply to national court proceedings relating to the application of Articles 81 and 82 EC Treaty, there may be a 'barrier' to the possibility for the Commission to deploy against the investigated parties evidence obtained from domestic jurisdictions and especially from domestic courts.[381]

However, it may be argued that this conclusion may be inconsistent with the principle of 'equivalent protection' of the rights of the defence enshrined in Council Regulation No 1/2003, on which the obligations of cooperation between the Commission and the national enforcement agencies are based.[382] Kerse and Khan suggested that the enactment of the Modernisation Regulation may justify a revision of *Otto v Postbank* to ensure that the principles of EC law protecting the rights of defence of the investigated undertakings receive full and uniform application in all proceedings concerning the application of the Treaty antitrust rules.[383]

It is submitted that, although the concerns for the uniform and effective application of Articles 81 and 82 EC Treaty not only in administrative but also in judicial proceedings cannot be underplayed, the need to uphold the principle of national procedural autonomy in an area as sensitive as that of due

---

378 *Id.*, para. 16.

379 *Id.*, para. 17.

380 *Id.*, para. 20. For commentary, see KERSE and KHAN, *EC Antitrust Procedure*, pp. 269–70, especially fn. 38.

381 KERSE and KHAN, *EC Antitrust Procedure*, p. 271.

382 Recital 16, Preamble to Council Regulation No 1/2203.

383 KERSE and KHAN, *EC Antitrust Procedure*, p. 271.

process of law before domestic courts may still constitute a sound basis for the application of domestic procedural guarantees in the interest of the courts' independence and of the protection of the parties' right to a fair trial in the determination of private rights and obligations.[384]

It may be concluded that more recent case law of the ECJ and the CFI may be interpreted as a signal towards the convergence of the scope of the privilege against self-incrimination recognised in EC law with that enshrined in Article 6 ECHR and interpreted in the light of the *Saunders* judgment.

However, it would appear that the limits placed by the Luxembourg courts on the nature of the information which may or may not benefit from the cover of the privilege cannot be reconciled with the position adopted by the European Court of Human Rights[385] and consequently raise relevant questions with respect to the compliance of the notion of the rights of defence enjoyed by the undertakings concerned by competition proceedings before the Commission with that of 'fair procedure' enshrined in Article 6(1) ECHR.[386]

The implications of the continuing adoption of different requirements for the application of the right not to incriminate oneself in the EC and, in national jurisdictions, in the context of the 'modernised' framework for the application of Articles 81 and 82 EC Treaty will be illustrated in detail in later chapters. However, the examination of the *Otto v Postbank* preliminary ruling has already demonstrated some of the difficulties that could potentially arise from the absence of a 'common solution' as regards the scope of the privilege in the context of the decentralised enforcement of Articles 81 and 82 EC Treaty.[387]

6. LAWYER–CLIENT CONFIDENTIALITY AND PRIVILEGE AGAINST SELF-INCRIMINATION IN EC LAW AND IN THE ECHR: TENTATIVE CONCLUSIONS

The previous sections demonstrated the importance of the protection of lawyer–client confidentiality and of the right not to incriminate oneself for the purpose of safeguarding the rights of the defence of the undertakings being investigated by the Commission for suspected violation of the competition rules. However, the comparative analysis of the Community law standards in

---

[384] *Inter alia*, HOGAN, 'The use of compelled evidence in European competition law cases', in HAWK (ed.), *International Antitrust Law and Policy*, pp. 663–64.

[385] VESTERDORF, 'Legal professional privilege and the privilege against self-incrimination in EC law', p. 713.

[386] HOGAN, 'The use of compelled evidence in European competition law cases', pp. 672–73.

[387] *Id.*, pp. 663–64.

the light of the principles enshrined in the European Convention on Human Rights as regards the right to a 'fair procedure' illustrated that, despite being recognised as general principles of EC law, the notions of legal professional privilege and the privilege against self-incrimination enshrined in the case law of the ECJ are not entirely consistent with the degree of protection afforded by Article 6(1) ECHR.

With respect to the protection of lawyer–client confidentiality, sections 2 and 3 illustrated that despite providing at an interim stage a golden opportunity for the reformulation of the EU notion of LPP, the *AKZO Nobel* judgment resulted in a setback for the proponents of a more generous concept of privilege. However, the circumstance that the CFI has indicated the continuous judicial control of the Commission's decisions concerning privilege claims as an indispensable guarantee for the protection of the rights of defence is extremely telling. Not only does it constitute an additional check over the Commission officers' discretion in the course of the preliminary investigation, but it could also pave the way for future litigation and eventually lead to the further reconsideration of this issue.

The analysis conducted in section 4 illustrated the degree of uncertainty still existing as regards the rationale and scope of application of the privilege against self-incrimination.[388] The analysis of more recent case law of the European Court of Human Rights indicated that the interpretation of the privilege as concerned with the protection of the personal autonomy of the accused adopted in *Saunders* does not seem to have been entirely accepted in later judgments and therefore does not shed enough light on its exact scope and manner of application.[389]

A degree of uncertainty appears also to characterise the case law of the ECJ: whereas the decisions adopted in the *Re: PVC II* appeal and the *SGL Carbon* cases can be taken as supporting an approach to the assessment of claims of infringement of the privilege which is not too dissimilar from that applied by the Strasbourg Court, the Court has been adamant in upholding the limits on the scope of the privilege imposed by the *Orkem* and *Mannesmannrohren-Werke* decisions.[390]

Although the arguments deployed by the supporters of the current EC concept to justify a less generous attitude to the interpretation of the privilege

---

388 WARD and GARDNER, 'The privilege against self-incrimination: in search of legal certainty', at 394.

389 *Ibid.* See Appl. No 31827/97, *JB v Switzerland*, judgment of 8 March 2001, reported in 3 ITL Report 663, para. 62.

390 VESTERDORF, 'Legal professional privilege and the privilege against self incrimination in EC law', p. 713.

are not totally devoid of merit,[391] it is submitted that if the rights of the defence enjoyed by the investigated parties are to be effectively upheld, the focus of the assessment of the scope of the privilege should not perhaps lie on the nature of the information concerned – i.e. whether it is 'purely factual' or 'directly incriminating' – but on the nature of the proceedings.[392] It is argued that if EC competition proceedings are to be considered 'criminal' in nature for the purposes of the Convention,[393] it would then become necessary to reopen the discussion as to the extent to which the protection against 'coercive' methods of questioning currently afforded by ECJ case law is sufficient to ensure the overall fairness of the procedure in the light of ECHR standards.[394]

It is concluded that although the effectiveness of the enforcement of Articles 81 and 82 EC Treaty should remain paramount to the interpretation of the rules governing the investigative powers exercised by the Commission, it is also imperative to ensure that, even in the preliminary stages of the investigation the rights of the defence of the concerned parties are not irremediably impaired. Accordingly, whether, as a result of the enactment of the Modernisation Regulation, with its emphasis on decentralisation and on stringent fact-finding powers for the Commission, the ECJ should provide 'novel limitations that were not necessary under Regulation 17' to the Commission powers,[395] remains an open question.

---

391 WILS, 'Self-incrimination in EC antitrust enforcement', p. 577; also EMBERLAND, pp. 192–93.

392 HOGAN, 'The use of compelled evidence in European competition law cases', pp. 672–73.

393 *Supra*, Chapter 1, Part 2, sect. 7.

394 *Ibid.*

395 VESTERDORF, 'Legal professional privilege and the privilege against self-incrimination in EC law', p. 730.

5. Judicial review of competition decisions: a guarantee of fairness in EC competition enforcement?

INTRODUCTION

The previous chapters illustrated that the concept of 'administrative fairness' enshrined in Article 6(1) of the European Convention on Human Rights encompasses administrative as well as judicial elements. The 'composite approach' adopted by the European Court of Human Rights[1] requires not only that adequate safeguards be in place in proceedings before the administrative authority but also that the final decision be subject to the scrutiny of a properly constituted court which is both independent and impartial.[2]

The CFI stated in *Siderurgica Aristrain*[3] that 'the fact that the Commission combines the functions of prosecutor and judge (. . .) [would not be] contrary to the procedural safeguards provided for by Community law'[4] on the ground that the general principles of EC law ensured that any decision of the Commission finding and sanctioning an infringement of competition law would be subject to effective judicial review on the part of the Community courts.[5] Accordingly, since the Treaty confers on the Community courts the power to scrutinise carefully and exhaustively the impugned decisions, especially 'with respect to the accuracy and relevance of the facts established by the Commission',[6] the system for the enforcement of the competition rules contained in the Treaty was considered compatible

---

1 *Inter alia*, Appl. No 19178/91, *Bryan v United Kingdom*, [1996] 21 EHRR 342 at para. 44.

2 HOUSE of LORDS SELECT COMMITTEE on the EUROPEAN UNION, *XIX Report*, para. 55.

3 Case T-156/94, *Siderurgica Aristrain Madrid SL v Commission*, [1999] ECR II-645.

4 *Id.*, para. 102.

5 *Id.*, para. 105.

6 *Id.*, para. 115. For commentary, *inter alia*, WILS, *Principles of European Antitrust Enforcement* (2005) Oxford, Portland, OR, Hart Publishing, pp. 157–58.

with the 'due process' standards enshrined in the general principles of EC law and in Article 6(1) ECHR.[7]

However, it should be borne in mind that in several judgments the Strasbourg organs held that national antitrust proceedings, despite being classified as 'administrative' in the respective domestic laws, were in fact 'criminal' in nature.[8] Consequently, it was argued in earlier sections that in consideration of their characteristics, this conclusion could also be extended to the antitrust proceedings before the European Commission.[9]

As regards merger proceedings, instead, it was suggested that given their function and features, they could be considered to be concerned with the 'determination of civil rights and obligations'.[10] Therefore, it may be suggested that the adherence to the 'composite approach' emerging from *Aristrain*[11] requires that the right to seek the judicial scrutiny of competition decisions be practically and effectively available to the undertakings affected by the decision, and that the extent of the powers of control exercised by the Community courts conforms to the criteria of 'full jurisdiction' in matters of both fact and law.[12]

This chapter examines the standing requirements which applicants must satisfy to challenge antitrust and merger decisions and the scope of the powers of judicial scrutiny exercised by the Luxembourg courts. Thereafter, it will consider the standards governing the access to a court and the judicial scrutiny of administrative decisions having a 'civil' or 'criminal' character in accordance with Article 6(1) ECHR with a view to assessing the compatibility of the EC requirements with the principles enshrined in the Convention.

---

[7] HOUSE of LORDS SELECT COMMITTEE on the EUROPEAN UNION, *XIX Report: Strengthening the Role of the Hearing Officer*, sess. 1999/2000, published on 24 February 2000, para. 56. *Inter alia*, LENAERTS & VANHAMME, 'Procedural rights of private parties in the Community administrative process', (1997) 34 *CMLRev* 531 at 561.

[8] *Inter alia*, Appl. No 11598/85, *Société Stenuit v France*, [1992] ECC 410.

[9] *Supra*, Chapter I, Part 2, section 4.

[10] Cf., *inter alia,* series A No 13, *Ringeisen v Austria*, [1979–80] 1 EHRR 455 at para. 94, with respect to proceedings in the field of environmental planning and development.

[11] Case T-156/94, *Siderurgica Aristrain Madrid SL v Commission*, [1999] ECR II-645 at para. 105.

[12] Appl. Nos 7299/75 and 7496/76, *Albert & LeCompte v Belgium*, [1983] 5 EHRR 533 at para. 29. *Mutatis mutandis*, Per AG Vesterdorf, case T-7/89, *SA Hercules Chemicals NV v Commission (Re: the Polypropylene Cartel)*, [1991] ECR II-867 per AG Vesterdorf, para. 3, footnote 11.

1. JUDICIAL REVIEW OF COMPETITION DECISIONS IN EC LAW: ACCESS TO THE LUXEMBOURG COURTS AND SCOPE FOR JUDICIAL SCRUTINY

1.1. Challenging Antitrust Decisions: the General Test and its Drawbacks and the Solution Adopted in *Metro (I)*

The 'right to obtain an effective remedy in a competent court'[13] was recognised by the ECJ as 'a general principle of law which underlies the constitutional traditions common to the Member States'[14] and is also enshrined in Articles 6 and 13 of the European Convention of Human Rights.[15] As regards the conditions of standing governing direct actions against antitrust and merger decisions, it is clear from the case law that 'the fact that the contested decision was addressed to the applicant suffices to confer on it an interest in bringing proceedings and in having the legality of that decision examined by the Community judicature'.[16]

Different issues may arise for third parties whose involvement constitutes an important feature, and sometimes an indispensable factor, to ensure effective enforcement.[17] The fact that they are not the immediate addressees of the impugned decision exposes them to the risk that their action may be declared inadmissible due to the restrictive standing conditions laid down by the ECJ.[18]

The notion of 'direct concern' does not present particular problems:[19] a measure will be of direct concern to the applicant when it 'directly affects the legal position of the parties concerned'[20] by 'leav[ing] no discretion to the addressees of that measure who are entrusted with the task of implementing it,

---

13 Case 222/84, *Johnston v Chief Constable of the Royal Ulster Constabulary*, [1986] ECR 1651 at para. 19.

14 *Id.*, para. 18.

15 *Ibid.*

16 Case T-22/97, *Kesko Oy v EC Commission*, [1999] ECR II-3775 at para. 57. See also, *inter alia*, joined Cases T-374, 375, 384, 388/94, *European Night Services and Others v Commission*, [1998] ECR II-3141 at para. 61.

17 *Inter alia*, ALBORS-LLORENS, *Private Parties in European Community Law, Challenging Community Measures* (1996) Oxford: Clarendon Press, p. 79.

18 Case 25/62, *Plaumann v Commission*, [1963] ECR 95; Case 50/00 P, *Union de los Pequenos Agricultores v Council*, [2002] ECR I-6677.

19 ALBORS-LLORENS, *Private Parties in European Community Law, Challenging Community Measures* (1996) Oxford: Clarendon Press, p. 70.

20 Joined Cases 41-44/70, *NV International Fruit Company and Others v Commission*, [1971] ECR 411, para. 28.

such implementation being purely automatic and resulting from Community rules without the application of other intermediate rules'.[21]

By contrast, satisfying the requirement of individual concern laid down in *Plaumann v Commission*[22] is regarded as presenting 'an incontestable barrier to private actions'.[23] The ECJ held:

> Persons other than those to whom a decision is addressed may only claim to be individually concerned if that decision affects them by reason of certain attributes which are peculiar to them or by reason of circumstances in which they are differentiated from all other persons and by virtue of these factors distinguishes them individually just as in the case of the person addressed.[24]

Regrettably, despite leaning towards the adoption of a more lenient approach in later cases,[25] in *Union de los Pequenos Agricultores v Council*[26] the ECJ rejected the call for a reformulation of the notion of individual concern made by the Advocate General[27] and held instead that different standing conditions could be introduced only through an amendment to Article 230(4) of the EC Treaty.[28]

Nonetheless, it could be argued that the standing requirements in question may be ill-suited to the effective enforcement of competition law, which is aimed at the protection of the public interest as well as of the interests of competitors and ultimately of the consumers and therefore relies significantly on the involvement of third parties.[29] The ECJ was mindful of the features of competition enforcement when it adopted more relaxed standing conditions to

---

21 Case C-386/98 P, *Société Louis Dreyfus & Cie v Commission*, [1998] ECR I-2308.

22 Case 25/62, [1963] ECR 95.

23 CRAIG, 'Legality, standing and substantive review in Community law', (1994) 14 *OJLS* 507 at 509. See also GINTER, 'Access to Justice in the European Court of Justice in Luxembourg', (2002) 4 *Eur. Journal of Law Reform* 381 at 392.

24 Case 25/62, *Plaumann v Commission*, [1963] ECR 95, subpara. VIII (p. 107).

25 Case C-309/89, *Codorniu v Council*, [1994] ECR I-1853, paras. 19–22.

26 Case C-50/00 P, *Union de los Pequenos Agricultores v Council*, [2002] ECR I-6677.

27 *Ibid.*, per AG Jacobs at para. 59.

28 *Id.*, paras. 36–37, 44–45 of the judgment. See Draft Constitutional Treaty, IGC 1/07, Brussels, 23 July 2007, point 218: 'Article 230 shall be amended as follows: (. . .) (c) the fourth paragraph shall be replaced by the following: "Any natural or legal persons may (. . .) institute proceedings against an act addressed to that person or which is of direct and individual concern to him or her, and against a regulatory act which is of direct concern to him or her and does not entail implementing measures."'

29 ALBORS-LLORENS, *Private Parties in European Community Law, Challenging Community Measures*, p. 79.

allow third party applicants and especially complainants to challenge competition decisions.[30]

In his opinion in the *Metro I* case[31] Advocate General Reischl had suggested that individual concern should be established by reference to the peculiar circumstances of the case and especially to the role played by the applicant in the enforcement proceedings. He emphasised the circumstance that Metro had lodged a complaint and had taken an active part in the proceedings.[32] However, the ECJ took the different view that complainants should be allowed 'to institute proceedings in order to protect their legitimate interest'[33] and to satisfy the needs 'of a satisfactory administration of justice and of the proper application of Articles 85 and 86 [now 81 and 82]' of the EC Treaty.[34]

The late judge Federico Mancini argued that 'the formula employed in *Metro* introduces an exception of a special nature, which is justified by the overriding interest of verifying in court proceedings whether the competition rules have been properly applied'.[35] However, many commentators suggested that, rather than emphasising the active role played by the complainants,[36] the Courts should have allowed standing to applicants who could establish that 'the Commission's action would prejudice (. . .) their legal position (. . .) that is directly protected by Community antitrust rules'.[37] The circumstance that the applicant had lodged a complaint would be only one of the factors to be taken into account to ascertain that prejudice.[38]

Although the 'narrow' interpretation of individual concern in *Metro* initially prevailed,[39] later judgments indicated the adoption of a more flexible view of the standing conditions. In *Metropole*[40] the Court of First Instance held:

---

30 Case 26/76, *Metro SB-Grossmarkte GmbH & Co KG v Commission*, [1977] ECR 1875, per AG Reischl, p. 1923.

31 Case 26/76, *Metro SB-Grossmarkte GmbH & Co KG v Commission*, [1977] ECR 1875.

32 *Ibid.*

33 *Id.*, para. 13 of the judgment.

34 *Ibid.*

35 MANCINI, 'Access to Justice: individual undertakings and EEC Antitrust law – problems and pitfalls', (1988–89) 12 *Fordham Int'l LJ* 189 at 203.

36 DINNAGE, 'Locus standi and article 173 EEC: the effect of *Metro SB Grossmarkte v Commission*', (1979) 4 *ELRev* 15 at 33.

37 *Ibid.*

38 *Ibid.*

39 *Inter alia*, Case 210/81, *Demo-Studio Schmidt v Commission*, [1983] ECR 3045, paras. 5, 8 and 16; more recently, Case C-70/97 P, *Kruidvat BVBA v Commission*, [1998] ECR I-7183, paras. 19, 21, 23 and 46.

40 Joined Cases T-528/93, T-542 and 543/93, T-546/93, *Metropole Television SA and Others v Commission*, [1996] ECR II-649.

> the truly relevant question is not whether or not a party participated in the administrative procedure for the adoption of a decision, but to what extent such participation helps to put third parties which were not addressees of the Decision in what the judgment in *Plaumann* describes as 'circumstances in which they are differentiated from all other persons and [the decision] by virtue of these factors distinguishes them individually just as in the case of the person addressed'.[41]

In declaring the application admissible, the Court relied on the fact that the applicant had unsuccessfully applied to join the associations of undertakings in question before the decision had been adopted[42] and was in direct competition with their existing members.[43] It is submitted that *Metropole* constitutes a positive development in the assessment of the standing conditions. The Court moved from a purely 'mechanical' appraisal of the position of the applicant, based almost entirely on its participation in the proceedings, to a more flexible assessment of its overall position in the relevant market which appears far more suitable to reflect the importance of third parties in competition enforcement.

The fact that the applicant had taken an active part in the proceedings no longer seems to be an essential condition to establish standing. Equally relevant are other factors, namely the position of the applicant on the market vis-à-vis that of the addressees of the impugned decisions,[44] whether or not, in cases concerning selective distribution agreements, the applicant had been refused access to the system[45] and the fact that the applicant had already initiated damages proceedings before the competent national court.[46] It could be argued that the increased degree of flexibility in assessing *locus standi* could increase the complexity of the existing test, thus undermining their clarity and coherence.[47] However, it is submitted that any drawback of the more flexible attitude as regards standing is likely to be compensated by the benefits of the new approach.

1.2. Challenging Merger Decisions

With respect to the challenge of merger decisions by third parties, the position

---

41 *Id.*, para. 57.

42 *Id.*, para. 58.

43 *Id.*, para. 61.

44 *Ibid.*

45 *Inter alia,* case 210/81, *Demo-Studio Schmidt v Commission*, [1983] ECR 3045.

46 Case T-231/99, *Joynson v EC Commission*, [2002] ECR II-2085. Case T-131/99, *Shaw and Falla v EC Commission*, [2002] ECR II-2023.

47 WARD, '*Locus standi* under Article 230(4) of the EC Treaty: crafting a coherent test for a "wobbly polity"', (2003) 22 *YEL* 45.

of the Court as regards standing requirements appears similar to that expressed in recent judgments in the area of antitrust law. Applicants will enjoy *locus standi* if they can establish that they have been involved in the procedure leading to the adoption of the measure and that the latter affects their economic position on the market to a significant degree, for example, by imposing on them obligations in order to allow the concentration to go ahead.

In the early *Air France (Re: Dan Air)*[48] judgment, the applicant was granted standing to challenge the statement made by a Commission official to the effect that the Merger Task Force would not commence a Phase II investigation concerning the proposed concentration between British Airways and Dan Air. The Court held that 'since the contested statement enabled . . . the proposed operation to be put into effect immediately, it was such as to bring about an immediate change in the situation in the market or markets concerned, depending solely on the wishes of the parties'[49] and was therefore of direct concern to the applicant as a direct competitor of the merging parties.

With respect to individual concern, central to the Court's assessment were the impact of the concentration on the economic position of Air France, which was the main competitor to BA on these routes,[50] and the circumstance that by declaring that the concentration in question did not satisfy the 'Community dimension' thresholds, the applicant had been deprived of its procedural rights which it would have enjoyed as an 'interested party'.[51]

In the other *Air France (re: TAT)*[52] decision, the CFI added that the applicant was individually concerned by the impugned decision in consideration of its close involvement in the proceedings at issue. Air France had 'informed the Commission by letters . . . of its critical observations, supported by figures and statistical data, regarding the concentration at issue'[53] and the Commission had taken its observations into significant account while examining the compatibility of the transaction with the rules of competition.[54] Most importantly, Air France had undertaken 'to give up the whole of its interest in TAT'[55] before the concentration was actually notified.

Similarly, in *Re: Kali und Salz*[56] the ECJ, following the advice of the

---

48 Case T-3/93, *Air France v Commission*, [1994] ECR II-121.

49 *Id.*, para. 80. For commentary, BROWN, 'Judicial review of Commission decisions under the Merger Regulation: the first cases', (1994) 15 *ECLR* 296 at 299.

50 See para. 82 of the judgment. Also, BROWN, *ibid.*, at 299.

51 Para. 81 of the judgment.

52 Case T-2/93, [1994] ECR II-323.

53 *Id.*, para. 44.

54 *Id.*, para. 45.

55 *Id.*, para. 46.

56 Joined cases C-68/94 and C-30/95, *France and Others v Commission*, [1998] ECR I-1375.

Advocate General,[57] held that the decision individually and directly concerned the applicants since they had taken an active part in the proceedings leading to the adoption of the impugned decision and their position on the market had been specifically taken into account by the Commission, especially for the purpose of devising the conditions attached to the clearance of the notified merger.[58]

However, establishing standing has proved difficult in actions brought by minority shareholders. In *Zunis Holding*[59] the action was declared inadmissible on the ground that the impugned decision was 'not of such nature as by itself to affect the substance or extent of the rights or the ability to participate in the company management conferred on them by such rights'.[60] In addition, the Court, being aware of the significantly tight time-constraints to which the notifying undertakings were subject, decided that the 'request of the reopening of the proceedings on the ground of the discovery of an allegedly new fact' could not be allowed since it had not been submitted 'within a reasonable period'.[61]

Commentators argued that to establish individual concern, minority shareholders would be obliged to 'prove two things. First (. . .) that the Commission decision has some material effect on the substance or effect of the proprietary or voting rights attaching to its minority shareholding'.[62] And second, that the shareholder can 'exhibit special attributes peculiar to itself, which distinguish that shareholder from all the other minority shareholders, so that it is individually concerned'.[63]

It is suggested that the main problem in that judgment may have been lack of direct concern: the Court did not expressly rule out the possibility that a minority shareholder whose procedural role was analogous to that played by the applicant in *Metro* could bring an action for the annulment of the final decision on the merger. Rather, it questioned the ability of that decision to immediately affect the legal position of the applicant. Nonetheless, it would appear that, if the applicant held a minority share to which 'special rights' were attached (for instance, the right to veto strategic decisions or to appoint senior members of the management organs of the firm), standing to challenge the decision should be granted.[64]

---

57 Per AG Tesauro, paras. 59–60.

58 *Id.*, paras. 54–55 of the Advocate General's Opinion.

59 T-83/92, *Zunis Holding v Commission*, [1993] ECR II-1169.

60 *Id.*, para. 35.

61 *Id.*, para. 38.

62 BROWN, 'Judicial review of Commission decisions under the Merger Regulation: the first cases', (1994) 15 *ECLR* 296 at 298.

63 *Ibid.*

64 Joined Cases C-68/94 and C-30/95, *France v Commission (re: Kali und Salz)*, [1998] ECR I-1375, per AG Tesauro, para. 35.

However, the attitude of the Court appears to be changing. The *Royal Philips NV* judgment[65] indicates that the CFI adopts an increasingly flexible attitude in assessing direct concern which focuses on the purpose of the impugned decision and on its impact on the rights granted to the applicant by the Merger Regulation and the Treaty.[66] In that case, a referral decision adopted under Article 9 of the Merger Control Regulation was held to be of direct concern to the applicant since it had resulted in depriving the applicant 'of the opportunity to have the Commission review the lawfulness of the concentration'[67] and 'of the procedural rights'[68] conferred on third parties under the Regulation as well as of 'the judicial protection which they enjoy under the Treaty'.[69]

Royal Philips can be interpreted as supporting the view that the trends governing the standing of third parties in the area of merger control may be in the process of converging with those underlying *locus standi* vis-à-vis the Commission's antitrust decisions.[70] This trend seems to have been confirmed by more recent case law of the CFI. In *BaByliss*[71] the CFI held that the third-party applicant was entitled to challenge an approval decision subject to commitments on the ground that the measure '[brought] about an immediate change in the situation [of] the markets concerned'.[72]

With respect to individual concerns, the Court held that participation in administrative proceedings, despite not being sufficient on its own, was one of the factors 'regularly taken into account (. . .) to establish in conjunction with other specific circumstances the admissibility of the action'.[73] Among those 'other specific circumstances' the CFI emphasised the position of the applicant on the relevant market as an actual or potential competitor[74] and the impact of the applicant's participation on the outcome of the proceedings and on the final decision.[75]

The issue of *locus standi* remains controversial for the recognised representatives of the employees of the merging undertakings, who are granted special consultation rights under Article 18(4) of the Regulation. In the

---

65 Case T-119/02, *Royal Philips Electronics NV v Commission*, [2003] ECR II-1433.

66 *Id.*, para. 276.

67 *Id.*, para. 282.

68 *Id.*, para. 284.

69 *Id.*, para. 285.

70 *Id.*, at paras. 276, 280, 282 and 284.

71 Case T-114/02, *BaByliss SA v Commission*, [2003] ECR II-1279.

72 *Id.*, para. 89.

73 *Id.*, para. 95.

74 *Id.*, para. 96.

75 Case T-158/00, *ARD v Commission*, [2003] ECR II-3825, para. 72, 76.

Grandes Sources[76] judgment, the CFI took the view that the applicants were individually concerned by the impugned decision on the basis of the 'express mention . . . among the third parties showing a sufficient interest to be heard by the Commission',[77] and 'without it being necessary to establish . . . whether the concentration is at least prima facie liable to affect adversely the social objectives referred to in the Treaty'.[78]

The application, however, fell partially for lack of direct concern. It was stated that 'even supposing that the concentration brings about a reduction in the resources of the various applicant councils following job losses as alleged, that circumstance cannot in any event be regarded as adversely affecting those councils' own rights'.[79] The CFI concluded:

> only a decision which may have an effect on the status of the employees' representative organisations or on the exercise of the prerogatives and duties given them by the legislation in force can affect such organisations' own interests. That cannot be the case with a decision authorising a concentration.[80]

However, the applicant associations were granted limited standing on the basis of the principle that, 'where a regulation gives procedural rights to third persons, they must have a remedy available for the protection of their legitimate interests'.[81] They were therefore allowed 'to bring proceedings against that decision for the specific purpose of examining whether the procedural guarantees which they are entitled to assert, during the administrative procedure . . . have been infringed'.[82]

This solution was criticised as being 'wholly inappropriate'[83] and inconsistent with the existing case law concerning the standing requirements of third

---

[76] Case T-96/92, *Comité Central d'Enterprise de la Société Generale des Grandes Sources and Others v Commission*, [1995] ECR II-1213.

[77] *Id.*, para. 31.

[78] *Ibid.* See ARNULL, case comment to T-96/92, *Comité Central d'Enterprise de la Société Generale des Grandes Sources and others v Commission*, Judgment of 27 April 1995 ; Case T-12/93, *Comité Central d'Enterprise de la Société Anonime Vittel and Others v Commission*, Judgment of 27 April 1995, (1996) 33 *CMLRev* 319 at 324.

[79] Case T-96/92, *Comité Central d'Enterprise de la Société Generale des Grandes Sources and Others v Commission*, [1995] ECR II-1213 at para. 38.

[80] *Ibid.*

[81] *Ibid.*

[82] *Id.*, para. 46.

[83] ARNULL, case comment to T-96/92, *Comité Central d'Enterprise de la Société Generale des Grandes Sources and Others v Commission*, Judgment of 27 April 1995; Case T-12/93, *Comité Central d'Enterprise de la Société Anonime Vittel and Others v Commission*, Judgment of 27 April 1995, (1996) 33 *CMLRev* 319 at 332.

parties in the field of merger control.[84] Despite the similarity to the *Chernobyl*[85] decision, where the ECJ had 'held that the Parliament had standing to challenge acts of the Council and the Commission under Article 173 where the purpose of the proceedings was to protect the Parliament's prerogatives',[86] the *Grandes Sources* decision was viewed as detrimental to the effective judicial protection of the representatives of the workforce and of their involvement in the proceedings.[87]

1.3. The Scope of Judicial Control of Antitrust Decisions: the Unlimited Jurisdiction under Article 229 of the EC Treaty

Having regard to the scope of judicial control exercised by the ECJ on competition decisions, the 'composite approach' advocated by the European Court of Human Rights and endorsed in *Aristrain* demands that the court competent for reviewing administrative measures aimed at, in the case of competition infringements, the determination of a criminal charge enjoy 'full jurisdiction'. A court must therefore be 'able not only to control fully the objective legality of an act but at least to *review fully the facts* upon which a decision is based'.[88]

Article 229 of the EC Treaty allows the Council to enact regulations conferring on the ECJ 'unlimited jurisdiction with regard to penalties provided for in such regulations'. On that basis, Article 31 of Regulation No 1/2003 endows the ECJ with unlimited jurisdiction over 'decisions whereby the Commission has fixed a fine or a periodic penalty payment' and consequently with the power to 'cancel, reduce or increase' their amount.

Despite the potentially sweeping scope of this jurisdiction, the Community courts have appeared rather reluctant to second-guess the Commission. In the *LR AF* judgment[89] the CFI recognised that the Commission enjoyed wide

---

84 WARD, '*Locus standi* under Article 230(4) of the EC Treaty'.

85 Case C-70/88, *European Parliament v Council*, [1991] ECR I-4529.

86 ARNULL, case comment to T-96/92, *Comité Central d'Enterprise de la Société Generale des Grandes Sources and Others v Commission*, Judgment of 27 April 1995 ; Case T-12/93, *Comité Central d'Enterprise de la Société Anonime Vittel and Others v Commission*, Judgment of 27 April 1995, (1996) 33 *CMLRev* 319 at 332.

87 HOUSE of LORDS SELECT COMMITTEE on the EUROPEAN UNION, *XXXII Report: the review of the EC Merger Regulation*, Session 2001/2002, 30/7/2002 at para. 226.

88 WAELBROECK and FOSSELARD, 'Should the decision-making power in EC Antitrust procedures be left to an independent judge? – the impact of the European Convention of Human Rights on EC antitrust procedures', (1994) 14 *YEL* 111 at 132 (emphasis in the text).

89 Case T-23/99, *LR AF 1998 A/S v Commission*, [2002] ECR II-1705.

discretion in setting the financial penalties for antitrust violations[90] for the purpose of furthering the implementation of the Community's competition policy.[91] Consequently, the Court held that, so long as the fine did not go beyond the limits set by the Implementing Regulation, the Court would not be prepared to alter its amount.[92]

In the later *Cheil Jedang* case[93] the CFI added that, although the Fining Guidelines[94] adopted in 1998 laid down limitations on its discretion,[95] the Commission was nonetheless entitled to apply the relevant criteria in the light of the circumstances of each case.[96] Accordingly, the Commission could take into account the overall turnover figures of the undertakings involved in a cartel to assess the actual impact of the infringement on the market, although the Guidelines did not indicate these figures as a means to calculate the fines.[97] The Court concluded that the amount of the financial penalty imposed on the applicant had been appropriate and proportionate to the magnitude of the infringement.[98]

In its appeal decision in the *Re: Pre-Insulated Pipe Cartel* case[99] the ECJ substantially confirmed the view of the CFI and reiterated that, so long as a departure from the Commission's Guidelines did not entail a violation of the criteria laid down by the applicable legislative rules, it could not lead to the reassessment of the penalty already imposed.[100] However, in the later *Daichii Pharma v Commission*[101] judgment the CFI took the different view that, by adopting the Guidelines, the Commission had defined 'while complying with higher ranking law, the criteria which [it proposed] (. . .) to apply in the exercise of its discretion'[102] from which it could not depart, despite not being 'required to apply a precise mathematical formula (. . .)'.[103]

---

90 *Id.*, paras. 234–35.

91 *Id.*, para. 237.

92 *Id.*, para. 241, 248.

93 Case T-220/00, *Cheil Jedang v Commission*, [2003] ECR II-2473.

94 Guidelines on the method of setting fines imposed pursuant to Article 15(2) of Regulation No 17 and Article 65(5) of the ECSC Treaty, [1998] OJ C9/3.

95 *Id.*, para. 79.

96 *Id.*, para. 81.

97 *Id.*, para. 83.

98 *Id.*, para. 103. Also case T-224/00, *Archer Daniels Midland and Others v Commission*, [2003] ECR II-2611, para. 206.

99 Joined cases C-189/02, 202/02, 205-208/02 and 213/02, *Dansk Rorindustri and Others v Commission*, [2005] ECR I-5425.

100 *Id.*, para. 278; also para. 177.

101 Case T-26/02, judgment of 15 March 2006, not yet reported.

102 *Id.*, para. 49.

103 *Ibid.*

Although the appeal failed on the merits,[104] the Court found that the Commission, by not recognising the applicability to it of one of the attenuating circumstances listed in the Guidelines, had incorrectly assessed the dimension of the fine to be inflicted on the applicant[105] and as a result redetermined that amount, in the ambit of its jurisdiction under Article 229 EC Treaty.[106]

The decisions under comment suggest that, unless there has been a manifest error of fact or the fine clearly disregards the limits set in Article 23(2) of Regulation No 1/2003 the Courts will not determine afresh its amount.[107] Even when the Commission has been found to have departed from the limits which it imposed on its own discretion, the applicants would have to provide unequivocal and convincing proof that the amount should have been different in the light of the Fining Guidelines.[108]

1.4. Judicial Scrutiny of Antitrust Infringement Decisions: the Jurisdiction under Article 230 EC Treaty

Having regard to the 'substantial' review of the decisions of the Commission finding a competition infringement, Article 230 EC Treaty confers on the CFI and the ECJ only limited, supervisory jurisdiction to review the decision on the basis of five grounds of annulment, namely lack of competence, infringement of an essential procedural requirement or of the Treaty or of any rule of law related to its application and misuse of powers.[109] Consequently, the Court cannot substitute its own assessment to the economic and legal appraisal contained in the decision.[110] Its jurisdiction will be limited to ensuring that the

---

104 *Id.*, paras. 129–30.

105 *Id.*, paras. 109–11.

106 *Id.*, paras. 112–13.

107 Joined Cases C-189/02, 202/02, 205–08/02 and 213/02, *Dansk Rorindustri and Others v Commission*, [2005] ECR I-5425, paras. 178–9.

108 Case T-26/02, *Daichii Pharma v Commission*, judgment of 15 March 2006, not yet reported, paras. 129–30.

109 *Inter alia*, CRAIG and DeBÙRCA, *EU Law: Text, Cases and Materials*, 3rd edn (2003) Oxford University Press, p. 540.

110 Case 74/74, *CNTA SA v Commission*, [1975] ECR 533 at paras. 21–22; more recently, *inter alia*, Case T-155/04, *SELEX Sistemi Integrati SpA v Commission*, judgment of 12 December 2006, not yet reported, available in [2007] 4 CMLR 10, para. 28. For commentary, see CRAIG and DeBÙRCA, p. 539. *Inter alia,* BAILEY, 'Scope of judicial review under Article 81 EC', (2004) 41 *CMLRev* 1327 at pp. 1330–31; TIILI and VANHAMME, 'The "power of appraisal" (*pouvoir d'appreciation*) of the Commission of the European Communities vis-à-vis the powers of judicial review of the Communities' Court of Justice and Court of First Instance', (1998–1999) 22 *Fordham Int'l L. J.* 885 at 886.

Commission did not overstep the limit of its discretion and did not commit any error of law or of fact in the assessment of the evidence before it.[111]

The case law of the Community courts suggests that the intensity of the powers of judicial review varies in relation to the grounds of appeal raised before them by the applicants. When it is alleged that the Commission committed an error in the statement of the facts at issue in an individual case or erred in the interpretation of Articles 81 and 82 EC Treaty, the CFI will exercise a 'comprehensive review' of the decision, namely a careful and exhaustive examination of the findings of fact and of the assessment of whether the Treaty rules have been complied with.[112]

In *Bayer*[113] the CFI examined the existing case law concerning the concept of 'agreement' within the framework of Article 81 EC Treaty and concluded that even apparently 'unilateral measures' adopted by two or more undertakings could constitute prohibited conduct,[114] provided that that unilateral behaviour constituted the expression of a 'concurrence of wills'[115] between the parties 'to conduct themselves on the market in a specific way'.[116]

Thereafter, the Court thoroughly assessed the accuracy of the facts adduced as evidence and of the legal reasoning contained in the decision and concluded that the Commission had failed to prove '"to the requisite legal standard" the existence of an agreement between undertakings', namely of the 'concurrence of wills between economic operators on the implementation of a policy'[117] on the relevant market. In the appeal judgment, the ECJ[118] confirmed the CFI's 'exclusive jurisdiction first to establish the facts except where the substantive inaccuracy of its findings is apparent from the documents submitted to it and, second, to assess those facts'.[119]

A comprehensive review is also exercised with respect to allegations that the Commission failed to comply with the procedural rules: in *La Cinq* the CFI explained that 'in cases where the institutions of the Community have a power of appraisal in order to be able to fulfil their tasks, respect of the rights

111 KERSE and KHAN, *EC Antitrust Procedure*, pp. 467–68. Also BAILEY, 'Scope of judicial review under Article 81 EC', (2004) 41 *CMLRev* 1327 at 1332.

112 *Inter alia*, case T-44/02, *Dresdner Bank AG and Others v Commission*, judgment of 27 September 2006, not yet reported, paras. 66–67. For commentary, see BAILEY, 'Scope of judicial review under Article 81 EC', at 1332.

113 Case T-41/96, *Bayer AG v Commission*, [2000] ECR II-3383.

114 *Id.*, para. 71.

115 *Id.*, para. 69.

116 *Id.*, para. 67.

117 *Id.*, para. 174.

118 Case C-2/01, *BAI and Commission v Bayer*, [2004] ECR I-23, para. 48.

119 Case C-7/95 P, *John Deere Ltd v Commission*, [1998] ECR I-3111, para. 21; also Case C-2/01, *BAI and Commission v Bayer*, [2004] ECR I-23, para. 47.

guaranteed by the Community legal order in administrative procedures is of even more fundamental importance'.[120] It is incumbent on the Courts to ensure that the Commission fulfils its obligation 'to examine carefully and impartially all the relevant aspects in the individual case'[121] and to state 'clearly and unequivocally'[122] the grounds for its conclusions so as to enable 'the parties affected to know the justification for the measure taken and the Court to carry out its review'.[123]

Commentators suggested that the 'full jurisdictional control' exercised by the Community courts over matters of law stems from their function within the institutional framework of the EC. Vesterdorf, speaking extra-judicially, argued that 'it is for the Community courts to provide the definitive interpretation of Community law . . . and this goes to both procedural and substantive legal provisions'.[124] Review of matters of law thus entails the power for the CFI to 'interpret the law and then check whether the Commission has applied the correct legal principles'[125] to individual cases.

By contrast, when the applicants seek to challenge the 'complex economic assessments' conducted by the Commission, the power of judicial control exercised by the Community courts appears to be far less intense. In *Remia* the ECJ took the view that, unlike matters of fact or procedure, the assessment of the available evidence made by the Commission and the conclusions as to whether a competition infringement indeed occurred entails complex evaluation of an economic nature which the Commission, in consideration of its expertise, is best equipped to carry out.[126] Judicial review will accordingly be restricted to 'verifying whether the relevant procedural rules have been complied with, whether the statement of the reasons for the decision is adequate, whether the facts have been accurately stated and whether there has been any manifest error of appraisal or a misuse of powers'.[127]

---

120 Case T-44/90, *La Cinq SA v Commission*, [1992] ECR II-1, para. 48.

121 *Id.*, para. 86.

122 Case T-7/92, *Asia Motor France SA and Others v Commission*, [1993] ECR II-669, para 22.

123 *Id.*, para. 30.

124 VESTERDORF, 'Standard of proof in merger cases: reflections in the light of recent case law of the Community courts', (2005) 1(1) *Eur. Comp. Journal* 3 at 12.

125 *Ibid.*

126 *Inter alia*, case T-112/99, *Metropole Television and Others v Commission*, [2001] ECR II-2459, para. 114; BAILEY, 'Scope of judicial review under Article 81 EC', (2004) 41 *CMLRev* 1327 at 1335; SIRAGUSA, 'Judicial review of competition decisions under EC law', Speech given at the Competition Commission on 21 September 2004, available at: http://www.competition-commission.org.uk/our_role/cc_lectures/judicial_control_210904_Siragusa.pdf.

127 Case 42/84, *Remia v Commission*, [1985] ECR 2585, para. 26.

In its appeal judgment against the *Re: Italian Flat Glass* cartel decision the CFI explained that it was 'not for itself . . . to carry out a comprehensive re-assessment of the evidence before it, nor to draw conclusions from that evidence in the light of the rules on competition'.[128] To allow the Court any more extensive powers of review 'could disturb the inter-institutional balance established by the Treaty and would risk prejudicing the rights of the defence'.[129]

Commentators considered that although the Court must be allowed to carry out a review of the legality of the decision, it cannot usurp the role of the Commission as the institution endowed with specific powers and expertise and therefore responsible for conducting the 'complex economic assessments' required by the enforcement of competition law.[130] The Commission's appraisal of the facts will be called into question only if there has been a manifest error of assessment, the facts have not been accurately stated or there has been misuse of powers.[131]

It is noteworthy that the same standard of judicial review has been applied to exemption decisions adopted under Article 81(3) EC Treaty. In *Van den Bergh*[132] the ECJ recognised that the adoption of these decisions entailed 'accommodating and balancing what can sometimes be incommensurate, or indeed conflicting, policies'[133] which were best left to the Commission in the exercise of its powers of implementation of competition policy. Accordingly, the breadth of judicial review over the impugned measure should be restrained.[134]

Therefore, it would appear that the need to ensure that the division of powers within the EC institutional framework and the nature of competition enforcement as requiring 'complex economic assessments' justifies the exercise by the Community courts of a 'limited' review of the assessment of the evidence conducted by the Commission.[135] Nevertheless, it is submitted that this

---

128 Joined Cases T-68, 77-78/89, *Società Italiana Vetro SpA and Others v Commission*, [1992] ECR II-1403 at para. 320.

129 *Id.*, para. 319.

130 BAILEY, 'Scope of judicial review under Article 81 EC', at 1338. *Inter alia*, case T-17/93, *Matra Hachette SA v Commission*, [1994] ECR II-595 at para. 104.

131 *Inter alia*, cases 142/84 and 156/84, *British American Tobacco Co Ltd and RJ Reynolds Industries Inc v Commission*, [1987] ECR 4487 at para. 62.

132 Case T-65/98, *Van den Bergh v Commission*, [2003] ECR II-4653.

133 BAILEY, 'Scope of judicial review under Article 81 EC', at 1338–39.

134 Case T-65/98, *Van den Bergh v Commission*, [2003] ECR II-4653 at para. 135.

135 *Id.*, p. 1336. *Inter alia*, case T-17/93, *Matra Hachette SA v Commission*, [1994] ECR II-595 at para. 104; C-194/99 P, *Thyssen Stahl v Commission,* judgment of 2 October 2003, unreported, para. 73; more recently, case T-168/01, *Glaxosmithkline Services Unlimited v Commission*, judgment of 27 September 2006, not yet reported, available at [2006] 5 CMLR 29, para. 57.

approach is open to the criticism that it may not always be clear what constitutes a 'complex economic assessment'. Especially when a simultaneous plea is raised that the Commission failed to give an adequate statement of the reasons supporting its decision, it could be argued that the 'procedural' and the 'substantial' allegations may be so closely connected as to become interdependent.[136] Furthermore, not in every case does the Commission adopt 'policy decisions' for which a 'restrained' type of judicial review could be appropriate.[137]

Although Article 230 EC Treaty does not allow for a re-hearing of competition cases, it could be speculated as to whether the standard adopted to review the 'complex economic appraisals' conducted by the Commission to justify a prohibition decision is entirely suited to the objective nature of the conditions laid down in Articles 81 and 82 EC Treaty and to the 'criminal' nature of antitrust proceedings.[138]

1.5. The Breadth of Judicial Control over Decisions Adopted under the Merger Control Regulation

The case law concerning the judicial review of merger decisions indicates that, as in the area of antitrust enforcement, the Community courts have developed varying standards of judicial scrutiny depending on the grounds of review raised by the applicants before them. Whereas a 'comprehensive review' is exercised with respect to matters of law, both procedural and substantial,[139] a more 'restrained' approach is applied when the applicant seeks to challenge the 'complex economic assessments' conducted by the Commission to ascertain whether the notified concentration would significantly impede effective competition.[140]

In the *Re: Kali & Salz* appeal, the ECJ, after carrying out a 'considered review' of the interpretation of Article 2 of the Merger Regulation, concluded that cases of joint dominance fell within its scope.[141] With respect to the

---

136 E.g. Joined Cases T-68, 77-78/89, *Società Italiana Vetro SpA and Others v Commission*, [1992] ECR II-1403 at para. 95.

137 Cf., *inter alia*, Case C-129/85, *Ahlstrom Osakeyhtio and Others v Commission*, [1993] ECR I-1307 at paras. 31–32 and 126–27.

138 *Inter alia,* case T-41/96, *Bayer AG v Commission*, [2000] ECR II-3383 at para. 174. *Infra*, this chapter, para. 3.1, footnote 281 and accompanying text.

139 *Inter alia*, BAY and RUIZ CALZADO, '*Tetra Laval II*: the coming of age of the judicial review of merger decisions', (2005) 28(4) *W. Comp.* 433 at 434.

140 *Inter alia*, NICHOLSON, CARDELL and McKENNA, 'The scope of review of merger decisions under Community Law', (2005) 1(1) *Eur. Comp. Journal*, 123 at 140.

141 Joined Cases C-68/94 and 30/95, *France and Others v Commission*, [1998] ECR I-1375, para. 178. *Inter alia,* NICHOLSON et. al., (footnote 140), p. 128.

compliance of the decision with the relevant procedural rules, Advocate General Tizzano had suggested that the 'twofold nature of the Commission's functions – a power of inquiry and investigation coupled with a decision-making power'[142] required strict adherence to the rules governing the 'fair hearing' of the affected parties and the exercise of stringent powers of control on the part of the courts.[143]

In *MCI v Commission* the CFI annulled the decision prohibiting the merger between WorldCom and Sprint on the ground that the Commission had disregarded the formal withdrawal of the parties' notification and therefore had exceeded the limits of its powers.[144] In the other *Schneider* judgment the CFI engaged in a careful review of the Statement of Objections and concluded that the failure of the Commission to address adequately one of the allegations had violated the applicants' rights of defence and therefore justified the annulment of the decision.[145]

Having regard to the review of the 'complex economic assessments' of the facts and evidence gathered by the Commission, it is noteworthy that the approach of the ECJ and CFI has evolved from a 'restrained' type of judicial control, akin to that exercised over antitrust decisions, to a more careful and stringent review.[146] Earlier judgments had indicated that judicial review was confined to 'ruling on important issues of law or procedure'[147] and to verifying that the Commission had not committed any manifest error of fact or of law.[148]

In *Gencor*[149] the CFI held that to establish that a collective dominant position existed as a result of the notified transaction, the Commission was obliged to prove, 'using a prospective analysis of the relevant market',[150] whether that transaction would result in the competition in the relevant market being significantly restricted and concluded that, since the Commission enjoys a 'certain discretion especially with respect to assessments of an

---

142 Per AG Tizzano, para. 21.

143 VESTERDORF, 'Standard of proof in merger cases: reflections in the light of recent case law of the Community courts', (2005) 1(1) *Eur. Comp. Journal*, 3 at 13–14.

144 T-310/00, *MCI v Commission*, judgment of 28 September 2004, not yet reported, para. 107.

145 T-310/01, *Schneider Electric v Commission*, [2002] ECR II-4071, paras. 440 and 462; NICHOLSON, CARDELL and McKENNA, 'The scope of review of merger decisions under Community Law', at 127.

146 *Inter alia*, Case T-102/96, *Gencor v Commission*, [1999] ECR II-753 at para. 165. BROWN, 'Judicial review of Commission decisions under the Merger Regulation: the first cases', (1994) 15 *ECLR* 296 at 305.

147 BROWN, *ibid.*, at 305.

148 BROWN, *supra*, footnote 146.

149 T-102/96, *Gencor v Commission*, [1999] ECR II-753.

150 *Id.*, para. 163.

economic nature'[151] implicit in the rules governing concentrations, judicial scrutiny should necessarily be limited.[152]

More recent judgments, however, have demonstrated a more proactive approach to the scrutiny of merger decisions. In *Airtours* the CFI annulled the decision prohibiting the merger between the applicant and its competitor First Choice on grounds that a collective dominant position had been established as a result of the transaction.[153] The Court stated that its review should encompass 'the way in which the law has been applied to the facts and adjudicate on the merits on the Commission's findings concerning the effects of the concentration on competition'.[154] Consequently, although the Commission enjoyed a discretionary margin in the assessment of the notified transaction,[155] it was obliged to 'produce convincing evidence' that a collective dominant position is likely to result from the proposed concentration.[156]

However, the CFI held that the Commission had failed to establish 'to the requisite legal standard'[157] that the notified transaction had given rise to such a collective dominant position: in fact, no 'convincing evidence' had been produced to demonstrate, *inter alia*, 'the lack of effective competition between the operators alleged to be members' of the oligopoly and the weakness of the competitive pressure likely to be exercised by other market players.[158]

Airtours was hailed by commentators as a 'warning call' for the Commission's approach to reviewing concentrations allegedly giving rise to collective dominance.[159] Vesterdorf, speaking extra-judicially, commented that the close scrutiny exercised by the CFI was justified by the 'novelty and/or controversial or contested nature of the economic theory or data' on which the Commission's reasoning rests.[160] He argued that when novel theories are advanced to support the prohibition of a notified merger, 'it is the duty and responsibility of the CFI, so as to ensure effective judicial review, to scrutinise closely the convincing nature of the evidence relied upon (. . .)'.[161]

---

151 *Id.*, para. 164.

152 *Id.*, para. 165. Also case T-22/97, *Kesko Oy v EC Commission*, [1999] ECR II-3775, para. 142.

153 Case T-342/99, *Airtours v Commission*, [2002] ECR II-2585.

154 *Id.*, para. 53.

155 *Id.*, para. 64.

156 *Id.*, para. 63.

157 *Id.*, para. 294.

158 *Id.*, para. 63.

159 See, *inter alia*, STROUD, 'Collective dominance under the Merger Regulation: a serious evidentiary reprimand for the Commission', (2002) 27(6) *ELRev* 736 at 744.

160 VESTERDORF, 'Standard of proof in merger cases', at 24.

161 *Ibid.*

In *Tetra Laval*[162] the CFI reiterated this approach and held that, just as in cases of mergers giving rise to collective dominance, a proposed concentration suspected of having a 'conglomerate effect', namely resulting in the creation or strengthening of a dominant position in a neighbouring market due to the dominant position already held in the relevant market,[163] would have to be subjected to 'a particularly close examination (. . .)'.[164]

Consequently, even though under Article 2 of the Merger Regulation the Commission enjoys a 'certain discretion, especially with respect to assessment of an economic nature',[165] which the Community judiciary must take into account while reviewing its decisions, it is nonetheless obliged to provide 'convincing evidence' of the circumstances giving rise to the alleged conglomerate effects.[166] On appeal[167] the ECJ endorsed the standard of review adopted by the CFI and held:

> Whilst the Court recognises that the Commission has a margin of discretion with regard to economic matters, that does not mean that the Community Courts must refrain from reviewing the Commission's interpretation of information of an economic nature. Not only must the Community Courts, *inter alia*, establish whether the evidence relied on is factually accurate, reliable and consistent but also whether that evidence contains all the information which must be taken into account in order to assess a complex situation and whether it is capable of substantiating the conclusions drawn from it.[168]

Accordingly the CFI, far from overstepping the boundaries of its own jurisdiction, 'merely drew attention to the essential function of evidence, which is to establish convincingly the merits . . . of a decision on a merger'.[169] The strength of the evidence adduced by the Commission is all the more important when 'conglomerate effects' are at issue, since their analysis is necessarily 'prospective' and focused on the establishment of 'chains of cause and effect [that] are dimly discernible, uncertain and difficult to establish'.[170]

However, this conclusion should not be interpreted as imposing on the Commission a duty to prove with absolute certainty that the concentration will lead to the creation or strengthening of a dominant position on the relevant

---

162 Case T-5/02, *Tetra Laval BV v Commission*, [2002] ECR II-4381.
163 *Id.*, para. 154.
164 *Id.* para. 155.
165 *Id.*, para. 119.
166 *Id.*, para. 155.
167 Case C-12/03, *Commission v Tetra Laval*, [2005] ECR I-987.
168 *Id.*, para. 39.
169 *Id.*, para. 42.
170 *Id.*, para. 44.

market.[171] In his opinion in the *Tetra Laval* appeal AG Tizzano suggested that the Commission should 'base its conviction on elements gathered in the course of a thorough and painstaking investigation',[172] to assess the relevant market carefully, to examine all the relevant factors and to state fully its reasons, 'disclosing the various passages of logical argument supporting the decision'.[173] Without going as far as to 'enter into the merits of the Commission's complex economic assessments or to substitute its own point of view for that of the institution',[174] fulfilling 'those duties ... make it possible for the Community judicature to exercise an adequate review'.[175]

The importance of the *Tetra Laval* judgments cannot be sufficiently highlighted. Despite acknowledging the margin of discretion enjoyed by the Commission in the assessment of concentrations and the resulting 'restrained' judicial scrutiny over its decisions, the ECJ made clear that the CFI will examine carefully 'the Commission's assessment based on the interpretation of economic information'[176] and focus on the accuracy and reliability of the evidence gathered for the purpose of 'substantiating the conclusions drawn from it'.[177]

Commentators suggested that the *Tetra Laval* decisions, far from constituting 'an invitation of judicial activism by the CFI that will disturb the separation of powers of the European Community institutions',[178] should instead be read as a reminder of the importance of evidence in merger control and, overall, of the role of the judiciary as 'the primary element of the various checks and balances' to protect the legitimate interests of the notifying parties.[179] It could be argued that merger control discloses an 'inevitable tension between the administrative nature of individual Commission decisions and the Commission's desire to push the boundaries of competition law through the decision-making process'[180] and therefore justifies the 'margin of discretion' enjoyed in this area.[181]

---

171 Per AG Tizzano, para. 74.

172 *Id.*, para. 87.

173 *Id.*, para. 87.

174 *Id.* para. 89.

175 *Id.*, para. 88.

176 BAY and RUIZ CALZADO, '*Tetra Laval II*', at 437.

177 Case C-12/03, *Commission v Tetra Laval*, [2005] ECR I-987, para. 39.

178 BAY and RUIZ CALZADO, '*Tetra Laval II*', at 452.

179 *Id.*, para. 453. For commentary, VESTERDORF, 'Standard of proof in merger cases', at 31.

180 NICHOLSON et al., 'The scope of review of merger decisions under Community Law', at 148.

181 Joined Cases C-68/94 and 30/95, *France and Others v Commission*, [1998] ECR I-1375, paras. 223–24.

Nonetheless, it is submitted that the nature of the interests at stake and the 'twofold nature of the Commission's functions' as both investigator and decision-maker[182] seem capable of justifying this 'more intense and exacting' standard of review.[183] In addition, such an 'exacting' standard of review appears consistent with the mandate of the CFI as a 'specialised competition court'[184] for which it is appropriate to provide a meticulous and stringent review of the substance of the Commission's analysis.[185] Judicial review in merger control constitutes therefore a key element of the checks and balances in this area,[186] being 'an integral part of an overall merger control system that has truly come of age'.[187]

Separate issues could arise with respect to the scrutiny of merger clearance decisions adopted subject to the acceptance of commitments. As noted above,[188] Articles 6(2) and 8(2) of Regulation no 139/2004 allow the Commission to approve the notified concentration following modifications agreed by the concerned parties within, respectively, Phase I and Phase II proceedings. However, concerns have been raised about the possibility that the time limits provided by the Regulation 'could impose a straitjacket in some cases, where more time to produce suitable remedies could prevent the outright prohibition of a deal'.[189] Although the 'stop-the-clock' clause[190] goes some way toward minimising that risk, it is suggested that judicial scrutiny of these decisions should be all the more careful to ensure that the undertakings are not 'forced' into accepting commitments as a result of the tight time limits and reasons of business convenience.[191]

However, the case law of the CFI could be read as suggesting that scrutiny

---

182 *Id.* per AG Tizzano, para. 21.

183 VESTERDORF, 'Standard of proof in merger cases', at 33.

184 Case C-12/03, *Commission v Tetra Laval*, [2005] ECR I-987, paras. 40–41.

185 BAY and RUIZ CALZADO, '*Tetra Laval II*', at 453.

186 VESTERDORF, 'Standard of proof in merger cases', at 33. See more recently case T-210/01, *General Electric v Commission*, [2002] ECR II-4071, para. 63.

187 BAY and RUIZ CALZADO, '*Tetra Laval II*', at 453.

188 *Supra*, Chapter 2, section 1.4, footnote 305 and accompanying text.

189 HOUSE of LORDS SELECT COMMITTEE on the EUROPEAN UNION, *XXXII Report: the review of the EC Merger Regulation*, Session 2001/2002, 30/7/2002 at para. 189.

190 Article 10, Council Regulation (EC) No 139/2004 of 20 January 2004 on the control of concentrations between undertakings, which has repealed Article 10 of Council Regulation No 4064/89.

191 HOUSE of LORDS SELECT COMMITTEE on the EUROPEAN UNION, *XXXII Report: the review of the EC Merger Regulation*, Session 2001/2002, 30/7/2002 at para. 189. See below for analysis of, *inter alia*, ser. A No 35, *Deweer v Belgium*, [1979–1980] 2 EHRR 439 at para. 49.

of commitments remains by and large restrained. In *ARD v Commission*[192] the CFI held that Articles 6(2) and 8(2) of the Merger Regulation conferred on the Commission the discretionary power to examine on a case-by-case basis the modifications proposed by the notifying parties.[193] The Court thus concluded that the decision approving the merger subject to commitments would be annulled only if it was shown that 'the Commission has committed a manifest error of assessment'.[194] So long as 'the Commission was reasonably entitled to conclude that the commitments contained in the decision dispel the serious doubts' the decision would not be annulled.[195]

Similarly, in the later *Petrolessence* case[196] the CFI held that, although in principle the approval of a merger upon the acceptance of modifications to the transaction called for a 'close examination . . . of the circumstances which, in each individual case, are relevant for assessing the effects of the concentration on competition'[197] in the relevant market, the decision could not be quashed unless it is shown that 'the Commission's appraisal . . . is clearly mistaken (. . .)'[198] on the basis of 'concrete evidence adduced by the applicants'.[199]

It could be queried whether the approach to judicial scrutiny applicable to approval decisions subject to commitments is consistent with the standard of review applied to prohibition decisions. It may be argued that the language used by the CFI in rulings such as *ARD* and *Petrolessence* appears far more cautious than that adopted by the ECJ in *Tetra Laval* and could therefore disclose the application of a less intensive standard of review.

However, it is submitted that the standard of judicial control is in fact not very different from that applied to merger prohibitions. Like the ECJ in *Tetra Laval*, the CFI emphasised the importance of the quality of the evidence adduced by the applicant to demonstrate that the commitments were not capable of dispelling the anti-competitive concerns raised by the proposed transaction.[200] Just as the Commission is obliged to point to 'convincing evidence' to prove that a concentration is liable to substantially lessen competition, it appears that the applicant seeking to have the approval decision overturned

---

[192] Case T-158/00, [2003] ECR II-3825.

[193] *Id.*, paras. 193–94.

[194] *Ibid.* Also, case T-119/02, *Royal Philips NV v Commission*, [2003[ECR II-1433, para. 78.

[195] Case T-158/00, *ARD v Commission*, [2003[ECR II-3825, para. 329.

[196] Case T-342/00, *Petrolessence and Others v Commission*, [2003] ECR II-1161.

[197] *Id.,* para. 102.

[198] *Id.*, para. 103.

[199] *Id.*, para. 112.

[200] Cf. Case C-12/03, *Commission v Tetra Laval*, [2005] ECR I-987, para. 44 with Case T-342/00, *Petrolessence and Others v Commission*, [2003] ECR II-1161, para. 112.

would have to present concrete proof of the inadequacy of the proposed modifications.[201]

In a recent Opinion[202] AG Kokott added that, given the voluntary nature of the commitments offered by the undertakings seeking approval of the concentration, there are legitimate reasons to suppose that the parties concerned regard them as 'appropriate, necessary and reasonable for resolving a competition problem identified by the Commission'[203] and a 'less onerous' alternative to the outright prohibition of the transaction.[204] Consequently, she suggested that, before declaring the commitments 'disproportionate' and thus inappropriate to address the anti-competitive concerns highlighted by the case-handling officials, the applicant must adduce 'extraordinary circumstances',[205] going well beyond the threat of fines or of divestiture following the unlawful implementation of the transaction.[206] The fact that the Commission mentioned these consequences did not constitute an 'extraordinary step' but rather only an indication of the consequences of the implementation of an unauthorised concentration and therefore did not affect the voluntary nature of the modifications agreed by the parties.[207]

The above analysis therefore indicates that the judicial review exercised over approval of commitments is consistent with the more vigilant approach adopted by the ECJ and with the overall effectiveness of the checks and balances provided by EC law for the overall fairness of decision-making in merger control.[208] With respect to the scrutiny of approval decisions subject to commitments, the scope of the powers enjoyed by the CFI appears to be consistent with the voluntary nature of the merger remedies agreed by the parties and likely to justify a more pervasive power of control only in exceptional circumstances.[209]

---

201 BAY and RUIZ CALZADO, '*Tetra Laval II*', at 448–49.

202 Case C-202/06 P, *Cementbouw Handel & Industrie BV v Commission*, Opinion of 26 April 2007, not yet reported.

203 *Id.*, para. 69.

204 *Ibid.*

205 *Ibid.*

206 *Id.*, para. 71.

207 *Ibid.*

208 NICHOLSON et al., 'The scope of review of merger decisions under Community Law', at 148.

209 Case C-202/06 P, *Cementbouw Handel & Industrie BV v Commission*, Opinion of 26 April 2007, not yet reported, paras. 69–71.

1.6. Judicial Scrutiny of the Commission Decisions: Summary Conclusions

The previous sections assessed the two separate questions of whether judicial control is adequately available to both the undertakings concerned and the interested third parties, and whether the Community courts are empowered to exercise a sufficiently extensive scrutiny of the impugned measures. With respect to the conditions governing *locus standi* to challenge antitrust decisions, the position of the Courts supports the conclusion that a judicial remedy is readily available to the undertakings to which the decision is directly addressed, who are entitled to bring an action for the mere fact of being on the receiving end of the decision.[210]

As regards actions for annulment brought by third parties, the original judicial position laid down in *Metro No 1*, according to which the applicants had to demonstrate that they were involved in the competition proceedings, appears to have given way to a more flexible approach. Other elements such as the economic position of the applicant in the relevant market, together with any legal relations vis-à-vis the undertakings concerned, are now taken into account to conclude that the applicant was directly and individually concerned by the impugned measure.[211]

Nevertheless, in the field of merger control, judgments such as *Zunis Holding*[212] and *Grandes Sources*[213] evidence the difficulties encountered by the Community Courts in establishing that the impugned clearance decisions were of direct concern to the applicants. However, the recent decisions allowing annulment actions to be brought against commitments and referrals decisions would seem to pave the way towards an increasingly flexible attitude in assessing the standing conditions.[214]

Having regard to the intensity of the power of judicial scrutiny of antitrust decisions, the case law indicates that its degree varies depending on the grounds of appeal against which the impugned measure is tested: when alle-

---

210 *Inter alia*, Joined Cases T-374, 375, 384, 388/94, *European Night Services and Others v Commission*, [1998] ECR II-3141 at para. 61.

211 *Inter alia*, Joined Cases T-528/93, T-542 and 543/93, T-546/93, *Metropole Television SA and Others v Commission*, [1996] ECR II-649; Case 210/81, *Demo-Studio Schmidt v Commission*, [1983] ECR 3045; Case T-231/99, *Joynson v EC Commission*, [2002] ECR II-2085; Case T-131/99, *Shaw and Falla v EC Commission*, [2002] ECR II-2023.

212 T-83/92, *Zunis Holding v Commission*, [1993] ECR II-1169.

213 Case T-96/92, *Comité Central d'Enterprise de la Société Generale des Grandes Sources and Others v Commission*, [1995] ECR II-1213.

214 *Inter alia*, Case T-119/02, *Royal Philips Electronics NV v Commission*, [2003] 5 CMLR 2 at paras. 282 and 284.

gations of procedural impropriety or of error in the interpretation of Articles 81 and 82 EC Treaty are raised, the CFI and the ECJ will exercise a 'comprehensive review' of the decision, in conformity with their function of 'ultimate arbiters' in interpreting Community law.[215] When, instead, the applicants seek to challenge the Commission's 'complex economic assessments' judicial scrutiny will be limited to ascertaining the respect for the rules of procedure, the adequacy of the statement of reasons, the accuracy of the facts and the absence of any manifest error of appraisal or of misuse of powers.[216]

Coming to the review of merger decisions, although the position as regards allegations of procedural impropriety and of error of law on the part of the Commission is consistent with that taken in the field of antitrust, the approach adopted by the Courts as regards the assessment of 'complex economic appraisals' has moved from a restrained to a far more vigilant type of judicial control. In *Tetra Laval* the ECJ made it clear that although the Commission enjoys some discretion in assessing the notified concentrations, that discretion will be subject to careful judicial supervision. The Commission will thus be obliged to provide evidence of the merger's anti-competitive effects which is clear, convincing, complete and accurate and thus capable of supporting its conclusions.[217]

Accordingly, after defining the standards governing access to the Luxembourg courts on the part of the undertakings directly affected by competition decisions and third parties and the breadth of judicial scrutiny exercised by the CFI, the following sections will address the requirements of the 'right to a court' and the degree of control exercised by judicial authorities over administrative decisions having a civil or criminal character enshrined in Article 6(1) ECHR. Thereafter, the two sets of standards will be compared with a view to establishing the extent to which the relevant EC rules comply with the Convention principles.

215 VESTERDORF, 'Standard of proof in merger cases', at 12.

216 *Inter alia*, Cases 142/84 and 156/84, *British American Tobacco Co Ltd and RJ Reynolds Industries Inc v Commission*, [1987] ECR 4487, para. 62; Case 42/84, *Remia v Commission*, [1985] ECR 2585, para. 26; more recently, Case T-168/01, *Glaxosmithkline Services Unlimited v Commission*, judgment of 27 September 2006, not yet reported, available at [2006] ECR 11-2969.

217 Case C-12/03, *Commission v Tetra Laval*, [2005] ECR I-987, paras. 39, 42.

2. JUDICIAL CONTROL OF NON-JUDICIAL DECISIONS HAVING A 'CRIMINAL' AND 'CIVIL' CHARACTER ACCORDING TO ARTICLE 6(1) ECHR: WHAT ARE THE REQUIREMENTS OF A 'FULL JURISDICTION'?

2.1. The Right to a Court in Challenging the Validity of Administrative Acts in the Case Law of the Strasbourg Court

The previous sections illustrated that in the context of administrative proceedings leading to the determination of civil rights and obligations or of a criminal charge, Article 6(1) ECHR could be interpreted either as imposing that those proceedings be judicial *tout court*[218] or as ensuring at a minimum a right of appeal on the merits against the final decision before a court which meets the requirements of Article 6(1) ECHR.[219] According to the 'composite approach' adopted by the European Court of Human Rights it is necessary to examine whether the right to 'due process' afforded to individuals by the Convention is respected in the judicial phase of the proceedings.[220]

With respect to the availability of a judicial remedy, the Strasbourg Court has long and forcefully established that the Convention enshrined 'the "right to a court", of which the right of access . . . constitutes one aspect (. . .)'.[221] In fact, 'it would be inconceivable . . . that Article 6(1) should describe in detail the procedural guarantees afforded to parties in a pending lawsuit and should not first protect that which alone makes it in fact possible to benefit from such guarantees, that is, access to a court'.[222]

In *Ashingdane* the Court held that the right 'of access to the courts is not absolute but may be subject to limitations'.[223] However, although the Contracting States are allowed a certain margin of appreciation,[224] any restriction imposed by domestic law 'must not . . . reduce the access left to the individual in such a way or to such an extent that the very essence of the right is

---

218 BOYLE, 'Administrative justice, judicial review and the right to a fair hearing under the European Convention on Human Rights', (1984) *PL* 89, at 100.

219 Appl. Nos 7299/75 and 7496/76, *Albert & LeCompte v Belgium*, [1983] 5 EHRR 533, para. 29.

220 BOYLE, 'Administrative justice', at 105.

221 Ser. A No 18, *Golder v United Kingdom*, [1979–80] 1 EHRR 524, para. 36.

222 *Id.*, para. 36. Also ser. A No 32, *Airey v Ireland*, [1979–80] 2 EHRR 305, para. 26. See LeSUEUR, 'Access to justice in the United Kingdom', (2000) *EHRLR* 5 457 at 467–68.

223 Appl. 8225/78, *Ashingdane v United Kingdom*, [1985] 7 EHRR 528, para. 57.

224 *Ibid.*

impaired',[225] must 'pursue a legitimate aim' and bear 'a reasonable relationship of proportionality between the means employed and the aim sought to be achieved'.[226]

When a 'vetting system' for the admissibility of judicial claims is established to pursue goals of public interest it is not sufficient that 'the existence of a requirement that prior authorization be given by a court is in principle justified'. It is also necessary that each decision is supported by adequate reasoning in relation to the position and the circumstances of the individual applicant.[227] In addition, any conditions governing the admissibility of appeals against administrative decisions falling within the scope of Article 6(1) ECHR should respect criteria of legal certainty, clarity and coherence.

In *Geouffre de la Pradelle v France*[228] the European Court of Human Rights held that 'the applicant was entitled to expect a coherent system that would achieve a fair balance between the authorities' interests and his own',[229] a system which ought to have provided him with 'a clear, practical and effective opportunity to challenge an administrative act that was a direct interference with his right of property'.[230] A breach of Article 6(1) ECHR was thus found in the 'extreme complexity of the positive law'[231] governing the nature of the impugned measure, its manner of notification to the applicant and the time limits governing the action.[232]

This judgment suggests that the standing requirements which must be satisfied in order to challenge administrative measures affecting individual rights and obligations must be sufficiently clear and express a reasonable relation of proportionality between individual and public interests, in order to render the right to a court practical and effective.[233] The absence of legal certainty in this respect will therefore cause the proceedings in question to violate Article 6(1) ECHR.[234]

---

225 *Ibid.* See McBRIDE, 'Access to justice and Human Rights treaties', (1998) 17 *CJQ* (Jul) 235 at 239.

226 *Ibid.* See also BREMS, 'Conflicting human rights: an exploration in the context of the right to a fair trial in the European Convention for the protection of Human Rights and Fundamental Freedoms', (2005) 27 *Hum. Rts. Quart.* 294 at 302–05.

227 McBRIDE, *supra*, footnote 226, at 240–41. For a critique to the approach of the European Court of Human Rights see HICKMAN, 'The 'uncertain shadow': throwing light on the right to a court under Article 6(1) ECHR', (2004) *PL* (SPR) 122 at 136–41.

228 Appl. No 12864/87, [1993] Series A, Judgments and Decisions, vol. 253.

229 *Id.*, para. 34.

230 *Ibid.*

231 *Id.*, para. 33.

232 *Ibid.*

233 WARD, '*Locus standi* under Article 230(4) of the EC Treaty'.

234 McBRIDE, 'Access to justice and Human Rights treaties', at 266.

The Strasbourg Court also dealt with cases in which the applicant had waived his right to a court in proceedings having a 'criminal nature' by paying an administrative fine after entering into negotiations with the public authorities.[235] In *Deweer v Belgium*[236] it was held that this right could not 'be forfeited solely by reason of the fact that an individual is a party to a settlement reached in the course of a procedure ancillary to court proceedings'[237] and that any waiver agreed with the public authorities to avoid criminal proceedings[238] should be closely scrutinised especially as regards the 'absence of constraint'.[239]

In *Deweer* the European Court of Human Rights found a violation of Article 6(1) of the Convention on the ground that the applicant had entered into the waiver under the threat of execution of an order of closure of his trade effective until the date of the judgment and would have caused him significant economic loss,[240] and had therefore been forced to settle the matter due to the harshness of the measure adopted against him.[241] Consequently, the waiver, despite having complied with the requirements laid down by national law, was 'tainted by constraint'[242] and was incompatible with the Convention.

2.2. The Intensity of Judicial Control over Administrative Measures having a 'Civil' or 'Criminal' Character

The European Court of Human Rights emphasised in *Albert & LeCompte* that the court competent for reviewing administrative measures aimed at the determination of the individual's civil rights and obligations or of a criminal charge must enjoy 'full jurisdiction', namely the 'power to give full consideration to issues of law, facts and merits'.[243] Although this requirement could be interpreted as justifying an extremely expansive form of review, extending also to questions about the expediency of the impugned measure, a slightly narrower approach seems to have prevailed.

---

235 Ser. A No 35, *Deweer v Belgium*, [1979–1980] 2 EHRR 439, para. 49.
236 Ser. A No 35, [1979–1980] 2 EHRR 439.
237 *Id.*, para. 49.
238 *Ibid.*
239 *Ibid. Mutatis mutandis*, Appl. No 10096/82, *Pinder v United Kingdom*, [1985] 7 EHRR CD 464, Report of the European Commission on Human Rights, paras. 6–7. For commentary, *inter alia*, McBRIDE, 'Access to justice and Human Rights treaties', (1998) 17 *CJQ* (JUL) 235 at 244–45.
240 *Id.*, para. 51.
241 *Id.*, para. 52.
242 *Id.*, para. 54.
243 BOYLE, 'Administrative justice, judicial review and the right to a fair hearing under the European Convention on Human Rights', (1984) *PL* 89 at 105.

With respect to measures determining the individual's civil rights and obligations, the European Commission for Human Rights recognised in *Kaplan* that the 'legitimate concern to protect the citizen against arbitrary administrative action'[244] justifies the provision for 'judicial review of administrative action'.[245] However, the scope for scrutiny cannot extend as far as to encompass 'certain elements of administrative discretion'.[246] Provided that 'the administrative authority has acted properly and within the limits of the law', the court cannot, except in rare cases 'decide whether or not the administrative decision was well-founded in substance'.[247]

Nonetheless in later decisions the Court took the view that this review should not be limited to the 'formal' scrutiny 'of the administrative authorities' exercise of their discretionary powers'.[248] In *Obermeier*[249] it was held that judicial review limited only to ensuring that 'the discretion enjoyed by the administrative authorities [was] used in a manner compatible with the object and purpose of the law'[250] did not satisfy the demands of Article 6(1) ECHR since it did not allow the court to 'enter . . . into the merits of the administrative law issue'.[251]

Similarly, in *Zumtobel*[252] the European Court considered that, since the legality of the expropriation decision at issue in the case was determined in relation to conditions laid down by the applicable law and was thus amenable to the legal assessment on the part of the courts,[253] there had been no violation of Article 6(1) ECHR. In fact, 'the Administrative Court (. . .) [had] considered these submissions on their merits, point by point, without ever having to decline jurisdiction in replying to them or in ascertaining various facts'.[254]

In *Bryan v United Kingdom* the Strasbourg organs had to deal with the compatibility of English law judicial review proceedings in the area of town and environmental planning and development. The Court noted that this remedy, 'being on points of law, was not capable of embracing all aspects of

---

244 Appl. No 7598/76, *Kaplan v United Kingdom*, [1982] 4 EHRR 64, para. 159.

245 *Ibid.*

246 *Ibid.*

247 *Ibid.*

248 ZUPANCIC, 'Access to court as a human right according to the European Convention of Human Rights', (2000) 9(2) *NLJ* 1 at 9.

249 Appl. No 11761/85, *Obermeier v Austria*, [1991] 13 EHRR 290, para. 70.

250 *Id.* para. 70.

251 ZUPANCIC, 'Access to court as a human right', at 10.

252 Appl. No 12235/86, *Zumtobel v Austria*, [1994] 17 EHRR 116.

253 *Id.*, para. 31.

254 *Id.*, para. 32. See also Appl. No 18064/91, *Ortenberg v Austria*, [1995] 19 EHRR 524, para. 70.

the inspector's decision'[255] and did not envisage any 'rehearing as such of the original complaints'[256] or the readoption of the inspector's decision in case of annulment.[257]

However, the proceedings were considered compatible with Article 6(1) ECHR on the grounds that the impugned decision could have been annulled by the High Court if it had been adopted 'by reference to irrelevant factors or without regard to relevant factors',[258] or on the basis of insufficient evidence, or if it had been 'based on an inference from facts which was perverse or irrational'.[259] The European Court of Human Rights also stressed the importance of the possibility for the High Court to examine allegations concerning the violation of the 'uncontested safeguards attending the procedure before the inspector'.[260]

It is submitted that the *Bryan* decision confirms in full the 'composite approach' advocated by the European Court of Human Rights.[261] Without allowing the applicants to challenge the expediency of the final decision, the Court pointed out that the availability of appropriate procedural safeguards at the administrative level, together with the provision of judicial control based on grounds of legality of the impugned decision, ensured the overall 'fairness' of the proceedings.[262]

However, it is not entirely clear whether similar standards of judicial review should apply to other types of administrative proceedings, including those 'more directly involving the determination of rights'[263] and especially to those leading to the determination of a 'criminal charge'.[264] The European Court of Human Rights held in *Belilos*[265] that the proceedings before the 'Criminal Cassation Division' did not satisfy the standards laid down by Article 6(1) of the Convention. In fact, recourse to that court did

---

255 Appl. No 19178/91, *Bryan v United Kingdom*, [1996] 21 EHRR 342, para. 44.
256 *Ibid.*
257 *Ibid.*
258 *Id.*, para. 45.
259 *Ibid.*
260 *Id.* para. 46.
261 Also *R (on the application of Holding and Barnes plc), R (on the application of Premier Leisure UK), R (on the application of Alconbury Developments Ltd) v Secretary of State for the Environment, Transport and the Regions*, House of Lords, 9 May 2001, [2001] HRLR 45, *inter alia*, per Lord Clyde, para. 152.
262 POUSTIE, 'The rule of law or the rule of lawyers? *Alconbury*, article 6(1) and the role of courts in administrative decision-making', (2001) 6 *EHRLR* 657 at 663–64.
263 *Id.*, p. 669.
264 *Ibid.* See also, *mutatis mutandis*, Appl. No 9749/82, *W v United Kingdom*, [1988] 10 EHRR 29, para. 79.
265 Appl. No 10328/83, *Belilos v Switzerland*, [1988] 10 EHRR 466, para. 68.

not allow for a 'ruling on the merits but solely for review of (. . .) [the] lawfulness'[266] or provide for 'oral argument [or] the taking of evidence'[267] supporting the decision. Nor did the proceedings before the Federal Court, since the Court's powers were 'limited to ensuring that there had been no arbitrariness'.[268]

Similarly in *Schmautzer* – another case relating to an administrative decision concerning motoring offences – a violation of Article 6(1) ECHR was found in the lack on the part of the competent administrative court of the power to annul the final decision 'in all respects, on questions of fact and law'.[269] Although 'in civil matters a somewhat limited review of the decisions of administrative authorities may, in certain circumstances, satisfy the requirements of Article 6 of the Convention',[270] when the impugned decisions concern the punishment of offences that are 'criminal' in nature, jurisdiction should be entrusted to 'a court which could consider all the facts of the case'.[271] Accordingly, there must be 'no room for limitation on the scope of review required of the decisions of administrative authorities'.[272]

The case law of the European Court of Human Rights analysed so far seems to support the view that the appropriate standard of judicial review which must be afforded to applicants wishing to challenge administrative decisions falling under Article 6(1) ECHR is different depending on whether the impugned decision determines the individual's civil rights and obligations or a 'criminal charge'. Nonetheless, a limited scope of judicial oversight such as that characterising 'judicial review-type' proceedings appears to be acceptable only in the former case. The decisions in *Belilos* and *Schmautzer* justify the conclusion that, where 'criminal matters' are concerned, the competent court should be able to assess the validity of the measure both in fact and in law in accordance with an adversarial procedure and without being limited to testing merely the legality of the decision.[273]

---

266 *Id.*, para. 70.
267 *Ibid.*
268 *Id.*, para. 71.
269 Appl. No 15523/89, *Schmautzer v Austria*, [1996] 21 EHRR 511, para. 36.
270 *Id.*, Report of the Commission, para. 53.
271 *Ibid.*
272 *Ibid.*
273 Appl. No 15523/89, *Schmautzer v Austria*, [1996] 21 EHRR 511, para. 36.

3. JUDICIAL REVIEW OF EC COMPETITION DECISIONS AND THE CONVENTION: DIFFERING STANDARDS?

3.1. EC 'Due Process' and Convention 'Administrative Fairness' in the Judicial Stage of the Proceedings: Elements for a Comparative Analysis

Section 1 analysed the requirements governing *locus standi* and the intensity of the powers of judicial scrutiny of Commission decisions in the field of antitrust enforcement and of merger control. Section 2 instead examined the conditions governing the 'right to a court' and the standards of judicial review exercised over administrative decisions having a 'civil' or 'criminal' character enshrined in Article 6(1) ECHR. On this basis, it is possible to attempt a comparative assessment on whether the existing standards of judicial review of competition decisions comply with the requirements of fairness enshrined in the Convention.

With respect to the conditions governing *locus standi* to challenge the antitrust decisions, the current position appears by and large consistent with the ECHR.[274] Issues of concern remain, however, in the field of merger control. Although annulment actions have been allowed against commitments and referrals decisions, in accordance with an increasingly flexible attitude in assessing the standing conditions,[275] judgments such as *Zunis Holding*[276] and *Grandes Sources*[277] evidence the difficulties encountered by the Community Courts in establishing that the impugned clearance decisions were of direct concern to the applicants.

The inconsistency of the position adopted by the CFI in these cases as regards the question of direct concern under the standing test normally applicable to third parties also suggests that the Court's conclusions in the *Grandes Sources* appeal decision[278] could be detrimental to the effective protection of

---

274 *Inter alia*, joined Cases T-374, 375, 384, 388/94, *European Night Services and Others v Commission,* [1998] ECR II-3141 at para. 61; joined Cases T-528/93, T-542 and 543/93, T-546/93, *Metropole Television SA and Others v Commission*, [1996] ECR II-649; case 210/81, *Demo-Studio Schmidt v Commission*, [1983] ECR 3045; Case T-231/99, *Joynson v EC Commission*, [2002] ECR II-2085; Case T-131/99, *Shaw and Falla v EC Commission*, [2002] ECR II-2023.

275 *Inter alia*, Case T-119/02, *Royal Philips Electronics NV v Commission*, [2003] 5 CMLR 2 at paras. 282 and 284.

276 T-83/92, *Zunis Holding v Commission*, [1993] ECR II-1169.

277 Case T-96/92, *Comité Central d'Enterprise de la Société Generale des Grandes Sources and Others v Commission*, [1995] ECR II-1213.

278 Case T-96/92, *Comité Central d'Enterprise de la Société Generale des*

the rights of that category of applicants and could undermine the coherence of the relevant standing conditions.[279]

Having regard to the intensity of the power of judicial scrutiny exercised over antitrust decisions, the 'comprehensive review' provided by the Luxembourg Courts in respect to allegations of procedural impropriety or of error in the interpretation of Articles 81 and 82 EC Treaty appears to provide effective checks on the Commission's decision-making processes.[280] However, it is the more restrained approach adopted for the review of the 'complex economic assessments' made by the Commission[281] that does not seem consistent with the concept of 'full jurisdiction' enshrined in Article 6(1) ECHR.[282]

It is argued that although the rights enshrined in Article 6(1) ECHR are not absolute,[283] this 'limited' power of control may not conform entirely to the requirements of 'full jurisdiction' enshrined in the composite approach to Article 6(1) ECHR[284] and could therefore jeopardise the overall consistency of EC antitrust proceedings with the Convention, despite the reassurance offered by the CFI in its *Aristrain* decision.[285]

The position adopted with respect to the review of Commission antitrust decisions can be contrasted with the recent achievements in the area of merger control. The *Tetra Laval* appeal judgment must clearly be welcomed since it ensures that a stringent and exhaustive scrutiny of the Commission's decision, extending to the substance of the economic analysis and to the relevance and sufficiency of the evidence.[286]

Grandes Sources and others v Commission, [1995] ECR II-1213 at para. 38. *Supra*, this chapter, para. 1.2, footnote 76 and accompanying text.

279 *Inter alia,* ARNULL, case comment to T-96/92, *Comité Central d'Enterprise de la Société Generale des Grandes Sources and others v Commission*, Judgment of 27 April 1995; Case T-12/93, *Comité Central d'Enterprise de la Société Anonime Vittel and Others v Commission*, Judgment of 27 April 1995, (1996) 33 *CMLRev* 319 at 332; WARD, '*Locus standi* under Article 230(4) of the EC Treaty'.

280 VESTERDORF, 'Standard of proof in merger cases', at 12.

281 *Inter alia*, cases 142/84 and 156/84, *British American Tobacco Co Ltd and RJ Reynolds Industries Inc v Commission*, [1987] ECR 4487, para. 62; case 42/84, *Remia v Commission*, [1985] ECR 2585, para. 26.

282 *Inter alia*, Appl. No 10328/83, *Belilos v Switzerland*, [1988] 10 EHRR 466, paras. 70–71; Appl. No 15523/89, *Schmautzer v Austria*, [1996] 21 EHRR 511, Opinion of the Commission, para. 53, para. 36 of the judgment.

283 Cf., *inter alia*, Appl. No 8225/78, *Ashingdane v United Kingdom*, [1985] 7 EHRR 528, para. 57; Appl. No 12864/87, *Geouffre de la Pradelle v France*, [1993] ser. A, Judgments and Decisions, vol. 253, paras. 33–34.

284 *Inter alia*, Appl. No 10328/83, *Belilos v Switzerland*, [1988] 10 EHRR 466, paras. 70–71.

285 Case T-156/94, *Siderurgica Aristrain Madrid SL v Commission*, [1999] ECR II-645.

286 Case C-12/03, *Commission v Tetra Laval*, [2005] ECR I-987, paras. 39–40. For commentary, BAY and RUIZ CALZADO, '*Tetra Laval II*', at 442–43.

However, the overall examination of the case law mentioned above appears to suggest that the Luxembourg Courts, while exercising a more stringent review of decisions regarding the control of concentrations and therefore 'civil' in nature, exercise a lower standard of control with regard to decisions ascertaining the violation of Articles 81 and 82 EC Treaty that have been deemed to have a 'criminal' character.

Some commentators argued that the shift in approach in the judicial control of antitrust decisions towards a more restrained type of scrutiny may be explained in relation to the changing role of the CFI as competition court from 'guarantor of regulatory rigour and fair dealing' to a 'sentencing moderator',[287] whose powers of scrutiny are likely to concentrate more on the sufficiency of the evidence than on the observance of the procedural rules on the part of the Commission.[288] This new attitude to judicial control could also be motivated by the more aggressive attitude in policing cartels and the emergence of new enforcement tools, such as the 2002 Leniency programme.[289]

Nonetheless, it is submitted that despite sounding convincing, this argument does not address the main issue of how to ensure the compatibility of the existing standards of control of antitrust decisions with the safeguards enshrined in Article 6(1) ECHR for the judicial scrutiny of administrative decisions having a 'criminal character'.[290] Although it is legitimate to take the view that under Article 230 EC Treaty the Community courts are not to be allowed to substitute their own judgment for that of the Commission, it is apparent that the scope of judicial review exercised over antitrust decisions appears at variance with the position of the Strasbourg Court.

It could be argued that the more 'vigilant' attitude developed by the CFI and ECJ with respect to the judicial control of merger decisions should be extended to the review of antitrust decisions. However, it is clear from the *Tetra Laval* appeal judgment[291] that the stringent standards of judicial scrutiny applicable to merger decisions are justified mainly by the characteristics of the system for the control of concentrations,[292] namely its administrative, forward-looking nature, the presence of tight time limits and the impossibility

---

[287] HARDING and GIBBS, 'Why go to court in Europe? An analysis of cartel appeals 1995–2004', (2005) 30(3) *ELRev* 349 at 369.

[288] HARDING and JOSHUA, *Regulating Cartels in Europe: a Study of Legal Control of Corporate Delinquency* (2003) Oxford University Press, p. 174–75.

[289] *Id.*, pp. 185–86. Also HARDING and GIBBS, 'Why go to court in Europe?', at 369.

[290] Appl. No 15523/89, *Schmautzer v Austria*, [1996] 21 EHRR 511 at para. 36; also, Opinion of the European Commission of Human Rights, para. 53.

[291] Case C-12/03, *Commission v Tetra Laval*, [2005] ECR I-987, para. 42.

[292] BAY and RUIZ CALZADO, '*Tetra Laval II*', at 449–50.

for the interested parties to challenge the decisions of the Commission in national courts.[293]

By contrast, antitrust enforcement entails an *ex post* assessment of allegations of anti-competitive conduct and seeks to detect and sanction the infringement of Articles 81 and 82 EC Treaty. Accordingly, it is argued that the application of a *Tetra Laval*-type standard of review would not be entirely appropriate and, especially in consideration of the 'criminal nature' of these measures, would not ensure compliance with the relevant ECHR standards.[294]

Consequently, the question emerges of how the compatibility of the existing standards of judicial scrutiny of Commission antitrust decisions with Article 6(1) ECHR can be attained. On this point, the recent debate sparked by the proposal made by the Confederation of British Industry[295] to the House of Lords Select Committee on the European Union for the creation of an EU Competition Court in the form of a specialised 'judicial panel' attached to the CFI, in accordance with Article 225a EC Treaty, provided very useful insights into the effectiveness of judicial scrutiny in the field of competition.[296]

The inquiry explored the viability of the proposal for the creation of a specialised court whose jurisdiction, despite being concerned initially with the review of merger decisions, would be extended in the future to all competition matters raised by private parties. The Select Committee looked with interest at the British Competition Appeals Tribunal (CAT) as a blueprint for a 'competition court',[297] and supported the proposal to confer on the CFI the power to decide cases on the merits in limited circumstances.[298] It is therefore suggested that the possibility of introducing a similar form of jurisdiction in the field of EC antitrust enforcement should be explored, since it could succeed in accommodating the needs of effective competition enforcement with respect for the right to a 'fair hearing' enjoyed by the undertakings affected by the Commission's competition decisions. The implications of this proposal will be examined in Chapter 7.

---

293 VESTERDORF, 'Standard of proof in merger cases', at 30. See also, *mutatis mutandis*, Case T-351/03, *Schneider Electric v Commission*, judgment of 11 July 2007, not yet reported, especially para. 132.

294 *Id.*, p. 27.

295 CBI Brief, 'The need for an EU Competition Court', 15 June 2006.

296 HOUSE of LORDS SELECT COMMITTEE, *XV Report: an EU Competition Court*, session 2006–07, 23 April 2007 (hereinafter referred to as *XV Report*). *Infra*, Chapter 7, section 2.

297 *Id.*, para.135.

298 Competition Act 1998, Schedule 8, para. 3(1). See HOUSE of LORDS SELECT COMMITTEE, *XV Report*, para. 210.

4. 'DUE PROCESS' IN COMPETITION PROCEEDINGS: FROM 'CENTRALISATION' TO MODERNISATION

So far the examination has concentrated on the standards of 'due process' relevant for antitrust and merger proceedings before the European Commission. The application of the 'composite approach' advocated by the European Court of Human Rights and by the ECJ consequently called for the examination both of the administrative and the judicial stage of the proceedings.

However, the enactment of Council Regulation No 1/2003 and the consequent implementation of the 'Modernisation Plan', with its emphasis on the decentralised application of Articles 81 and 82 of the EC Treaty, demands an examination of the impact of the operation of the European Competition Network (hereinafter referred to as ECN) and of the measures of cooperation between the Commission and the NCAs on the EC 'due process' requirements.

The following chapter will therefore address the implications of the rules governing the allocation of cases and the exchange of information and evidence within the ECN for the procedural rights enjoyed by the parties affected by the application of the Treaty antitrust rules.

6. The Modernisation of the enforcement of Articles 81 and 82 EC Treaty and the right to a 'fair procedure'*

INTRODUCTION

Although the focus of the present work is on the right to a 'fair procedure' before the European Commission, the implementation of the 'Modernisation' plan demands an examination of the implications of the decentralised application of Articles 81 and 82 EC Treaty for the 'due process' rights enjoyed by the investigated firms.

This chapter, after having outlined the main characteristics of the new enforcement framework, will investigate the functioning of the mechanisms of case allocation and of exchange of information within the European Competition Network (hereinafter referred to as ECN). The analysis will focus on their implications for the procedural rights of the investigated undertakings, including leniency applicants.[1] Special consideration will be given to the impact of those mechanisms on the level of protection of legal professional privilege and of the privilege against self-incrimination to assess whether the assumption of 'equivalent protection' of the rights of the defence throughout the Community made by Regulation No 1/2003 is fully justified.

Thereafter, the chapter will address the general question of which fundamental rights standards should be applied to proceedings before NCAs when Articles 81 and 82 EC Treaty are at issue, in the light of the ECJ's *Wachauf* case law. In conclusion, an attempt will be made to predict the overall effect of the Modernisation Regulation on the future standards of due process in competition enforcement, especially as regards the treatment of evidence and the protection of privileged information. It is not the purpose of this chapter to

---

* A shorter version of this chapter was published in (2006) 31 (3) *ELRev* 342 with the title: 'The impact of the Modernisation Regulation on the guarantees of due process in competition proceedings'.

[1] Commission Notice on the non-imposition or reduction of fines in cartel cases, [1996] OJ C207/04; replaced by Commission notice on immunity from fines and reduction of fines in cartel cases, [2002] OJ C45/03.

examine the different procedural laws applicable in the Member States. Instead its focus will lie in the impact of the application of the rules concerning case allocation and exchange of information on the procedural rights of the undertakings concerned by antitrust proceedings, given the absence of harmonised rules on procedures and sanctions before the individual Network members.

1. THE MAIN CHARACTERISTICS OF THE NEW FRAMEWORK FOR THE ENFORCEMENT OF ARTICLES 81 AND 82 OF THE EC TREATY: THE EUROPEAN COMPETITION NETWORK

Council Regulation No 1/2003 introduced substantial changes in the framework for the enforcement of Articles 81 and 82 EC Treaty by abolishing the Commission's 'monopoly' in the application of Article 81(3) EC Treaty and strongly encouraging the NCAs and the national courts to take a much more active role in the application of EC competition rules[2] to secure the efficient implementation of EC antitrust policy.[3]

These reforms envisaged the achievement of effectiveness, coherence and uniformity in the application of Community competition law within a new landscape characterised by the increasing involvement of the national agencies acting in 'close cooperation' with the Commission and with each other in the context of a 'European Competition Network'.[4] The ECN, however, has no independent legal existence.[5] It was created as a forum for discussion and cooperation for the enforcement of EC competition policy by the European competition agencies[6] and functions as 'a kind of shell for various mechanisms of mutual assistance and consultation'[7] to facilitate the efficient handling of cases, foster collaboration between the Commission and the NCAs

---

2 Recital VI, Council Regulation 1/2003.

3 EHLERMANN, 'The Modernization of EC antitrust policy: a legal and cultural revolution', (2000) 37 *CMLRev* 537 at 560.

4 Joint Statement of the Council and the Commission made at the time when Regulation No 1/2003 was adopted (hereinafter referred to as Joint Statement), Brussels 3.3.2003 (13.03), para. 2,5,7.

5 GAUER, 'Due process in the face of divergent national procedures and sanctions', paper presented at the International Bar Association 2005 Conference: 'Decentralisation of EC Competition Law: a year in practice', p. 1.

6 Commission Notice on cooperation within the Network of competition authorities (hereinafter referred to as the 'Network Notice'), [2004] OJ C101/43 at para. 1.

7 GAUER, *supra*, footnote 5, p. 1.

and amongst the NCAs themselves and ensure the uniform interpretation of the competition rules.[8]

At the heart of that close cooperation, Regulation No 1/2003 envisages an effective method of case allocation and the sharing of information and evidence across the ECN. With respect to case allocation, Article 11(3)[9] obliges the NCAs to inform the Commission without delay of the initiation of any proceeding involving the application of the Treaty so that the information can be made available to all the members of the ECN. Its purpose is to permit the detection of parallel proceedings and allow the reallocation of each case to the NCA which is well placed to deal with it.[10]

Article 12 of the Regulation provides the legal basis for the exchange and use as evidence of information between the Commission and the NCAs and amongst the NCAs themselves.[11] By ensuring that the enforcement agencies proceed on the basis of the fullest information[12] it constitutes 'a key element of the functioning of the network' and a 'precondition for efficient and effective allocation and handling of cases'.[13]

Article 22 of Regulation 1/2003 lays down the third device aimed at ensuring close cooperation within the parties to the ECN by conferring on each NCA the power to 'carry out any inspection or other fact-finding measure under its national law on behalf and for the account of the competition authority of another Member State'; any evidence so collected will then be transmitted to the requesting authority in accordance with Article 12. Likewise, the

---

8 Network Notice, para. 3.

9 'The competition authorities of the Member States shall, when acting under Article 81 or Article 82 of the Treaty, inform the Commission in writing before or without delay after commencing the first formal investigative measure. This information may also be made available to the competition authorities of the other Member States.'

10 BURNSIDE and CROSSLEY, 'Cooperative mechanisms within the EU: a blueprint for future cooperation at the international level', (2004) 10 *Int'l Trade Law and Regulation* 25 at 27.

11 VAN der WOUDE, 'Exchange of information within the European Competition Network: scope and limits', in EHLERMANN and ATANASIU (eds), *European Competition Law Annual 2002: Constructing the EU Network of Competition Authorities* (2004) Oxford, Portland, OR: Hart Publishing, p. 369 at 378. Cf. Case C-67/91, *Direccion General de la Defensa de la Competencia v Asociacion Espanola de Banca Privada and others*, [1992] ECR I-4785 at para. 41; for commentary, *inter alia*, WILLIS, 'Transfer of information between authorities in the modernised network', (2004) 2(4) *Competition Law Journal* 310 at 319.

12 DEKEYSER and DALHEIMER, 'Cooperation within the European Competition Network – taking stock after 10 months of case practice', paper presented at the International Bar Association 2005 Conference: 'Decentralisation of EC Competition Law, a year in practice', p. 11.

13 Network Notice, footnote 6, para. 26.

Commission may request the NCAs to undertake inspections or other measures of inquiry on its own behalf in their own territory and in accordance with the authority's national law.[14]

The Modernisation Regulation resulted in Articles 81 and 82 EC Treaty becoming a common set of substantive rules applicable at national and at Community level to all forms of anti-competitive conduct adversely affecting interstate trade within the EC in a framework in which the national enforcement agencies are 'closely associated' with the Commission and with each other. However, it did not provide for uniform rules governing procedures and sanctions: harmonisation in these areas was not considered a precondition to the functioning of the new 'decentralised' framework.[15] Consequently, the operation of the Network and the enhanced level of cooperation raises the question of whether adequate standards of due process can be maintained where no common rules exist as regards the scope of the rights of the defence enjoyed by the investigated undertakings.[16]

2. CASE ALLOCATION AND COMMUNITY 'DUE PROCESS' IN COMPETITION PROCEEDINGS

2.1. The Impact of 'Flexible' Case Allocation Criteria on the Procedural Rights of the Investigated Parties

Regulation 1/2003 confers the power to apply Articles 81 and 82 EC Treaty to individual cases on both the Commission and the NCAs,[17] thus making the task of enforcing the Community competition rules a 'shared responsibility'.[18] However, since the practices caught by the application of the Treaty rules have an impact on interstate trade and are therefore capable of adversely affecting competition in markets falling within the jurisdiction of more than one NCA,

---

14 *Id.*, paras. 29–30. *Inter alia*, LOWE, 'Current issues of EU Competition law: the new competition enforcement regime', (2003–2004) 24 *Nw. J. Int'l L. & Bus.* 567 at 572.

15 GAUER, 'Does the effectiveness of the EU network of competition authorities require a certain degree of harmonisation of national procedures and sanctions?', in EHLERMANN and ATANASIU (eds), *European Competition Law Annual 2002*, at 201.

16 *Inter alia*, IDOT, 'A necessary step towards common procedural standards of implementation for Articles 81 and 82 EC within the network', in *ibid.*, p. 213 at 214–15.

17 Respectively, Article 4 and 5, Council Regulation No 1/2003.

18 KERSE and KHAN, *EC Antitrust Procedure*, p. 47.

the new framework is characterised by the likelihood of parallel proceedings.[19]

To allow an efficient case allocation, the NCAs are obliged to inform the Commission and hence the ECN of the initiation of new proceedings involving the application of EC competition rules.[20] Nevertheless, their power to prosecute and sanction suspected infringements remains unaffected:[21] the fact that one authority is already dealing with a case constitutes 'sufficient ground' for other NCAs to suspend proceedings or reject a complaint with respect to the same allegation, but does not entail an obligation to relinquish its jurisdiction.[22] Only the Commission can seize jurisdiction to deal with a particular infringement by initiating proceedings.[23]

Although in principle each case should be dealt with by a single authority,[24] Regulation 1/2003 does not provide any rules concerning the 'division of work'[25] among the members of the ECN. According to the Joint Statement 'cases will be dealt with by an authority, or by authorities, able to restore or maintain competition in the market'.[26] An authority will be 'well-placed to act' when a restrictive practice has 'substantial direct actual or foreseeable effects on competition' within the authority's jurisdiction, or is 'implemented within or originate from its territory'.[27] The agency must be able to 'effectively bring to an end the entire infringement',[28] to 'gather, possibly with the assistance of other authorities, the evidence required to prove the infringement'[29] and to sanction it adequately.

---

[19] DEKEYSER and DALHEIMER, 'Cooperation within the European Competition Network', p. 5.

[20] Article 11(3), Regulation 1/2003.

[21] Case 14/68, *Walt Wilhelm v Commission*, [1969] ECR 1, para. 11.

[22] *Inter alia*, VENIT, 'Brave new world: the Modernisation and decentralisation of enforcement under Articles 81 and 82 of the EC Treaty', (2003) 40 *CMLRev* 545 at 564–65.

[23] Article 11(6), Council Regulation 1/2003: 'The initiation by the Commission of proceedings for the adoption of a decision under Chapter III shall relieve the competition authorities of the Member States of their competence to apply Articles 81 and 82 of the Treaty. If a competition authority of a Member State is already acting on a case, the Commission shall only initiate proceedings after consulting with that national competition authority.' See, *inter alia*, GERBER and CASSINIS, 'The 'Modernization' of European Community competition law: achieving consistency in enforcement. Part I', (2006) 27(1) *ECLR* 10 at 16–18.

[24] Recital XVIII of the Preamble to Council Regulation 1/2003.

[25] GAUER, 'Due process in the face of divergent national procedures and sanctions', p. 2.

[26] Para. 15, Joint Statement of the Council and the Commission.

[27] Network Notice, *supra*, footnote 6, para. 8.

[28] *Ibid.*

[29] *Ibid.*

Normally, provided that its action is adequate to end the infringement[30] the notifying authority will remain responsible for the case[31] unless there are grounds for action by the Commission.[32] Joint or parallel action is justified for restrictive practices having 'effects on competition mainly in the territories of two or more Member States' for which action by a single NCA 'would not be adequate to bring the infringement to an end or to sanction it adequately'.[33]

The Commission will normally take action with respect to restrictive practices having anti-competitive effects in the territories of more than three Member States, when a case 'is closely linked to other Community provisions which may be exclusively or more effectively applied by the Commission'[34] and where 'the Community interest requires the adoption of a Commission decision to develop Community competition policy when a new competition issue arises or to ensure effective enforcement'.[35]

Reallocation is likely to constitute a last resort at the early stages of the procedure 'where either that authority considered that it was not well placed to act or (. . .) other authorities also considered themselves well placed to act'[36] and if it is 'necessary for an effective protection of competition and of the Community interest'.[37]

In the absence of a 'clearing house where the Network would decide where a specific case would be handled',[38] the efficient division of labour is in fact entrusted to the single members of the ECN.[39] Nor is there any such thing as a 'reallocation decision': once proceedings are started in a specific jurisdiction, the allocation of a case depends on the decision of the individual agency on whether or not to pursue that case.[40]

Although the Joint Statement indicates that the 'mutual recognition' of the Member States' standards constitutes the 'basis for cooperation' within the

---

30 *Id.*, para. 11. Joint Statement, para. 16.

31 *Id.*, para. 6. Joint Statement, para. 17.

32 *Id.*, paras. 6 and 9. NAZZINI, *Concurrent Proceedings in Competition Law – procedure, evidence and remedies* (2004) Oxford University Press, p. 72.

33 NAZZINI, op. cit. Network Notice (footnote 6), para. 12.

34 *Id.*, para. 14.

35 *Ibid.* Joint Statement, para. 18.

36 Network Notice, footnote 6, para. 6.

37 *Id.*, para. 7. For an example of reallocation to the Commission, see the complaint lodged with the Office of Fair Trading by the consumers' association Which?, concerning the *Apple-iTunes* service (http://www.oft.gov.uk/news/press+releases/statements/2004/itunes.htm).

38 GAUER, 'Due process in the face of divergent national procedures and sanctions', p. 3.

39 DEKEYSER and DALHEIMER, 'Cooperation within the European Competition Network', p. 6.

40 *Ibid.* But note Article 11(6), Council Regulation No 1/2003.

ECN,[41] no harmonisation of the domestic rules governing procedures and sanctions was provided. Consequently, the possibility of reallocation could significantly affect the position of the investigated undertakings. In fact, competition authorities have different powers and the degree of their independence and manner of composition vary from jurisdiction to jurisdiction.[42]

In some Member States 'independent administrative authorities' are entrusted with competition enforcement and enjoy powers similar to those of the Commission, as is the case in Italy, Germany and the United Kingdom,[43] whereas others, like Ireland, have opted for 'splitting' investigation and prosecution from the decision-making function between, respectively, the Irish Competition Authority and the national courts.[44]

Furthermore, whereas in some legal systems the NCAs may enter premises only upon a judicial warrant,[45] in the majority of the Member States their investigative powers resemble those enjoyed by the Commission, namely the power to request written information, to enter premises and to seize documents[46] without the need for prior judicial authorisation.[47] Consequently although national courts can exercise only a limited scrutiny on investigative measures ordered by NCAs,[48] the reallocation of a case from Ireland to Italy, for example, would deprive the investigated firms of the possibility to challenge these investigative measures in court.

Even this brief overview demonstrates the significant impact of the possibility of reallocation on the position of the investigated undertakings vis-à-vis the authority 'well-placed' to investigate the allegations made against them. The flexible nature of the case allocation criteria and the lack of harmonisation of the domestic laws governing procedures and sanctions are likely to

---

41 Para. 8, Joint Statement.

42 For commentary, see, *inter alia*, PERRIN, 'Challenges facing the network of competition authorities: insights from a comparative criminal law perspective', (2006) 31 *ELRev* 540 at 559.

43 CAHILL and COOKE (eds), *The Modernisation of EU Competition Law Enforcement in the EU*: FIDE 2004 National Reports (2004) Cambridge University Press, National Reports, pp. 305–06.

44 *Id.*, p. 276.

45 E.g. Ireland, United Kingdom. *Id.*, National Reports, pp. 277–78; pp. 605–06.

46 *Id.*, General Report, pp. 633–34.

47 *Id.*, pp. 309–10.

48 KERSE and KHAN, *EC Antitrust Procedure*, pp. 284–85. See case C-94/99, *Roquette Frères SA v Directeur General de la Concurrance*, [2002] ECR I-9011, para.74; Commission Notice on cooperation between the Commission and the courts of the EU member states in the application of Articles 81 and 82 EC, [2004] OJ C101/54 at para. 39. For the approach adopted by the English courts in reviewing the investigative measures ordered by the OFT, see *Office of Fair Trading v X* (Queen's Bench Division), [2004] ICR 105, especially paras. 8–10.

result in legal uncertainty regarding the extent of the rights enjoyed by the investigated undertakings and ultimately could threaten the effectiveness of their rights of defence.[49]

2.2. Case Reallocation and Legal Certainty: the Case of Leniency Applicants

The impact of the flexible mechanism of case allocation envisaged by the 'Modernisation Plan' on the legal position of the investigated undertakings may be illustrated in relation to those firms who have lodged or are considering lodging a leniency application with any of the members of the ECN. The introduction of a Leniency programme by the Commission,[50] providing the undertakings with the possibility to obtain partial or total immunity from fines in exchange for full, continuous and expeditious cooperation during competition proceedings represented a significant breakthrough in the fight against cartels, resulting in more efficient detection and deterrence.[51]

The Commission grants full immunity to the first undertaking to submit evidence which the Commission considers will justify it launching a targeted inspection related to the alleged breach or will allow it to find an infringement of Article 81 of the EC Treaty,[52] provided that at that time the Commission did not have sufficient evidence to carry out that inspection or had not already done so.[53] A reduction of the fine is instead granted to undertakings which, despite not complying with the conditions for full immunity, provide the Commission with information on an alleged infringement constituting 'significant added value' to the evidence already available to the officials and which have ended their involvement in the cartel.[54]

The success of the Notice has led to the proliferation of analogous programmes in many, but not all, of the Member States. However, their

---

49 *Inter alia*, PERRIN, 'Challenges facing the EU network of competition authorities', at 556.

50 Commission Notice on immunity from fines and reduction of fines in cartel cases, [2006] C298/17, replacing the Notice on Immunity from fines and reduction of fines in cartel cases, [2002] OJ C45/03. For a consideration of the 2002 Notice see RILEY, 'Cartel whistle blowing: toward an American model', (2002) 9 *Maastricht Journal of European and Comparative Law* 1.

51 LEVY and O'DONOGHUE, 'The EU leniency programme comes of age', (2004) 27 *W. Comp.* 75 at 76. See Commission Notice on the non-imposition or reduction of fines in cartel cases, [1996] OJ C207/04.

52 Commission Notice on immunity from fines and reduction of fines in cartel cases, [2006] C298/17, para. 8.

53 *Id.*, para. 10.

54 *Id.*, paras. 24–25.

requirements differ substantially in each jurisdiction. For instance, full immunity is available under the Irish Leniency policy to the first applicant who confesses its involvement in a cartel and takes effective steps to terminate it, provided it was not the instigator of the cartel, that it fully and timely cooperates with the investigation and does not alert the other cartel members.[55] Instead the programme issued by the Italian Competition Authority requires the applicant to disclose evidence which the Authority considers 'decisive for the finding of an infringement' and will grant immunity from fines only provided that, at the time of the disclosure, it did not have sufficient proof of the alleged violation.[56]

Furthermore, the decisions of the NCAs granting immunity from fines are ineffective beyond the boundaries of the jurisdiction within which they were adopted.[57] Hence, successful whistle-blowers remain exposed to the risk of being prosecuted and fined by another NCA for the same infringement[58] and are in fact obliged to file applications in all the jurisdictions potentially affected by the restrictive practices to secure immunity within the ECN.[59] Also, since immunity from administrative fines is not always accompanied by immunity from criminal prosecution of the officers of the undertakings,[60] the threat of criminal liability provided in some jurisdictions could discourage the employees of potential applicants from assisting in preparing a leniency application.[61]

Although the information supplied to the Network as regards new proceedings initiated following a leniency application cannot be used as a basis for filing a new case in a different European jurisdiction,[62] the applicants are not

---

55 Irish Competition Authority, Cartel Immunity Programme, 20 December 2001; for commentary, see MEDINGER, 'Antitrust leniency programs: a call for increased harmonisation as proliferating programs undermine deterrence', (2003) 52 *Emory L. J.* 1439, p. 1453.

56 AUTORITA' GARANTE della CONCORRENZA e del MERCATO, 'Notice on the non-imposition and reduction of fines under section 15 of Law No 287 of 10 October 1990', para. 2.

57 See EUROPEAN COMMISSION, European Competition Network, 'Model leniency programme', Memorandum of 29 September 2006 No 06/356, p. 4 of the memorandum.

58 Case 14/68, *Walt Wilhelm v Commission*, [1969] ECR 1, para. 11. NAZZINI, *Concurrent Proceedings in Competition Law*, p. 123.

59 MEDINGER, 'Antitrust leniency programs', at 1458.

60 LEVY and O'DONOGHUE, 'The EU leniency programme comes of age', at 96.

61 *Ibid.* See also GARZANITI, GUDOFSKY and MOFFAT, 'Dawn of a new era? Powers of investigation and enforcement under Regulation 1/2003', (2004–2005) 72 *Antitrust L J* 159 at 200.

62 Network Notice, footnote 6, para. 39.

protected from the danger of being tipped off by other sources, such as complainants.[63] Apart from the more general issues which parallel competence could raise with respect to the principle of *ne bis in idem*,[64] multiple filings not only would appear costly for the potential applicants but could also jeopardise the effectiveness of the promise of immunity in uncovering cartels.[65]

It is submitted that the impact of the flexible mechanism of case allocation in the context of the 'Modernised' landscape for the enforcement of Articles 81 and 82 EC Treaty constitutes a telling example of the implications of the transfer of an investigation across the ECN on the legal position of leniency applicants. In this respect, it is noteworthy that in September 2006 the ECN launched a 'Model Leniency Programme' to foster convergence throughout the Member States with respect to the requirements governing the grant of immunity or of reductions of fines, and the procedures to be followed in assessing the applications.[66]

The Model programme sets out conditions for the grant of full or partial immunity that are by and large similar to those contained in the Commission's own Leniency Notice, both as regards the 'first-come-first-served' basis and the standards of 'quality' of the evidence necessary to obtain immunity.[67] It also envisages that the NCAs grant a 'marker' for summary applications so that the 'place in the queue' of potential whistleblowers can be protected for the time necessary to gather the necessary evidence to qualify for immunity.[68]

Nonetheless, it should be emphasised that the Model programme does not provide any solution to the problem of multiple filings arising from the absence of a 'one-stop-shop' for transnational cartels.[69] Accordingly, it is submitted that although it is perhaps premature to draw any conclusion as to

---

63 *Ibid.* See HENRY, 'Leniency programmes: an anaemic carrot for cartels in France Germany and the UK', (2005) 26(1) *ECLR* 13 at 22.

64 WAELBROECK, '"Twelve feet dangling down and six necks exceeding long". The EU network of competition authorities and the European Convention on Fundamental Rights', in EHLERMANN and ATANASIU (eds), *European Competition Law Annual 2002*, p. 465 at 470ff., *inter alia*, Appl. No 37/950/97, *Franz Fischer v Austria*, judgment of 29 May 2001, unreported, paras. 22, 25, 29. Cf. WILS, 'The EU network of competition authorities, the European Convention on Human Rights and the Charter of Fundamental Rights of the EU', in EHLERMANN and ATANASIU (eds), *Competition Law Annual 2002*, p. 433 at 449. *Infra*, para. 4.2.

65 HENRY, 'Leniency programmes: an anaemic carrot for cartels in France Germany and the UK', at 23.

66 European Competition Network, 'Model leniency programme', Memorandum of 29 September 2006 no 06/356.

67 *Id.*, sections III and IV.

68 *Id.*, section VI, paras. 16–18.

69 *Ibid.*; see ECN memorandum, p. 4.

its impact, the Model Leniency Programme does not appear wholly able to address the main difficulties stemming from the lack of procedural harmonisation and of a sole clearing house for leniency applications within the Network, with potentially adverse effects on the effectiveness of the promise of immunity as a means to boost cartel detection.

3. THE EXCHANGE OF INFORMATION WITHIN THE ECN AND THE PROTECTION OF FUNDAMENTAL RIGHTS. THE CASE OF LEGAL PROFESSIONAL PRIVILEGE

3.1. Exchanging Information within the Network of Competition Authorities: Efficient Enforcement versus Effective Protection of the Undertakings' Rights of Defence?

The accessibility of the information exchanged within the ECN represents a key element of the 'Modernised' framework.[70] Article 11(4) of Regulation 1/2003 allows the NCAs and the Commission to exchange any information necessary for the assessment of cases involving the application of Articles 81 and 82 EC Treaty.[71] Alongside that general clause, Council Regulation No 1/2003 provides a new power to transmit information to another jurisdiction so that the receiving competition agency can use it as evidence in its proceedings.[72] According to its Article 12(1): 'For the purpose of applying Articles 81 and 82 of the Treaty the Commission and the competition authorities of the Member States shall have the power to provide one another with and use in evidence any matter of fact or of law, including confidential information.'

The rules provided by Regulation 17/62 did not allow for the 'horizontal' flow of information, namely the transmission of information between the various NCAs.[73] In accordance with its Article 20(1), the information collected by the Commission could only be used for 'the purpose of the relevant request or investigation'.[74] In the *Spanish Banks*[75] preliminary ruling the ECJ interpreted that provision as precluding that evidence from being deployed beyond 'the

70 Para. 10, Joint Statement.

71 Article 11(4), Regulation 1/2003.

72 KERSE and KHAN, *EC Antitrust Procedure*, pp. 266–67.

73 VAN der WOUDE, 'Exchange of information within the European Competition Network', at 374.

74 Article 20(1), Regulation 17/62.

75 Case C-67/91, *Direccion General de Defensa de la Competencia v Asociacion Espanola de Banca Privada and others*, [1992] ECR I-4785.

legal scope of the procedure'[76] in which it had originally been gathered, and concluded that evidence exchanged 'vertically' between the Commission and the NCAs could be relied upon solely 'to decide whether or not it [was] appropriate to initiate a national procedure'.[77]

Commentators, however, pointed out that the view taken in *Spanish Banks* could only be justified in an enforcement framework largely centralised on the Commission. It could not, on the other hand, fulfil the needs of the 'Modernised' enforcement system which, due to the increased involvement of the NCAs in the application of Articles 81 and 82 EC Treaty,[78] demands that the information gathered by the members of the ECN be allowed to 'change hands' within the Network.[79]

Consequently, Article 12 of Council Regulation No 1/2003 represents a departure from the previous state of the law since it allows for the 'horizontal' transfer of information. Nevertheless, it is subject to limits: the exchanged information can be relied upon only 'for the purpose of applying Article 81 and 82 of the Treaty and in respect of the subject-matter for which it was collected by the investigating authority'[80] save in cases where the receiving Authority is seeking to enforce national competition law that is applied in parallel with the Community rules and does not 'lead to a different outcome'.[81]

Also, the use in evidence of exchanged information against individuals cannot result in the imposition of custodial sanctions and is limited to cases when 'the law of the transmitting authority foresees sanctions of a similar kind' for infringements of Articles 81 and 82 EC Treaty or, 'in absence thereof, the information has been collected in a way which respects the same level of protection of the rights of the defence of natural persons' as in the law of the receiving authority.[82]

The structure and the function of Article 12 of Regulation 1/2003 supports

---

[76] *Id.*, para. 36.

[77] *Id.*, para. 42. Cf. NAZZINI, *Concurrent Proceedings in Competition Law*, p. 212.

[78] *Ibid.*

[79] SCHAUB, 'Modernization of EC Competition law: reform of Regulation No. 17', (1999–2000) 23 *Fordham Int'l L J* 752 at 767. Cf. NAZZINI (footnote 32), p. 214. For the possible issue arising from the UK Competition Act 1998 see RODGER, 'Interrelationship with Community competition law enforcement', in RODGER and MacCULLOCH (eds), *The UK Competition Act: a New Era for UK Competition Law* (2000) Oxford, Portland, OR: Hart Publishing, pp. 64–66.

[80] Article 12(1), Regulation 1/2003.

[81] Article 12(3), Regulation 1/2003.

[82] *Ibid. Inter alia*, WILS, 'Powers of investigation and procedural rights and guarantees in EU antitrust enforcement', at 23.

a broad interpretation of the scope of the exchange of information which allows the free flow[83] of evidence within the ECN, subject only to the exceptions listed in Article 12(2) and (3) and providing that such evidence is acquired for the purpose of applying Articles 81 and 82 EC Treaty.[84]

However, the Regulation lacks rules governing the use of that evidence. The Network Notice only suggests that, once it can be demonstrated that the evidence is admissible under the rules applicable in the jurisdiction of the collecting authority, the receiving NCA should be able to use it regardless of any more protective rules in force in its own jurisdiction.[85] According to the Commission, the obligation of confidentiality enshrined in Article 27 of the Regulation[860] and the existing guarantees for the secrecy of correspondence laid down by Article 8 ECHR to which all the Member States are signatories, were regarded as providing a uniform minimum standard applicable across the Network.[87] The fact that more extensive safeguards provided by national law may be set aside due to the operation of the Network would not be inconsistent with the Convention.[88]

Nevertheless, the solution adopted in the Notice, despite being consistent with the principle of 'mutual recognition' of national procedural rules,[89] would seem to overlook the consequences of the absence of harmonisation of the rules concerning the legal treatment of evidence collected during competition proceedings in the national jurisdictions.[90] The implications of this broad interpretation of Article 12, Regulation 1/2003 for the protection of the rights of the defence of the investigated undertakings enshrined in EC law will be examined in the next section.

---

83 VAN der WOUDE, 'Exchange of information within the European Competition Network', at 385.

84 See, *inter alia*, BURNSIDE and CROSSLEY, 'Cooperation in competition: a new era?', (2005) 30 (2) *ELRev* 234 at 239.

85 Network Notice (footnote 6), para. 27. VESTERDORF, 'Legal professional privilege and the privilege against self-incrimination in EC law', p. 721.

86 *Inter alia*, case C-36/92 P, *SEP v Commission*, [1994] ECR I-1991 at paras. 38–39.

87 WILS, 'The EU network of competition authorities, the European Convention on Human Rights and the Charter of Fundamental Rights of the EU', in EHLERMANN and ATANASIU (eds), *European Competition Law Annual 2002*, pp. 457–58.

88 *Ibid.*

89 Para. 8, Joint Statement. Cf., *mutatis mutandis*, Proposal for a Council Framework Decision on the European Evidence Warrant for obtaining objects, documents and data for use in proceedings in criminal matters, COM/2003/0688 final – CNS 2003/0207, para. 39.

90 *Inter alia,* ARAUJO, 'The respect for fundamental rights within the European network of competition authorities', in HAWK (ed.), *International Antitrust Law and Policy*, p. 511 at 527ff.

3.2. Legal Professional Privilege and Decentralised Competition Enforcement: a Case in Point?

It will be recalled that EC law restricts the scope of application of legal professional privilege to communications made for the purpose and in the interest of the clients' rights of defence and which emanate from independent lawyers; EC law does not shield legal advice given by employed counsel from forced disclosure to the Commission.[91] Chapter 4 illustrated that, despite being based on principles common to the laws of the Member States,[92] the Community concept of privilege differs significantly from that provided by some domestic laws, under which employed legal advisers are permitted to be members of the local 'Bar' and therefore enjoy the same rights as independent lawyers.[93]

However, despite confirming in substance the existing position as regards the scope of privilege,[94] the recent judgment in the *AKZO Nobel* case[95] has not directly dealt with the issues arising from the possibility to exchange within the ECN evidence that may be covered by lawyer–client confidentiality in accordance with the differing standards enshrined in the laws of each Member State.[96] On this point, the President of the CFI had already observed extra-judicially that Article 12, Regulation 1/2003, could result in allowing the deployment of information against the investigated undertakings which 'has been collected under rules which are less protective than those of the Commission or the receiving NCA'[97] subject only to the limits established by Article 12(3).

It should be added that this interpretation was endorsed by the Office of Fair Trading. According to the OFT *Guidelines governing powers of investigation*:[98]

> Whilst UK privilege rules would apply to cases being investigated in the UK by the OFT on its own behalf under national and EC law, the OFT could be sent the

---

[91] Case 155/79, *AM & S Europe Limited v Commission of the European Communities*, [1982] ECR 1575, para. 21.

[92] *Id.*, para. 18.

[93] FAULL, 'In-house lawyers and legal professional privilege: a problem revisited', (1998) 4 *Colum. J. of Eur. L.* 139 at 142. *Supra*, Chapter 4, sections 1 to 3.

[94] Case 155/79, *AM & S Europe Limited v Commission of the European Communities*, [1982] ECR 1575, paras. 18, 21.

[95] Joined Cases T-125/03 and T-253/03, *AKZO Nobel and Ackros Chemicals v Commission*, judgment of 17 September 2007, not yet reported.

[96] *Supra*, Chapter 4, section 1.4.

[97] VESTERDORF, 'Legal professional privilege and the privilege against self-incrimination in EC Law', p. 721.

[98] OFFICE of FAIR TRADING, *Powers of Investigation,* Draft competition law guidelines for consultation, April 2004, OFT 404a.

> communications of in-house lawyers by a NCA from another Member State where the communications of in-house lawyers are not privileged. Under those circumstances, the OFT may use the documentation received from the other NCA in its investigation.[99]

Consequently, if the Commission or an NCA in whose jurisdiction that material can be disclosed were to transmit communications between an investigated undertaking and its in-house counsel to the OFT, the latter would be able to deploy that evidence despite the higher degree of protection afforded in its jurisdiction to lawyer–client confidentiality.

Commentators suggested that the OFT *Guidelines* are justified by the need to ensure the 'useful effect' of Article 12, Regulation 1/2003: to prevent the Office from using as evidence the information received from another NCA even though it would be privileged under English law, would override the purpose of that provision and conflict with the principle of supremacy of EC law.[100] However, several other NCAs expressed concern at the possibility that information obtained through the application of Article 12, Regulation 1/2003, could be used when it could not have been collected according to national law.[101]

Although there seems to be a general recognition that information received under Article 12 will have the same evidential value as evidence gathered within their own jurisdictions,[102] some of the national authorities questioned the extent to which the effective application of Regulation No 1/2003 can render the domestic evidential rules inapplicable.[103]

Difficulties could emerge, for example, if the Spanish NCA were required to transfer confidential information to its Irish counterpart: whereas the former would be obliged by national law to obtain the consent of the undertakings affected by the transfer,[104] the latter would be under no such obligation.[105] The Irish Competition Authority also stated that, due to the considerable differences

---

[99] Para. 6.3 of the Guidelines.

[100] BLOOM, 'Exchange of confidential information among members of the EU network of competition authorities', in EHLERMANN and ATANASIU (eds), *European Competition Law Annual 2002*, p. 399.

[101] E.g. Italy; CAHILL and COOKE (eds), *The Modernisation of EU Competition Law Enforcement in the EU*, National Reports, p. 328.

[102] CAHILL and COOKE (eds), *ibid.*, General Report, p. 655. *Inter alia*, National Reports: Austria, p. 54; Estonia, p. 125; Finland, p. 143.

[103] *Id.* General Report, p. 655.

[104] *Id.*, National Reports, Spain, p. 551.

[105] CAHILL and COOKE (eds), *The Modernisation of EU Competition Law Enforcement in the EU*, National Reports, Ireland, p. 302. See, *inter alia*, ARAUJO, 'The respect for fundamental rights within the European network of competition authorities', p. 529.

still existing among the procedural rules in force across the ECN, it would generally be reluctant to transmit information to a jurisdiction where, for instance, no leniency programme is provided.[106] However, the Authority also noted that its domestic antitrust law provides for a range of remedies and sanctions, both criminal and civil, and that, with respect to criminal penalties, the Competition Act 2002 confers on the national courts the discretion as to whether a custodial sanction should be imposed.[107] Accordingly, it took the view that Article 12 should not be interpreted as preventing it from receiving evidence from other jurisdictions even though criminal proceedings were contemplated.[108]

It is submitted that the position adopted by the Irish Competition Authority appears consistent with the view recently expressed by the CFI in the *AKZO Nobel* judgment, according to which the protection of confidentiality of certain kinds of evidence gathered during competition investigations constitutes an exception to the wide investigative powers enjoyed by the Commission and exercised in cooperation with its national counterparts.[109] It should therefore be narrowly interepreted to allow the effective enforcement of the Treaty competition rules in accordance also with the principle of supremacy of EC law.[110]

On this point, it may be argued, however, that although an extensive construction of Article 12 appears to be required by the general principles governing the application of the Community rules, it does not appear to take into account the circumstance that procedural rules governing the gathering of evidence are not uniform across the ECN.[111]

With respect especially to the privilege against self-incrimination, Judge John Cooke, speaking extrajudicially, expressed concern at the circumstance that evidence obtained in accordance with Article 12 of Regulation No 1/2003 from Member States in which no penal sanctions are provided for similar violations could be used by the authorities in a jurisdiction where these sanctions can be imposed even though the person giving that evidence had not been duly 'cautioned' as would have been required in the receiving jurisdiction.[112]

---

106 CAHILL and COOKE (eds), *The Modernisation of EU Competition Law Enforcement in the EU*, National Reports, p. 301.

107 *Id.*, p. 302.

108 *Ibid.*

109 Joined Cases T-125/03 and T-253/03, *AKZO Nobel and Ackros Chemicals v Commission*, judgment of 17 September 2007, not yet reported, para. 172.

110 *Id.*, para. 176.

111 For commentary, see most recently PERRIN, 'Challenges facing the EU network of competition authorities', at 557.

112 *Id.*, General Report, pp. 655–56. Also, *inter alia*, GARZANITI, GUDOFSKY and MOFFAT, 'Dawn of a new era? Powers of investigation and enforcement under Regulation 1/2003', (2004–2005) 72 *Antitrust L J* 159 at 206.

Commentators observed that the reference contained in the Preamble to the Modernisation Regulation to the observance of fundamental rights guaranteed by the general principles of EC law and interpreted in the light of the ECHR and the EU Charter of Fundamental Rights would ensure the observance of certain 'minimum standards' such as, *inter alia*, the right not to incriminate oneself, as it results from the *Orkem v Commission*[113] judgment.[114]

However, the case may well arise out of evidence being transmitted to jurisdictions where the scope of the privilege is wider than that provided by EC law. It will be recalled that, according to the European Court of Human Rights in *Saunders v United Kingdom*,[115] statements obtained from an individual in the course of non-judicial investigations under forms of coercion or oppression of his or her will[116] cannot be deployed against him or her in later proceedings and regardless of the fact that the statements in question were not explicitly incriminating.[117] The Strasbourg Court's position can be contrasted with the the *Orkem* concept of privilege, which extends only to statements involving an admission of guilt in respect of an infringement of the EC Treaty competition rules and excludes statements concerning 'purely factual' information, regardless of whether or not they may be later used in a manner that may be incriminating.[118]

Consequently, it could be argued that an NCA could rely on Article 12, Regulation 1/2003, in order to obtain from a different jurisdiction evidence which it could not otherwise have collected as a result of the greater safeguards provided by the law governing the use of evidence in its own jurisdiction.[119] Although, as was stated above, this outcome may be consistent with the supremacy of EC law,[120] the extent to which the application of that principle could result in fundamental guarantees of 'due process' enshrined in domestic law being set aside could still be questioned.[121]

---

113 Case 27/88, *Orkem v Commission*, [1989] ECR 3355, para. 35.

114 KERSE and KHAN, *EC Antitrust Procedure*, p. 269.

115 Case 43/1994/490/572, *Saunders v United Kingdom*, [1997] 23 EHRR 313. *Supra*, Chapter 4, section 2.

116 *Id.*, para. 68.

117 *Id.*, para. 71.

118 Case 27/88, *Orkem v Commission*, [1989] ECR 3355. *Supra*, Chapter 4, section 4.2.

119 KERSE and KHAN, *EC Antitrust Procedure*, p. 270; also VESTERDORF, 'Legal professional privilege and the privilege against self-incrimination in EC law', pp. 722–23.

120 Joined Cases T-125/03 and T-253/03, *AKZO Nobel and Ackros Chemicals v Commission*, judgment of 17 September 2007, not yet reported, paras. 176–77.

121 KERSE and KHAN, *EC Antitrust Procedure*; also WILS, 'Powers of investigation and procedural rights and guarantees in EU antitrust enforcement', (2006) 29 *W. Comp.* 3 at 19–20.

It is clear from Article 12(3), Regulation 1/2003, that exchanged evidence cannot be used against individuals and to impose custodial sentences unless 'the law of the transmitting authority foresees sanctions of a similar kind' for infringements of Articles 81 and 82 EC Treaty or, 'in absence thereof, the information has been collected in a way which respects the same level of protection of the rights of the defence of natural persons' as in the law of the receiving authority. However, the above analysis appears to suggest that the lack of uniform evidential rules could have unforeseen consequences for the rights of defence of the undertakings concerned.[122]

In this respect, it is argued that a wide interpretation of Article 12, Regulation 1/2003, inspired by the need to ensure the effective application of the Modernisation Regulation could create the risk that the protection of legal professional privilege or of the privilege against self-incrimination be watered down and, more generally, could be read as demonstrating that the assumption of 'equivalent protection', on which the framework of cooperation is based, is seriously questionable.[123]

4. DECENTRALISED APPLICATION OF ARTICLES 81 AND 82 EC TREATY IN THE FACE OF NATIONAL AUTONOMY AS REGARDS PROCEDURES AND SANCTIONS AND ITS CONSEQUENCES FOR THE POSITION OF THE INVESTIGATED UNDERTAKINGS

4.1. Introductory Remarks

This section analyses some of the issues arising from the application of the norms of Regulation 1/2003 governing case allocation and exchange of information. It will concentrate on the implications of the cooperation envisaged by the Regulation on the process of shaping the future standards of due process in EC competition enforcement. The absence of binding rules governing case allocation and of harmonised rules concerning competition procedures and sanctions raises substantial issues for the impact of the framework introduced

---

[122] ANDREANGELI, 'The impact of the Modernisation Regulation on the guarantees of due process in competition proceedings', (2006) 31 *ELRev* 342 at 355–56. Also, ARAUJO, 'The respect for fundamental rights within the European network of competition authorities', in HAWK (ed.), *International Antitrust Law and Policy*, pp. 530–31.

[123] E.g. the Netherlands, CAHILL and COOKE (eds), *The Modernisation of EU Competition Law Enforcement in the EU*, p. 436.

by Regulation No 1/2003 on the standards of protection of the rights of the defence of the undertakings concerned by proceedings before both the Commission and the NCAs.

4.2. Parallel Proceedings and the Principle of *Ne Bis in Idem*

It was noted above that Regulation No 1/2003 introduced a framework for the enforcement of Articles 81 and 82 EC Treaty characterised by the likelihood of parallel proceedings due to the flexible nature of the criteria governing case allocation and to the circumstance that Article 11(3), Regulation 1/2003, merely introduces a duty to notify new proceedings without prejudicing the investigative power of other members of the ECN.[124] Consequently, it could be argued that the possibility of the Commission and of the NCAs to prosecute and fine undertakings for the same infringement is incompatible with the principle of *ne bis in idem*, that is, the right not to be tried or convicted twice for the same offence enshrined in Article 4, Protocol VII to the ECHR and Article 50 of the EU Charter of Fundamental Rights.[125]

Supporters of the Modernisation Regulation argued that the very nature of the infringements of Articles 81 and 82 EC Treaty and the need to ensure their efficient detection and sanction required parallel action.[126] Competition infringements could not be treated in the same way as 'traditional crimes, which are committed by one or more specific offenders at a specific time and place':[127] their specificity as 'trans-national infringements', whose effects extend beyond the boundaries of the jurisdictions of each NCA,[128] could not justify an interpretation of the rule of *ne bis in idem* which impeded the 'sanctioning of all effects of an infringement'.[129]

Importantly, in recent judgments the Luxembourg Courts have recognised that this rule constitutes a general principle of EC law. In the *PVC II Cartel* appeal[130] the ECJ took the view that this rule precluded the Commission from bringing fresh proceedings against or sanctioning an undertaking for a breach of competition rules 'a second time on the ground of anti-competitive conduct

---

124 *Supra*, this chapter, para. 2.1.

125 WAELBROECK, '"Twelve feet dangling down and six necks exceeding long"', pp. 470ff.

126 GAUER, 'Due process in the face of divergent national procedures and sanctions', pp. 7–8.

127 *Id.*, p. 8.

128 *Id.*, p. 9.

129 *Id.*, p. 8.

130 Cases C-238/99, C-244/99, C-245/99, C-247/99, C-250/99 to 252/99, C-254/99, *Lymburgse Vinyl Maatschappij and Others v Commission*, [2002] ECR I-8375.

in respect of which it has been penalised or found not liable' with an earlier unappealable decision.[131]

However, it was not interpreted as far as to prevent the Commission from taking action in respect of facts that have already formed the subject matter of proceedings before national competition agencies. According to the Opinion of AG Mayras in *Boehringer v Commission*, antitrust breaches often consist of 'a large number of acts committed over a long period'[132] and having an impact on the territories of several states. Consequently, they are likely to fall within the jurisdiction of the NCAs of each Member State concerned.[133]

The Advocate General therefore argued that even if it was established that the same undertakings were involved in proceedings before the Commission and the competent national agencies in respect of the same allegations of anti-competitive conduct,[134] the other requirements for the application of the principle of *ne bis in idem*, namely, the unity of offender and of the legal interest protected by the rule infringed would not be fulfilled.[135]

Accordingly the ECJ held in the other *Walt Wilhelm* judgment[136] that the requirements of 'natural justice' did not exclude that an undertaking could be prosecuted and sanctioned twice for the same competition infringement in different jurisdictions. The principle of *ne bis in idem* was interpreted as requiring only that in setting the level of the fine for the second violation, the dimension of the sanction already imposed be taken into account.[137]

It was suggested that multiple proceedings with respect to the same cartel or abuse of dominance appear most likely at the primary stages of an investigation, when the breadth of their impact is not entirely known to the enforcement agencies and it is not possible to determine which agency is competent to deal with the case.[138] Hence, until such time as any of these proceedings has reached its final stage, that is, a finding of 'acquittal or conviction', parallel proceedings would not be inconsistent with the principle of *ne bis in idem*.[139]

Commentators added that only decisions imposing fines would probably raise *ne bis in idem* issues as they would be the only ones containing a finding

---

131 *Id.*, para. 59; see KERSE and KHAN, *EC Antitrust Procedure*, p. 431.

132 *Id.*, para. 3.

133 *Id.*, para. 4.

134 *Id.*, para. 5.

135 *Id.*, para. 6. See DEKEYSER and GAUER, 'The new enforcement system for Articles 81 and 82 and the rights of defence', in HAWK (ed.), *International Antitrust Law and Policy*, pp. 578–79.

136 Case 14/68, *Walt Wilhelm v Commission*, [1969] ECR 1.

137 *Id.*, para. 11

138 WILS, 'The EU network of competition authorities, the European Convention on Human Rights and the Charter of Fundamental Rights of the EU', p. 449.

139 *Ibid.*

of infringement with regard to past conduct and would impose a sanction for that infringement on the addressee of the decision. Consequently, other measures, such as the rejection of complaints or decisions accepting commitments, would not raise concerns in the light of this principle.[140]

However, it could be argued that these views may not be consistent with the case law of the European Court of Human Rights, according to which the rule of *ne bis in idem* should be interpreted as enshrining not only the right not to be sanctioned twice, but also the right not to be prosecuted twice for the same conduct.[141] Although none of the members of the ECN has the power to sanction competition infringements that occurred outside its jurisdiction, they all have the power to proceed against undertakings that have allegedly violated the same norms, namely Articles 81 and 82 EC Treaty and sometimes to impose the same level of fine for that infringement.[142] Consequently, it was submitted that, since there could be identity of conduct, of rule breached and even of sanction, the possibility to impose a parallel sanction constituted a case of double jeopardy.[143]

It is suggested that with the enactment of Council Regulation No 1/2003, these conclusions might hold true especially with respect to parallel proceedings before the Commission and the NCAs. The Modernisation Regulation did not overrule the conclusions reached in the *Walt Wilhelm* judgment.[144] Therefore, although Article 11(6) states that the initiation of proceedings by the Commission as regards a specific infringement relieves national authorities of their jurisdiction to deal with that breach, it is not excluded that the Commission could start fresh proceedings to prosecute a competition violation with which a NCA has already dealt.[145]

---

140 DEKEYSER and GAUER, 'The new enforcement system for Articles 81 and 82 and the rights of defence', pp. 582–83.

141 *Inter alia*, Appl. No. 37/950/97, *Franz Fischer v Austria*, judgment of 29 May 2001, not yet reported, paras. 22, 25, 29; Appl. No 15963/90, *Gradinger v Austria*, judgment of 23 October 1995, ser. A, no 328-C (HUDOC Reference No 33/1994/480/562), paras. 53–55. But cf. *Oliveira v Switzerland*, judgment of 30 July 1998 (HUDOC Reference No 84/1997/868/1080), [1998] 28 EHRR 289, para. 27. See, *inter alia*, WILS, *Principles of European Antitrust enforcement* (2005) Oxford, Portland, OR: Hart Publishing, p. 96.

142 WAELBROECK, '"Twelve feet all dangling down and six necks exceeding long"', p. 470.

143 *Ibid.*

144 Case 14/68, *Walt Wilhelm v Commission*, [1969] ECR 1 at para. 11. For commentary, *mutatis mutandis*, EISMANBERGER and THYRI, 'Third-country antitrust sanctions and EC law – Comments on the Advocate General's Opinion in C-308/04 P SGL Carbon/Commission', (2006) 27 *ECLR* 397 at 399.

145 WILS, 'The principle of *ne bis in idem* in EC antitrust enforcement: a legal and economic analysis', (2003) 26(2) *W. Comp.* 131 at 144.

On this point, the appeal judgment in the *Lysine Cartel* case concerning parallel proceedings pending before the Commission, the US and the Canadian antitrust authorities[146] can be read as confirming the possibility for the same undertaking to 'be made defendant to two parallel sets of proceedings concerning the same infringement and, thus, incur concurrent sanctions',[147] imposed respectively by the Commission and by the national enforcement agencies. Consequently, it could be argued that the ECJ favours an interpretation of the principle of *ne bis in idem* as prohibiting double prosecutions for the same breach only within the same jurisdiction and not as preventing fresh proceedings being initiated by different NCAs or indeed by the Commission itself at EC level.[148]

This position may, however, be contrasted with the interpretation of the principle of *ne bis in idem* adopted in the context of the Convention implementing the Schengen Agreement into the EU legal framework. According to Article 54 of the Convention:

> A person whose trial has been finally disposed of in one Contracting Party may not be prosecuted in another Contracting Party for the same acts provided that, if a penalty has been imposed, it has been enforced, is actually in the process of being enforced or can no longer be enforced under the laws of the sentencing Contracting Party.

In the *Gozutok* judgment the ECJ recognised that the objective of this provision is 'to ensure that no one is prosecuted on the same facts in several Member States on account of him having exercised his right to freedom of movement'.[149]

Therefore, it was held that the provision should be given an extensive interpretation encompassing not only cases that have already been 'finally disposed of' with a judicial decision, but also those in which the prosecution was discontinued with a decision of the public prosecution, perhaps following a 'criminal settlement' between the authorities and the accused.[150] Nonetheless,

---

[146] Case T-224/00, *Archer Daniels Midland Co and Another v Commission*, [2003] ECR II-2597, para. 90.

[147] *Id.*, para. 89. Confirmed in, *inter alia*, case C-289/04 P, *Showa Denko v Commission*, judgment of 29 July 2006, not yet reported, available in [2006] 5 CMLR 14, paras. 50–51; case C-308/04 P, *SGL Carbon AG v Commission*, judgment of 29 June 2006, not yet reported, available in [2006] 5 CMLR 16, paras. 26–27.

[148] Also, *id.*, para. 93. For commentary, *inter alia*, CANENBLEY and ROSENTHAL, 'Cooperation between antitrust authorities in and outside the EU: what does it mean for multinational corporations? Part 2', (2005) 26 *ECLR* 178 at 181–84.

[149] Joined Cases C-187/01 and C-385/01, *Criminal Proceedings against Husein Gozutok and Klaus Brugge*, [2003] ECR I-1345, para. 38.

[150] *Id.*, paras. 27–28. See also Case C-150/05, *Van Straaten v Staat der Nederlanden und Republiek Italie*, [2006] ECR I-9327, paras. 53, 57.

the ECJ made clear in the later *Miraglia* ruling[151] that Article 54 would not apply to cases in which a criminal prosecution was closed 'on the sole ground that (. . .) proceedings had been started in another Member State' for the same violation but without there having been any determination on the merits of the allegations.[152]

Even though any further examination of Article 54 of the Convention Implementing the Schengen Agreement into EU law is beyond the scope of this work, it is clear that the interpretation given to the principle of *ne bis in idem* in the context of the Third Pillar is more generous than that applicable to parallel antitrust proceedings. However, despite it being acknowledged that the rule against double jeopardy belongs to the general principles of EC law,[153] it remains unclear whether the reading adopted in the case law concerning the Third Pillar could be applicable to other areas of EU law, including competition enforcement.[154] It is suggested that, in any event, Article 54 should bar parallel criminal prosecutions for the same violation in Member States where competition breaches constitute criminal offences.

Furthermore, it is questionable whether the interpretation of the principle of *ne bis in idem* applicable to parallel antitrust proceedings in the ECN can be reconciled with Article 50 of the EU Charter of Fundamental Rights according to which the protection against being tried and punished twice extends 'within the Union'.[155] Whereas it could be argued that each set of proceedings takes into consideration only the effects of the competition violation within the jurisdiction of the NCA concerned, it is clear that the principle of *ne bis in idem* 'prohibits multiple prosecution or punishments for the same offence, not merely for the same effects of an offence'.[156] Accordingly, it is submitted that it should prevent further proceedings being initiated in another Member State for the 'same facts' for which the accused has already been found guilty or

---

[151] Case C-469/03, *Criminal Proceedings against Filomeno Mario Miraglia*, [2005] ECR I-2009.

[152] *Id.*, para. 28.

[153] *Inter alia*, Case C-436/04, *Criminal Proceedings against Leopold Henri Van Esbroeck*, [2006] ECR I-2333, para. 40.

[154] See, e.g., Case C-328/05, *SGL Carbon v Commission*, judgment of 10 May 2005, not yet reported, para. 29. Also, COMMISSION of the EUROPEAN COMMUNITIES, *Green Paper on Conflicts of Jurisdiction and the Principle of ne bis in idem in Criminal Proceedings*, 23 December 2005, SEC(2005) 1767, COM(2005) final 696, pp. 8–9.

[155] Case C-308/04 P, *SGL Carbon AG v Commission*, judgment of 29 June 2006, not yet reported, available in [2006] 5 CMLR 16, para. 93.

[156] WILS, 'The principle of *ne bis in idem* in EC antitrust enforcement: a legal and economic analysis', at 146. Cf. GARZANITI, GUDOFSKY and MOFFAT, 'Dawn of a new era? Powers of investigation and enforcement under Regulation 1/2003', at 203–04.

acquitted, regardless of their legal classification in the domestic jurisdictions concerned.[157]

It is concluded that, although the need to ensure the effective enforcement of the Treaty's antitrust rules should not be overlooked,[158] the possibility of multiple proceedings regarding the same infringement within the ECN, despite taking place in different jurisdictions, could be considered incompatible with the right not to be prosecuted and sanctioned twice for the same competition violation[159] resulting from the case law of the European Court of Human Rights and also from Article 50 of the Charter. Given the increasing influence of the EU Charter in the case law of the Luxembourg Courts and the current jurisprudential developments in the interpretation of this principle in the context of the Third Pillar, it is not excluded that the current position will be questioned again in the future.[160]

4.3. Challenging Allocation Decisions: a Remedy Against the Uncertainty Affecting the Handling of Cases within the ECN?

The implications of the handling of a case in a specific jurisdiction within the ECN for the legal position of the undertakings concerned by the proceedings could prompt the question whether the decision by which a case is reallocated from the Commission to a NCA could be open to judicial challenge before the Community courts.[161] Even though the Joint Statement emphasised the informal nature of the cooperation within the Network,[162] it is not excluded that the Commission's measure could possess the characteristics of a 'decision', namely the ability to produce 'legal effects (. . .) which are binding on, and capable of affecting the legal interests of, the applicant by bringing about a distinct change in his legal position'.[163]

---

157 See, *mutatis mutandis*, case C-150/05, *Van Straaten v Staat der Nederlanden und Republiek Italie*, [2006] ECR I-9327, paras. 44–45.

158 DEKEYSER and GAUER, 'The new enforcement system for Articles 81 and 82 and the rights of defence', pp. 584–85.

159 WILS, 'The principle of *ne bis in idem* in EC antitrust enforcement: a legal and economic analysis', (2003) 26(2) *W. Comp.* 131 at 146.

160 *Inter alia*, T-112/98, *Mannesmannrohren-Werke v Commission*, [2001] ECR II-729; per AG Mischo, joined Cases C-20/00 and C-64/00, *Booker Aquaculture Ltd v Scottish Ministers*, [2003] ECR I-7411 at para. 126; Case C-540/03 P, *European Parliament v Council*, judgment of 27 June 2006, [2006] ECR I-5769, para. 38.

161 *Ibid.*

162 Paras. 3 and 7, Joint Statement.

163 Case 60/81, *International Business Machines Corp v Commission*, [1981] ECR 2639 at para. 9. Also case T-377/00, *Philip Morris and Others v Commission*, [2003] ECR II-1, paras. 79, 80 and 110.

This suggestion was rejected by some commentators who regarded the 'decision' with which the Commission reallocates a case to a NCA as being merely preparatory and adopted on the basis of flexible, not binding criteria.[164] Also, the investigated firms affected by the transfer of a case to a national jurisdiction would be afforded the procedural rights provided by the national law of the receiving NCA.[165]

Nonetheless, it might be argued that the recent decision of the CFI adopted in the *Royal Philips* case in the area of merger control could cast doubt on these conclusions. The CFI declared admissible an action for annulment against a decision referring the assessment of a concentration from the Commission to an NCA which resulted in 'transfer[ring] responsibility for the examination of certain aspects of the concentration to the national authorities which have requested the referral in order that they may give a ruling in accordance with their national competition law'.[166] Consequently, the referral decision was considered capable of affecting the legal position of the undertakings in accordance with the *IBM* test[167] since it had resulted in the notifying parties being deprived of the opportunity to obtain the approval of the proposed concentration by the Commission[168] and of the right to be heard and to seek the judicial review of the final decision provided by EC law.[169]

It is suggested that there are strong similarities between a referral decision and the 'decision' to reallocate a case within the ECN, since both determine the competent authority and the law applicable to the case as regards, *inter alia*, the procedures and the available judicial remedies. However, unlike referrals reallocation decisions do not have the effect of submitting the alleged anti-competitive conduct to the assessment of national competition law: the Treaty rules on competition will continue to apply although the parallel application of national law remains a possibility allowed by Article 3 of Regulation No 1/2003.

However, the reasoning at the basis of the *Royal Philips* judgment could be interpreted as supporting the argument that the reallocation of a case from the Commission to an NCA constitutes a 'decision' amenable to judicial review. Just as with a referral, reallocation results in the undertakings concerned being

---

164 GAUER, 'Due process in the face of divergent national procedures and sanctions', p. 5.

165 *Ibid.*

166 Case T-119/02, *Royal Philips Electronics NV v Commission*, [2003] ECR II-1433 at para. 276.

167 Case 60/81, *International Business Machines Corporation v Commission*, [1981] ECR 2639 at para. 9.

168 Case T-119/02, *Royal Philips Electronics NV v Commission*, [2003] ECR II-1433 at para. 282.

169 *Id.* paras. 284–85.

subject to national procedural norms and judicial remedies and being denied the procedural rights which they would have enjoyed under Community law.[170]

It is submitted that, despite its importance in the reformed competition enforcement framework, case allocation could threaten the right to a 'fair procedure' of the undertakings concerned. The analysis of the position of leniency applicants suggests that the lack of procedural harmonisation could expose them to considerable legal uncertainty regarding the extent of the procedural rights available under the applicable national law.[171] The possibility of challenging the 'allocation decision' could go some way towards resolving these problems, although it seems unlikely that this view will be endorsed by the ECJ.[172]

4.4. Exchange of Information and the Undertakings' Rights of Defence: Tilting the Balance

The analysis conducted in earlier sections illustrated the adverse impact that the application of Article 12 of Regulation No 1/2003 could have on the rights of defence of the investigated undertakings. Although Article 12 of the Regulation now provides a firm legal basis for the exchange and use in evidence of information among the members of the Network, the absence of common rules as regards the admissibility of that evidence could threaten the effectiveness of the procedural rights of the firms concerned, regardless, it would appear, of the overall assumption of the 'equivalent protection' of the rights of the defence of the investigated parties, which lies at the basis of Council Regulation 1/2003.[173]

To strike a balance between the competing interests of the investigated undertakings and the competition authorities in the event of a transfer of evidence from the Commission to an NCA, two contrasting solutions have been envisaged. On the one hand, there is the current position of the Commission which tilts that balance in favour of the enforcement agencies by enabling them to deploy against the investigated undertakings the transferred

---

170 *Mutatis mutandis, id.*, para. 282.

171 *Inter alia*, WAELBROECK, '"Twelve feet dangling down and six necks exceeding long"', pp. 473 and 482; LEVY and O'DONOGHUE, 'The EU leniency programme comes of age', at 95.

172 *Inter alia*, WILS, 'Community Report', in CAHILL and COOKE (eds), p. 703. See, *mutatis mutandis*, Case T-377/00, *Philip Morris and others v Commission*, [2003] ECR II-1, paras. 79, 80 and 110.

173 *Inter alia*, PERRIN, 'Challenges facing the EU network of competition authorities', at 556–57.

information only on condition that its collection complied with the law of the transmitting authority.[174]

According to some commentators, this interpretation of Article 12, Regulation 1/2003, would not lead to the 'erosion' of the undertakings' rights of defence since all the Member States are signatories to the ECHR as well as bound by the fundamental rights principles enshrined in Community law, which would provide a 'minimum guarantee' of fairness across the ECN.[175] It was also argued that any such 'erosion' would only affect rights of corporate entities 'which are recognised neither in the case law of the European Court of Human Rights nor in the fundamental rights case-law of the Court of Justice', and not rights enjoyed by natural persons.[176]

It is, however, submitted that this view appears to overlook the broad construction given by the ECJ to the notion of 'undertaking' encompassing both individuals and corporate entities, and could therefore lead to the questionable conclusion that differing standards should apply to the investigated parties depending on whether they are natural or legal persons.[177]

In addition, the examination of the case law of the Strasbourg Court conducted in earlier chapters clearly indicated that business entities are entitled to some of the safeguards provided by the ECHR, including the protection of lawyer–client confidentiality.[178] Consequently, it could be argued that the view adopted by the Commission may be questioned in the light of the purposive interpretation of the safeguards enshrined in the European Convention and especially of the effective protection of the right to secrecy of information covered by LPP which is recognised by both individuals and legal entities.[179]

It is submitted that similar considerations could be made at least in part with respect to evidence attracting the application of the privilege against

---

174 Network Notice, footnote 6, para. 27.

175 *Inter alia*, WILS, 'Powers of investigation and procedural rights and guarantees in EU Antitrust enforcement', at 23–24.

176 *Id.*, p. 24. Cf. PERRIN, 'Challenges facing the EU network of competition authorities', at 554–55.

177 See, *mutatis mutandis*, MacCULLOCH, 'The privilege against self-incrimination in competition investigations: theoretical foundations and practical implications', (2006) 26(2) *Leg. Stud.* 211 at 234–35.

178 Appl. No 14369/88, *Noviflora Sweden AB v Sweden*, Commission Decision, [1993] 15 EHRR CD6; paras. 2(b) and 4; also, Report of the Commission adopted on 8 July 1993; paras. 13–16 of the report. For further commentary, *inter alia*, ANDREANGELI, 'The protection of legal professional privilege in EU law', at 36–37. *Supra*, Chapter 1, section 6.

179 See, *mutatis mutandis*, Appl. No 13710/88, *Niemitz v Germany*, ser. A No 251-B, [1993] 16 EHRR 17, para. 29, 31; Appl. No 10572/83, *Markt Intern Verlag GmbH and Klaus Bermann v Germany*, judgment of 20 November 1989, ser. A No 165, [1990] 12 EHRR 161, para. 35.

self-incrimination. Although the application to the corporate context of the standards governing the right not to incriminate oneself remains controversial,[180] it cannot be excluded that, even taking into account the more recent developments regarding the application of the privilege,[181] the restrictive view prevailing in the case law of the ECJ could, as a result of the application of Article 12 of the Regulation, determine a weakening of the levels of protection required by the ECHR.[182]

More generally, it may be argued that in the absence of common rules governing the use of evidence transferred in accordance with the Modernisation Regulation, 'no Community guarantee exists that the rights of the defence will be respected at national level'[183] and that, despite the limits enshrined in Article 12(3), Regulation 1/2003, it is not totally excluded that lawfully gathered evidence in jurisdictions where less stringent guarantees of the right against self-incrimination are in place, could be transmitted and later used against the investigated parties although the procedural safeguards required by the law of the receiving NCA have not been complied with.[184]

Consequently, it was suggested that Article 12 should not prevent the investigated firms from seeking a 'complete transfer',[185] that is, the application of more extensive safeguards applicable to confidential or privileged information in the jurisdiction of the receiving authority, even though that evidence had been lawfully collected by the transmitting NCA.[186] It was feared that the exchange of information could be relied on by the requesting authority so as to bypass any higher degree of protection in force in its own jurisdiction.[187]

---

180 See, *inter alia*, MacCULLOCH, 'The privilege against self-incrimination in competition investigations: theoretical foundations and practical implications', (2006) 26(2) *Leg. Stud.* 211 at 234–35.

181 *Inter alia,* Case C-238/99, *LVM NV and Others v Commission*, [2002] ECR I-8375, para. 275.

182 *Inter alia*, VESTERDORF, 'Legal professional privilege and the privilege against self-incrimination in EC Law', pp. 722–23.

183 VAN der WOUDE, 'Exchange of information within the European Competition Network: scope and limits', p. 382.

184 CAHILL and COOKE (eds), *The Modernisation of EU Competition Law Enforcement in the EU*, General Report, pp. 655–56. Also, *inter alia*, GARZANITI, GUDOFSKY and MOFFAT, 'Dawn of a new era? Powers of investigation and enforcement under Regulation 1/2003', (2004–2005) 72 *Antitrust L J* 159 at 206.

185 VAN der WOUDE, 'Exchange of information within the European Competition Network', p. 385.

186 *Id.*, p. 387. Also, more recently, PERRIN, 'Challenges facing the EU network of competition authorities', at 556–57.

187 LAGE and BROKELMANN, 'The possible consequences of a relatively broad scope for exchange of confidential information on national procedural law and antitrust sanctions', in EHLERMANN and ATANASIU (eds), *European Competition*

However, it should be noted that such an 'overprotective' interpretation appears incompatible with the conclusions reached by the CFI in its *AKZO Nobel* judgment:[188] by declining to accept the arguments, advanced by the applicants and some of the interveners, that the personal scope of LPP should be determined in accordance with national law,[189] the Court clearly preferred an extensive reading of the provisions of Council Regulation No 1/2003.[190] Consequently, it could be argued that in the light of *AKZO Nobel*, communications covered by privilege in the jurisdiction in which they were gathered can lawfully be collected in accordance with Article 12 of Regulation 1/2003 and used as evidence in jurisdictions whether they would not benefit from it.

However, it is noteworthy that in the same decision the CFI emphasised the importance of LPP in the context of the rights of defence of the investigated parties and the resulting need for the continuous judicial supervision of decisions withholding this safeguard.[191] Consequently, this raises the question of whether a middle-ground option could be proposed to reconcile the smooth exchange of information within the Network with the protection of the rights of the defence and the rule of *audi alteram partem* enshrined in the general principles of EC law.[192]

It is suggested that when evidence is transferred from the Commission to an NCA, the procedure devised by the ECJ in the *AKZO Chemie* judgment[193] for the disclosure of confidential information to a third party should be applied, since it would allow the investigated firms to be heard on the transfer of 'sensitive information' and to seek judicial control of the decision ordering the transfer.[194] Support for this solution could be found in the *SEP* judgment, where the ECJ held that the Commission would be obliged 'if it [wished] to

---

Law Annual 2002, p. 412. Cf., *mutatis mutandis*, European Parliament legislative resolution on the proposal for a Council framework decision on the European Evidence Warrant for obtaining objects, documents and data for use in proceedings in criminal matters, P5_TA (2004) 0243, Amendment 13, Article 19a (new): 'Subsequent use of evidence – The use of the evidence acquired pursuant to this Framework Decision shall in no way prejudice the rights of the defence in subsequent criminal proceedings in which that evidence is used, in particular as regards the admissibility of the evidence, the obligation to disclose the evidence and the ability of the defence to challenge that evidence.'

[188] Joined Cases T-125/03 and T-253/03, *AKZO Nobel and Ackros Chemicals v Commission*, judgment of 17 September 2007, not yet reported.

[189] *Id.*, para. 176.

[190] *Id.*, para. 172.

[191] *Id.*, paras. 46, 77, 87.

[192] VAN der WOUDE, 'Exchange of information within the European Competition Network', pp. 386–87.

[193] Case 53/85, *AKZO Chemie v Commission*, [1986] ECR 1965.

[194] *Id.*, para. 29.

transmit a document to the competent national authorities' for which confidential treatment had been requested, 'to adopt a properly reasoned decision amenable to judicial review' authorising that transfer.[195]

It is added that this solution could also be consistent with the emphasis placed by the CFI in *AKZO Nobel* on the need to provide effective judicial supervision over decisions of the Commission rejecting claims of LPP advanced by the investigated undertakings.[196] Not only did the Court affirm that these measures constituted a 'reviewable act' for the purpose of Article 230 EC Treaty actions,[197] but it also made clear that if the officials propose to reject a claim for privilege and thus to examine evidence whose nature is contested, they must adopt a formal determination on the matter and allow the parties concerned an opportunity to challenge that decision before the Court.[198]

Accordingly, it may be concluded that in the light of the findings of *AKZO Nobel*, and in the absence of a common notion of what is confidential or privileged, the availability of a judicial remedy against the decision authorising the transfer of evidence from the Commission to a different jurisdiction would constitute the only viable solution to tilt the balance between the effective antitrust enforcement and the protection of the rights of defence of the investigated firms. It is argued that the possibility of seeking scrutiny of the decision authorising the exchange of information would provide a check over whether a 'fair balance' was struck between the efficient application of Articles 81 and 82 EC Treaty and the interests of a 'fair procedure'.[199] It would also conform to the protection of the confidentiality of business secrets and especially of the secrecy of communications between lawyer and client[200] and thus benefit the undertakings' rights of defence.[201]

---

[195] C-36/92 P, *SEP v Commission*, [1994] ECR I-1911, para. 39. See also PERRIN, 'Challenges facing the EU network of competition authorities', at 563.

[196] Joined Cases T-125/03 and T-253/03, *AKZO Nobel and Ackros Chemicals v Commission*, judgment of 17 September 2007, not yet reported, paras. 46–48.

[197] *Id.*, para. 47.

[198] *Id.*, paras. 87–88.

[199] VAN der WOUDE, 'Exchange of information within the European Competition Network', p. 387.

[200] *Inter alia*, case C-36/92, *SEP v Commission*, [1994] ECR I-1911, para. 39: '(. . .) analogous considerations require the Commission, if it wishes to transmit a document to the competent national authorities, notwithstanding the claim that in the particular circumstances of the case that document is of a confidential nature with respect to those authorities, to adopt a properly reasoned decision amenable to judicial review by means of an action for annulment'. Also, VAN der WOUDE, 'Exchange of information within the European Competition Network: scope and limits', p. 382.

[201] Joined Cases T-125/03 and T-253/03, *AKZO Nobel and Ackros Chemicals v Commission*, judgment of 17 September 2007, not yet reported, para. 86.

5. THE MODERNISATION OF ENFORCEMENT OF EC COMPETITION LAW: WHAT FUTURE FOR THE RIGHTS OF DEFENCE?

On the basis of the analysis conducted so far, it is now appropriate to attempt to speculate on the future of standards of 'due process' in a framework characterised by the application of common substantive rules in the face of differing procedural standards and sanctions. By emphasising the importance of the 'decentralised enforcement' of Articles 81 and 82 EC Treaty and increasing the degree of cooperation between the Commission and the NCAs, Regulation No 1/2003 has dramatically changed the enforcement structure of EC competition law, with somewhat unforeseen consequences for the procedural rights of the investigated undertakings.

As was noted above,[202] one of the foundations on which the 'modernised' framework for the application of Articles 81 and 82 EC Treaty rests is the 'equivalent protection' of the rights of defence in proceedings before the Commission and the NCAs,[203] as a result of which each NCA is 'responsible for ensuring due process in the cases it deals with'[204] in accordance with national law.[205] However, the likelihood of parallel proceedings could cause divergences in the protection of the rights of due process enjoyed by the investigated undertakings in view of the differing domestic norms governing procedures and sanctions.[206]

The impact of Article 12, Regulation 1/2003 on the evidentiary rules in force across the Network appears particularly problematic and questions the very assumption of 'equivalent protection'.[207] Consequently, it should be ensured that, even in the absence of procedural harmonisation, the rights of defence enjoy a minimum standard of protection within the ECN. It could be argued that the case law of the ECJ concerning the protection of fundamental rights in the context of Community law may provide that standard.

According to the Court, EC fundamental rights bind not only the Community institutions but also the Member States 'when they implement

---

[202] *Supra*, this chapter, para. 2.1.

[203] Recital XVI, Preamble to Council Regulation No 1/2003.

[204] Network Notice (footnote 6), para. 4.

[205] GAUER, 'Due process in the face of divergent national procedures and sanctions', paper presented at the International Bar Association 2005 Conference: 'Decentralisation of EC Competition Law: a year in practice', p. 18.

[206] WAELBROECK, ' "Twelve feet all dangling down and six necks exceeding long" ', pp. 473–74.

[207] *Inter alia*, PERRIN, 'Challenges facing the EU network of competition authorities', at 556–57.

Community rules'[208] and adopt national measures falling 'within the scope of Community law'.[209] It is submitted that the decentralised application of EC competition rules constitutes one such case. Since the NCAs are obliged to apply Articles 81 and 82 EC Treaty to all forms of anti-competitive behaviour having an appreciable effect on trade between the Member States to achieve goals of competition policy set out at Community level,[210] their action would fall within the scope of Community law and should be compatible with the fundamental rights standards developed by the ECJ.[211]

It is therefore suggested that the standards of protection of the rights of defence elaborated by the ECJ should be applicable to proceedings concerning the application of Article 81 and 82 EC Treaty not only before the Commission, but also before the NCAs, so that until such time as procedural harmonisation is achieved, the investigated undertakings could enjoy a common set of procedural rights throughout the ECN in a manner more consistent with the tenet of 'equivalent protection' contained in the Preamble to the Modernisation Regulation.[212]

Nevertheless, it could be argued that the adoption of this solution does not eliminate all doubts concerning the compatibility of the Community level of protection with the right to a 'fair procedure' with the European Convention on Human Rights. As regards case allocation, some commentators criticised the possibility of seizing jurisdiction on antitrust cases pending before the NCAs conferred on the Commission by Article 11(6)[213] and argued that, since the EC is not a party to the Convention, the reallocation of cases to Brussels

---

[208] Case 5/88, *Wachauf v Bundesamt fur Ernährung und Fortwirtschaft*, [1989] ECR 2609, para. 19.

[209] Case 260/89, *ERT AE v DEP and Sotirios Kouvelas*, [1991] ECR I-2925, para. 42.

[210] Article 3(1), Regulation 1/2003. *Inter alia*, KERSE and KHAN, *EC Antitrust Procedure*, pp. 47–48.

[211] *Mutatis mutandis*, case C-60/00, *Carpenter v Secretary of State for the Home Department*, [2002] ECR I-6279. See, *inter alia*, WILS, 'Powers of investigation and procedural rights and guarantees in EU Antitrust enforcement', at 17–18.

[212] Also, Article 51(1), EU Charter of Fundamental Rights, proclaimed at Nice on 7 December 2000, [2000] OJ C364/1: 'The provisions of this Charter are addressed to the institutions and bodies of the Union with due regard for the principle of subsidiarity and to the Member States only when they are implementing Union law. They shall therefore respect the rights, observe the principles and promote the application thereof in accordance with their respective powers.' *Inter alia*, per AG Mischo, joined Cases C-20/00 and C-64/00, *Booker Aquaculture Ltd v Scottish Ministers*, [2003] ECR I-7411, para. 126. Also, T-112/98, *Mannesmannrohren-Werke v Commission*, [2001] ECR II-729.

[213] *Supra*, this chapter, section 4.3, footnote 163 and accompanying text.

would result in preventing the investigated firms from accessing the Strasbourg Court.[214]

It is submitted, however, that, although the concerns for the effective protection of the Convention rights in the context of the ECN cannot be underplayed, the doctrine of 'equivalent protection' of human rights in the EC law framework should ensure the continued supervision of the observance of the ECHR by the European Court of Human Rights and prevent breakdowns in the safeguard of the Convention rights. It is recalled from Chapter 1 that in *Matthews v United Kingdom*[215] the Strasbourg Court declared admissible an application brought against a Contracting State in respect of an alleged violation of the ECHR arising from a Community measure, mainly on the ground that the applicant had no other judicial remedy available either before the ECJ or the national courts.[216]

Furthermore, the later *Bosphorus* judgment[217] confirmed that, although the membership of an international organisation could not result in the Contracting States being absolved of their obligations under the Convention,[218] the European Court of Human Rights would not depart from its presumption of 'equivalent protection' of fundamental rights in EC law vis-à-vis the ECHR unless it could be shown that the safeguarding of the applicant's rights in the case at hand had been 'manifestly deficient'.[219]

It could be argued that, although the Strasbourg Court appears to have preferred a hands-off approach to the assessment of standards of EC human rights protection,[220] relevant problems could still arise with respect to the exchange of information among members of the ECN. It is significant that, although the majority have expressed overall positive views on the conformity of Article 12 with their rules of procedure and with constitutional law,[221] some NCAs have already raised concerns regarding the use of exchanged evidence

214 See WAELBROECK, '"Twelve feet dangling down and six necks exceeding long"', p. 483.

215 Appl. No 24833/94, [1999] 28 EHRR 361. For commentary, *inter alia*, SCHERMERS, Case Comment: *Matthews v United Kingdom*, judgment of 18 February 1999, (1999) 36 *CMLRev* 673. *Supra*, Chapter 1, Part 2, section 5.

216 *Id.* paras. 33–34. Also, *mutatis mutandis*, Appl. No 26083/94, *Waite and Kennedy v Germany*, judgment of 18 February 1999, [1999] 30 EHRR 261 at para. 68.

217 *Supra*, Chapter 1, section 3.

218 *Id.*, para. 154.

219 *Id.*, para. 156.

220 *Inter alia*, ECKES, 'Does the European Court of Human Rights provide protection from the European Community? – The case of *Bosphorus Airways*', (2007) 13 *EPL* 47 at 61–62.

221 *Id.*, General Report, p. 655; National Reports, *inter alia*, pp. 268–69, 300–01.

in a manner which would be inconsistent with domestic law[222] and questioned the extent to which Article 12 could override the obligation of professional secrecy vis-à-vis the investigated undertakings.[223]

In consideration of the potential threat that the generous reading of Article 12, Regulation 1/2003, could pose to the secrecy of privileged information, whether the European Court of Human Rights will consider the approach suggested by the Commission compatible with Articles 6(1) and 8 of the Convention[224] could legitimately be doubted[225] due to the absence of a specific indication as to whether the decisions of the Commission to transfer evidence to an NCA are amenable to judicial scrutiny before the CFI.[226]

Although the recent *AKZO Nobel* judgment[227] seems to support the view that such a challenge may be admissible,[228] it is argued that until the Luxembourg courts take a clear stance on this matter, the lack of an effective judicial remedy against decisions denying in substance fundamental safeguards such as LPP or the privilege against self-incrimination may irremediably prejudice the rights of defence of the undertakings concerned. Accordingly, it may be concluded that although a 'full transfer' of the standards of protection of the rights of defence may not be compatible with the need to ensure the effective application of Articles 81 and 82 of the EC Treaty throughout the ECN,[229] the 'pro-enforcement' interpretation of Article 12 of Council Regulation No 1/2003 appears likely to lead to results that are not entirely consistent with the legislative assumption of 'equivalent protection' of the right to fair legal process, and could perhaps diverge from the standards enshrined in the ECHR.

---

222 CAHILL and COOKE (eds), *The Modernisation of EU Competition Law Enforcement in the EU*, National Reports, *inter alia*, p. 328.

223 *Id.*, National Reports, pp. 551 and 569.

224 I.e. the right to a fair trial 'in the determination of civil rights and obligations or of a criminal charge' and the right to respect of, *inter alia*, the secrecy of correspondence. See WAELBROECK, ' "Twelve feet dangling down and six necks exceeding long" ', pp. 477–78.

225 See, VESTERDORF, 'Legal professional privilege and the privilege against self-incrimination in EC Law', p. 722.

226 ECKES, 'Does the European Court of Human Rights provide protection from the European Community?', p. 56–57.

227 Joined Cases T-125/03 and 253/03, *AKZO Nobel Ltd and Ackros Chemicals Ltd v Commission*, judgment of 17 September 2007, not yet reported.

228 See especially *id.*, paras. 47–48.

229 GAUER, 'Due process in the face of divergent national procedures and sanctions', p. 14. Also BLOOM, 'Exchange of confidential information among members of the EU network of competition authorities', p. 399.

6. CONCLUSIONS. REGULATION 1/2003 AND NCAS: TOWARDS NEW (JUDICIAL) CHALLENGES?

The Modernisation of EC competition enforcement seeks the effective application of Articles 81 and 82 EC Treaty through the increasing involvement of the NCAs and the enhanced cooperation between them and the Commission. However, the radical structural reforms brought about by Regulation No 1/2003 have not been matched by the harmonisation of national rules regarding procedure, evidence and sanctions. They have relied instead on the rather questionable assumption of 'equivalent protection' of the rights of defence of the investigated undertakings.

The analysis conducted in this chapter illustrated how the extensive cooperation within the ECN could jeopardise the effective protection of the rights of defence enjoyed by the investigated undertakings as a result of the lack of a common discipline of competition procedures and sanctions. The absence of binding rules governing allocation of cases among the Network's members emerges as a source of significant legal uncertainty for firms affected by antitrust proceedings as well as a factor adversely affecting the effectiveness of leniency programmes for cartel detection.

More serious issues could however arise from the exchange and use in evidence of information by the members of the ECN. Examination of the impact of Article 12, Regulation 1/2003, on the protection of confidential information and especially of evidence covered by legal professional privilege and by the privilege against self-incrimination demonstrated that the generous approach taken by the Commission in its Network Notice could threaten the right of the investigated firms to the secrecy of their 'sensitive' documents, unless judicial review is expressly extended to decisions effecting the transfer of that evidence.

However, until such time as these concerns are addressed in a way which is both consistent with practical and effective fundamental rights' protection and uniform throughout the ECN, it is submitted that the possibility that the European Court of Human Rights may claim jurisdiction with respect to measures adopted to fulfil the Community law obligations dictated by the Modernisation Regulation cannot be completely ruled out. Accordingly, it is necessary to assess the extent to which the standards of 'due process' enshrined in EC law and applicable to competition proceedings are compatible with the concept of administrative fairness provided by Article 6(1) ECHR.

7. Conclusions: 'Article 6-proofing' EC competition proceedings?

INTRODUCTION

The previous chapters discussed the current standards governing the notion of a 'fair procedure' enshrined in the European Convention on Human Rights and Community law. With respect to the ECHR, the analysis of the case law indicated that, given the silence of the Convention, the Strasbourg Court constructed the notion of a 'fair administrative procedure' on the basis of the purposive interpretation of Article 6(1) ECHR and particularly of an extensive reading of the concepts of 'determination of civil rights' and 'criminal charge'.[1]

The ECJ instead elaborated the basic tenets of that notion on the basis of the general principles of EC law and especially of the constitutional traditions common to the laws of the Member States.[2] Having regard to competition proceedings, secondary legislation as well as administrative practices played a significant part in setting out rules governing hearings, access to the file and the protection of confidentiality of documents submitted to the Commission during both antitrust and merger control proceedings. The case law of the Community courts has also contributed to the current standards for the protection of the procedural rights of investigated firms by emphasising the importance of an effective right to be heard and to obtain access to the Commission's case file in accordance with the principle of 'equality of arms' as well as the scope of its power of judicial review of both antitrust and merger decisions.

However, the comparative analysis conducted in the earlier chapters illustrated that there are still significant areas of variance between the principles laid down in the case law of the ECJ and the European Court of Human Rights. With respect to the administrative stage of the proceedings, the issues of concern include the absence of direct judicial control over the decisions of

1 *Inter alia,* Appl. No 8790/79, *Sramek v Austria*, [1985] 7 EHRR 380; Appl. No 15223/89, *Schmautzer v Austria*, [1996] 21 EHRR 511.

2 Case 17/74, *Transocean Marine Paint Association and Others v Commission*, [1974] ECR 1063; per AG Warner, [1974] 2 CMLR 459 at 469.

the Hearing Officer regarding the disclosure of evidence held by the Commission to the investigated parties, the scope of the privilege against self-incrimination and of lawyer-client confidentiality.[3]

In the area of merger control, the extent to which the negotiations of commitments between the notifying parties and the Commission officials are immune from pressure and thus inherently fair was also questioned.[4] With respect to the application of the Treaty antitrust rules, Chapter 6 illustrated the implications of the enactment of the Modernisation regulation for the uniform and effective protection of the rights of defence and questioned whether the observance of current human rights standards is secured in practice across the ECN.

It was, however, the examination of the 'judicial phase' of competition enforcement proceedings that perhaps highlighted the most pressing concerns. The examination of the intensity of the judicial review exercised by the ECJ and the CFI in light of the principles elaborated by the European Court of Human Rights illustrated that, whereas the currents standards of scrutiny of merger decisions are consistent with Article 6(1) ECHR and provide an adequate check on the Commission's discretion, the degree of control exercised over antitrust decisions does not appear to comply entirely with the Convention rules. It was argued that, although the concerns for the integrity of the inter-institutional balance of the EU cannot be downplayed,[5] the 'restrained' review exercised over the 'complex economic assessments' made by the Commission cannot be easily reconciled with the need to ensure the full re-examination of matters of fact and law required for decisions of a 'criminal nature'.[6]

This chapter will therefore discuss options for the improvement of the current rules with a view to ensuring compatibility with ECHR standards. It will conclude that, even though enhancing the intensity of the judicial control exercised by the Luxembourg Courts over antitrust decisions could constitute an adequate response to the human rights concerns hitherto highlighted, it may nonetheless be necessary to consider reforms to the administrative stage of the proceedings in consideration of the implications that the creation of a specialised 'jurisdiction on the merits' in competition matters could have on the judicial architecture established by the Treaty.

---

3 *Supra*, Chapter 4.

4 *Supra*, Chapter 2, section 3.2. *Inter alia*, ser. A No 35, *Deweer v Belgium*, [1979–1980] 2 EHRR 439, para. 49.

5 E.g. joined cases T-68, 77-78/89, *Società Italiana Vetro SpA and Others v Commission*, [1992] ECR II-1403, para. 319. *Supra*, Chapter 5, section 1.3, footnote 128 and accompanying text.

6 E.g. Appl. No 15223/89, *Schmautzer v Austria*, [1996] 21 EHRR 511. *Supra*, Chapter 5, section 2.

1. HUMAN RIGHTS AND EU COMPETITION ENFORCEMENT: TOWARDS A NEW EU 'DUE PROCESS' CLAUSE?

1.1. 'Administrative Fairness': from the General Principles of EC Law to the Draft Constitutional Treaty

Part 2 of Chapter 1 illustrated the development of fundamental rights principles in the EC/EU legal system. It identified the EU Charter of Fundamental Rights as the culmination of a process of 'human rights consolidation' initiated by the ECJ with its *Internationale Handelsgesellschaft*[7] and *Nold*[8] judgments and highlighted the role of the European Convention on Human Rights as a primary source of inspiration in the interpretation of Community law principles.

It was also suggested that the recent *Bosphorus* judgment of the European Court of Human Rights[9] could be read as confirming the vital function of the Convention in this process of 'consolidation', as a result of which the Strasbourg Court may have felt able to return to the 'trusting approach' to the human rights supervision of EC action that it had adopted up to the *Matthews* decision.[10] Accordingly, even though the EU is not a party to the Convention, it was argued that the principles governing the concept of 'fair procedure' enshrined in its Article 6(1) ECHR constitute a relevant benchmark for the assessment of standards of 'due process' guaranteed to the undertakings concerned by the Commission's antitrust and merger proceedings.[11]

Nonetheless, the analysis conducted in earlier chapters demonstrated that although in principle the 'composite approach' to the definition of a 'fair procedure' elaborated by the European Court of Human Rights in its case law concerning Article 6(1) ECHR[12] has been endorsed by the ECJ,[13] there are still significant differences between the standards advocated in the two jurisdictions. Especially in consideration of the challenges posed by Council

---

[7] Case 11/70, *Internationale Handelsgesellschaft*, [1970] ECR 1125, para. 4.

[8] Case 4/73, *Nold v Commission*, [1974] ECR 491, para. 13. *Supra*, Chapter 1, Part 2, section 2.

[9] Appl. No 45036/98, *Bosphorus Hava Yollari Turizm ve Ticaret Anonim Sirketi v Ireland*, judgment of 30 June 2005, [2006] 42 EHRR 1.

[10] Appl. No 24833/94, *Matthews v United Kingdom*, [1999] 28 EHRR 361.

[11] *Supra*, Chapter 1, section 5.

[12] Appl. Nos 7299/75 and 7496/76, *Albert & LeCompte v Belgium*, [1983] 5 EHRR 533, para. 29. *Supra*, Chapter 2, section 2.

[13] Case T-156/94, *Siderurgica Aristrain Madrid SL v Commission*, [1999] ECR II-645, para. 102. *Supra*, Chapter 2, section 3.2.

Regulation No 1/2003, it is thus indispensable to secure the application at Community level of rules of 'administrative fairness' that are consistent with the Convention.[14]

It is submitted that although it is not legally binding,[15] the EU Charter of Fundamental Rights could provide the 'way forward' to the establishment of a new 'due process' clause applicable to competition proceedings within the Community framework. It will be recalled that the Charter is rooted in the case law of the ECJ and its relationship of continuity with the existing human rights' guarantees is reflected in the role of the ECHR itself as a minimum standard for the protection of human rights which are common to both instruments.[16]

Furthermore, its scope of application encompasses both the EU institutions and the national authorities when they act in the pursuit of their obligations under EU law. Most importantly, it enshrines a common catalogue of human rights supported by the consensus of all the Member States binding on both the EU institutions and on the national authorities when they act within the scope of EC/EU law.[17] It is also recalled that the Charter provides for an express and free-standing 'right to good administration', including the right to a hearing, to have access to the individual's file, subject to the protection of the legitimate interests of confidentiality of other persons or undertakings, and to obtain a reasoned final decision within a reasonable time, as a result of which it was suggested that its function is to mirror the guarantees of administrative 'fair procedure' which the European Court of Human Rights has read in Article 6(1) ECHR.[18]

---

[14] *Supra*, Chapter 7, see, e.g., section 2.1.

[15] *Inter alia*, DOUGLAS-SCOTT, 'The Charter of Fundamental Rights as a constitutional document', (2004) *EHRLR* 37 at 42. *Supra*, Chapter 1, section 4.

[16] Article 52(3) EU Charter: 'Insofar as this Charter contains rights which correspond to rights guaranteed by the Convention for the Protection of Human Rights and Fundamental Freedoms, the meaning and scope of those rights shall be the same as those laid down by the said Convention. This provision shall not prevent Union law from providing more extensive protection.' For commentary, see, *inter alia*, PERNICE, 'Integrating the Charter of Fundamental Rights into the Constitution of the European Union: practical and theoretical propositions', (2003) 10 *Colum. J Eur L* 5 at 14. *Supra*, Chapter I, Part 2, section 1.

[17] *Inter alia*, per AG Mischo, Joined Cases C-20 and 64/00, *Booker Aquaculture v Scottish Ministers*, [2003] ECR I-7411, para. 126; Case C-540/03, *European Parliament v Council*, judgment of 27 June 2006, not yet reported, para. 38. See EECKHOUT, 'The EU Charter of Fundamental Rights and the federal question', (2002) 39 *CMLRev* 945 at 950–51.

[18] Lord MILLETT, 'The right to good administration in European Law', (2002) *PL* Summer 309 at 318.

In addition, the current developments concerning the reform of the Founding Treaties are likely to bring about far-reaching changes in the current standards of protection of the right of 'due process' in competition proceedings before the Commission and in the context of the ECN. According to Article 6 of the Draft Constitutional Treaty agreed at the July 2007 Inter-Governmental Conference,[19] not only will the EU Charter of Fundamental Rights become binding in its entirety on the EU institutions and on the Member States' Authorities within the limits set out by its General Provisions,[20] but Paragraph 2 of that provision also creates the legal basis for the Union's accession to the ECHR, as a result of which the European Commission's action will become amenable to the scrutiny of the European Court of Human Rights.[21]

At this stage it is perhaps premature to assess the full implications of the Draft Constitutional Treaty for the protection of fundamental rights and of the rights of defence. Nevertheless it could already be suggested that, as a result of its entry into force, the ECHR will provide the minimum standards governing the notion of 'administrative fairness' that will be binding on the Commission and also uniform across the ECN, since all the Member States are parties to the Convention.[22] Moreover, following accession by the EU, individual applicants will become able to hold the Union to account before the Strasbourg Court which will ensure the application of the 'administrative due process' rules enshrined in Article 6(1) ECHR to the Commission's action in the context of both individual proceedings and its cooperation within the Network.[23]

---

[19] Conference of the Representatives of the Member States, Brussels, 23 July 2007, Draft Treaty amending the Treaty of the European Union and the Treaty establishing the European Community, CIG 1/07.

[20] *Inter alia*, EECKHOUT, 'The EU Charter of Fundamental Rights and the federal question', (2002) 39 *CMLRev* 945 at 968–69; also, DEFEIS, 'A Constitution for the European Union? A transatlantic perspective', (2005) 19 *Temp. Int'l & Comp. L J* 351 at 379–80.

[21] For commentary, see, *inter alia*, CARRUTHERS, 'Beware of lawyers bearing gifts: a critical evaluation of the proposals on fundamental rights in the EU constitutional treaty', (2004) *EHRLR* 424 at 433–34; also, ARNULL, 'From Charter to Constitution and beyond: fundamental rights in the new European Union', (2003) *PL* Winter 774 at 786.

[22] *Inter alia*, LEMMENS, 'The relation between the Charter of Fundamental Rights of the European Union and the European Convention of Human Rights – substantive aspects', (2001) 8 *Maastricht J. of Euro. and Comp. L.* 49 at 54; also, PERNICE, 'Integrating the Charter of Fundamental Rights into the Constitution of the European Union', at 12–13.

[23] See, *inter alia*, HOUSE of LORDS SELECT COMMITTEE on the EUROPEAN UNION, *VI Report: the future status of the EU Charter of Fundamental Rights*, session 2002–03, paras. 110–11.

However, it is undeniable that until the Draft Constitutional Treaty is ratified by all Member States, the issues arising from the divergent 'due process standards' provided by, respectively, EU law and the ECHR as well as from the uneven protection afforded to the rights of defence in competition proceedings across the ECN, remain open and thus call for an interim solution. On this point, it is argued that the right to 'good administration' recognised by the EU Charter, examined above, could serve as the 'due process' clause of the EC/EU legal system, since it would provide a set of minimum guarantees to the individuals or undertakings affected by administrative proceedings before the EU institutions and bodies.[24]

Referring to Article 41 as a source of inspiration for the development of 'due process' guarantees in competition proceedings before the Commission would ensure consistency with the concept of 'fairness' enshrined in the Convention[25] while being rooted in the general principles of EC law. It is also suggested that, although the Charter limits the reach of Article 41 only to the action of the EU institutions and bodies, its application to the action of the Commission could also foster the achievement of the objective of 'equivalent protection' of the rights of defence in proceedings before the NCAs concerning the application of Articles 81 and 82 EC Treaty through a process of dialogue within the ECN.[26]

However, it is undeniable that the reliance on Article 41 by the Luxembourg Courts and the ensuing possibility of a deeper interpenetration of the European Convention on Human Rights in the context of the general principles of EC law governing fundamental rights resulting from the influence of the Charter[27] could have far-reaching consequences for the existing rules.[28] The implication of a new 'EU due process clause' for the rules governing the enforcement of antitrust and merger rules will be examined in the next sections.

---

[24] *Inter alia*, KANSKA, 'Towards administrative human rights in the EU. Impact of the Charter of Fundamental Rights', (2004) *ELJ* 296 at 306.

[25] See LEMMENS, 'The relation between the Charter of Fundamental Rights of the European Union and the European Convention of Human Rights', at 54.

[26] *Inter alia*, NAZZINI, 'Some reflections on the dynamics of Due Process discourse in EC Competition law', (2005) 2(1) *CompLRev* 5.

[27] Per AG Mischo, Joined Cases C-20/00 and C-64/00, *Booker Aquaculture Ltd v Scottish Ministers*, [2003] ECR I-7411, para. 126; T-112/98, *Mannesmannrohren Werke v Commission*, [2001] ECR II-729; T-54/99, *max.mobil Telekommunikation Service v Commission*, [2002] ECR II-313.

[28] *Inter alia*, WAELBROECK, ' "Twelve feet all dangling down and six necks exceeding long" ', pp. 473–74.

1.2. The New EU 'Due Process Clause' and the Commission: Towards New Administrative Practice Rules?

The previous section illustrated how the current judicial developments as well as the ongoing constitutional evolution taking place in the field of EU fundamental rights protection may call for a reformulation of the currents standards of 'due process' in competition enforcement. With respect to the Commission's practice, it is submitted that these trends could eventually result in significant modifications of the current rules governing access to the file and the treatment of evidence.

It is submitted that the existing position regarding internal documents would have to be revisited so as to allow the investigated undertakings to have wider access to them.[29] Furthermore, although strengthening the role of the Hearing Officer could improve the fairness of the proceedings,[30] the absence of judicial control over her decisions concerning the disclosure of evidence could be detrimental to the effective protection of the undertakings' rights of defence and inconsistent with the principle of 'equality of arms' in access to the evidence gathered by the case-handling officials.[31]

In *Bryan v United Kingdom* the European Court of Human Rights emphasised the importance of the quasi-judicial features characterising the inquiry before the planning inspector as a decisive factor for the overall fairness of the proceedings[32] and in its *Fortum* judgment reiterated the importance of the exercise of powers of judicial supervision on decisions concerning the disclosure of evidence to ensure the observance of the principle of 'equality of arms'.[33] Consequently, it is suggested that allowing judicial control over the Hearing Officer's decisions as regards access to the file would become necessary in the light of a new concept of 'fair procedure' inspired by Article 41 of the EU Charter.

It is added that a 'new-style due process clause' could demand a re-

---

[29] Joined Cases 142 and 156/84, *British American Tobacco Company Ltd and RJ Reynolds Industries Inc v Commission of the European Communities*, (interim order) [1986] ECR 1899, para. 10–11. See also Notice on Access to the File, para. 15. *Supra*, Chapter 3, section 2.4.

[30] COMMISSION of the EUROPEAN COMMUNITIES, *XXXIII Report on Competition Policy*, Brussels: 1994, p. 116. 'Commission Decision 2001/462/EC, ECSC, on the terms of reference of hearing officers in certain competition proceedings', [2001] OJ L162/21, Arts. 4–7, 16.

[31] Cases T-10-12/92 & 15/92, *Cimenteries CBR SA and Others v EC Commission*, [1992] ECR II-2667, para. 47.

[32] Appl. No 19178/91, *Bryan v United Kingdom*, [1996] 21 EHRR 342, para. 46.

[33] Appl. No 32559/96, *Fortum Corp v Finland*, judgment of 15 July 2003, [2004] 38 EHRR 36, paras. 41, 43.

examination of the current rules governing the privilege against self-incrimination[34] and legal professional privilege.[35] With specific respect to the right not to incriminate oneself, although it was acknowledged that a 'more lenient' approach to the application of the ECHR in the corporate context may be explained in the light of the need to allow the public authorities to exercise a degree of control over economic activities,[36] it could be questioned whether the restrictive interpretation given by the ECJ is entirely justified in the light of the need to ensure the effective protection of 'everyone' from the arbitrary or disproportionate exercise of public power.[37]

On this point, it is regrettable that so far the Luxembourg Courts have been adamant in reaffirming their restrictive stance as regards the scope of rights against self-incrimination in competition proceedings. Acoordingly, it is suggested that only the entry into force of the Draft Constitutional Treaty and the resulting accession to the ECHR will ensure consistency between the EU concept of privilege and Convention standards.

1.3 A New Concept of 'Fairness' in Competition Enforcement: What are the Consequences for Judicial Review of the Commission's Decisions?

Section 1.2 discussed some of the implication that a 'new-style due process clause' in EU competition enforcement could have for the administrative stage of proceedings. However, it could be argued that the challenges posed by the new 'Due Process' clause inspired by Article 41 of the EU Charter may be even more urgent in the context of the judicial phase of antitrust proceedings.[38] It could be speculated whether it should perhaps be for the CFI and the

---

34 *Supra*, Chapter 4, section 5.2. Case 27/88, *Orkem v Commission*, [1989] ECR 3355, paras. 28, 33–34.

35 *Supra*, Chapter 4, section 1. Case 155/79, *AM & S Europe Limited v Commission of the European Communities*, [1982] ECR 1575; Case T-125/03, *AKZO Nobel Chemicals Ltd and Ackros Chemicals Ltd v Commission*, [2003] ECR II-4771; joined Cases T-125/03 and 253/03, *AKZO Nobel Chemicals Ltd and Ackros Chemicals Ltd v Commission*, judgment of 17 September 2007, not yet reported; *supra*, Chapter 4, section 2–3.

36 EMBERLAND, *The Human Rights of Companies*, pp. 128–30; see *inter alia*, Appl. No 10572/83, *Markt Intern Verlag GmbH and Klaus Bermann v Germany*, judgment of 20 November 1989, ser. A No 165, [1990] 12 EHRR 161; also TRAINOR, 'A comparative analysis of a corporation's right against self-incrimination', (1994–1995) 18 *Fordham Int'l L J* 2139. *Supra*, Chapter 1, section 6.

37 EMBERLAND, *ibid.*, p. 47. *Supra*, Chapter 1, section 6.

38 Appl. No 15523/89, *Schmautzer v Austria*, [1996] 21 EHRR 511; cf. joined Cases T-68, 77-78/89, *Società Italiana Vetro SpA and Others v Commission*, [1992] ECR II-1403. *Supra*, Chapter 5, section 3.

ECJ to adopt a more proactive stance in policing the fairness of the Commission's action.

With regard to the role of the Hearing Officer with respect to the exercise of the right of access to the file of the investigated parties, it could be argued that the Luxembourg Courts should accept jurisdiction over actions brought against these measures because that would provide the 'judicial supervision' over the disclosure of evidence in antitrust cases required by the ECHR in criminal proceedings.[39] Although the strict notion of 'reviewable act' adopted by the ECJ could stand in the way of this achievement, it is respectfully submitted that effective protection of the rights of defence may eventually result in the revision of the test laid down in the *IBM* judgment.[40]

The emergence of new standards of 'due process' based on Article 41 of the EU Charter could also have a significant impact on the scope of powers of judicial control exercised by the Luxembourg courts over competition decisions. Whereas the stance taken in the *Tetra Laval* judgment[41] with regard to merger prohibition decisions is to be welcomed, the current position with respect to antitrust decisions may instead have to be reconsidered.

Although it is recognised that Article 230 EC Treaty only confers on the ECJ powers of supervisory jurisdiction over the acts of the institutions, the 'restrained' scrutiny of the 'complex economic assessments' contained in decisions applying Articles 81 and 82 EC Treaty appears to be at variance vis-à-vis the standards laid down by the European Court of Human Rights as regards appeals against administrative decisions determining a criminal charge, such as minor motoring offences.[42]

It could be asked whether an alternative standard of review might be devised to bring Community law into line with the Convention in respect of decisions having a 'criminal character'. It is submitted that the introduction of a 'jurisdiction on the merits', similar to that envisaged by the UK Competition Act 1998, could be an option worth considering. The Competition Appeals Tribunal (hereinafter referred to as CAT) was created as a specialised competition court competent to hear appeals against decisions of the Director General of Fair Trading. According to Schedule 8, para. 3(2) of the Act, it

---

[39] *Inter alia,* Appl. No 27052/95, *Jasper v United Kingdom*, [2000] 30 EHRR 441, para. 52.

[40] Case 60/81, *International Business Machines Corp v Commission*, [1981] ECR 2639, para. 9. Also Case T-377/00, *Philip Morris and Others v Commission*, [2003] ECR II-1, paras. 79–80.

[41] Case T-5/02, *Tetra Laval BV v Commission*, [2002] ECR II-4381; C-12/03, *Commission v Tetra Laval*, [2005] ECR I-987.

[42] Appl. No 11598/85, *Stenuit v France*, [1992] ECC 401, paras. 56, 61; also Appl. No 15523/89, *Schmautzer v Austria*, [1996] 21 EHRR 511, para. 36. *Supra*, Chapter 5, section 2.2.

enjoys the power, *inter alia*, to 'give any direction, take any step or make any other decision which the Office of Fair Trading (or regulator) could have given, taken or made'.[43]

In its *NAPP* judgment[44] the Tribunal acknowledged that competition proceedings under the Act involved the determination of a 'criminal charge' for the purpose of the ECHR[45] and consequently, the seriousness of the matter justified the circumstance that once an appeal was lodged, 'what was previously an administrative procedure, in which the Director combines the roles of "prosecutor" and "decision-maker" becomes a judicial proceeding'[46] in which 'the Tribunal for its part is not limited to the traditional role of judicial review but is required to decide the case "on the merits" '.[47]

So wide a power of scrutiny constituted 'an essential part of ensuring the fairness and transparency of the new regime'[48] especially in cases 'where it is believed that a failure on the part of the Director General to follow proper procedures has led him to reach an incorrect conclusion'.[49] It is submitted that the link between the existence of a 'jurisdiction on the merits' and the needs of a 'fair trial' in the light of Article 6(1) ECHR emerges clearly from the Tribunal's argument. Given the 'criminal nature' of the proceedings under the Competition Act, the CAT is allowed the full review on the merits of the infringement decisions to comply with the requirements of 'full jurisdiction' laid down by the ECHR.[50]

However, it could be argued that such a pervasive form of judicial scrutiny seems difficult to reconcile with the principles governing the judicial architecture established by the EC Treaty and especially with the limited powers of review conferred on the Luxembourg Courts by Article 230 EC Treaty.[51] At

---

43 Schedule 8, para 3(2), Competition Act 1998; for commentary, *inter alia*, FREEMAN and WHISH, *A Guide to the Competition Act 1998* (1999) London: Butterworths, pp. 80ff.

44 *NAPP Pharmaceuticals v Director General of Fair Trading*, [2002] ECC 13.

45 *Id.*, para. 93.

46 *Id.*, para. 117.

47 *Ibid.*

48 *Id.*, para. 118.

49 *Ibid.*

50 Appl. Nos 7299/75 and 7496/76, *Albert & LeCompte v Belgium*, [1983] 5 EHRR 533 at para. 29. Also Marion Symmons, Chair of the CAT, speech given at the British Institute of International and Comparative Law conference on 'Antitrust Litigation: Where do we stand?', 3 February 2006.

51 *Inter alia*, joined Cases T-68, 77-78/89, *Società Italiana Vetro SpA and Others v Commission*, [1992] ECR II-1403. See also HOUSE of LORDS SELECT COMMITTEE, *XV Report: an EU Competition Court*, session 2006–07, 23 April 2007 (hereinafter referred to as *XV Report*); e.g. Minutes of Evidence given before Subcommittee E by Judge Bo Vesterdorf, p. 99; also Minutes of Evidence given before Subcommittee E by Judge John Cooke, p. 98.

the same time, one could speculate as to whether the recent reforms to the EU judiciary introduced by the Treaty of Nice could provide a means by which to introduce a more stringent form of scrutiny. According to Article 225a of the EC Treaty, the Council is empowered to 'create judicial panels to hear and determine at first instance certain classes of actions or procedures brought in specific areas', attached to the CFI, which will be competent to hear appeals against their decisions.

It could be argued that a judicial panel may constitute a specialised forum for the hearing of antitrust appeals and, equipped with powers of scrutiny 'on the merits', could succeed in ensuring the 'Article 6-proofing'[52] of the proceedings for the application of Articles 81 and 82 EC Treaty. The fact that the Council has already relied on Article 225a to create the EU Civil Service Tribunal and is discussing the possibility of introducing a 'Community Patent Court'[53] could be interpreted as providing further support for this proposal. It is added that the creation of a 'competition court' would be consistent with the trend established by the Treaty of Nice towards a 'three-tier Community judicial system' in specific areas to counterbalance, at least in part, the workload imposed on the CFI by its role of general forum to hear all direct actions.[54]

It may be recalled from Chapter 5 that a proposal for the creation of an 'EU competition court' responsible for the review of merger appeals was recently discussed before the House of Lords Select Committee on the European Union.[55] Nevertheless, it should be recognised that, even though the call for fairer and speedier competition proceedings cannot be dismissed outright, the introduction of a specialised judicial body on the basis of Article 225a EC Treaty does not resolve all the questions concerning the compatibility of its potentially wide powers of review with the existing institutional framework.[56] Consequently, the next section will assess the extent to which the introduction of an 'antitrust court' in the EU context constitutes an appropriate and viable response to the need to ensure a 'fair procedure' before the Commission in the light of the principles enshrined in Article 6(1) ECHR.

---

52 Marion Symmons, *supra*, footnote 50.

53 VESTERDORF, 'The Community court system ten years from now and beyond: challenges and possibilities', (2003) 28(3) *ELRev* 303 at 312.

54 *Id.*, p. 313.

55 CBI Brief, 'The need for an EU Competition Court', 15 June 2006. HOUSE of LORDS SELECT COMMITTEE, *XV Report: an EU Competition Court*, session 2006–07, 23 April 2007 (hereinafter referred to as *XV Report*). *Supra*, Chapter 5, section 3.

56 See e.g. Minutes of Evidence given by Mr Tim Cowen before the House of Lords Select Committee on the EU, p. 3.

2. IS A 'COMPETITION COURT' THE RESPONSE TO THE NEEDS OF THE NEW 'EU DUE PROCESS CLAUSE'? THE PROS AND CONS OF A 'JURISDICTION ON THE MERITS' IN ANTITRUST ENFORCEMENT*

The previous section recalled some of the possible implications of the 'limited review' exercised by the ECJ on antitrust decisions and argued that given the 'criminal' nature of the proceedings for the application of Articles 81 and 82 of the EC Treaty, it may become necessary to consider the introduction of a form of control 'on the merits' over the Commission decisions.

It is undeniable that the British Competition Appeals Tribunal could represent an ideal blueprint for any proposal of reform in this area[57] as it would ensure appropriate checks and balances on the Commission's discretion both during the administrative procedure, by being empowered to oversee the decisions of the Hearing Officer concerning the disclosure of the evidence contained in the 'file', and after its conclusion, by exercising powers of scrutiny on all matters of fact and of law over the decision, including the power to readopt the impugned measure in case of annulment.[58] However, it was also pointed out that the introduction of such wide powers of judicial review may not be compatible with the limited judicial powers conferred on the Luxembourg Courts by the Treaty and would therefore raise fundamental questions of consistency vis-à-vis the existing EU institutional architecture.

The recent *XV Report* of the House of Lords Select Committee on the European Union, despite being concerned with the proposal made by the Confederation of British Industry to introduce a specialised panel responsible only for the review of merger decision, provides useful insights on the impact of the possible institution of a new judicial body on the existing framework laid down by the Treaty.[59] In its proposal the CBI envisaged the creation of a specialised panel composed of nine judges, divided into three chambers and

* A shorter version of this section is forthcoming with the title 'Toward an EU Competition court: "Article-6-proofing" antitrust proceedings before the Commission?', in (2007) 30(4) *World Competition* 595.

57 *Inter alia*, VESTERDORF, 'The Community court system ten years from now and beyond', at 313.

58 See, *mutatis mutandis*, Marion Symmons, *supra*, footnote 50.

59 CBI Brief, 'The need for an EU Competition Court', 15 June 2006. HOUSE of LORDS SELECT COMMITTEE, *XV Report*. For an analysis of the implications of a "competition court" in the field of EC antitrust see, *inter alia*, ANDREANGELI, 'Toward an EU Competition court: "Article-6-proofing" antitrust proceedings before the Commission?', in (2007) 30(4) *World Competition* 595.

responsible for the review of merger decisions and, perhaps at a later stage, of all competition matters raised by private applicants.

The new body would enjoy the same jurisdictional powers as the CFI, in accordance with Article 230 EC Treaty, and its decisions would be subject to appeal before the CFI. In accordance with Article 225(3) of the EC Treaty, there would also be the possibility of an exceptional 'review' and 'preview' of these appeals on the part of the ECJ, upon the initiative of the first Advocate General.[60]

Given the limited remit of this work, it is not possible to address in detail all the implications raised by the proposal. Nonetheless, it is noteworthy that despite recognising the need in principle for the timely and final review of merger decisions,[61] several witnesses during the Select Committee inquiry doubted that the new judicial body would constitute an appropriate and proportionate response to these concerns.[62] They argued that a new court would result almost inevitably in another layer of judicial review being added to the existing framework and would therefore increase its complexity.[63] Furthermore, in consideration of the central role played by the competition rules in the context of EC law as a whole, it was questioned whether the limited powers of review enjoyed by the ECJ vis-à-vis the appeal decisions of the CFI could ensure the unitary and coherent interpretation of the EC Treaty.[64]

In respect of the scope of the panel's jurisdiction, it is noteworthy that the CBI proposal did not envisage the conferral of the power to decide merger appeals 'on the merits' but instead opted to remain within the remit of Article 230 of the EC Treaty.[65] On this specific point, the final Report and the evidence gathered during the inquiry did not express uniform views. Certain witnesses and the Select Committee itself favoured the conferral of a power to re-examine the impugned decision as regards all matters of fact and of law and

---

60 CBI Brief, 'The need for an EU Competition Court', 15 June 2006.

61 See, *inter alia*, HOUSE of LORDS SELECT COMMITTEE on the EUROPEAN UNION, *XXXII Report: the review of the EC Merger Regulation*, sess. 2001/2002, paras. 242–43. Also HOUSE of LORDS SELECT COMMITTEE, *XV Report*, para. 16.

62 See, e.g. written evidence submitted to the inquiry by Sir David Edward, p. 3.

63 Written evidence submitted by the International Bar Association to the House of Lords Select Committee, Subcommittee E, pp. 3–4.

64 *Inter alia*, written evidence submitted to the inquiry by the Office of Fair Trading, p. 4; see also HOUSE of LORDS SELECT COMMITTEE, *XV Report*, para. 71.

65 *Inter alia*, written evidence submitted to the inquiry by John Temple Lang and Robert O'Donoghue, p. 2.

thus to readopt it in limited circumstances[66] – for example, 'where (. . .) there has been no substantial alteration in the circumstances nor other factors apparently requiring a fresh investigation'.[67]

Other witnesses, instead, pointed out that this proposal would entail a radical departure from the powers of judicial scrutiny conferred on the Community courts and consequently would require an amendment to the Treaty.[68] In addition, it was argued that conferring on the proposed judicial panel powers of scrutiny 'on the merits' over antitrust decisions would probably encourage the new court to adopt a proactive stance in the review of the impugned measures and therefore could endanger the discretion enjoyed by the Commission as the chief competition policy maker and enforcer in the EU institutional framework.[69]

Despite doubting that the Commission would allow such a significant shift to occur, the Select Committee recognised in its final Report that the conferral of powers of control on matters of fact and law would be likely to be met by opposition from the Member States.[70] As Judge Vesterdorf put it, the only way that amendment could be introduced would be

> if Member States were willing to accept that the institutional balance, which has been set up carefully under the Treaty, allowing the Commission as a quasi-administrative political body to take those decisions, that specific power should be taken away and given to judges . . . but that is not of actuality because it cannot be done, and I fail to see Member States accepting that as a change.[71]

In the light of the inquiry before the House of Lords EU Select Committee, it could be argued that the introduction of a form of 'jurisdiction on the merits', despite constituting perhaps the most appropriate response to the concerns for the fairness of EC antitrust proceedings, does not appear viable in practice, in consideration of its impact on the current interinstitutional balance of the EU and, perhaps most importantly, the perceived lack of consensus on the part of the Member States with respect to the changes entailed by the proposal.[72]

---

66 See, e.g., minutes of Evidence given before Subcommittee E by Sir Christopher Bellamy, p. 40.

67 HOUSE of LORDS SELECT COMMITTEE, *XV Report*, para. 161.

68 See Minutes of Evidence given before Subcommittee E by Judge Bo Vesterdorf, pp. 98–99.

69 See, e.g., written evidence submitted to the inquiry by the Office of Fair Trading, p. 6.

70 See, *inter alia*, Minutes of Evidence given before Subcommittee E by Michel Petite and Philip Lowe, pp. 74–75.

71 Minutes of Evidence given before Subcommittee E by Judge Bo Vesterdorf, p. 99.

72 *Inter alia*, joined Cases T-68, 77–78/89, *Società Italiana Vetro SpA and*

In this respect, it is telling that during the Select Committee inquiry the very parallel between the UK Competition Appeals Tribunal and the proposed judicial panel was questioned in view of the significant differences existing between the EC and the British enforcement structures. Sir Christopher Bellamy argued that the CAT enjoyed several distinct advantages over the proposed panel, including having only one working language, having started with a 'complete clean sheet' and enjoying pervasive powers of review extending to the merits of each case which are accepted as being compatible with the existing domestic judicial structure.[73]

It can therefore be concluded that, although the demands of fairness in the context of antitrust enforcement may justify the introduction of a specialised judicial body responsible for the scrutiny of the Commission decisions, and in case of the annulment of the impugned measure, for their readoption, there seem to be strong arguments against what appears to be a major reform for which an amendment to the Treaty is very likely to be necessary.

However, it could equally be argued that the progressive human rights consolidation taking place at the EU level does not allow these concerns for the existing standards of due process in antitrust proceedings to be downplayed.[74] Consequently, the next section will consider whether, rather than being concerned with the 'judicial phase' of the enforcement proceedings, the suggestions for reform should instead focus on the 'administrative stage' and should thus aim to ensure the fairer handling of individual cases before the Commission itself.

3. REDESIGNING DG COMPETITION: A SEPARATE INVESTIGATIVE TASK FORCE FOR ANTITRUST CASES?

Section 2 examined the implications arising from the proposal to introduce a form of specialised jurisdiction 'on the merits', aimed at the review of antitrust decisions in the EU institutional framework, and suggested that despite constituting perhaps the most appropriate means to 'Article-6-proof' the Commission proceedings for the application of Articles 81 and 82 of the EC

Others v Commission, [1992] ECR II-1403 at para. 319. Also, written submission made by the OFT to Subcommittee E, p. 6 (para. 24). Cf. HOUSE of LORDS SELECT COMMITTEE on the EUROPEAN UNION, *XV Report*, paras. 78–79.

[73] Minutes of Evidence given before Subcommittee E by Sir Christopher Bellamy, p. 41; also Written evidence submitted to the inquiry by John Temple Lang and Robert O'Donoghue, p. 2.

[74] *Supra*, this chapter, section 1.

Treaty, it could not be easily reconciled with the existing judicial and institutional architecture.

Consequently, it raised the question of whether a solution to the ongoing concerns for speedy, effective and overall fair competition enforcement should be sought by means of a wide-ranging reform of the system for the application of the EC antitrust rules resulting in the separation of the investigative from the decision-making phase of the proceedings, along the lines of the US system for the enforcement of the Sherman Act.[75]

It is noteworthy that before the EU Select Committee several witnesses to the inquiry on the proposal for an EU competition court had forcefully argued in favour of the introduction of a system whereby the Commission would only be empowered to carry out the necessary inquiries in order to make a case against a notified merger or in support of allegations of a breach of the antitrust rules, and that a separate decision-maker would assess the evidence and adopt a final decision on the matter.[76] Although this option was not considered in detail in the final Report, it is recognised that a similar change would bring in the benefits of a de-politicised decision-making mechanism in the context of competition enforcement, namely 'a more efficient and effective quality control of fact-finding and economic assessment'[77] without entailing the creation of a new judicial body.[78]

However, it may be doubted whether this suggestion, just as that for an 'EU competition court', could be met with the necessary political support. In this respect, it is recalled that the broadly similar proposal for the introduction of a 'European Cartel Office' was rejected in 1997.[79] Although it is not possible to examine it in detail, it may be remembered that at the core of the call for the creation of the Office was the need to ensure that the enforcement of the Community competition rules can take place away from political pressures[80] and in a more objective, transparent and efficient manner.[81] It was thus envisaged that the Office would have exercised exclusively the power to apply Articles 81 and 82 of the EC Treaty and the Merger Regulation (but not the rules concerning, for instance, industrial liberalisation or state aids) and that

---

75 See, *inter alia*, MEADE, 'Modelling a European Competition Authority', (1996) 46 Duke L J 153.

76 Minutes of Evidence given before the Subcommittee by Dr William Bishop, pp. 33–34.

77 Minutes of Evidence given to the Subcommittee by Sir David Edward, p. 52.

78 *Id.*, p. 53.

79 For an examination of the proposal, see, *inter alia*, RILEY, 'The European Cartel Office: a guardian without weapons', (1997) 18 *ECLR* 3.

80 *Inter alia*, RODGER, 'Competition policy, liberalism and globalisation: a European perspective', (2000) 6 *Colum. J. Eur. L.* 289 at 293.

81 RILEY, 'The European Cartel Office: a guardian without weapons', at 4–5.

its decisions would be subject to the review of the Commission and to further judicial appeal before the CFI.[82]

Although the significant concerns arising from often lengthy and opaque proceedings before the Commission were generally acknowledged,[83] the proposal for a European Cartel Office failed to attract both political consensus and the support of practitioners and academics. It was argued that the creation of a separate competition enforcement body would result in the marginalisation of antitrust and merger policy and practice from the overall economic policies pursued by the Commission, would increase the risk of inconsistent interpretation of the competition rules vis-à-vis the EC Treaty as a whole[84] and therefore increase the complexity of the existing institutional structure.[85]

In the light of the above proposal, legitimate doubt could therefore be cast on the possibility that the creation of a 'US-style' system for the application of Articles 81 and 82 EC Treaty, characterised perhaps by a distinct authority responsible for the investigation of antitrust infringement claims and by the Commission as decision-maker, could find the approval of the Member States.[86]

However, it is submitted that, to achieve better standards of fairness and impartiality in this area, a satisfactory and less controversial alternative could be found in the adoption of measures of internal reorganisation of DG Competition, aimed at separating the two phases of investigation and adoption of a final decision, and entrusting each stage to a different unit within the Directorate. In this respect it is noteworthy that in accordance with Council Regulation 659/1999[87] the Commission already exercises its powers of prior control over new state aid measures by way of a two-phase procedure articulated in a preliminary investigation and a formal procedure. The latter is initiated by a formal decision which states the doubts raised by the Commission with regard to the compatibility of the aid with the competition rules.[88]

---

82 *Id.*, p. 7.

83 *Inter alia*, MONTAG, 'The case for a reform of Regulation 17/62: problems and possible solutions from a practitioner's point of view', (1999) 22 *Fordham Int'l L J* 819 at 833–34.

84 RODGER, 'Competition policy, liberalism and globalisation: a European perspective', at 310.

85 RILEY, 'The European Cartel Office: a guardian without weapons', at 11–12.

86 MEADE, 'Modelling a European Competition Authority', (1996) 46 *Duke L J* 153 at 194.

87 Council Regulation No 659/1999 of 22 March 1999 laying down detailed rules for the application of Article 93 (now Article 88) of the EC Treaty, [1999] OJ L83/1.

88 See generally ARNULL et al. *Wyatt and Dashwood's European Union Law* (2006) London: Thomson/Sweet & Maxwell, pp. 1176ff.

It is further added that the proposal could gather support from the blueprint offered by the European Anti-Fraud Office (hereinafter referred to as OLAF), the Commission's department responsible for the investigation of serious allegations of fraud, corruption and professional misconduct in all the institutions and bodies of the EU.[89] The Office was established in the wake of the Santer Commission scandal by Commission decision No 1999/352 and its powers were later disciplined by Regulation No 1973/1999.[90]

The Regulation confers on OLAF the power to obtain 'unannounced access' to the premises of the EU institutions and bodies, to examine documents and records and to ask for on-the-spot explanations from their staff.[91] However, the Office has no decision-making powers, being only in charge of gathering evidence concerning the serious allegations of fraud, corruption and other professional misconduct threatening the EU financial interests. Its powers are thus limited to reporting its findings to the competent authorities of the Member States and to recommending appropriate action to be taken against the concerned individuals.[92]

Despite being formally a department of the Commission, it enjoys significant operational independence from EU institutions and bodies and national governments and performs its functions under the supervision of a Surveillance Committee appointed for this purpose from amongst independent outside persons with appropriate skills and expertise.[93] OLAF is headed by a Director appointed by the Commission upon recommendation of the Supervisory Committee, and after consulting the European Parliament and the Council, for a term of five years. She enjoys extensive management powers, including limited autonomy as regards the budget of the Office and the Staff, and is responsible in full independence for the initiation of new investigations.[94]

---

[89] Commission Decision 1999/352/EC, ECSC, Euratom of 28 April 1999, [1999] OJ L136/20; Regulation 1073/1999 of 25 May 1999 of the Council and the European Parliament, concerning investigations conducted by the European Anti-Fraud Office (OLAF), [1999] L136/1.

[90] For a general examination of the structure and function of OLAF, see, *inter alia*, WAKEFIELD, 'Good governance and the European Anti Fraud Office', (2006) 12(4) EPL 549.

[91] See READER, 'Moving forward, never backwards: preventing fraud in the European Union and defining European Central Bank independence', (2004) 27 *Fordham Int'l L J* 1509 at 1529–30.

[92] WAKEFIELD, 'Good governance and the European Anti Fraud Office', at 553.

[93] *Id.*, pp. 551–52.

[94] *Inter alia*, ODUDU, Case comment to C-11/00, *Commission v European Central Bank*, judgment of 10 July 2003, (2004) 41 *CMLRev* 1073 at 1081–82.

A thorough examination of the role of OLAF is clearly beyond the scope of this work. Nevertheless, its manner of composition and its position vis-à-vis the Commission is of particular interest in the light of the 2003 ECJ decision in the *Commission v European Central Bank* case.[95] In that judgment the ECJ was asked to decide, *inter alia*, whether the exercise of powers of investigation by OLAF with respect to the European Central Bank (hereinafter referred to as ECB) threatened the independence enjoyed by the ECB.[96]

The Bank had alleged that, by being subjected to the investigative powers of the Office, its autonomy as central bank would be irremediably undermined; in this respect, the ECB pointed to the circumstance that OLAF remained a department within the Commission and retained 'certain links, in particular budgetary links, with the Commission'.[97] It also expressed concern at the 'guarantees attendant upon the exercise of OLAF's powers' and claimed that as a result it may be open to the Office to launch investigations in the absence of 'serious suspicions' of fraud or other misconduct.[98]

The ECJ rejected the ECB's arguments.[99] It took the view that being exposed to the possibility of an investigation on the part of OLAF could not threaten the functional autonomy conferred on it by the Treaty to allow it to perform its role of central bank. Although the Office existed as a department of the Commission, the rules contained in Regulation 1053/1999 were inspired by a clear legislative commitment 'to subject the powers conferred on OLAF, first, to guarantees intended to ensure (. . .) [its] complete independence and, second, the strict observance of the rules of Community law' affecting the exercise of these powers.[100]

The Court attached great importance to the limited remit of the powers enjoyed by the Office and to the fact that an investigation could only begin upon a decision of the Director on the basis of a 'sufficiently serious suspicion' of fraud, corruption or other unlawful conduct, and should be conducted in accordance with the internal rules of procedure adopted by each institution.[101] Also, the safeguards attending the independence of OLAF vis-à-vis the Commission, including the rules governing the appointment of its Director, the guarantees protecting her autonomy and the role of the Surveillance Committee,[102] ensured that the investigative powers enjoyed by the Office

---

95 Case C-11/00, [2003] ECR I-7147.
96 *Id.*, paras. 113–14, 119–20.
97 *Id.*, para. 120.
98 *Id.*, para. 121.
99 *Id.*, para. 138.
100 *Id.*, para. 139.
101 *Id.*, paras. 140–41, 143.
102 *Id.*, para. 143.

would be exercised without any risk of political pressure being put on the investigated institutions.[103]

It is submitted that the *ECB* judgment could provide support to the suggested proposal to separate the investigative and decision-making functions in antitrust cases and entrust each stage to a separate unit within the Commission for the benefit of the quality, impartiality and fairness of competition decision-making. Short of the creation of a separate body responsible for the investigation stage of EC antitrust proceedings, which would perhaps be as controversial as establishing a new 'EU competition court',[104] it is argued that, provided 'OLAF-type' guarantees are in place to safeguard the independence of each unit, the allocation of the fact-finding and of the decision-making phase to separate teams within DG Competition could foster fairer and more efficient enforcement of Articles 81 and 82 of the EC Treaty.

The fact that OLAF was established by way of a decision of the Commission and that its powers were regulated through legislation suggests that a similar change in the area of competition enforcement could be introduced via legislative measures without requiring Treaty amendment. It is thus regrettable that the EU Select Committee did not address the possibility of reforming the overall system for the control of concentrations or, more generally, for competition enforcement.[105] Although the *XV Report* briefly mentions the possibility of removing decision-making from the Commission, at least as regards the prohibition of mergers, the viability of this proposal is not examined, probably due to the perceived lack of support shown by the EU institutions.[106]

It is therefore concluded that adopting a middle-ground solution inspired by the composition and functioning of OLAF could constitute a satisfactory option to address concerns over the fairness of the EC antitrust enforcement system and be more consistent with the existing institutional arrangements, in addition to, as a result, being less 'politically charged' than other proposals.

---

103 Case C-11/00, *Commission v European Central Bank*, [2003] ECR I-7147, per AG Jacobs, para. 165. For commentary, see READER, 'Moving forward, never backwards', at 1551.

104 Minutes of Evidence given by Mr M Petite to Subcommittee E, *supra*, fn. 44, pp. 54–55.

105 HOUSE of LORDS SELECT COMMITTEE on the EUROPEAN UNION, *XV Report*, para. 155.

106 *Ibid.*

Conclusions: the future of Community 'due process' in competition cases

The underlying focus of this work has been the examination of how the standards of Community 'due process' in competition cases can be maintained consistent with the concept of 'administrative fairness' elaborated in the ECHR. The consideration of the role of the Convention in the process of 'human rights consolidation' taking place in the EU legal system and the challenges posed by the implementation of the Modernisation plan emphasised the need to ensure a common approach to the protection of the rights of defence of the undertakings concerned by competition proceedings inspired by Article 6(1) ECHR.

Accordingly, it was suggested that, until the ECHR standards become binding on the Commission and thus directly applicable to EU antitrust and merger enforcement as a result of the entry into force of the Draft Constitutional Treaty, consistency between the 'due process' rules governing the action of the Commission and the NCAs and those enshrined in Article 6(1) of the Convention could be attained through the medium of the 'right to good administration' enshrined in Article 41 of the EU Charter of Fundamental Rights.

The analysis of the 'administrative phase' of EC competition proceedings demonstrated that whereas the right to be heard ensures an overall meaningful and effective participation of the investigated parties to the proceedings, significant issues arise with respect to their right to obtain disclosure of the evidence gathered by the Commission. Although the ECJ pointed out that access to the Commission file should conform to the principle of 'equality of arms', it is submitted that the Court's interpretation of this rule is not entirely consistent with that enshrined in the Convention. Since no judicial supervision is ensured over the decisions of the Hearing Officer concerning access to the file of the investigated parties, it may be doubted that limitations on their right to be acquainted with the evidence in conditions of parity with the Commission are adequately counterbalanced by the available procedural safeguards, as is required by the Convention.

The restrictive scope of the privilege against self-incrimination and of legal professional privilege, emerges as another cause of concern for 'due process' in EC competition enforcement. It is submitted that the ongoing process of 'human rights consolidation' recalled above, together with the challenges posed by cooperation between the Commission and the NCAs within the ECN, may strengthen the argument in favour of a more generous interpretation of these guarantees.

As regards the judicial phase of competition proceedings, the consideration of standing conditions governing the appeals against antitrust and merger decisions illustrated that although the requirements of the 'right to a court' enshrined in Article 6(1) are satisfied, the *locus standi* of the representatives of the employees of the notifying parties in merger cases for the purpose of challenging the decisions appears to contradict the generally applicable conditions and should therefore be made more consistent with them.

With respect to the scope of powers of judicial control assigned to the Community courts, although the careful scrutiny of merger decisions endorsed in the ECJ's *Tetra Laval* judgment is to be welcomed, the comparison of the 'limited' standard of review applied to antitrust decisions with the review 'on the merits' advocated by the European Court of Human Rights for administrative decisions determining a 'criminal charge' raised concerns as to the 'Article 6-proofing' of proceedings for the application of Articles 81 and 82 EC Treaty.

Although the example offered by the 'jurisdiction on the merits' enjoyed by the British Competition Appeals Tribunal was hailed as being, in principle, appropriate to ensure the conformity of EC antitrust proceedings with Article 6(1) ECHR, the examination of the potential implications of this option for the judicial architecture established by the Founding Treaties revealed that its introduction may not be viable in practice. It was thus argued that the adoption of an intermediate solution entailing only the internal reorganisation of DG Competition to ensure separation of the investigative from the decision-making stages of the proceedings between different units within the Directorate, together with appropriate guarantees to ensure their reciprocal independence, could provide a less controversial and perhaps equally satisfactory solution to the problems of 'administrative fairness' highlighted by the comparative analysis.

Consequently, it is respectfully concluded that, at least for the time being, the emergence in competition enforcement of a new 'due process' clause increasingly inspired by the European Court of Human Rights and in continuity with the general principles of EC law could have positive, yet far-reaching consequences for the existing standards and is likely to pose a welcome challenge not only for the Commission, but also for the ECJ and perhaps for the Community legislature.

Bibliography

BOOKS

ALBORS-LLORENS, *Private Parties in European Community Law, Challenging Community Measures* (1996) Oxford: Clarendon Press.

ARNULL, DASHWOOD, DOUGAN, ROSS, SPAVENTA & WYATT, *Wyatt and Dashwood's European Union Law* (2006) London: Thomson/Sweet & Maxwell.

CAHILL and COOKE (eds), *The Modernisation of EU Competition Law Enforcement in the EU* (2004) Cambridge: Cambridge University Press.

CRAIG and DeBÙRCA, *EU Law: Text, Cases and Materials*, 3rd edn (2002) Oxford: Oxford University Press.

CURTIN and HEUKELS (eds), *Institutional Dynamics of European Integration, Essays in Honour of Henry G. Schermers*, Vol. 2 (1994) Dordrecht, London: Nijhoff.

DOUGLAS-SCOTT, *The Constitutional Law of the European Union* (2002) London and New York: Longman.

EHLERMANN and ATANASIU (eds), *European Competition Law Annual 2002: Constructing the EU Network of Competition Authorities* (2004) Oxford, Portland, OR: Hart Publishing.

EMBERLAND, *The Human Rights of Companies* (2005) Oxford: Oxford University Press.

FREEMAN and WHISH, *A Guide to the Competition Act 1998* (1999) London: Butterworths.

HARDING and JOSHUA, *Regulating Cartels in Europe: a Study of Legal Control of Corporate Delinquency* (2003) Oxford: Oxford University Press.

HARTLEY, *The Foundations of European Community Law*, 5th edn (2003) Oxford: Oxford University Press.

HAWK (ed.), *International Antitrust Law and Policy, Annual Proceedings of the Fordham Corporate Law Institute* (2005) New York: Juris Publishing.

JONES and SUFRIN, *EC Competition Law* (2001) Oxford: Oxford University Press.

KERSE and COOK, *EC Merger Control*, 4th edn (2005) London: Sweet and Maxwell.

KERSE and KHAN, *EC Antitrust Procedure*, 5th edn (2004) London: Sweet and Maxwell.

KORAH, *An Introductory Guide to EC Competition Law and Practice*, 8th edn (2004) Oxford, Portland, OR: Hart Publishing.

KORAH, *Cases and Materials on EC Competition Law* (2001) Oxford, Portland, OR: Hart Publishing.

LENAERTS and VAN NUFFEL, *Constitutional Law of the European Union*, 2nd edn (2004) London: Sweet and Maxwell.

MIDDLETON, RODGER and MacCULLOCH, *Cases and Materials on UK and EC Competition Law* (2003) Oxford: Oxford University Press.

NAZZINI, *Concurrent Proceedings in Competition Law – Procedure, Evidence and Remedies* (2004) Oxford: Oxford University Press.

NEHL, *Principles of Administrative Procedure in EC Law* (1999) Oxford, Portland, OR: Hart Publishing.

OVEY & WHITE, *Jacobs and White: The European Convention on Human Rights*, 3rd edn (2002) Oxford: Oxford University Press.

RODGER and MacCULLOCH, *The UK Competition Act: a New Era for UK Competition Law* (2000) Oxford, Portland, OR: Hart Publishing.

SCHWARZE, *European Administrative Law* (1992) London: Sweet and Maxwell.

TRIDIMAS, *The General Principles of EC Law* (1998) Oxford: Oxford University Press.

WHISH, *Competition Law*, 5th edn (2003) London: Butterworths.

WILS, *Principles of European Antitrust Enforcement* (2005) Oxford, Portland, OR: Hart Publishing.

ARTICLES

ACIERNO, 'The Carpenter judgment: fundamental rights and the limits of the Community legal order', (2003) 28 *ELRev* 398.

AIBEL, 'Corporate counsel and business ethics: a personal review', (1994) 59 *Mo. L. Rev.* 427.

ALLOTT, 'Fundamental rights in the EU', (1996) 55 *CLJ* 409.

ALONSO GARCIA, 'The general provisions of the Charter of Fundamental Rights of the European Union', (2002) 8 *ELJ* 492.

ANDREANGELI, 'Strasbourg versus Brussels: Human Rights, the right of access to the file and legal professional privilege', (2004) 11 *IJEL* 362.

ANDREANGELI, 'Fairness and timing in Merger control proceedings: will the "stop-the-clock" clause work?', (2005) 26(7) *ECLR* 403.

ANDREANGELI, 'The protection of legal professional privilege in EU law and the impact of the rules on the exchange of information within the

European Competition Network on the secrecy of communications between lawyer and client: one step forward, two steps back?', (2005) 2(1) *CompLRev* 31.

ANDREANGELI, 'The impact of the Modernisation Regulation on the guarantees of due process in competition proceedings', (2006) 31 *ELRev* 342.

ANDREANGELI, 'Toward an EU Competition Court: "Article-6-proofing" antitrust proceedings before the Commission?', (2007) 30(4) *W.Comp.* 595.

ANDREWS, 'Legal advice privilege's broad protection – the House of Lords in *Three Rivers* (no. 6)', (2005) 24 (Apr) *CJQ* 185.

ARAUJO, 'The respect of fundamental rights within the European network of competition authorities', in HAWK (ed.), *International Antitrust Law and Policy, Annual Proceedings from the Fordham Corporate Law Institute* (2005) New York: Juris Publishing, p. 511.

ARNULL, case comment to T-96/92, *Comité Central d'Enterprise de la Société Generale des Grandes Sources and others v Commission*, Judgment of 27 April 1995 ; Case T-12/93, *Comité Central d'Enterprise de la Société Anonime Vittel and Others v Commission*, Judgment of 27 April 1995, (1996) 33 *CMLRev* 319.

ARNULL, 'From Charter to Constitution and beyond: fundamental rights in the new European Union', (2003) *PL* Winter 774.

BAILEY, 'Scope of judicial review under Article 81 EC', (2004) 41 *CMLRev* 1327.

BANNER and THOMPSON, 'Human rights' review of state acts performed in compliance with EC Law: Bosphorus Airways v Ireland', (2005) 6 *EHRLR* 649.

BARBOT, 'Money laundering: an international challenge', [1995] 3 *Tul. J. Int'l & Comp L* 161.

BAUM, 'An economic analysis of corporate lawyer client privilege', paper presented at the EALE Conference, Ljubjana, Slovenia, on 14 September 2005, available at: http://www.eale-slovenia.org/papers/Baum.pdf.

BAY and RUIZ CALZADO, '*Tetra Laval II*: the coming of age of the judicial review of merger decisions', (2005) 28(4) *W. Comp.* 433.

BERG, 'The new EC Merger regulation: a first assessment of its practical impact', (2004) 24 *NW. J. of Int'l L. and Bus.* 683.

BERG and OSTENDORF, 'The Reform of EC Merger Control: substance and impact of the proposed new procedural rules', (2003) 24 *ECLR* 594.

BESSON, 'The European Union and human rights: towards a post-national human rights institution?', (2006) 6 *Hum. Rts. L Rev.* 323.

BIONDI, 'Free trade, a mountain road and the right to protest: European economic freedoms and fundamental individual rights', (2004) *EHRLR* 51.

BLOOM, 'Exchange of confidential information among members of the EU network of competition authorities', in EHLERMANN and ATANASIU, (eds), *European Competition Law Annual 2002: Constructing the EU Network of Competition Authorities* (2004) Oxford, Portland, OR: Hart Publishing, p. 389.

BOYLE, 'Administrative justice, judicial review and the right to a fair hearing under the European Convention on Human Rights', (1984) *PL* 89.

BRAND, 'Professional responsibility in a transnational transactions practice', (1998) 17 *J. L. & Com.* 301.

BREMS, 'Conflicting human rights: an exploration in the context of the right to a fair trial in the European Convention for the protection of Human Rights and Fundamental Freedoms', (2005) 27 *Hum. Rts. Quart.* 294.

BROWN, 'Judicial review of Commission decisions under the Merger Regulation: the first cases', (1994) 15 *ECLR* 296.

BURNSIDE and CROSSLEY, 'Cooperative mechanisms within the EU: a blueprint for future cooperation at the international level', (2004) 10 *Int'l Trade Law and Regulation* 25.

BURNSIDE and CROSSLEY, 'Cooperation in competition: a new era?', (2005) 30 (2) *ELRev* 234.

CALVANI, 'Devolution and convergence in competition enforcement', (2003) 24 *ECLR* 415.

CANENBLEY and ROSENTHAL, 'Cooperation between antitrust authorities in and outside the EU: what does it mean for multinational corporations? Part 2', (2005) 26 *ECLR* 178.

CANOR, '*Primus inter pares*. Who is the ultimate guardian of Fundamental Rights in Europe?', (2000) 25 *ELRev* 3.

CARR, 'Should in-house lawyers have lawyer-client privilege?', (1996) 24 *Int'l Business Lawyer* 522.

CARRUTHERS, 'Beware of lawyers bearing gifts: a critical evaluation of the proposals on fundamental rights in the EU constitutional treaty', (2004) *EHRLR* 424.

CHRISTOFOROU, 'Protection of legal privilege in EEC competition law: the imperfections of a case', (1985–86) 9 *Fordham Int L J* 1.

COHEN, 'In-house counsel and the attorney-client principle: how Sarbanes-Oxley misses the point', (2004) 9 *Stanford Journal of Law, Business and Finance* 297.

COPPELL and O'NEILL, 'The European Court of Justice: taking rights seriously?', (1992) 29 *CMLRev* 669.

CORNER and BROWN, 'Applying *Alconbury*: Article 6, third parties and development plans', (2002) *Journal of Planning and Environment Law*, Jun 661.

COSTELLO, 'The Bosphorus ruling of the European Court of Human Rights: fundamental rights and blurred boundaries in Europe', (2006) 6 *Hum. Rts. L. Rev.* 87.

CRAIG, 'Legality, standing and substantive review in Community law', (1994) 14 *OJLS* 507.

CROSSLAND, 'Three major decisions given by the Bunderverfassungsgericht (Federal Constitutional Court)', (1994) 19 *ELRev* 202.

CUMMINGS, 'Automobiles Peugeot SA v Commission of the European Communities', case comment, (1998) 19 *ECLR* 106.

CURTIN, SAVRIN and BIGELOW, 'Collateral consequences of expanded European antitrust investigative authority for defendants in US proceedings', in HAWK (ed.), *International Antitrust Law and Policy, Annual Proceedings from the Fordham Corporate Law Institute* (2005) New York: Juris Publishing, p. 533.

DALY, 'The cultural, ethical and legal challenges in lawyering for a global organization: the role of the general counsel', (1997) 46 *Emory L. J.* 1057.

DAUSES, 'The protection of fundamental rights in the Community Legal Order', (1985) 10 *ELRev* 398.

DeBÙRCA, 'Fundamental rights and the reach of EC Law', (1993) 13 *Oxford J. Legal Stud.* 283.

DeBÙRCA & ASCHENBRENNER, 'The development of European constitutionalism and the role of the EU Charter of Fundamental Rights', (2003) 9 *Colum. J. Eur. L.* 355.

DEFEIS, 'A Constitution for the European Union? A transatlantic perspective', (2005) 19 *Temp. Int'l & Comp. L J* 351.

DEKEYSER and DALHEIMER, 'Cooperation within the European Competition Network – taking stock after 10 months of case practice', paper presented at the International Bar Association 2005 Conference: 'Decentralisation of EC Competition Law, a year in practice', available at: http://www.ibanet.org/images/downloads/A04824516v1.IBA_dekeyser_dalheimer.pdf.

DEKEYSER and GAUER, 'The new enforcement system for Articles 81 and 82 and the rights of defence', in HAWK (ed.), *International Antitrust Law and Policy, Annual Proceedings from the Fordham Corporate Law Institute* (2005) New York: Juris Publishing, p. 549.

DENNIS, 'Instrumental protection, human right or functional necessity? Reassessing the privilege against self-incrimination', (1995) 54 (2) *CLJ* 342.

DINNAGE, 'Locus standi and article 173 EEC: the effect of *Metro SB Grossmarkte v Commission*', (1979) 4 *ELRev* 15.

DOLMANS, 'Attorney-client privilege for in-house counsel: a European proposal', (1998) 4 *Colum. J. of Eur. L.* 125.

DOUGLAS-SCOTT, 'The Charter of Fundamental Rights as a constitutional document', (2004) *EHRLR* 37.

DRABEK, 'A fair hearing before EC institutions', (2003) 4 *ERPL* 529.

DRYWOOD, 'Giving with one hand, taking with the other: fundamental rights, children and the family reunification decision', (2007) 32(3) *ELRev* 396.

DUTHEIL de la ROCHERE, 'The EU and the individual: fundamental rights in the Draft Constitutional Treaty', (2004) 41 *CMLRev* 345.

DUVIGNEAU, 'From Advisory Opinion 2/94 to the Amsterdam Treaty: human rights protection in the European Union', (1998) 25 *LIEI* 61.

ECKES, 'Does the European Court of Human Rights provide protection from the European Community? – the case of *Bosphorus Airways*', (2007) 13 *EPL* 47.

EECKHOUT, 'The EU Charter of Fundamental Rights and the federal question', (2002) 39 *CMLRev* 945.

EHLERMANN, 'Developments in Community competition law procedures', (1994) 1 *EC Comp. Policy Newsl.* 2.

EHLERMANN, 'The Modernization of EC antitrust policy: a legal and cultural revolution', (2000) 37 *CMLRev* 537.

EHLERMANN and DRIJBER, 'Legal protection of enterprises: administrative procedure, in particular access to files and confidentiality', (1996) 17 *ECLR* 375.

EISMANBERGER and THYRI, 'Third-country antitrust sanctions and EC law – comments on the Advocate General's Opinion in C-308/04 P SGL Carbon/Commission', (2006) 27 *ECLR* 397.

ERLANDSSON, 'The defendant's right of access to the Commission's file in Competition cases', (1998) *LIEI* 139.

FAULL, 'In-house lawyers and legal professional privilege: a problem revisited', (1998) 4 *Colum. J. of Eur. L.* 139.

FELDMAN, 'The developing scope of Article 8 of the European Convention on Human Rights', (1997) 3 *EHRLR* 265.

FENNELLY, 'Lawyers and employed lawyers: the application of legal professional privilege', (1998) 1 *Irish Bus. L.* 2.

FORRESTER, 'The reform of the implementation of Articles 81 and 82 following publication of the Draft Regulation', (2001) 28 *LIEI* 173.

GALE, 'The Leniency regime and the fight against cartels by the Directorate General for Competition', (2004) 25 *Company Lawyer* 324.

GARZANITI, GUDOFSKY and MOFFAT, 'Dawn of a new era? Powers of investigation and enforcement under Regulation 1/2003', (2004–2005) 72 *Antitrust L J* 159.

GAUER, 'Does the effectiveness of the EU network of competition authorities require a certain degree of harmonisation of national procedures and sanctions?', in EHLERMANN and ATANASIU (eds.), *European Competition Law Annual 2002: Constructing the EU Network of Competition Authorities* (2004) Oxford, Portland, OR: Hart Publishing, p. 187.

GAUER, 'Due process in the face of divergent national procedures and sanctions', paper presented at the International Bar Association 2005 Conference: 'Decentralisation of EC Competition Law: a year in practice', available at: http://www.ibanet.org/images/downloads/A04824516v1.IBA_gauer.pdf.

GERBER and CASSINIS, 'The "Modernization" of European Community competition law: achieving consistency in enforcement. Part I', (2006) 27(1) *ECLR* 10.

GIANNAKOPOULOS, 'The right to be orally heard by the Commission in antitrust, merger, anti-dumping/anti-subsidies and State Aid Community Procedures', (2001) 24 *W. Comp.* 541.

GIESEL, 'The legal advice requriement of the attorney-client privilege: a special problem for in-house counsel and outside attorneys representing corporations', (1997) 48 *Mercer L. Rev.* 1169.

GINTER, 'Access to justice in the European Court of Justice in Luxembourg', (2002) 4 *Eur. Journal of Law Reform* 381.

GIPPINI FOURNIER, 'Legal professional privilege in competition proceedings before the European Commission: beyond the cursory glance', (2005) 28 *Fordham Int'l L J* 967.

Lord GOLDSMITH, 'A Charter of rights, freedoms and principles', (2001) 38 *CMLRev* 1201.

HARDING and GIBBS, 'Why go to court in Europe? An analysis of cartel appeals 1995–2004', (2005) 30(3) *ELRev* 349.

HARLOW, 'Global administrative law: the quest for principles and values', (2006) 17 *Eur. J. Int'l L.* 187.

HARMSEN, 'National responsibility for European Community acts under the European Convention on Human Rights: recasting the accession debate', (2001) 7 *EPL* 625.

HEFFERNAN, 'The Treaty of Nice: arming the Courts to defend a European Bill of Rights?', (2002) 65 *Law & Contemp Probs* 189.

HENRY, 'Leniency programmes: an anaemic carrot for cartels in France Germany and the UK', (2005) 26(1) *ECLR* 13.

HICKMAN, 'The 'uncertain shadow': throwing light on the right to a court under Article 6(1) ECHR', (2004) *PL* (Spr) 122.

HILL, 'A problem of privilege: in-house counsel and the attorney-client privilege in the United States and the European Community', (1995) 27 *Case W. Res. J. of Int'l L.* 145.

HINAREJOS PARGA, '*Bosphorus v Ireland* and the protection of fundamental rights in Europe', (2006) 31(2) *ELRev* 251.

HOFFMEISTER, Case comment to German Bundesverfassugsgericht: *Alcan*, Decision of 17 February 2000: *Constitutional review of EC Regulation on bananas*, Decision of 7 June 2000, (2001) 38 *CMLRev* 791.

HOFFMEISTER, '*Bosphorus Hava Yollari Turizm Ve Ticaret Anonim Sirket v Ireland*', case comment, (2006) 100 *Am J Int'l L* 442.

HOFMANN, 'Good governance in EC Merger Control: due process and checks and balances under review', (2003) 24 *ECLR* 114.

HOGAN, 'The use of compelled evidence in European competition law cases', in HAWK (ed.), *International Antitrust Law and Policy, Annual Proceedings from the Fordham Corporate Law Institute* (2005) New York: Juris Publishing, p. 659.

IDOT, 'A necessary step towards common procedural standards of implementation for Articles 81 and 82 EC within the network', in EHLERMANN and ATANASIU (eds), *European Competition Law Annual 2002: Constructing the EU Network of Competition Authorities* (2004) Oxford, Portland, OR: Hart Publishing, p. 213.

JACOBS, 'European Community Law and the European Convention of Human Rights', in CURTIN and HEUKELS (eds), *Institutional Dynamics of European Integration*, Vol. 2 (1997) Dordrecht, London: Nijhoff, pp. 516–72.

JELLEMA, 'The redheaded stepchild of Community competition law: the third party and its right to be heard in competition proceedings', (2002) 20 *Boston University International Law Journal* 211.

JOSHUA, 'The right to be heard in EEC Competition procedures', (1991–1992) 15 *Fordham Int'l L. J.* 16.

JOSHUA, 'Balancing the public interest: confidentiality, trade secret and disclosure of evidence in EC Competition procedures', (1994) 15 *ECLR* 68.

JOSHUA, 'A Sherman Act bridgehead in Europe, or a ghost ship in mid-Atlantic? A close look at the United Kingdom proposals to criminalise hardcore cartel conduct', (2002) 23 *ECLR* 231.

JOSHUA, 'Privilege in multi-jurisdictional cartel investigations: are European courts missing the point?', (2004) 7 *Global Comp. Rev.* 39.

KANSKA, 'Towards administrative human rights in the EU. Impact of the Charter of Fundamental Rights', (2004) *ELJ* 296.

KEKELEKIS, 'The rights of notifying parties and third parties during the preliminary investigation procedures under the ECMR', (2003) *EBLRev* 429.

KEKELEKIS, 'The statement of objections as an inherent part of the right to be heard in EC merger proceedings: issues of concern', (2004) 25 *ECLR* 518.

KERSE, 'Procedures in EC competition cases: the oral hearing', (1994) 15 ECLR 40.

KINGSTON, 'A "new division of responsibilities" in the proposed Regulation to modernise the rules implementing Articles 81 and 82 EC? A warning call', (2001) 22 *ECLR* 340.

KRAULAND and HUTMAN, 'Money Laundering enforcement and policy', (2004) 38 *Int'l Law* 509.

LAGE and BROKELMANN, 'The possible consequences of a relatively broad scope for exchange of confidential information on national procedural law and antitrust sanctions', in EHLERMANN and ATANASIU (eds), *European Competition Law Annual 2002: Constructing the EU Network of Competition Authorities* (2004) Oxford, Portland, OR: Hart Publishing, p. 405.

LAMBERT, 'Parallel Antitrust investigations: the long arm of the DOJ from the perspective of an EU defence counsel', (2002) 14 *Loy. Consumer L. Rev.* 509.

LAVOIE, 'The investigative powers of the Commission with respect to business secrets under Community Competition rules', (1992) 17 *ELRev* 20.

LEMMENS, 'The relation between the Charter of Fundamental Rights of the European Union and the European Convention of Human Rights – Substantive aspects', (2001) 8 *Maastricht J. of Euro. and Comp. L.* 49.

LENAERTS and DeSMIJTER, 'A Bill of Rights for the European Union', (2001) 38 *CMLRev* 273.

LENAERTS and GERARD, 'Decentralisation of EC competition law enforcement: judges on the frontline', (2004) 27 *W. Comp.* 313.

LENAERTS and VANHAMME, 'Procedural rights of private parties in the Community administrative process', (1997) 34 *CMLRev* 531.

LeSUEUR, 'Access to justice in the United Kingdom', (2000) *EHRLR* 5 457.

LEVITT, 'Access to the file: the Commission's administrative procedures in cases under Articles 85 and 86', (1997) 34 *CMLRev* 1413.

LEVITT, 'Commission Notice on internal rules of procedure for access to the file', (1997) 18 *ECLR* 187.

LEVITT: 'Commission Hearings and the role of the Hearing Officer: suggestions for reform', (1998) 19 *ECLR* 397, pp. 404–5.

LEVY and O'DONOGHUE, 'The EU leniency programme comes of age', (2004) 27 *W. Comp.* 75.

LEWIS, 'Harmonisation and its limits', in HAWK (ed.), *International Antitrust Law and Policy, Annual Proceedings from the Fordham Corporate Law Institute* (2005) New York: Juris Publishing, p. 7.

LOWE, 'Current issues of EU Competition law: the new competition enforcement regime', (2003–2004) 24 *Nw. J. Int'l L. & Bus.* 567.

MacCULLOCH, 'The cartel offence and the criminalisation of United Kingdom competition law', (2003) *Journal of Business Law*, Nov 616.

MacCULLOCH, 'The privilege against self-incrimination in competition investigations: theoretical foundations and practical implications', (2006) 26(2) *Legal Studies* 211.

MACDONALD, 'Judicial review and procedural fairness in administrative law', (1979–80) 25 *McGill L. J.* 520, (1980) 26 *McGill L. J.* 1.

MACDONALD, 'Procedural due process in Canadian constitutional law: natural justice and fundamental justice', (1987) 39(2) *U. Fla. L. Rev.* 217.

MAHER, 'Professional privilege – without prejudice letters and statutory inroads on the common law', (1990) 35 *Journal of the Law Society of Scotland* 108.

MAHLMANN, 'Renewed? Prospects of the protection of human rights in Europe', (2004) 11 *Cardozo J. Int'l & Comp. L.* 903.

MANCINI, 'Access to Justice: individual undertakings and EEC Antitrust Law – problems and pitfalls', (1988–89) 12 *Fordham Int'l L. J.* 189.

McBRIDE, 'Access to justice and human rights treaties', (1998) 17 *CJQ* (Jul) 235.

MEADE, 'Modelling a European Competition authority', (1996) 46 *Duke L. J.* 153.

MEDINGER, 'Antitrust leniency programs: a call for increased harmonisation as proliferating programs undermine deterrence', (2003) 52 *Emory L. J.* 1439.

MESTMACKER, 'The EC Commission's Modernization of Competition policy: a challenge to the Community's constitutional order', (2000) 1(3) *Euro. Bus. Organization L. Rev.* 401.

Lord MILLETT, 'The right to good administration in European Law', (2002) *PL* Summer 309.

MONTAG, 'The case for a radical reform of the infringement procedure under Regulation 17', (1996) 17 *ECLR* 428.

MONTAG, 'The case for a reform of Regulation 17/62: problems and possible solutions from a practitioner's point of view', (1999) 22 *Fordham Int'l L. J.* 819.

MORTMAN, 'Putting starch in European efforts to combat money laundering', (1992) 60 *Fordham L. Rev.* S429.

MURPHY, 'CFI signals possible extension of professional privilege to in-house lawyers', (2004) 25 *ECLR* 447.

NASH and FURSE, 'Partners in crime – the cartel offence in UK law', (2004) 15 *International Company and Commercial Law Review* 138.

NAZZINI, 'Some reflections on the dynamics of due process discourse in EC Competition law', (2005) 2(1) *CompLRev* 5.

NICHOLSON, CARDELL and McKENNA, 'The scope of review of merger decisions under Community Law', (2005) 1(1) *Eur. Comp. Journal*, 123.

ODUDU, Case comment to C-11/00, *Commission v European Central Bank*, judgment of 10 July 2003, (2004) 41 *CMLRev* 1073.

PATTENDEN, 'Litigation privilege and expert opinion evidence', (2000) 4 *Int'l J. of Ev. and Proof* 213.

PERNICE, 'Integrating the Charter of Fundamental Rights into the Constitution of the European Union: practical and theoretical propositions', (2003) 10 *Colum. J Eur L* 5.

PERRIN, 'Challenges facing the EU network of competition authorities: insights from a comparative criminal law perspective', (2006) 31 *ELRev* 540.

PHELPS, 'Reflections on Bosphorus and human rights in Europe', (2006) 81 *Tul. L. Rev.* 251.

POUSTIE, 'The rule of law or the rule of lawyers? *Alconbury*, Article 6(1) and the role of courts in administrative decision-making', (2001) 6 *EHRLR* 657.

POWER, 'Representing clients after the Modernisation of EC Competition law', (2003) 14 *ICCLR* 335.

RAGOLLE, '*Schneider Electric v Commission*: the CFI'S response to the Green Paper on Merger Review', (2003) 24 *ECLR* 176.

READER, 'Moving forward, never backwards: preventing fraud in the European Union and defining European Central Bank independence', (2004) 27 *Fordham Int'l L. J.* 1509.

REDISH and MARSHALL, 'Adjudicatory independence and the values of procedural due process', (1986) 95 *Yale L. J.* 455.

RILEY, 'The European Cartel Office: a guardian without weapons', (1997) 18 *ECLR* 3.

RILEY, 'Saunders and the power to obtain information in Community and United Kingdom competition law', (2000) 25 *ELRev* 264.

RILEY, 'The ECHR implications of the investigation provisions of the Draft Competition Regulation', (2002) 51 (1) *ICLQ* 55.

RILEY, 'Cartel whistle blowing: toward an American model?', (2002) 9 *Maastricht Journal of European and Comparative Law* 1.

RILEY, 'EC antitrust Modernisation: the Commission does very nicely – thank you! Part 1: Regulation 1 and the Notification burden', (2003) 24 *ECLR* 604.

RODGER, 'Competition policy, liberalism and globalisation: a European perspective', (2000) 6 *Colum. J. Eur. L.* 289.

RODGER, 'Interrelationship with Community Competition law enforcement', in RODGER and MacCULLOCH, *The UK Competition Act: a New Era for UK Competition Law* (2000) Oxford, Portland, OR: Hart Publishing, p. 45.

RODGER and WYLIE, 'Taking the Community interest line: decentralisation and subsidiarity in competition law enforcement', (1997) 18 *ECLR* 485.

RYAN, 'Reform of the EU Merger Control System – a comprehensive package of proposals', (2003) (issue 1) *EC Competition Policy Newsletter* 9.

SCHAUB, 'Modernisation of EC competition law: reform of Regulation No 17', (1999–2000) 23 *Fordham Int'l L. J.* 752.

SCHERMERS, *Matthews v United Kingdom*, judgment of 18 February 1999, case comment, (1999) 36 *CMLRev* 673.

SCHWARZE, 'Tendencies towards a common administrative law in Europe', (1991) 16 *ELRev* 3.

SHAUGHNESSY, 'The new EU Money Laundering directive: lawyers as gate-keepers and whistle-blowers', (2002) 34 *Law & Pol'y Int'l Bus.* 25.

SHAW, 'Decentralization and law enforcement in EC competition law', (1995) 15 *Legal Studies* 128.

SIRAGUSA, 'A critical overview of the White Paper on the reform of the EC competition law enforcement rules', (1999–2000) 23 *Fordham Int'l L. J.* 1089.

SIRAGUSA, 'Judicial review of competition decisions under EC law', Speech given at the Competition Commission on 21 September 2004, available at: http://www.competition-commission.org.uk/our_role/cc_lectures/judicial_control_210904_Siragusa.pdf.

SLOT, 'A view from the mountain: 40 years of developments in EC competition law', (2004) 41 *CMLRev* 443.

STESSENS, 'The obligation to produce documents versus the privilege against self-incrimination: human rights protection extended too far', (1997) 22 SUPP (Human Rights survey).

STEVER, 'Protecting human rights in the European Union: an argument for Treaty reform', (1997) 20 *Fordham Int'l L. J.* 919.

STROUD, 'Collective dominance under the Merger Regulation: a serious evidentiary reprimand for the Commission', (2002) 27(6) *ELRev* 736.

SYMMONS, 'The role of the UK's Competition Appeals Tribunal', speech given at the British Institute of International and Comparative Law conference on 'Antitrust Litigation: Where do we stand?' on 3 February 2006.

TIILI and VANHAMME, 'The 'power of appraisal' (*pouvoir d'appreciation*) of the Commission of the European Communities vis-à-vis the powers of judicial review of the Communities' Court of Justice and Court of First Instance', (1998–1999) 22 *Fordham Int'l L. J.* 885.

TODINO, 'Modernisation from the perspective of national competition authorities: impact of the reform on decentralised application of EC competition law', (2000) 21 *ECLR* 348.

TOTH, 'The European Union and human rights: the way forward', (1997) 34 *CMLRev* 491.

TRAINOR, 'A comparative analysis of a corporation's right against self-incrimination', (1994–1995) 18 *Fordham Int'l L. J.* 2139.

VAN der WOUDE, 'Hearing Officers and EC antitrust procedures: the art of making subjective procedures more objective', (1996) 33 *CMLRev* 531.

VAN der WOUDE, 'Exchange of information within the European Competition Network: scope and limits', in EHLERMANN and ATANASIU (eds), *European Competition Law Annual 2002: Constructing the EU Network of Competition Authorities* (2004) Oxford, Portland, OR: p. 369.

Van OVERBEEK, 'The right to remain silent in competition investigations:

the *Funke* decision of the Court of Human Rights makes revision of the ECJ's case law necessary', (1994) 15(3) *ECLR* 127.

VENIT, 'Brave new world: the Modernisation and decentralisation of enforcement under Articles 81 and 82 EC Treaty', (2003) 40 *CMLRev* 545.

VENIT and LOUKO, 'The Commission's new power to question and its implications on human rights', in HAWK (ed.), *International Antitrust Law and Policy, Annual Proceedings from the Fordham Corporate Law Institute* (2005) New York: Juris Publishing, p. 675.

VESTERDORF, 'The Community court system ten years from now and beyond: challenges and possibilities', (2003) 28(3) *ELRev* 303.

VESTERDORF, 'Legal professional privilege and the privilege against self-incrimination in EC Law: recent developments and current issues', in HAWK (ed.), *International Antitrust Law and Policy, Annual Proceedings from the Fordham Corporate Law Institute* (2005) New York: Juris Publishing, p. 701.

VESTERDORF, 'Standard of proof in merger cases: reflections in the light of recent case law of the Community courts', (2005) 1(1) *Eur. Comp. Journal* 3.

WAELBROECK, ' "Twelve feet dangling down and six necks exceeding long". The EU network of competition authorities and the European Convention on Fundamental Rights', in EHLERMANN and ATANASIU (eds.), *European Competition Law Annual 2002: Constructing the EU Network of Competition Authorities* (2004) Oxford, Portland, OR: Hart Publishing, p. 465.

WAELBROECK and FOSSELARD, 'Should the decision-making power in EC antitrust procedures be left to an independent judge? – the impact of the European Convention on Human Rights on EC Antitrust procedures', (1994) 14 *YEL* 111.

WAKEFIELD, 'Good governance and the European Anti Fraud Office', (2006) 12(4) *EPL* 549.

WARD, '*Locus standi* under Article 230(4) of the EC Treaty: crafting a coherent test for a "wobbly polity" ', (2003) 22 *YEL* 45.

WARD and GARDNER, 'The privilege against self-incrimination: in search of legal certainty', (2003) 4 *EHRLR* 388.

WEILER, 'Eurocracy and distrust: some questions concerning the role of the European Court of Justice in the protection of fundamental human rights within the legal order of the European Communities', (1986) 61 *Wash. Law Rev.* 1103.

WESSELING, 'The Draft-Regulation modernising the competition rules: the Commission is married to one idea', (2001) 26 *ECLR* 357.

WETZEL, 'Improving fundamental rights protection in the European Union: resolving the conflict and confusion between the Luxembourg and Strasbourg Courts', (2003) 71 *Fordham L. Rev.* 2823.

WILLIAMS, 'EU human rights policy and the Convention on the Future of Europe: a failure of design', (2003) 28 *ELRev* 794.

WILLIAMS, 'Four questions of privilege: the litigation aspect of legal professional privilege', (1990) 9 (Apr) *CJQ* 139.

WILLIS, ' "You have the right to remain silent . . ." or do you? The privilege against self-incrimination following *Mannesmannrohren-Werke* and other recent decisions', (2001) 22 *ECLR* 313.

WILLIS, 'Transfer of information between authorities in the modernised network', (2004) 2(4) *Competition Law Journal* 310.

WILS, 'Self-incrimination in EC antitrust enforcement: a legal and economic analysis', (2003) 26 *W. Comp.* 567.

WILS, 'The principle of *ne bis in idem* in EC antitrust enforcement: a legal and economic analysis', (2003) 26(2) *W. Comp.* 131.

WILS, 'The combination of the investigative and prosecutorial function and the adjudicative function in EC Antitrust enforcement: a legal and economic analysis', (2004) 27 *W. Comp.* 201.

WILS,' The EU network of competition authorities, the European Convention on Human Rights and the Charter of Fundamental Rights of the EU', in EHLERMANN and ATANASIU (eds), *Competition Law Annual 2002: Constructing the EU Network of Competition Authorities* (2004) Oxford, Portland, OR: Hart Publishing, p. 433.

WILS, 'Powers of investigation and procedural rights and guarantees in EU antitrust enforcement – the interplay between European and national legislation and case law', (2006) 29(1) *W. Comp.* 3.

WILS, 'Leniency in antitrust enforcement: theory and practice', (2007) 30 *W. Comp.* 25.

WINCKLER, 'Some comments on procedures and remedies under EC merger control rules: something rotten in the kingdom of EC merger control?', (2003) 26 *W. Comp.* 219.

YOUNG, 'The Charter, Constitution and human rights: is this the beginning or the end for human rights protection by Community law?', (2005) 11 *EPL* 219.

ZUPANCIC, 'Access to court as a human right according to the European Convention of Human Rights', (2000) 9(2) *NLJ* 1.

OTHER DOCUMENTS

CBI Brief, 'The need for an EU Competition Court', 15 June 2006.

CCBE, Action Points for EU Bars and Law Societies on the implementation of the Money Laundering Directive, January 2002, available at www.ccbe.org/doc/En/action_points_220102_en.pdf.

CCBE, Position on the requirements of a lawyer to report suspicions of money laundering and on the European Commission Proposal for a third EU Directive on Money Laundering Regulations, November 2004, available at www.ccbe.org/doc/En/ccbe_position_paper_money_laundering_%20051104_en.pdf.

CCBE, Position on the Consultation Paper of the FATF Forty Recommendations, September 2002, available at www.ccbe.org/doc/En/ccbe_response_110902_en.pdf.

ECLA, 'Legal privilege for in-house lawyers', position paper, December 2002, available at http://www.ecla.org/pages/position_paper.html.

EDWARD, 'The professional secret, confidentiality and legal professional privilege in the nine Member States of the European Community', report published by the Consultative Committee of the Bars and Societies of the European Community (CCBE), 1976.

Financial Action Task Force (FATF), 40 Recommendations, contained in the 1990–1991 FATF Report (31 May 1991), available at: http://www.fatf-gafi.org/dataoecd/20/18/33643115.pdf.

FISH, *Regulated legal professionals and professional privilege within the European Union, the European Economic Area and Switzerland and certain other European Jurisdictions* – report published by CCBE, 2004, available at: http://www.ccbe.org/en/comites/in_house_en.htm.

G-7 Task Force, Recommendations on Curbing Money Laundering – Paris Economic Summit: Economic Declaration, 16 July 1989, published in (1989) 28 *ILM* 1293.

MONTI, 'European Commission strengthens the role of the Hearing Officer in competition proceedings', Press release IP/01/736.

Marion Symmons QC, Chair of the Competition Appeals Tribunal, speech given at the Conference: *Competition Litigation in the EU: Where do we stand?* – Panel I: 'The role of the UK's Competition Appeal Tribunal', held on 3 February 2006 at the British Institute of International and Comparative Law.

Index